VIDÉO TONFA

SIC

PUBLISHED by FLOATING WORLD COMICS

EDITING & LAYOUT: JASON LEIVIAN
PRODUCTION ASSISTANCE: SHANNA MATUSZAK

FLOATING WORLD COMICS
400 NW COUCH STREET
PORTLAND, ORE. U.S.A.
WWW.FLOATINGWORLDCOMICS.COM

FIRST PAPERBACK EDITION: MAY 2016
PRINTED IN CANADA

ISBN: 978-1-942801-93-1

FOR
SHEA

RIP
DW

Rodney Dangerfield

The 4th Tenor

SO FAR AS I'V SEEN THIS'S THE MELLOWIST OF
OF THE BASIL/DANGERFIELD. FEEL GOOD CHUMP
RE-AWAKENING TRIUMPH OF THE HEART THING.
I LIKE IT. NO HEAVY FAIR BUT RODNEYS SO
LOVEABLE THAT THIS OLD CHESTNUT IS
STILL ENJOYABLE. CLASSIC SCHLUB W/A
HEART OF GOLD STAYS TRUE IN THE FACE OF
"REALITY". PG-13 IS A MISFIRE FOR THIS APP-
ROCHE. IT'S NOT GO'N ALL RAISINGARIZONA ON
IT BUT IT'S A BIG "GROWN" IN IT'S TONE. SEEMS
LIKE AN EDITING CHOICE GIVEN SWAY FOR
EXPERIMENTATION W/THE "NEW MARKET"
OR WHATEVER; BECAUSE THERES NO TEENY 'B'-
OPPER THING HERE. OLD TIMER
LATE AFTERNOON BURNOUT
ROMANCICK COMIDY.
SANGRIEEA
SWEET
HEART.
RODNEY DANGERFIELD ROBERT DAVI
ANITA DE SIMONE CHARLES FLEISCHER
ANNABELLE GURWITCH RICHARD LIBERTINI
WRITTEN BY RODNEY DANGERFIELD & HARRY BASIL
DIRECTED BY HARRY BASIL
PG-13 COLOR 97 minutes 2001 CC
P C DOLBY SURROUND

YOU WANNA KNOW WHAT HAPPENS WHEN YOU HESITATE ON SUICIDE? THE COPS CALL YOUR FOLKS TO COME PUT A HEAVY TRIP ON YOU, & THEN YOU GOTTA TALK ABOUT YOUR EX & IT'S A BIG PAIN. DAMN IT. THIS DUDE IS ALIENATED & SENCITIVE WITH THE ONSET OF NHILESM COMES A FORM OF MELODRAMATIC HALFASS SCEEMS TO OFF ONE'S SELF. THIS GUY DID'NT HAVE THIS EPHONY IN HIS TEEN'S & NOW IT'S AN EVEN TOUGHER PILL TO SWOLLOW. I DIG THE CAST.

THIS IS VERY PLAY'ESQUE. IN FACT I DON'T KNOW IF IT EVER WAS, BUT COULD VERYWELL. EMOUTIONALLY AGRESSIVE. I THINK I MAY HAVE SEEN THIS HELLZA YEARS AGO ON AMC, IT DID'NT RING A BELL UNTILL THE LAST ACT BUT THE I WAS ALL "OH YEAH" THE SAME THING HAPPENED WHEN I SAW GORE GORE GIRLS. BUT NOT ON AM

PAUL DOUGLAS RICHARD BASEHART BARBARA BEL GEDDES DEBRA PAGET AGNES MOOREHEAD ROBERT KEITH, JR HOWARD DA SILVA MARTIN GABEL GRACE P. KELLY FRANK FAYLEN

DIRECTED by HENRY HATHAWAY PRODUCED BY SOL C. SIEGEL
SCREENPLAY by JOHN PAXTON FROM A STORY BY JOEL SAYRE

DVD

20 FOX

FOX FILM NOIR
FROM THE EDGE OF THE LEDGE HE DEFIED THEM ALL!
14 HOURS
PAUL DOUGLAS
RICHARD BASEHART
BARBARA BEL GEDDES

976 EVIL
STEPHEN GEOFFREYS JIM METZLER
MARIA RUBELL PAT O'BRYAN SANDY DENNIS
WRITTEN BY
RHET TOPHAM & BRIAN HELGELAND
DIRECTED by
ROBERT ENGLUND

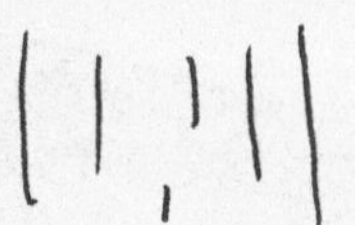

09873

SO TASTY, SO GOOD. ENGLUND KNOW HOW TO PUT IT TOGETHER. STARTS OFF W/CLASSIC 50'S/80'S THING THEN SHIFTS INTO A TALES FROM THE CRYP TYPE SITCHUATION. GEOFFREYS IS THE BEST OF HIS ERA IN EVIL TRANSFORMATIONS. PEEP FRIGHTNIGHT W/THIS FOR THE FULL DOSE. I LOVE THE PHOTOGRAPHY TOO. KINDA LIKE CREEPSHOW LIGHTING. I LIKE THE COMICBOOK STYLE OF MOVIES BETTER DURRING THIS TIME. I'M PRETTY SURE THIS IS MY FAV HELGELAND. OH... ITS ABOUT TEENS WHO CALL A 976 LINE FOR TIMELY EVIL ADVICE THAT RUINS ALL THEIR SHIT & EVERYTHING.

THE WORLD IS DEVISED TO TURN YOUR COMPULTIONS AGAINST YOU.

1988 (R) COLOR APPROX. 105 MINS.

DELUXE LETTER-BOX EDITION
MGM PRESENTS STANLEY KUBRICKS
2001:
a space odyssey
MGM
HOMEVIDEO

HONESTL, I PUT THIS ON AS A PREEMPTIVE STRIKE AGAINST DORA THIS, THE ULTIMATE WEIRD APPRIPO OLD'R PEOPLES MOVIE THAT YOUNG'R FOLKS CAN SEE. LIKE A HEAVY PAINTING THAT MAY NEVER END. I DIG IT. ARE YOU UNPATIANT? IF SO YOU MAY WANT TO GO CHILL OUT BEFORE PEEP'N OUT THIS ONE. I BELIEVE STALEY KUBRICK HAS NEVER MADE A MOVIE I DID'NT DIG. NOT THAT I CAN REMEMBER ANYTHING ABOUT THAT MOVIE SPARTACUS, BUT DON'T LET THAT GET IN THE WAY OF SEE'N THIS.

KEIR DULLEA
GARY LOCKWOOD
screenplay by STANLEY KUBRICK
and ARTHUR C. CLARK
Produced and DIRECTED by
STANLEY KUBRICK

APPROX. RUNNING TIME
2 hours 19 minutes
COLOR 1968 G
letterbox format

ACTUALL MOST OF THE CELEBRITY SINGINGIS'NT REALLY BAD, JUST NOT NORMAL, OR CHEESEY, OR WEIRD. SOME OF IT IS JUST DOWN RITE AMAZING. SOME FOLKS MAY GET HUNG UP ON A TOP 40 TYPE OF TASTE BUT I'M NOT ONE OF THEM. HERVE VILLECHAIZE IS SO GREAT. I LOVE THE GUY SO MUCH IT BREAKS MY HEART. I NEVER HAD A PROBLEM WITH TERRY BRADSHAW BUT HE NEVER REALLY GOT MY ATTENTION TOO MUCH IN THE PAST. DUDE CAN SING AND IS REALLY CHARASMATIC WITH A MIC IN HIS HAND. THE SING'N PART OF THIS DISC IS ALL WELL & GOOD BUT I REALLY GOT THE MOST FROM THE BLOOPERS, FLUBS, TYRAIDS, FREAKOUTS SECTION THAT COMES AFTER THE SINGING. AS A KID I'D WATCH SISKEL & EBERT AS OFTEN AS I COULD FIND IT. I LOVED MOVIE PREVIEWS & THEY SEEM'D TO HAVE THE DELUX SET UP. BUT I THOUGH SISKEL WAS TO SNOBBY {BOTH OF THEM ACTUALLY} BUT AFTER PEEP'N THE FLUB'S & OUT TAKES OF THEM HERE I WAS JUST FLOORED BY THERE UNCUT PERSONALITIES. DUDES JUST RIP ON EACH OTHER SO HARD. THEN WE HAVE THE RICHARD PRYOR. DAMN. DUDE IS FLYYYYY'N INTO THE EYE OF BLOWCAINIA. I WON'T EVEN TRY TO DISCRIBE THIS BIT BUT I WILL SAY "OH SHIT" NO FILTER AT ALL.

BOOTLEG

THE ABSOLUTE WORST OF THE DINAH SHORE SHOW

Celebrity Singers

including WILLIAMSHATNER TELLY SAVALAS, ROBERTBLAKE, HERVE VILLECHAIZE, CHAD EVERETT, JOHN TRAVOLTA, BURT REYNOLDS, DAVID CARRADINE, ANDYKAUFMAN TERRY BRADSHAW & MORE!

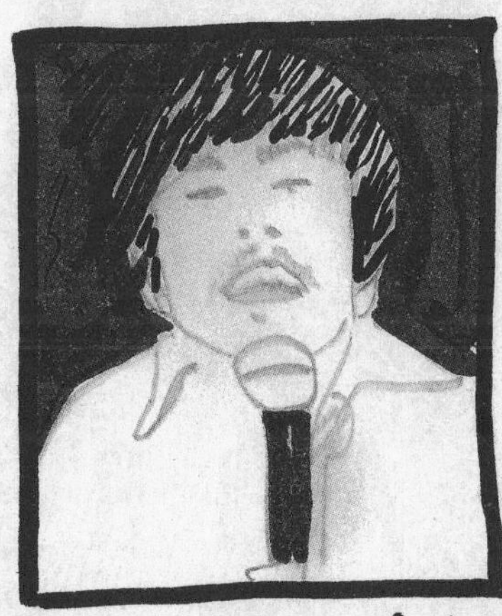

Plue bonus footage of celebs making fools of themselves from the likes of CRISPIN GLOVER, ORSON WELLES SISKEL & EBERT, ZSAZSA GABOR, JAMES BROWN and RICHARD PRYOR & more.

CHRISTOPHER
LAMBERT

NATASHA
HENSTRIDGE

ADRENALIN
FEAR THE RUSH

WISH I COULD GET INTO. BUT DISPITE LAMBERT; IT JUST NEVER GET'S TOO INTERESTING. SOMETIMES ALBERT PYUN MAKES A BAD MOVIE GOOD. BUT THERE IS'NT ENOUGH TOO THIS TO GET SOLID & A LITTLE TOO MUCH TO GO SPACEOUT ON. IT'S A TRICKY LINE TO PLAY & PYUN IS ONE OF THE MORE INTERESTING PEOPLE TO EXPERIMENT WITH THE LINES ON THIS END OF MOVIE MAKING. PYUN'S EYE IS STILL VERY STRONG HERE, & THAT'S WHAT HOLDS MY INTEREST IN THIS MOVIE. OKAY'ISH.

CHRISTOPHER LAMBERT NATASHA HENSTRIDGE
NORBERT WEISSER ELEZABETH BARONDES
CRAIG DAVIS XAVIER DECLIE
WRITTEN & DIRECTED BY
ALBERT PYUN

PERFECTION. IT JUST KEEPS ON GIVING, EVERY TIME I WATCH IT, I SEE SOMETHING NEW. IT'S SO DENSE'LY DETAILED YOU COULD WATCH IN SLOW MOUTION & STILL THERE WILL BE MISSED JEMS. SO MUCH SO, THAT I'D RECCOMEND EVERYONE SEE IT A MINIMUM OF THREE {3} TIMES. SERIOUSLY. AT THE END THERE IS A MENTION OF ANOTHER BANZAI MOVIE TO COME. IT HAS'NT. BUT, A SCRIPT WAS WRITTEN; WHICH IN TIME WAS RETOOLED BY RICHTER INTO "BIG TROUBLE IN LITTLE CHINA". I BELIEVE PETER WELLER IS THE QUINTESSENTIAL 1980'S SCI-FI ACTOR, HANDS DOWN. BELIEVE.

PETER WELLER JOHN LITHGOW ELLEN BARKIN

WRITTEN BY EARL MacRAUCH

DIRECTED BY W.D. RICHTER

DUDES, TOTAL SIDENOTE, I WAS FULL DRIZZZEED WHEN I DID THAT LEG & I'M SORRY IF YOU CAN'T DEAL WITH IT; BUT THAT'S MY FOR REAL SHIT. TRUST. IF YOU WANT SOME OTHER SHIT GO DO IT YOUR SELF.

THIS MOVIE IS A REAL JEM. APPRIECIEATE IT FULLY.

APPROXIMATE RUNNING TIME 1 HOUR 42 MINUTES 1984

SPECIAL EDITION

IF YOU SURVIVE THIS NIGHT...
NOTHING WILL SCARE
YOU AGAIN.

Alice, Sweet Alice

TOM SIGNORELLI LOUISA HORTON PAULA SHEPPARD
MILDRED CLINTON LINDA MILLER LILLIAN ROTH
BROOKE SHIELDS

CHILDREN PAY FOR THE SINS OF THEY'RE PARENTS. UPON MY 1ST VIEWING OF THIS I WAS NOT SURE IF THEY WERE GOING TO DO ANYTHING GOOD WITH IT. BUT NOW I KNOW. GOOD STUFF. A LITTLE TYPICAL @ POINTS BUT MOSTLY SMART W/

STARRING
TOM SIGNORELLI
LOUISA HORTON
PAULA SHEPPARD
MILDRED CLINTON
LINDA MILLER
LILLIAN ROTH
BROOKE SHIELDS

DIRECTED BY
ALFRED SOLE

SCREENPLAY BY
ROSEMARY RITVO
AND
ALFRED SOLE

GOOD MOMENTUM. IF YOUR INTO BROOK SHIELDS SHES IN THE FIRST SCENE & GETS KILLED & BURNED & SHE'S A KID {PERVERT}. THE REST OF THE CAST IS PRETTY COOL. FREAKY KID IN A WORLD OF PERVERTS, JERKS, CREEPS, PSYCHOS, NEGITIVE VIBE MERCHANTS, COPS, CHURCH HEADS & MAYBE ONE OR TWO O.K TYPES. HEAVY. GREAT MASK. I LOVE KNIFE MOVIES TOO. I THINK I LIKED THE SOUNDTRACK TOO.

ALPHA VIDEO DISTRIBUTERS

1976 COLOR 108 MINUTES

"HILARIOUS!"

NOT REALLY

JUST WATCH SAFE MEN

WELL, THIS ONE IS SORT OF TOUGH FOR ME. JOHN HAMBURG WROTE & DIRECTED THIS MOVIE, SO I WAS STOKED TO SEE IT BECAUSE HE ALSO MADE SAFEMEN WHICH I LOVE. SAFEMEN IS A MUST SEE IN MY OPPINION. I LIKED PARTS OF THIS BUT IT REALLY DID'NT COME TOGETHER. I BELIEVE IT WAS CRUSHED BY IT'S CAST. I'M A FAN OF STILLER EXPECIALY WHEN HE WRITES & DIRECTS. BUT HE'S NOT THE RIGHT GUY FOR THIS; NEATHER IS JENNIFER ANISTON. THE REST OF THE CAST IS PRETTY MUCH PERFECT. THE SUPPORTING CHARACTERS ARE WHAT KEEP THIS WATCHABLE. I HOPE HAMBURG RETURNS TO HIS EARLY'R SENSIBILITYS THIS SORT OF SMELLS LIKE AN ATTEMPT TO GET A HOLLYWOOD HIT, RATHER THEN MAKE A UNIQUE SMALL BUDGET. THE ONLY THING A BIGGER BUDGET GAVE HAMBURG WAS A NICE PILLOW TO HOLD OVER THE FACE OF THIS MOVIE.

Ben Stiller Jennifer Aniston Philip Seymour Hoffman
Debra Messing Hank Azaria Bryan Brown Alec Baldwin
Written and Directed by John Hamburg

PG-13 ©2003 color 91 mins.

DVD VIDEO

Ben Stiller Jennifer Aniston

Along Came Polly

AMERICAN CYBORG
STEEL WARRIOR

YOU KNOW WHEN YOUR WATCHING A MOVIE & IN IT THEY SHOW FOLKS MAKING A "BAD MOVIE" & YOU THINK "DANG I WANNA SEE THAT MOVIE": WELL THIS IS ONE OF THOSE. IF I WERE TO WATCH IT IN 2-5 MINUTE BURSTS I'D PROBABLY DIG IT MORE BUT WATCHING IT STRAIGHT THROUGH WAS A BIT DRAGY AFTER A BIT BECAUSE IT KEPT UP WITH A HOLLOW TENSION THAT YOU KNOW IS B.S. SOME GREAT VISUALS THOUGH & FUN FOR A PARTY SETTING W/ BEER
JOE LARA NKOLE HANSEN JOHN RYAN
STORY: BOAZ DAVIDSON & CHRISTOPHER PEARCE
THEN SCREENPLAY BY
BRENT FRIEDMAN & BILL CROUNSE & DON PEQUIGNOT
DIRECTED BY BOAZ DAVIDSON
WB R 1994 COLOR 95 MINUTES

AMERICAN
PSYCHO

I NEED TO RETURN SOME VIDEOS

I'M INTO MURDERS & EXICUTIONS MOSTLY

I ADMIT THAT THE FIRST TIME I SAW THIS I DID'NT KNOW WHAT I WAS WATCHING. I DID NOT GET IT. OVER THE YEARS I SAW IT A FEW MORE TIMES AFTER THE 3RD OR 4TH TIME I GOT IT. OR AT LEAST I START'D TO DIG IT. "BUT WHAT KIND OF MOVIE IS IT?" FUK'T IF I KNOW. I CAN ONLY SORT IT WITH OTHERS OF IT'S TYPE. IT'S A CRAZY COKE HEAD TALK MOVIE, LIKE HURLY BURLY, WITHNAIL & I, & MAYBE TITUS? IT'S TOUGH TO SAY IF SUCH A LIST IS GOOD, OR FAIR. I LIKE ALL THE MOVIES I'V SEEN WHICH COME FROM BRET ELLES BOOKS BUT THIS IS THE ONE THAT GETS BETTER EVERY TIME I SEE IT. THIS VIEWING WAS ACCIDENTAL, WE WERE GO'NG TO WATCH O'BROTHER WHERE ARE THOU? BUT FOREST GUMP WAS IN THE BOX. HAHAHA AMERICAN PSYCHO RULES. NO WHIMPS NEED BOTHER CHECKING IT OUT. IT IS BRUTAL. SICK.

CHRISTIAN BALE CHLOË SEVIGNY
JUSTIN THEROUX SAMANTHA MATHIS
JOSH LUCAS REESE WITHERSPOON BILL SAGE
JARED LETO & WILLEM DAFOE
SCREENPLAY BY MARY HARRON & GUINEVERE TURNER
DIRECTED BY MARY HARRON {AWESOME}

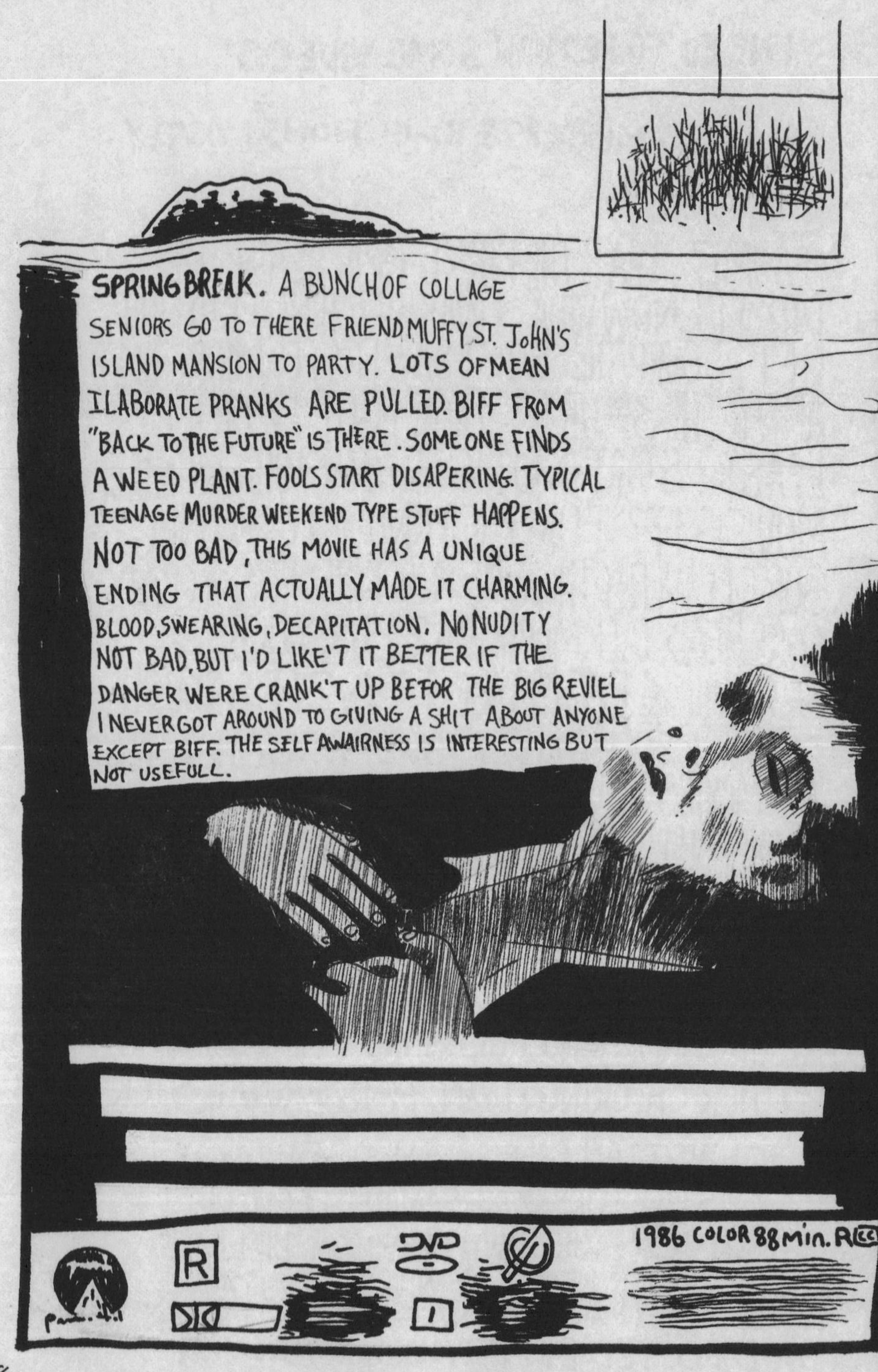
SPRING BREAK. A BUNCH OF COLLAGE SENIORS GO TO THERE FRIEND MUFFY ST. JOHN'S ISLAND MANSION TO PARTY. LOTS OF MEAN ILABORATE PRANKS ARE PULLED. BIFF FROM "BACK TO THE FUTURE" IS THERE. SOME ONE FINDS A WEED PLANT. FOOLS START DISAPERING. TYPICAL TEENAGE MURDER WEEKEND TYPE STUFF HAPPENS. NOT TOO BAD, THIS MOVIE HAS A UNIQUE ENDING THAT ACTUALLY MADE IT CHARMING. BLOOD, SWEARING, DECAPITATION. NO NUDITY NOT BAD, BUT I'D LIKE'T IT BETTER IF THE DANGER WERE CRANK'T UP BEFOR THE BIG REVIEL I NEVER GOT AROUND TO GIVING A SHIT ABOUT ANYONE EXCEPT BIFF. THE SELF AWAIRNESS IS INTERESTING BUT NOT USEFULL.
R
DVD
1986 COLOR 88 Min.

APRIL FOOL'S DAY

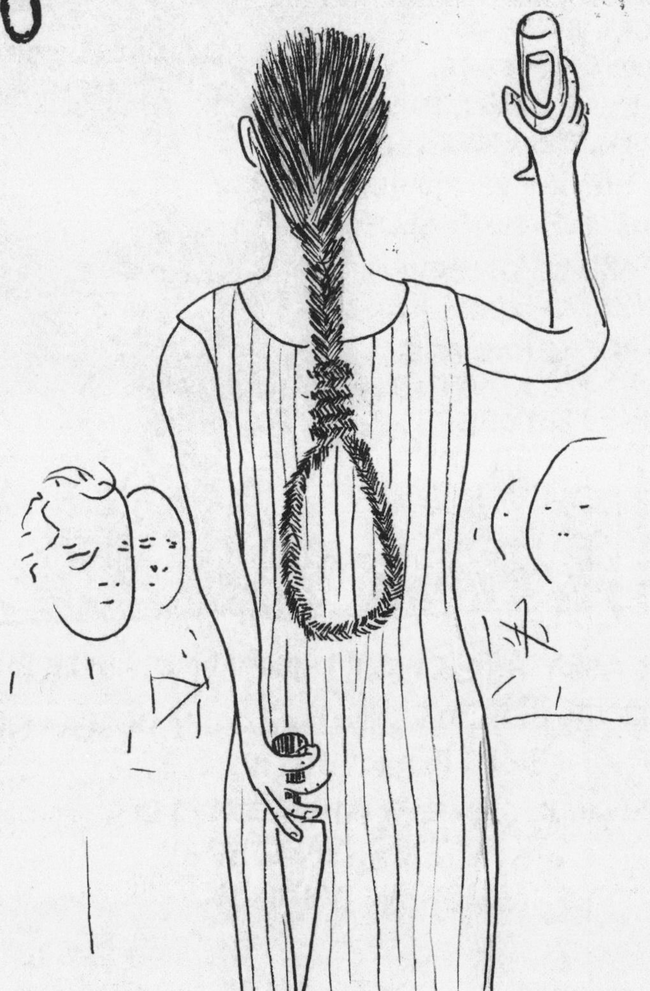

LAST ONE OUT'S... A GONER

I AVOIDED THIS MOVY FOR A LONGTIME BECAUSE I DON'T TEND TO DIG PITT IN SERIOUSE ROLLS. THEN DYLAN HIP'T ME TO IT BECAUSE IT'S THE DUDE WHO MADE CHOPPER. PITTS OVERBEARING FAMOUSNESS MAKES HIM TOUGH TO SWALLOW AS A REGULAR PERSON CHARACTER BUT JESSE JAMES IS'NT A REGULAR TYPE & SO I CAN DIG IT. DO YOU WANT A SLOW, BROODING, BRUTAL ART MOVY? WELL, THIS IS A GOOD ONE. LONG TOO. WHICH IS GOOD IN THIS CASE. OF THE JAMES MOVIES I'V SEEN THIS HAS THE MOST BELIEVABLE VERSION OF FORD. WHICH I'D ATTRIBUTE TO CASEY AFFLECK WHO DOSE A GREAT JOB. THE WINDOW SHOTS ARE BEAUTIFUL IN A WAY THAT I'V NOT EXPERIENCED BEFORE.

BRAD PITT CASEY AFFLECK SAM SHEPARD MARY-LOUISE PARKER
PAUL SCHNEIDER JEREMY RENNER ZOOEY DESCHANEL
SAM ROCKWELL

MUSIC BY NICK CAVE & WARREN ELLIS
WRITTEN & DIRECTED BY
ANDREW DOMINIK

DUAL-LAYER FORMAT
DVD

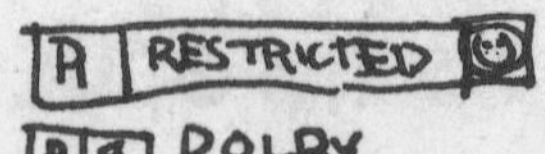

2007
COLOR 160 minutes

BRAD PITT CASEY AFFLECK

THE ASSASSINATION OF JESSE JAMES BY THE COWARD ROBERT FORD

HERE WE HAVE VAL GUEST DOING HIS DIRTY OLD MAN THING. VAL GUEST IS ALLWAYS A TREAT FOR ME. HIS WHOLE GAME IS SEW'N UP SO WELL. HIS TASTE & STYLE ARE LAZER REFINED.

HE'S REALLY IMPORTANT TO MY TASTE & THIS IS HIS NUDIE CUTIE PICTURE. WELL. ONE.

A VARIETY OF HOT "TEEN" AU PAIRS ARIVE IN 1970'S ENGLAND & MAKE BRITISH MEN BUG OUT/ACT LIKE DIPSHITS. AWESOME. BY THE END THEY ALL GET HOOKED UP W/A SMOOTH MID-EAST DUDE WHO LAYS GOOD PIPE & HAS MANNERS. HA,HA,HA. SHOT QUICK & WELL, KIND'A PUNK.

COLOR * 86 MINS. * 1972 UNRATED

DIRECTED BY VAL GUEST

SCREENPLAY by: VAL GUEST & DAVID ADNOPOZ

ASTRID FRANK, JOHNNY BRIGGS, GABRIELLE DRAKE, ME ME LAI, NANCY WAIT JOYCE HERON, DAPHNE ANDERSON, GEOFFREY BAYLDON, ROGER AVON, ROSALIE-CRUTCHLEY, HAROLD BENNETT, JULIAN BARNES, JOHN LeMESURIER, RICHARD-O'SULLIVAN, DEREK GRAY, CHARLES MORGAN, MARIANNE STONE, LYN-YELDHAM, NORMAN CHAPPELL, ROBIN FORD, FERDY MAYNE, JOHN STANDING STEVE PATTERSON, TREVOR BANNISTER, CHRISTINE DONNA, MILTON REID MARCIA FOX, CAROLE CATKIN

SEXY RETRO FROM THE SAUCY SEVENTIES

jezebel

SUS

SUS

VALGUEST'S

Au Pair

GIRLS

TYRESE IS A SPOILED IRRESPONCIBLE MAN/BOY THE MOVIE OPENS W/ A QUOTE ABOUT HOW THE BLACK MAN HAS BEEN EMOUTIONALLY STUNTED IN MODERN AMERICA, BUT I THINK ITS BIGGER THAN THAT. IT SEEMS TO ME THAT AMERICANS HAVE BECOME SPOILED IN GENERAL & HAVE BECOME BRATS. THIS MOVIE IS FANTASTIC. VING HAS ALL KINDS OF SEX W/ TYRESES MOM & PUTS HIM IN A SLEEPERHOLD. SNOOP GETS OUT OF JAIL & TAKES HIS GIRLFRIEND BACK FROM TYRESE. HE INTIMIDATES THE SHIT OUT OF TYRESE WHICH IS GREAT CONSIDERING HOW BUFF TYRESE IS. SINGLETONS UN-SUBTLE APROACH SEEMS TO RUN FOLKS OF OFF HIS MOVIES. BUT I THINK HE'S GREAT, EVEN THOUGH I DON'T ALLWAYS AGREE W/HIM. TOTALLY UNDERRATED. TYRESE IS GREAT, BUT VING TOTALLY STEALS THE MOVIE. HES SO COOL, TOUGH, FUNNY, SMART, CHARMING & HARDWORKING. OBVIOUSLY A PORTRAIT OF WHAT ONCE WAS & SHOULD BE AGAIN, A REAL MAN.

WRITTEN PRODUCED & DIRECTED by JOHN SINGLETON

R RESTRICTED

SPECIALEDITION

TYRESE GIBSON SNOOP DOGG AND VING RHAMES

A FILM BY JOHN SINGLETON

baby boy

TWENTIETH CENTURY FUXXXZZZZ
SELECTIONS
TOM HANKS ADRIAN ZMED
BACHELOR PARTY

SEE'N THIS AS A KID IT SEEMED WILDER & MORE SEXY THEN IT DOSE NOW. IT'S MOSTLY ABSTRACT SUGGESTION W/ A ZAINY DELIVERY. ITS THE CAST THAT'S MORE INT-ERISTING TO ME NOW. LIKE ADRIAN ZMED AS THE BIG STUD & BEST FRIEND JERK.

I DIDN'T KNOW HE WAS IN T.J. HOOKER TILL 5 YEARS AGO, WHICH IS PROBABLY HOW HE GOT BILLED OVER THE TITLE. WEIRD. I THINK THIS IS GONNA BE HOW HE'S REMEMBERED OVER T.J. WHICH IS MAYBE TOO BAD CUZ T.J. IS A LOT OF FUN. HANKS KEEPS TRYING TO PULL A SEX MOVE WITH AN EGGBEATER WHICH I STILL CAN'T FIGURE OUT. IF YOU KNOW PLEASE TELL ME. THE ANTAGONIST IS A RICHSHIT YUPPIE TYPE WHO FALLS VICTIM TO THE MOST UNFORTUNATE MEXICAN 80'S MOVIE CLECHE. I SAY THAT ITS UNFORTUNATE CUZ I HAVE NEVER FALLEN INTO ITS "CLUTCHS". MEXICAN DUDES WILL STEAL YOUR CAR & IMEDIEATLY SPEND TONS OF $ TURNING IT INTO A LOWRIDER THEN RETURN IT AS A PRANK. I WISH.

TOM HANKS ADRIAN ZMED
WILLIAM TEPPER TAWNY KITAEN
STORY BY BOB ISRAEL
SCREENPLAY BY
NEAL ISRAEL & PAT PROFT
105 mins.
1984 DIRECTED BY NEAL ISRAEL

HI-FI

R

20

RODNEY DANGEFIELD RANDY QUAID KIRSTIE ALLEY

BACK BY MIDNIGHT

RANDY QUAID

KIRSTIE ALLEY

PAUL RODRIGUEZ

GILBERT GOTTFRIED

ED BEGLEY JR.

RODNEY DANGERFIELD
RANDY QUAID
KiRSTiE ALLEY
THIS IS MAYBE MY FAV RODNEY, W/EASYMONEY. THIS IS MY GO TO. LOTS OF JOKES &, FUN. ITS A LAID BACK PRIVATIZED PRISON W/ RODNEY AS WARDEN. IT MAKES YOU WANT TO GO THERE, BUT EVIL CORPRATE JERKS MAKE TROUBLE & ON LIKE THAT. ITS A REAL COOL LAID BACK CHARMER W/ A CRUDE STREAK. IF YOU DON'T DIG THIS THEN YOU NEED TO TAKE A STEP BACK & CHILL OUT DUDE. PERFECTO!
MONARCH
COMEDY RUNTIME 90 MINS
R RESTRICTED
RODNEY DANGERFIELD KIRSTIE ALLEY TONY COX PHILLAMARR PAUL RODRIGUEZ GILBERT GOTTFRIED RANDY QUAID HARLAND WILLIAMS
2005
WRITTEN BY
RODNEY DANGERFIELD & HARRY BASIL
COLOR
DIRECTED BY HARRY BASIL

MCA UNIVERSAL
VHS
BACK IN ACTION
MAN, I WISH THESE TWO WOULD DO
MORE MOVIES TOGETHER. I REALLY DIG
THIS MOVIE A LOT. NICE CAMERA WERK
& FIGHT SCENES. TRIPPY 90'S FASHION
LIKE HOTPANTS W/A SLEEVLESS OVER-
COAT. BILLY WEARS BRIGHT BLUE DENEM
W/A PEACE SIGN VEST &
HE & HIS SISTER BOTH
HAVE FASHION BANDAGES
ON THEIR WRISTS. RODDY
IS GREAT AS USUAL &
HE HAS SOME COOL STR-
EIGHT LEGGED BLACK
JEANS TO EMPHISIZE
HIS EPIC SHOLDERS.
GOOD CHARISMA & NICE PACE
KEEP IT ALL HUMMING ALONG
A LOT OF SLOW-MO & SUN-
GLASSES ALL AROUND.
I LOVE IT.
COLOR 1 hr. 33 min
CC 1994
R Restricted

BILLY RODDY
BLANKS PIPER
BACK ACTION
RODDY PIPER BILLY BLANKS BOBBIE PHILLIPS
MATT BIRMAN NIGEL BENNETT
DAMON D'OLIVEIRA KAI SOREMEKUN
WRITTEN by KARL SCHIFFMAN
DIRECTED by STEVE DIMARCO
STEREO R

BACK TO SCHOOL

RODNEY DANGERFIELD SALLY KELLERMAN BURT YOUNG KEITH GORDON ADRIENNE BARBEAU ROBERT DOWNEY JR. SAM KINISON WRITTEN by STEVEN KAMPMANN, WILL PORTER, PETER TOROKVEI HAROLD RAMIS, RODNEY DANGERFIELD, GREG FIELDS, DENNIS SNEE

DIRECTED by ALAN METTER

AS YOU CAN PLAINLY SEE THE SCRIPT HAS A "TOO MENY COOKS IN THE KITCHEN" TYPE THING GO'N ON. BUT BETWEEN RODNEY, SAM, & ROBERT JR. THERES ENOUGH GOODNESS TO KEEP IT GO'N GOOD. I'LL GIVE RAMIS A SHOT AS AN OTHER ELEMENT OF FUN. WHO KNOWS? the shadow knows. OKWELL... THIS IS AN ICON OF RODNEYS & HE DOSE HAVE SOME GREAT ONES ~~HERE~~ BUT FOR ME IT'S A BIT FORMÜLE' LIKE STREIGHT SCEENS & STUFF W/OUT RODNEYS ~~HEART~~. WASTEFULL. BUT I LOVE IT. I'V GOT RODNEYITES SO FOR ME THIS IS PROBABLY MY FIRST & IT'S GOT HIM ON SCREEN MORE THAN MENY. THE STORY GO'S, RODNEY IS A SELFMADE SUCESS WHOS FROM THE SCHOOL OF HARD KNOCKS. HE SENDS HIS SON TO A STUFFY IVY LEAGUE SCHOOL & OUT OF LONELYNESS DECIDES TO GO TO. HE MEETS RESISTANCE BUT TURNS IT ON IT'S HEAD. BE TRUE TO YOURSELF IMPOWERMENT TYPE DEAL.

HBO
CANNON
VIDEO

RUNNING TIME: 96 MINUTES

VHS
HI-FI
ORION

PG-13 COLOR 1986

RODNEY
DANGERFIELD
BACK TO SCHOOL

DENNIS HOPPER - JODIE FOSTER
BackTrack
1992 DIRECTOR'S CUT BY DENNIS HOPPER

Back Track

APPROX. RUNNING TIME: 102 Min.

WHAT A COOL MOVIE. THE SET UP IS COMMON, BEAUTIFUL ARTIST WITNESS' A MOB HIT. GO'S ON THE RUN. MASTER HITMAN GO'S TO KILL HER BUT FALLS IN LOVE W/ HER INSTEAD. BUT FROM THIS COMES A GREAT MOVIE. UNIQUE CHARACTERS & LITTLE INTEREST IN HANDING YOU ENDLESS EXCUSES FOR ITS MOVEMENTS. THE CAST IS AS YOU CAN SEE, PERFECT. HOPPER DOSE A GREAT JOB INFRONT OF & BEHIND THIS MOVIE & I'M GO'N BACK THROUGH HIS DIRECTORIAL CATALOGUE. PRETTY INSPIRATIONAL ARTIST FOR ME. OUTSIDE OF THE CONCEPT THIS IS VERY MUCH AN ALEX COX MOVIE TOO. RECOMENDED

SCREENPLAY
RACHEL KRONSTADT & ANN LOUISE BARDACH
WASH & RINSE BY ALEX COX

R

DIRECTED BY
DENNIS HOPPER

TWO NITES BACK TO BACK CUT TOGETHER. AMAZING. DUDE IS ON FIRE, STOPS EVERYONE TO TELL A GUY WHO IS BLEEDING TO GO CLEAN HIMSELF. THERE A POWER OUTAGE. I DON'T KNOW HOW TO TALK ABOUT MUSIC SO MUCH BIT I LIKE THIS VIDEO ALOT & PUT IT ON TO GET SOME REAL DOING DONE. THIS LIVED AT THE BAD APPLE FOR YEARS AS PART OF THE STORE TV SET WE USED. REWARDING AFTER REPEATED PLAYINGS. IF YOU DON'T KNOW BAD BRAINS THEY ARE PUNK & RASTA TOO. GOOD COMBO, I DIG IT AT LEAST.

TRACK LISTING

- BIG TAKE OVER
- ATTITUDE
- I
- I AND I RASTA
- SUPERTOUCH/SHIT FIT
- KING of GLORY/w DAVE HAHN
- RIGHT BRIDGE
- F.U.K.
- BANNED IN DC
- HOW LOW CAN A PUNK GET
- THE MEEK SHALL INHERIT
- RIOT SQUAD
- WE WILL NOT
- COPTIC TIMES
- AT THE MOVIES
- RIGHT BRIDGE
- RALLY AROUND JAH THRONE
- RED BONE IN THE CITY
- PAY TO CUM

BONUS MATERIALS

- INTERVIEWS FROM 1982
- BONUS AUDIO TRACK: I AND I SURVIVE

DIRECTED BY RICHARD ORETSKY

CAMERAS BY RICHARD ORETSKY and DUNCAN KRUSE

MVD visual

CBGB
OMFUG

BAD BRAINS
LIVE AT
CBGB OMFUG
1982

NICOLAS CAGE EVA M

SMOKE

A FILM

VAL KILMER ALVIN "XZIBIT" J

CRACK

HERZOG

BAD LIEUTENANT

PORT OF CALL NEW ORLEANS

"BAD LIEUTENANT: PORT OF CALL NEW ORLEANS"

PRODUCED BY EDWARD R. PRESSMAN SCREENPLAY BY WILLIAM FINKELSTEIN DIRECTED BY WERNER HERZOG

COCAIN

RAD

ower 10 (633)
esenting
IEUTENANT
1 Wed 12/16/09
ult $10.50
5
100010004 MCR
/09 09:57 PM
customer copy

EVEN THOUGH I DID'NT BUY MY TICKET I CAN SAY I'D BUY THE NEXT TWO.

NICK CAGE IS A LITTLE SHITTY IN HIS MOVIE CHOICES RECENTLY, BUT HE'S TOTTALY BACK TO A CHARASMATIC REDICKULESS MANIAC; WHICH IS HOW I TEND TO PREFER HIM. SO, GOOD SHIT. HERZOG PROBABLY IS 85% RESPONCIBLE FOR THE RAD'NESS. HIS DAP LEVELS OUT THE INCONGRUINCE'S THAT MOVIES WITH A CAST AS DESPRATELLY VARRIED OFTEN CHOKE ON. PRETTY MUCH A COKEHEAD POWERTRIP MOVIE WITH A HAPPY ENDING TWISTED INTO A COLLAGE OF CAPTIVATING INCOUNTERS. YOU KNOW, HERZOG SHIT. THE ART'Y-NESS IS A LITTLE MORE OF A COLLAGE THAN THE O.G. PRETTY MEAN & FUNNY BUT NOT BRUTTAL. THE CAST IS PART OF THE APEAL FOR ME, I LIKE A LOT OF THE PEOPLE IN IT.

NICOLAS CAGE EVA MENDES RUSSELL HAEUSER VAL KILMER XZIBIT FAIRUZA BALK BRAD DOURIF

SCREENPLAY by WILLIAM FINKELSTEIN

DIRECTED by WERNER HERZOG

2009 R 2 HOURS 2 MINUTES

THE CRITERION COLLECTION, a bunch of movies with matching box's, has brought us...

THE bank DICK

IT IS SO GOOD. SO GOOOOOOOOOD. IT JUST JAMS. A BIG WASTIOD MAKES HIS WAY IN THE WORLD. A BLUE COLLER HERO W/ A DRINK & NO FRIENDS. RAD CHASE SCEEN. RECOMENDED.

1940 · 72 minutes
BLACK & WHITE
I'D SEE'N A FEW SHORTS BUT DIDN'T REAL'Y GET FIELDS UNTILL I SAW THIS. DUDE IS GREAT. TOP BILLING.

W.C. FIELDS
UNA MERKEL CORA WITHERSPOON SHEMP HOWARD
FRANKLIN PANGBORN GRADY SUTTON director: EDWARD CLINE
screenplay: MAHATMA KANE JEEVES

THE CRITERION COLLECTION

THE bank dick

W.C. FIELDS

from the director of NAKED GUN

I NEVER GAVE THIS MOVIE A SHOT. I WAS A BIT SOUTHPARK'T OUT. THEN OVER THE NEXT DOZEN YEARS FOLKS SAY IT'S WORTH WATCH'N. OK, OK. SO I COP A COPY. HEY, IT'S UNPRETENTIOUS GOOFBALL SATIRE GENRE-BENDER. IT'S FUN. GOOD. NO FUCK UPS. WHEN YOU REQUIRE A REDICKULESS CRASS SILLY MOVIE GIVE IT A SHOT IF YOU AINT TOO UPTIGHT. DUDES INVENT A GAME THEY CAN'T LOSE & IT CATCHES ON & THEY RULE IT W/A FLOCK OF FAME PARELS ON THEIR ASS.

TREY PARKER, MATT STONE
YASMINE BLEETH, JENNY McCARTHY
ROBERT VAUGHN, ERNEST BORGNINE, DIAN BACHAR

WRITTEN by
DAVID ZUCKER, ROBERT LoCASH, LEWIS FRIEDMAN, & JEFF WRIGHT
DIRECTED by DAVID ZUCKER

COLOR 1 hour 44 minutes 1998 CC R

BAT PUSSY/ BABY BUBBLES -Volume 23

BATPUSSY IS MORE LIKE A SESSION OF TERETS THERAPY THAN A PORNO. THE SAME INSULTS & THRETS ARE REWORKED THROUGH OUT. THERES ONE GUY & HE NEVER GETS A BONER DISPITE ORAL ASSISTANCE. THE WIFE HAS AN AWESOME HAIR-DO. BATPUSSY CUS'S, PUTS HER CLOATHS ON, RIDES AROUND ON A BALL W/A HANDEL, INTERUPTS A RAPE & SMACKS DUDE W/HER PONY BALL THING. THEN SHE INTERUPTS THIS SHIT TALK'N HEARTLESS ORAL SEX COUPLE. DUDE PRETENDS TO HAVE A BONER BUT WE CAN SEE THATS NOT SO.

BABY BUBBLES IS A SECRET AGENT OF **G**.IRLS **A**.GAINST **S**.LAVERY <G.A.S.> SO SHE ACTS LIKE AN IDIOT & HOOKS UP W/CREEPY PORNOGRAPHERS. BLOWS ONE OF THEM, MASTEBATES, MAKESOUT W/ THE NEW GIRL. THE NEW GIRL HAS ACTUAL COMMON SEX W/THE DUDE WHILE HIS BUDDY ALSO HAS SEX W/A WOMAN WHO GO'S UNEXPLAINED. A CLOSING VOICEOVER SAYS THAT THE DRUGPORNO DUDES GET BUSTED.

BUCKY BEAVERS
DRAGON
ART THEATRE
TRIPLE XXX-RATED
DOUBLE FEATURES

BAT PUSSY
BABY BUBBLES

MICHAEL KEATON
DANNY DeVITO
MICHELLE PFEIFFER

BATMAN
RETURNS

MICHAE KEATON DANNY DeVITO MICHELLEPFEIFFER
CHRISTOPHER WALKEN
WRITTEN BY
DANIEL WATERS & SAM HAMM
DIRECTED BY TIM BURTON

I'D FORGOTTEN ALLMOST THE WHOLE THING. IT WAS LIKE WATCHING IT NEW. I DIG IT. IT'S ALLVILLENS. BATMAN IS A FRAIMING DEVICE. IT'S A LITTLE LONG BUT I WISH THEY HAD MADE A FEW MORE LIKE IT. BATMAN IS DOING STREIGHT-UP MURDERS HERE. HE STUFFS LITE DYNAMITE DOWN DUDES PANTS THEN DROPS HIM HEAD FIRST DOWN A MANHOLE. TRIPLE VILLENS. PEEWEE CAMEO. WISH THEY'D MADE/MAKE SPIN OFF SHOW FOR DEVITOS PENGUIN. DIGGIN THROUGH FILTH.
VIDEO
WB
FBI
PG-13
DIGITALLY PROCESSED
1992

JOHN SAVAGE KIRA GLOVER PAUL DILLON

THERES A LOT OF MOVIES W/ THIS NAME, THE BEAT 1988 SEEMS THE BEST WAY TO DISTINGWISH. PAUL MONES WROTE & DIRECTED 2 OTHER MOVIES. THEN HE CO-WROTE A COUPLE VAN DAMME MOVIES. HE'S IN TUFF TURF.

102 MINUTES IT SAYS 1986 BUT IT MIGHT BE '88 [R]

WRITTEN & DIRECTED by PAUL MONES

A COMMING OF AGE IMPOWERMENT TALE ABOUT HIGHSCHOOL BADASSES. THEY FIGHT AMONG THEMSELVES OUT OF AIMLESSNESS & BOREDOM. THERE TEACHERS MOSTLY HATE THEM BUT ONE TRYS TO BE COOL W/THEM. THEN A NEW WEIRDO MOVES TO THE HOOD & THEY DUB HIM RETARD BECAUSE HE'S POETIC & POSI. HE'S GOT A FOLKY GURU RAP THING "THE BEAT THE BEAT, BOOM BOOM" HE'S INTO & CAN INSPIRE WITH. THE COOL TEACHER BACKS HIM UP. THE KIDS ARE VERBALLY RACIST BUT DON'T ACTUALLY ACT OUT ON IT. IT'S TRIPPY, BECAUSE NO ONE IS SPAIRED THE RACIST SLURS EXCEPT THE NEW KID WHO IS JEWISH I THINK HE'S A MAGICAL WANDERING JEW BUT THEY CALL HIM THE RETARD. IT'S ODD. LIKE, IS IT MORE RACIST THAT WAY? WERE THEY TRYING TO MAKE IT LESS? IT'S PRETTY OBVIOUS THAT THIS WAS A PLAY FIRST. THE STAGING, MONOLOGUES & PACE HOLD FORM. AT ONE POINT SOME OF THE KIDS GO SEE THE IRON SKULLS PLAY A SHOW & THE MOVIE TURNS INTO 3½ MINUTES OF A CRO-MAGS SHOW W/THE KIDS CUT IN. AGE OF QUARREL LINE UP. IT'S LIKE A SACCHARINE INNER-CITY S.E. HINTON TYPE THING. I DIG IT. IT MIGHT BE A PAIN IN THE ASS TO FIND. MY BUDDY ARLO LENT ME IT.

NASIR "NAS" JONES
EARL "DMX" SIMMONS TARAL HICKS
TIONNE "T-BOZ" WATKINS CLIFFORD "METHOD MAN" SMITH
STORY BY ANTHONY BODDEN, NAS, HYPE WILLIAMS
WRITTEN and DIRECTED by HYPE WILLIAMS

DOLBY  ARTISAN

OH MAN I SAW THIS IN THE THEATRE & FOLKS SEEMED CONFUSED BY IT. WELL I THOUGHT ABOUT IT & TO ME IT SEEMS LIKE THEY MUST

HEY DUDE. NEXT TIME YOUR PUTTING SCARFACE '83 ON JUST PUT THIS ON INSTED. IT'S HALF AS LONG & 5 TIMES BETTER. IT HAS GROWTH, INTELIGENCE, & WISDOM. AND IT'S NOT A BORING WANK OFF.

HAVE BEEN WAY HIGHER OR DRUNKER THAN ME. OR PERHAPS THEY WERE OVER WHELMED BY THE BEAUTIFUL HYPE PHOTOGRAPHY. SO, REAL QUICK, NASTY NAS & DMX ARE FLIPPING DRUGS & KNOCK'N OVER CLUBS. THEY SEEM TO BE GROWING APART. BUT THEY STEP UP THEIR GAME ANY WAYS. NASTY NAS IS GROWING UP & WANTS TO GET OUT TO MOVE HIS FAMILY TO AFRICA. DMX KEEPS GETTING MORE AGRESSIVE & NON-CHALANT W/ HIS LIFE. <u>THERES A TON OF VIOLENCE/WEED/GUNS</u>/WOMEN TO THE POINT WHERE IT'S HARD TO TELL HOW MUCH TIME PASS'S. IT SEEMS LIKE A LOT. DMX IS BUSTED, & THE FED'S GIVE HIM A DEAL IF HE WILL ASSASSINATE THE MINISTER {FARRAKHAN?}. HE ACCEPTS BUT CAN NOT FOLLOW THROUGH. IT SEEMS THAT NASTY NAS & DMX ARE WELL SUITED AS A TEAM. 2 SIDES, 1 COIN. A PRETTY CLASSIC STORY, W/ THE ACCEPTION OF DMX NOT TAKING THE SELFISH OUT. CREDIBILITY. PERHAPS IT'S THE BREVITY & DAP OF HYPE'S ARTISTRY THAT TAKES CENTERSTAGE IN THE MOVIE THAT HAS FOLKS OVERWHELMED. HE DOSENT HAVE ANY EXTRANIOUS CRAP ELEMENTS TO PAD OUT THE MOVIE. THE MEDITATIVE SHOTS SWITCH TO FORSHADOWING &/OR HEAVY CONFLICTS. UNRESTFUL. NO WONDER NASTY NAS WANT'S TO MOVE TO AFRICA. I HOPE HYPE MAKE MORE MOVIES.

GOD I WAS READY TO PUKE MOLTIN VENOM ALL OVER THIS THING. YES IT IS A FULLY BRO'D OUT VIDEO GAME. BUT IT'S SO WEIRD AND CREEPY. IT SEEMS LIKE IT MUST HAVE BEEN BORN OLD.

I CAN GET PRETTY UPTIGHT ABOUT THE CG BARRIER & PERHAPS THAT'S PART OF THE CHARM, BECAUSE IT'S SO IMBRACED. LOOK AT THAT LIST OF FOLKS WHO DID IT. ZEMECKIS IS STILL INTERESTING TO ME WHICH IS SUPRISING TO ME BASED ON THE CROUD HE OFTEN IS ACCOCICATED WITH. THE SPECIAL FEATURES ARE GREAT. GLOVERS ALONE IS A MUST.

RAY WINSTONE ANTHONY HOPKINS JOHN MALKOVICH
ROBIN WRIGHT PENN BRENDAN GLEESON CRISPIN GLOVER
ALISON LOHMAN &, ANGELINA JOLIE

SCREENPLAY BY NEIL GAIMAN &, ROGER AVARY.

DIRECTED BY ROBERT ZEMECKIS

UNRATED NTSC 2007 COLOR

BEOWULF
DIRECTORSCUT

20th Century Fox
SELECTIONS
John Cusack
Better off Dead

I CAN'T RECALL WHEN OR AT WHAT MIND STATE I WAS AT BUT THAT DRAWING IS A FRIEGHT. AS A LEAD IN TO THE MOVIE THE BOX IS SUPER WRONG ANYHOW BUT NOW IT LOOKS LIKE SOME SARTE SHIT. WELL, THIS IS A SILLYASS COMEDY WITH A SEMIBROODING LEAD. MOST LIKELY ONE OF THE BEST HIGHSCHOOL COMEDYS OF THE 80'S & PROBABLY BEYOND TOO. SAVAGE STEVE HOLLAND ONLY MADE ONE OTHER MOVIE FOR YEARS "ONE CRAZY SUMMER" & THEN HE WENT TO T.V. HE'S A HOOT. I ♡ IT WHEN DUDES USE CLAYMATION IN MOVIES & THIS IS A FANTASTIC EXAMPLE. I SAW THIS IN 5TH GRADE @ MY BUDDY TREVORS HOUSE. I HAD'NT SEEN ANYTHING LIKE IT. SCREWBALL/DARK ABSURD/EMO. HIS LITTLE BROTHER IS AWESOME & TAYLOR NEGRONE IS GREAT IN HIS 45 SECONDS OF SCREEN TIME. GOOD GOLLY WOULD YOU LOOK AT THAT PENMENSHIP
WRITTEN & DIRECTED by SAVAGE STEVE HOLLAND
1985 COLOR 97 MINUTES STEREO

PEEP'T THIS OUT IN THE THEATRE & WAS RELITIVLY INTO IT BUT SOME HOW WAS'NT INTO THE BLOW OFF STYLE OF THE "STORY". WHAT? DUDE I THINK I WAS TOO UPTIGHT IN THOSE DAYS. IT'S A SCREW-BALL SATIRE WITH FULL H.K. ACTION. TELL THE TRUTH IT'S GOT A LOT GO'N ON MAYBE TOO MUCH CUZ IT SEEMS LIKE A BIT MORE AIR-HEAD'D-NESS MIGHT FIT NICE BUT NO PROBLEM

MARK'Y'MARK IS GREAT AS THE BEST & MOST PATHETIC KILL'R ON THE TEAM. HE'S A PUSHOVER & GET'S HIMSELF IN DEEP SHIT. BOKEEM DISCOVERS THE POWERS OF JACK'N IT & SCORES SOME OF THE BEST LINES OF THE WHOLE MOVIE. ANTONIO IS THE PRETTY BOY & GETS THE WEAK JOKES TOO BAD I THINK HIS CHARACTER WAS DROPPED IN EDITING A BIT. LOU DIAMOND IS GREAT. I WISH I SAW HIM IN MORE MOVIES HE'S SO GOOD AT GETTING MAD. HE'S THE BIG DOG ON THE TEAM & SHITS ON MARK THE MOST. ELLIOTT GOULD STEELS EVERY SCEENE AS USUAL.

THERES SUCH A MANIC CAR-TOONY NESS HERE THAT IT SORT'A RAN ME OVER. NOW'A DAY'S I WATCH THIS MORE AS BACK-GROUND, PROBABLY CAUSE I'V SEEN IT ENOUGH THAT I CAN. THE CAST IS PRETTY GREAT BOBBY HAD ME CONVINCED THAT BET MIDLER WAS IN THIS BUT... SHE'S NOT. WESLEY IS A PRODUCER ON THIS BUT NOT IN IT WHICH IS A BUMMER. THERES SOME BONUS SCEENS OF ANTONIO TAKING IT FURTHER WHICH THEY SHOULD HAVE KEPT IN THE MOVIE. FUN/NUTS.

MARK WALBERG LOU DIAMOND PHILLIPS CHRISTINA APPLEGATE
AVERY BROOKS BOKEEM WOODBINE ANTONIO SABATO JR.
LAINE KAZAN ELLIOTT GOULD SAB SHIMONO LELA ROCHON

WRITTEN BY BEN RAMSEY PRODUCED BY WARREN ZIDE & WESLEY SNIPES
DIRECTED BY CHE-KIRK WONG
1998

R RESTRICTED CC Approx. 91 minutes COLOR 1

TRI STAR DVD VIDEO SONY

MARK WAHLBERG
LOU DIAMOND PHILLIPS
CHRISTINA APPLEGATE
BOKEEM WOODBINE
ANTONIO SABATO, JR.
the big hit
DVD VIDEO

JAN MICHAEL VINCENT · WILLIAM KATT
GARY BUSEY · PATTI D'ARBANVILLE
LEE PURCELL
SCREENPLAY by JOHN MILIUS & DENNIS AABERG
DIRECTED by JOHN MILIUS
1978 120 MINUTES PG
PANAVISION · METROCOLOR

MAN, THIS MOVIE MAKES ME WANT TO MOVE TO THE COAST. I'M SURE IT'S GOT A LOT TO DO W/ THE IDEALIZATION MILIUS IS DO'N IT SURE FEELS LIKE THERES MORE THAN A LITTLE AUTOBIO HERE. DUDES SURF AND TOPDOG ALL AROUND TOWN BEING ROWDY AND CHARMING. LIVING IN PARTYMODE, HAVING FUN FIGHTS. THEY DON'T LOOK IT BUT I THINK THEY'R TEENAGERS AT THE BEGINING & IN THEIR 20'S AT THE END. THEY EACH HAVE THEY'R OWN WAYS AND PATH'S THAT LEAD THEM INTO GROWING UP W/ THE POSSABLE EXCEPTION OF BUSEY WHO SEEMS TO JUST GET MORE WILD ALPHA. SOME NICE CHILLED OUT MACHO PHILOSOPHY FOR SURE, MORE IN-TOUCH W/ NATURE STYLE. THEY ALL GO IT ALONE BUT STAY TRUE TO THE PACK. THE DRAWING UP TOP HERE IS OFF A PRODUCTION PHOTO, MILIUS IS THE ONE W/ THE BEARD. THE OTHERS ARE THE SURFERS WITH THEIR ACTOR COUNTER PARTS. THEY HAVE A COOL GURU/OLDER DUDE NAMED BEAR WHO LIVES ON THE PIER AND BUILDS ALL THEIR SURF BOARDS. THERES EVEN A LITTLE EARLY "SIDEWALK SURFING". THEY HEAD DOWN TO MEXICO FOR A BIT AND GET INTO TROUBLE AND BUSEY IS A TOTAL ASSHOLE. BUMMER. THE CARS ARE BEAUTIFUL IN THIS MOVIE, WHICH MAKES SENSE SINCE IT TAKES PLACE IN THE 60'S. COOL MOVIE, KIND'A EPIC AND MELLOW AT THE SAME TIME, BREASY & HEAVY. THATS A TOUGH COMBO TO PULL OFF. FULLY RECOMENDED FOR ALL YOU BEEFCAKE LOVERS AND JOCK PUNKS.

Bill&Ted's
EXCELLENT
adventure
NELSON

ALEX WINTER KEANU REEVES GEORGE CARLIN

SCREENPLAY BY CHRIS MATHESON & ED SOLOMON

DIRECTED BY STEPHEN HEREK

ORION PG DICKWEED

COLOR COMEDY CLOSED CAPTIONED 90 MINUTES 1989

I SAW THIS MOVIE & DREW THIS BOX BUT BEFORE I WROTE ANYTHING THERE WAS A HUGE AMOUNT OF ATTENTION ON IT IN THE PEJORATIVE FANDOM TYPE WAY. I'M NOT ABOUT THAT "IT'S SO BAD ITS GOOD" JAM. I WANT NEW {TO ME} IDEAS, STYLES, FUN, TRUTH. BUDGET MEANS LITTLE TO QUALITY. SO, THIS MOVIE. DUDE MAKES AN INDEPENDENT BRUCHEIMER STYLE KNOKOFF. IT'S COOL THATS HIS JAM BUT THERES NOT MUCH THERE FOR ME. THIS MOVIE IS WEIRDLY SUPER NORMAL. I REALLY ENJOIED DRAWING THAT NEIGHBORHOOD IN FLAIMES. THIS DUDE SAYS THIS IS HIS HOMAGE OR SOMESUCH, TO THE BIRDS. SURE THAT MAKES SENCE. THE BIRDS WAS MY FIRST HITCHCOCK & IT DID'NT REALY EXCITE ME. SO I DID'NT PERSUE HIM TILL LATER & I SAW IT AGAIN ON CABLE & IT STILL WAS'NT PUSHING MY BUTTONS SO GOOD. THIS MOVIE IS A LOVESTORY W/ EXCITING CHAOTIC SERCUMSTANCES FOR THEM TO CONTEND WITH. BIRDS CAN BE SCARY BUT ITS NOT ONE OF THOSE FEARS I CARRY W/ ME DAILY. FOOL WOULD HAVE TO BE IN MY FACE BEFORE I FREAK OUT. I THINK I'D WANT A SWORD IN THIS MOVIE. A WHIP WOULD BE COOL BUT I'D PROLLY JUST HERT MY SELF. I DON'T SEE FOLKS ROCKING THE WHIP. OR MAYBE THEY JUST DO THEM CONCEILED CARRY. I'D FEEL SAFER IF EVERYONE CARRIED WHIPS. THATS SOME REAL SHIT, NOT SOME COWARD GUN POSE. WE COULD SWING FROM TREES. WHIP IT. WHIP IT GOOD.

A JAMES NGUYN FILM

BIRDDEMIC

SHOCK AND TERROR

PATRICK SWAYZE
BLACK DOG
RANDY TRAVIS
MEAT LOAF
Bob's
OK, SO CLEARLY THIS WAS BOB'S TAPE FIRST, BUT I GOT THIS AT GOODWILL. I HOPE BOB IS O.K. SOMETIMES I WORRY THAT THE PERSONALIZED BOX'S COME FROM SAD CIRCUMSTANCES. KEEP ON TRUCKING Bob. ♡ tim

FROM THE DIRECTOR OF "PASSENGER 57"

BLACK DOG

CHECK IT DUDE, I WAS WATCH'N & DIGG'N THIS ENOUGH BUT NOT ALL IMPRESS & BLOW'N AWAY. SWAYZE PICKS PRETTY GOOD ACTION MOVIES TO WERK ON & THIS WAS COMING ALONG O.K. THEN, THEY DO SOME AMAZING BIG RIG STUNTS & I REWOUND IT OVER & OVER. GREAT STUNTS, SOLID ACT'RS ALL THE WAY THROUGH. I ♡ MEATLOAF & RANDY TRAVIS IS ACTUALLY BETTER THAN I EXPECTED. I REALLY DIG THE CHARACTER "JUNIOR" I WISH HE HAD A BIGGER ROLL. SWAYZE COMES OFF KIND'A MEXICAN HERE, I DON'T KNOW IF IT'S THE SCRIPT OR HIM BUT I BET IT'S A BIT OF BOTH. COOL. SWAYZE HAS A COOL STUNT & MAY HAVE DONE A GOOD NUMBER OF HIS OWN HERE. NOT THAT I REALLY KNOW BUT I THINK HE'S ONE OF THOSE KIND'A GUY'S. FULLY SOLID ACTION MOVIE, NICE MANABEABLE CAMERA WORK A SMALL AMOUNT OF CHEESE'Y CG, BUT NO BIG PROBABLEM.

PATRICK SWAYZE RANDY TRAVIS MEAT LOAF
STEPHEN TOBOLOWSKY CHARLES DUTTON
WRITTEN BY WILLIAM MICKELBERRY & DAN VINING
DIRECTED BY KEVIN HOOKS

PG-13 COLOR 1 HR. 29 MINS. 1998 VHS dude!

WHEN I HEARD ABOUT THIS I SAID WHY & PUT IT OUT OF MY MIND. THEN ANTHONY KEPT TALKING ABOUT IT & I KEPT TELLING HIM TO WATCH THE ORIGINAL. THIS WENT ON A YEAR & A HALF AT LEAST. WHY, I GUESS I JUST FELT TIRED OF BEING STUBORN OR SOMETHING. I BORROWED IT OFF HIM. OH SHIT. YOU KNOW WHAT? IT'S GOOD. IT HAS ITS OWN THING AND IT'S PRETTY MUCH A SEQUAL, AND BOB CLARK WAS DOWN WITH IT THOUGH I DON'T THINK HE GOT TO SEE IT. ITS PERVEY BUT NOT WASTEFULY SO. IT PLAYS WITH A LOT OF THE MATERIAL FROM THE O.G. & USES SOME ELEMENTS IN A WAY THAT WAS THOUGHTFUL. THIS DUDE ALSO MADE THE CRISPIN GLOVER "WILLARD" WHICH I ALSO DUG. THAT EYEBALL UP THERE ↖ REMINDS ME OF THE JEEPERS CREEPERS BOX. ANYWAYS,

CHECK THIS OUT.

KATIE CASSIDY MICHELLE TRACHTENBERG MARY ELIZABETH WINSTEAD
OLIVER HUDSON LACEY CHABERT KRISTEN CLOKE ANDREA MARTIN

SCREENPLAY & DIRECTION by
GLEN MORGAN

DIMENSION 2929 COLOR DVD NOT RATED 2006 95 MINUTES

BLACK X-MAS

UNRATED

DAMON WAYANS'
BLANKMAN

DAMON WAYANS DAVID ALAN GRIER
ROBIN GIVENS JON POLITO JASON ALEXANDER
SCREENPLAY by DAMON WAYANS & J.F. LAWTON
DIRECTED by MIKE BINDER

CC PG-13 1995 COLOR APPROX 96 MIN. USA

BLOOD
& DONUTS

FULLLENGTHSCREENER

GREAT, DRY CAMP. THEY HIT MOST OF THE VAMPIRE TROPES W/OUT BEING PRETENTIOUS OR BORING WHICH IS TOUGH THESE DAYS. I DIG THE CAST. THERES A BOOKISH ROMANTIC MOPIE'NES THAT REALLY APPEALS TO ME, SEEMS LOVINGLY MADE WHICH IS ALSO UNUSUAL FOR VAMPIRE MOVYZ AFTER THE 70'S. I WAS HIP'T TO THIS MOVY BY MENTION THAT EDWARD GOREY WAS A FAN. IT'S LESS MEAN THAN GOREY BUT VERY MUCH IN LINE W/ HIS BOOKS.

GORDON CURRIE · JUSTIN LOUIS
HELENE CLARKSON · TIONA REID
FRANK MOORE · HADLEY KAY
DAVID CRONENBERG

89 MINUTES

COLOR
1995

WRITTEN BY
ANDREW RAI BERZINS
DIRECTEBY: HOLLY DALE

ULTRA-STEREO 

BLOOD BEACH

JUST WHEN YOU THOUGHT IT WAS SAFE
TO GO BACK IN THE WATER–YOU CAN'T GET TO IT.

DAVID HUFFMAN MARIANA HILL
JOHN SAXON AND BURT YOUNG
WRITTEN & DIRECTED by JEFFREY BLOOM

MEDIA HOME ENTERTAINMENT INC

BLOOD BEACH

COLOR 92 MINUTES

AS YOU CAN SEE I GOT SOME RAIN ON THIS ONE. MAYBE IF THERE WAS MORE JOHN SAXON THIS WOULD BE BETTER, BUT IT SEEMS LIKE ACTORS ARE KINDA WAITING AROUND FOR THEIR SCENE TO END. ITS THE RESULT OF SOME TYPE OF ORGANIZED PROCESS BUT ITS HAD SOME SPOILING EFFECT. IT'S JUST A MOVIE PRODUCTION THAT SEEMS TO PASS OVER A SERIES OF PEOPLE AND PLACES WITH A POSSIBLE PROMISE OF A CREATURE 1981©

MEDIA

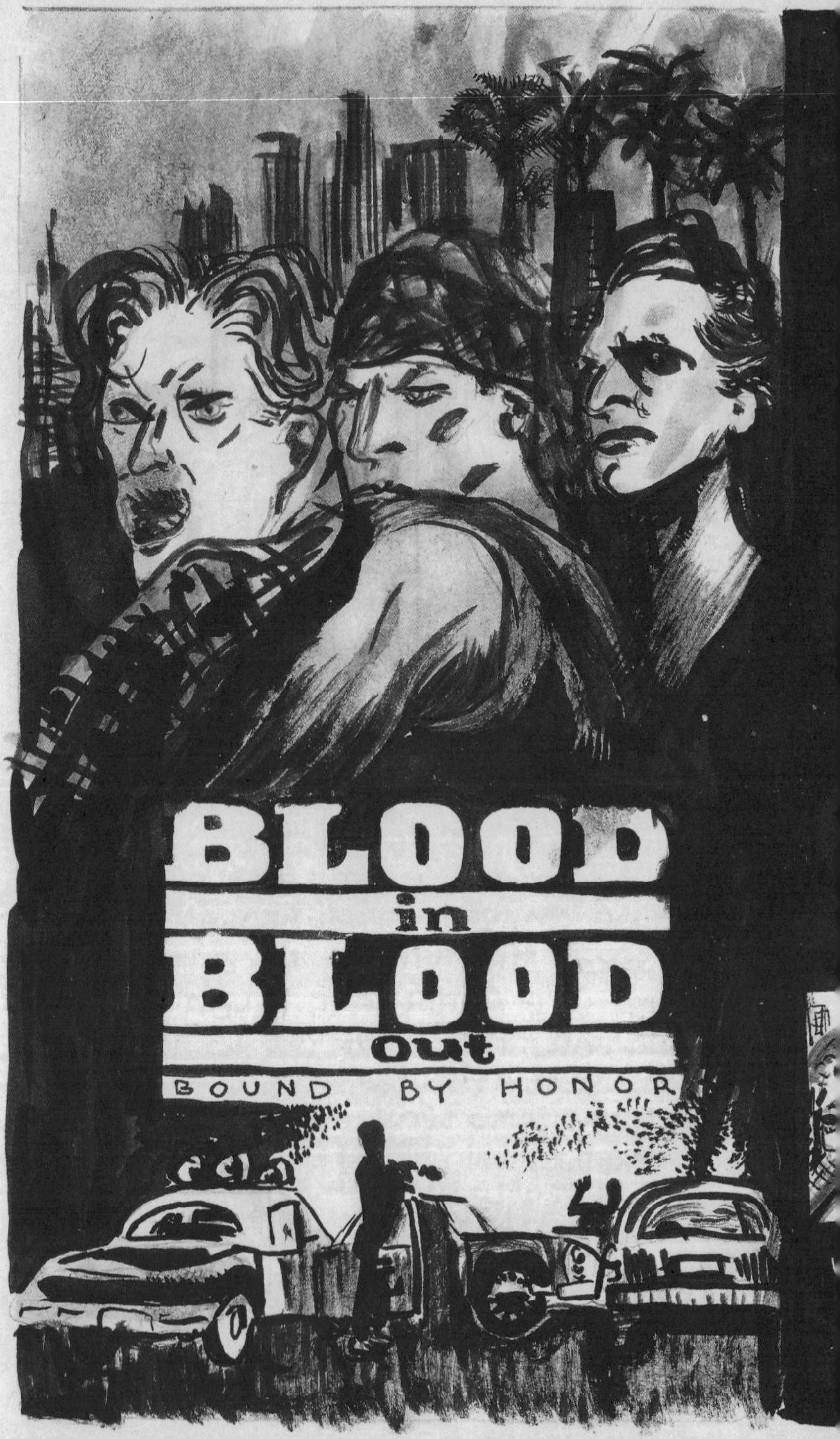

BLOOD

in

BLOOD

out

BOUND BY HONOR

MAN; THIS IS A REALLY GREAT MOVIE. EPIC CRIME DRAMA. I'D RATHER WATCH THIS THAN -GODFATHESCARFACEGOODFELLAS-. THIS MOVIE HAS HEART WHERE THE OTHERS HAVE ROMATIFICATION OF "DO'N CRIMES". WE START WITH 3 DUDES IN THE END TIMES OF THEY'R TEENAGE BAD ASS PHASE WHEN THINGS CHANGE EACH OF THEM. WE FOLLOW EACH OF THEM AS THEY FALL APART & OVER LIKE... 15 YEARS THEY HAVE CROSS OVER & CONFLICTS BUT STILL HAVE LOYAL CONECTION TO EACH OTHER. ALSO THERES HELLA RACISM, MURDER, DRUGS, KNIFES, FOOD, PRISON SEX, CARS, ART, HONOR & THE CAST IS AMAZING. THIS IS A DUDE MOVIE IN WAY WHERE LADIES POP IN TO THE MOVIE FOR PART OF A SCEEN. DOSE BLOOD IN BLOOD OUT SOUND LIKE A MELLOW MOVIE? I LOVE IT. THERES A REALLY COOL TREE IN IT TOO. PEEP IT OUT.

JESSE BORREGO, BENJAMIN BRATT
ENRIQUE CASTILLO & DAMIAN CHAPA
SCREENPLAY by JIMMY SANTIAGO BACA
JEREMY IACONE & FLOYD MUTRUX
Ⓡ DIRECTED by TAYLOR HACKFORD
RUNNING TIME 180 MINUTES COLOR 1993 CC

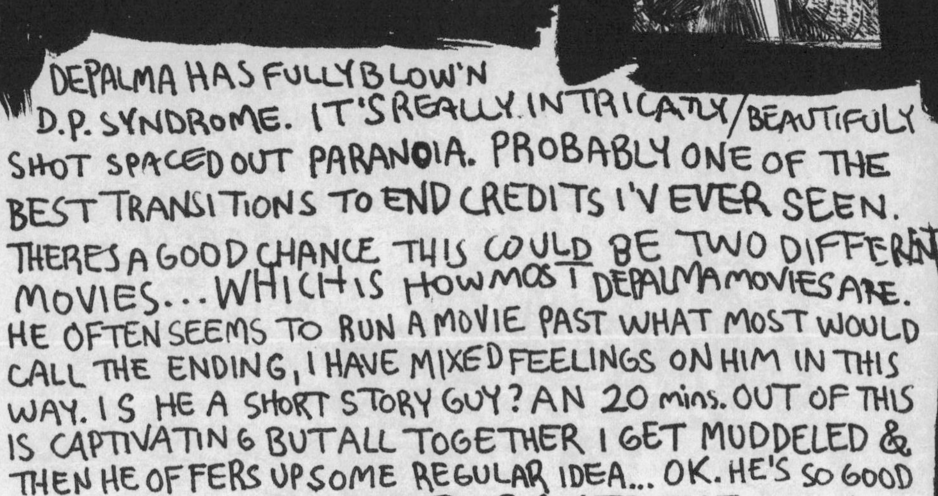

DEPALMA HAS FULLY BLOW'N D.P. SYNDROME. IT'S REALLY INTRICATLY/BEAUTIFULY SHOT SPACED OUT PARANOIA. PROBABLY ONE OF THE BEST TRANSITIONS TO END CREDITS I'V EVER SEEN. THERES A GOOD CHANCE THIS COULD BE TWO DIFFERENT MOVIES... WHICH IS HOW MOST DEPALMA MOVIES ARE. HE OFTEN SEEMS TO RUN A MOVIE PAST WHAT MOST WOULD CALL THE ENDING, I HAVE MIXED FEELINGS ON HIM IN THIS WAY. IS HE A SHORT STORY GUY? AN 20 mins. OUT OF THIS IS CAPTIVATING BUT ALL TOGETHER I GET MUDDELED & THEN HE OFFERS UP SOME REGULAR IDEA... OK. HE'S SO GOOD W/SO MENY OF THE ELEMENTS OF MOVIES THAT I GIVE HIM A LOT OF ROPE, BUT OFTEN FEEL LIKE HE'S JUST GIVE'N ME THE FLUFF JOB. SPACED OUT DINGY STORYTELLING. BUT HE'S GOT THIS DREAMY QUALITY THAT CAN SPIN YOU OFF YOUR FEET. ALL IN ALL THIS IS'NT A MOVIE I HAVE MUCH ATTRATION TO.

DEBORAH SHELTON
CRAIG WASSON GREGG HENRY MELANIE GRIFFITH
SCREENPLAY by ROBERT J. AVRECH & BRIAN DE PALMA
PRODUCED & DIRECTED by BRIAN DE PALMA

COLUMBIA PICTURES [CC] COLOR DOLBY SURROUND [R] DVD APPROX 114 MIN.

1984

BODY DOUBLE

THE FIRST TIME I WATCHED THIS I WAS TIRED & I WANTED TO SEE SNOOP, WHO POPS UP BREIFLY BUT DOSENT REALLY GET PROMINENT TILL THE 2nd ½ OF THE PICTURE. SO I GOT PISS'Y ABOUT THE YOUNG CHARACTERS BUT I WATCHED IT A FEW MORE TIMES WHILE DRAWING & NOW I'M DIG'N IT. IT'S GOT PROBLEMS BUT NOT ONES I FAULT IT FOR. DICKERSON CAME FROM BEING A D.O.P. & IT SHOWS, WILD, BEAUTIFUL COLORS, DRAMATICLY AGRESSIVE COMPOSITIONS. I GET THE FEELING THAT HE FOLLOWED THE SCRIPT WITHOUT MUCH EDITORIAL IMPUT. FOR ALL IT'S LIFE THIS A BIT TOO UNORGANIC FOR ME. ALL THOUGH I'M SURE IT COULD BE SAVED BY MORE SNOOP WHO RULES THE BACK ½ OF THIS MOVIE. NO SUPRISE. I'D LIKE TO SEE DICKERSON SPACE OUT A BIT MORE. HE'S GOT SUCH A GOOD EYE I THINK HE COULD FOLLOW IT MORE. IT FEELS LIKE HE'S GOT A LOT OF CLASSIC MIDCENTURY VISUAL STORYTELLING HEAR BUT I THINK HE FITS IN A MORE SEAMONAL WORLD OF VISUAL POWER, WHICH GIVES THIS AN ALMOST SILENT FEELING. IT MIGHT ALSO COME FROM THE OVER THE TOP SOUND RUNNING AT RAVE LIKE POWER I'D LOVE TO SEE IT IN A THEATRE.

SNOOP DOGG PAM GRIER KHAUL KAIN

CLIFTON POWELL BIANCA LAWSON MICHAEL T. WEISS

WRITTEN BY ADAM SIMON & TIM METCALFE

DIRECTED BY ERNEST DICKERSON

WIDESCREEN 2001 COLOR

DVD ENGLISH

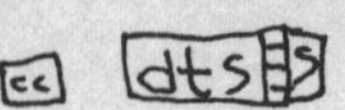

NEW LINE PLATINUM SERIES

SNOOP DOGG

Bones

UNLEASH THE DOGG

THE
BORROWER

EXTRATARESTRIAL INSECTS DECIDE TO RE-ASSIGN THE SPECIES OF THEY'R WORST CRIMINAL INTO HUMAN & DUMP HIM ON EARTH AS A PUNISHMENT LESS LENIENT THAN DEATH. AWESOME. BUT HIS HEAD KEEPS EXPLODING SO HE JUST RIPS THE HEAD OFF OF THE BEST SUPPORTING CHARACTER IN THE SCENE. RAE DAWN IS A COP AFTER HER OWN WORST CRIMINAL AROUND AND OF COURSE EVERY-ONE RUNS INTO EACHOTHER EVENTUALLY. GREAT WRITTING, ACTING, & DIRECTING MAKE THIS MOVIE A WINNER THAT IN OTHER HANDS COULD BE A TURD. I DON'T HAVE ANY PROBLEMS AT ALL W/ THIS MOVIE. I DID MISTAKE AN ACTOR FOR BRYON JAMES & WAS SUPER TRIPPED OUT TO FIND HE WAS'NT. OH, WELL. THAT DUDE DID A GREAT JOB. I THINK THIS' MY FAVORITE JOHN McNAUGHTON MOVIE THESE DAYS. I THINK THAT'S TOM TOWLES HEAD THERE ON THE COVER EVEN THOUGH HE IS'NT BILLED ON IT. BEAUTIFUL PHOTOGRAPHY. THE WHOLE THING IS TRIPPY PSYCHIDELIC, CREEPY, FUNNY.... YEAH WHAT CAN I SAY? I LOVE THIS MOVIE. PEEP IT OUT.

RAE DAWN CHONG DON GORDON ANTONIO FARGAS

MAKEUP EFFECTS by KEVIN YAGHER
SCREENPLAY BY MASON NAGE and RICHARD FIRE
DIRECTED BY JOHN McNAUGHTON

CANNON VIDEO

ULTRA*STEREO

R

COLOR 1991 97 mins

KIDS in the HALL
BRAIN CANDY
BRAIN CANDY
BRAIN CANDY
Chuck
Ave
PORTLAND OR
R

Hilarious Thumbs!

1/2 'o' SISKEL & EBERT

KIDS in the HALL BRAINCANDY

THE FIRST TIME I SAW THIS {THEATRE} I WAS DISIPOINTED. I DON'T RECALL WHY. YEARS LATER I SAW IT ON CABEL IN A MOTEL & IT FULLY HAD ME IN STITCHES. I COULD'NT BELIEVE IT WAS SO GOOD & THAT I HAD'NT DUG IT THE FIRST TIME. SO WE SCORED A COPY FOR THE HOUSE & WATCHED IT LIKE A MILLION TIMES <NO SHIT I SWEAR I'V SEEN THIS OVER 100 TIMES> DAVE FOLEY IS IN IT BUT HE'S THE ONLY CAST MEMBER WHO DID'NT WRITE IT, AT LEAST HE IS'NT CREDITED AS SUCH. IT'S MADE FROM MONKEY CUM. THIS BOX AS YOU MAY HAVE NOTICED HAS CHUCKS LABEL ON IT. I OBSCURED HIS ADDRESS SO FOLKS WOULD'NT BE ABLE TO SEND HIM LETTERS & MENACE HIM AT HOME FOR GETTING RID OF THIS. YOU SEE, THIS IS NOT MY FIRST COPY OF BRAINCANDY. THIS MOVIE IS PRONE TO MOVE ABOUT & PERHAPS DISAPPEAR ALL TOGETHER. SO IF YOUR READING THIS & YOU NEED TO PEEP THIS AGAIN, YOU CAN BORROW MINE DUDE. AS FOR EVERYONE ELSE, I WOULD SAY THIS IS AN AWESOME MOVIE & I THINK IT'S WORTH MORE THAN ONE VIEWING. I HAVE A SNEAKING SUSPISION THAT NORM HISCOCK IS DAVE FOLEY

WRITTEN BY
NORM HISCOCK & BRUCE McCULLOCK & KEVIN McDONALD
MARK McKINNEY & SCOTT THOMPSON
DIRECTED BY KELLY MAKIN

1996 COLOR [R] 89 MIN.

ANDREW DICE CLAY • TERI HATCHER

RESCUE A MODEL

BATTLE KILL'R "NINJAS"

SAVE A FLOWER

NO PROBLEMO

NOTSA

BRINSMASH'R

A LOVE STORY

RECORDED IN ULTRASTEREO

PG13

...A LOVE STORY

NOT MY FAV. PYUN, OR DICEMAN EITHER PRETTY TAME FOR BOTH. ITS THE NORMALIST PYUN. WHICH IS TRIPPY CUZ HE CO WROTE IT. MAYBE... HEWAS? I DON'T KNOW. IT'S NOT BAD, I JUST GO FOR PYUNS WEIRDNESS & HERE HE'S PLAY'N iT PRETTY STREIGHT. IT'S GOT A FEW LAUGHS & STUFF. FLOWER FIGHT

ITS TUFF BEING A CLECHE.

ANDREW DICE CLAY HARI THATCHER DEBORAH VAN VALKENBURGH YUJI OKUMOTO BRION JAMES TIM THOMERSON CHARLES ROCKET NICHOLAS GUEST

CO-WRITTEN, & DIRECTED BY ALBERT PYUN

COLOR 88 min'z ©1993

VIDMARK

BRING THE PAIN

NO CHILDREN
NC-17
UNDER SEVENTEEN

CONCERT COMEDY

CHRIS ROCK

ITS ALMOST EMBAR-
ASSING HOW MUCH I LOVE
CHRIS ROCK. ALMOST.
WHATS THAT THING WHEN
YOU GET EMBARASSED
BY/FOR SOMEONE ELSE
FUCK THAT. I HATE
THAT. WOOF. OK
SORRY. WATCHED
THIS ONE SO MUCH
I CANT WONT EVEN TRY TO COUNT.
I THINK THIS IS THE 2ND
ONE. I WISH HE HAD
A SHOW AGAIN...
THERE WAS A NAT X
ACTION FIGURE, I GOT
TO FIND ONE AGAIN.
SOMETIMES WHEN I
FEEL LIKE SHIT THIS
IS THE THING TO GET ME
LAUGHING. I HAVE
THE OTHERS BUT ON
DVD & THE TAPE HAS A BREAKGLASS IN AN
EMERGENCY
THING FOR ME.
CR
APPROXIMATE RUNNING TIME 58:00
1996 COLOR

BEAT TAKESHI OMAR EPPS CLAUDE MAKI
BROTHER
A FILM BY TAKESHI KITANO

SOME HOW OMAR EPPS MAKES THIS INTO ONE OF THE STRANGER BEAT TAKESHI KITANO MOVIES I'V SEEN. HE'S ODDLY INVOLVED & OUT OF PLACE IN MOST SITUATIONS & THEN AT THE END HE DOSE A SUPERHAM INTO THE CREDITS WHICH IS JARRING TO THE TONE THE LAST ACT HAS SET UP. BEAT ONCE AGAIN TURNS IN A UNIQUE CRIME MOVIE WHICH MOVES W/OUT THE BARS OF THE GENRE. EXILED GANGSTER REBUILDS HIMSELF & A GANG W/HIS LITTLE AMERICANIZED "BROTHER". HE'S DO'N WELL BUT IT GETS OUT OF CONTROLE ONCE THINGS GROW. COOL, BEAUTIFUL, A BIT WONKY

BEAT TAKESHI OMAR EPPS CLAUDE MAKI

WRITTEN & DIRECTED

TAKESHI KITANO

2001

THE FIRST TIME I WATCHED, I WAS A BIT UNDERWHELMED BY THE AMOUNT OF REPITITION FROM THE BORAT. I BITCHED ABOUT IT TO MARK & THEN I PUT IT ON TO PRODU IT & I WAS ALL LAUGHING AT IT. DAMN. SO YEAH AFTER THAT FIRST PEEP, PEEP AGAIN. IT'S STILL NOT AS CHARMING AS BORA BUT WHATEVERZ. STILL FUNNY THOUGH. BUT, IT'S SICKLY HUMOR THAT JUST REINFOURCES MY SHITTY'R ATTITUDES ABOUT HUMANS, THE END CREDITS ARE A HOOT & PROBABLY REASON ENOUGH TO PEEP IT ON A HALF ASS'D WEEKEND DOWNTIME I LOVE IT WHEN DUDE GET'S SHITHEADS GO'N. MAYBE I APPRECIEAT IT MORE THAN I ENJOY IT. FUCK! ARE YOU STILL READING THIS? LOOK JUST WATCH IT IF YOUR SO CURIOUS IT'S PRETTY GOOD.

SACHA BARON COHEN & GUSTAF HAMMERSTEN

STORY by

SACHA BARON COHEN & PETER BAYNHAM & ANTHONY HINES & DAN MAZER

SCREENPLAY by

SACHA BARON COHEN & ANTHONY HINES & DAN MAZER & JEFF SCHAFFER

[A]

DIRECTED by

LARRY CHARLES

2009

1 Hr 22 mins

the borat dude...

Sacha Baron Cohen

brüno

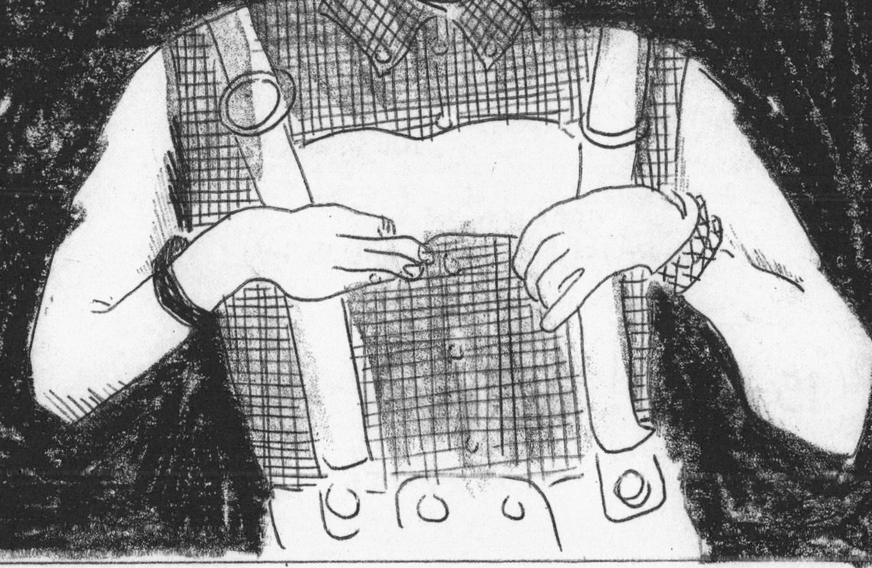

BLACK & WHITE / COLOUR

SUCH A GREAT SHOW. BUDGIE IS A PROFESSIONAL AMATURE CRIMINAL. HE'S A MOOCH, THEIF, FOOL, CHUMP, PRICK, DEADBEAT, DANDY, RUBE, CHEAT, SEX MACHINE, WIMP, SWEET HEART, COWARD, BADASS, YOU FALL IN LOVE WITH HIM JUST IN TIME TO BECOME COMPLETLY DISAPOINTED IN HIM.

IT WON'T MAKE YOU FEEL GOOD
BUT IT IS AWESOME... WERD UP.

DISC ONE
OUT
SOME MOTHERS SONS
BRAINS
GRANDEE HOTEL
DISC TWO
IN DEEP
COULD DO BETTER
BEST MATES

DISC THREE
EVERYBODY LOVES A BABY
A PAIR OF CHARLIES
FIDDLER ON THE ROOF PART ONE
DISC FOUR
FIDDLER ON THE ROOF PART TWO
SUNSET MANSIONS
... AND IN AGAIN

CREATED BY
KEITH WATERHOUSE & WILLIS HALL

COMPLETE FIRST SERIES
Budgie
COMPLETE & UNCUT • All 13 EPISODES
4 DISC SET
ADAM FAITH
IAN CUTHBERTSON
LYNN DALBY
DVD
VIDEO

YO... I WATCHED THE FIRST SEASON TOOFAST. & THIS SET HIT ME A LITTLE TOO MUCH. IF YOU WATCH THESE I RECOMEND YOU SPACE OUT EACH EPISODE WITH SOME DUMB ASS THINGS. THIS WAS A CRITICAL BEAT-DOWN AT FULL STEAM. VERY, VERY, POWERFULL & AMAZING. JUST SPACE IT OUT A BIT. THIS SEASON IS FULL TILT. SO, PEEP THIS SLOW'LY. GREAT ENDING. TRUE TRUE TRUE

DISC ONE
DREAMING OF THEE
AND THE LORD TAKETH AWAY
LOUIE THE RING IS DEAD AND BURIED IN KENSAL GREEN CEMETERY
THE JUMP-UP BOYS

DISC TWO
OUR STORY SO FAR
DO ME A FAVOUR
GLORY OF FULHAM

DISC THREE
TWENTY FOUR THOUSAND BALL POINT PENS
KING FOR A DAY
THE OUTSIDE MAN

DISC FOUR
THE MAN OUTSIDE
BRIEF ENCOUNTER
RUN RABBIT, RUN RABBIT, RUN RUN RUN

BUDGIE BIRD ADAM FAITH
HAZEL FLETCHER LYNN DALBY
JEAN BIRD GEORGINE HALE
CHARLIE ENDELL IAIN CUTHBERTSON
LAUGHING SPAM FRITTER JOHN RHYS-DAVIES

GRANADA Ventures

15

DVD

Network | THE COMPLETE SECOND SERIES

4 DISC SET

Budgie

CREEP

DIPSHIT

15

WESTERN LEGENDS
A BULLET
GENERAL

AWWW MAN... WATCH OUT, THIS ONE TRICKS YOU A FEW TIMES W/ . SOME MIGHT WANDER OFF ON THIS BUT LET'M. IT'S REALLY GREAT. THERE NO FLUFF BUT IT'S GOT A WANDERING ARTY STYLE {YOU KNOW, ITALIAN} & IT'S CHOCK FULL OF RUGGE BADASS WEIRDOS. THE STORY IS COMPLEX & BEAUTIFUL SO I'LL AVOID TRY'N TO EXPLAIN IT. I WILL SAY THAT IT'S GOT A LOT OF MORAL & POLITICAL THEMES W/ FOLKS DEALING IN A VARIETY OF WAYS. SOCIALLY THIS IS ONE OF THE MOST COMPLETE MOVIES I'V EVER SEEN. WELL WORTH MULTIPLE VIEWINGS & REALLY, NESISARY TOO BECAUSE TO EXPECT TO "GET IT" RIGHT OFF IS AN INDICATION THAT YOU HAVE TOO HIGH AN OPPINION OF YOURSELF. IF YOUR NOT "INTO" WESTERNS THEN THIS IS THE ONE FOR YOU. MAYBE BECAUSE IT'S AN ITALIN MOVIE ABOUT MEXICO THATS IN ENGLISH.

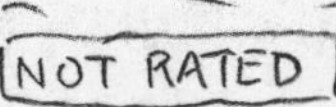

APPROXIMATE RUNNING TIME: 1 HOUR 55 MINUTES COLOR 1967

GIAN MARIA VOLONTE KLAUS KINSKI MARTINE BESWICK LOU CASTEL JAIME FERNANDEZ

SCREENPLAY & STORY by SALVATORE LAURANI

DIRECTED BY DAMIANO DAMIANI

I ♡ JACK ARNOLD. NO SHIT, HE'S TOP'S IN MY BOOK. I HAVE NOTICED THAT HIS WERK HAS A RE-OCCURING ELEMENT... THAT BEING A KEEN EYE FOR THEE LOW'R, BACK SECTION OF WOMEN. NOW, THIS IS A NUDIE CUTIE; WE CAN OBSERVE THIS IN FULL EFFECT. SO, THERE IS THIS TEEN NAMED BUNNY; & SHE JUMP'S MORE JOHNSONS THEN THE KKK. BELIEVE. THERE'S SOME STORY MIX'D IN BUT NOT TOO MUCH. IF YOU DON'T KNOW WHAT TO EXPECT, THINK OF A BEATLES MOVIE; EXCEPT THEY'V BEEN REPLACED WITH MOSTLY/FULLY NAKED GIRLS. SO THIS IS BEING RELEASED AS GAMES GIRLS PLAY, BUT WAS ORIGINALLY CALLED THE BUNNY CAPER. CALL IT WHAT YOU LIKE, JUST DON'T CALL ME LATE FOR A JACK ARNOLD MOVIE. I COULD'NT BRING MYSELF TO DRAW THE COVER OF THIS RELEASE, SO REPLACED IT WITH THE POSTER FROM IT'S ORIGINAL OUT'N. I LOVE THAT TWO DUDES WROTE THIS BECAUSE ANY NUMBER OF WRITERS OR REGULAR DUDE COULD WRITE THIS. IT IS THE STUFF OF LEGEND FOR TEENAGERS & DIRTY OLD MEN. TRUST.

Some have the urge... Some have the touch... These girls have it all!!
IT TAKES FOUR OF A KIND TO PULL OFF...
THE BUNNY CAPER
CHRISTINA HART · JANE ANTHONY · DRINA PAVLOVIC
JILL DAMAS
SCREENPLAY PE ER OPPENHEIMER & JAMESON BREWER
DIRECTOR JACK ARNOLD
R

la
noche del
TERROR

KARIN WELL-GIAN LUIGI CHIRIZZI
SIMONE MATTIOLI MARIA ANGELA GIORDAN

DIRECTOR ANDREA BIANCHI

EASTMAN COLOR

& THAT'S THE WAY I LIKE IT. ZENITH OF KILL.
UHMMM... SO LIKE, THERE'S A DUDE WITH A LITTLE PICK HAMMER & HE TAP'S IT ON A BIG STONE, THEN ZOMBIES KILL EVERYONE; FOR THE REST OF THE MOVIE. THE END. FIN. THIS THE CREAM OF HORROR PORN. WHERE SO MENY FAIL, THIS JUST SORES OVER THE WALL. THE "CHARACTERS" ARE GREAT. A GROUP OF CREEPS, JERKS, FOOLS, ASS HOLES, SLUTS, DIPSHITS, GREASEHEADS, TARDS, BACKSTAB'RS, LIARS, SUCKERS, GOOBS, BOOBS, RUBES, & A DUDE WHO'S "A KID" WHO NEEDS MOTHERS MILK. WOWY-WOW-WOW!! WHAT MORE CAN I SAY, TOP BILLIN! SUCH AWESOME ZOMBIES. THE MAKE UP HERE IS A HALLOWEEN FANTASY COME TRUE.

JAMES BROLIN
KATHLEEN LLOYD
JOHN MARLEY
RONNY COX
WHAT EVIL DRIVES
THE CAR

"OH GREAT BROTHERS OF THE NIGHT. WHO RIDETH OUT UPON THE HOT WINDS OF HELL, WHO DWELLETH IN THE DEVIL'S LAIR; MOVE & APPEAR."

ANTON LA VEY

THAT QUOTE STARTS THE MOVIE, EVEN BEFORE THE TITLE. I DON'T KNOW WHERE THIS FITS IN THE KILL'R CARS MOVIES BUT I DIG IT. FOR ONE, WHERE MOST MOVIES GET TIED UP IN A BUNCH OF "WHY" STORYTELLING. THE CAR JUST IS AND KILLS. NOT ALOT OF TIMEWASTING EATHER THEY GIVE YOU CHARACTERS & GET MOVING. WIDE VARIETY OF SUPPORT & VICTIM CHARACTERS {99%. HONKYS THOUGH} A NICE SINISTER SUPERNATURAL STREAK OF BARRIS DEATH WITH A BUMPER OFF A GUARD RAIL. AMAZING. 1970'S SUPERNATURAL WESTERN. NICE TIRE PHOTOGRAPHY TOO.

JAMES BROLIN
KATHLEEN LLOYD
JOHN MARLEY
ELIZABETH THOMPSON
RONNY COX
SCREENPLAY BY
DENNIS SHAYACK
MICHAEL BUTLER
LANE SLATE
DIRECTED BY
ELLIOT SILVERSTEIN

COLOR
96 MIN
1977
PG

HOW MANY TIMES
HAVE I SEEN THIS? I DON'T
KNOW, A LOT. MIA IS INTO IT SO
I WATCH IT WITH HER. HOW CAN I SAY NO TO
"CARE BEARYS"?
THESE DAYS MY FEELINGS ABOUT THIS MOVIE ARE
QUITE DIFFERENT THEN THEY ONCE WERE.
THE CARE BEARS ARE GREAT. EACH ONE
IS AN EMOUTION & WHEN THEY TEAM
UP THEY CAN OVERCOME THEY'R TROUBLES.
THIS MOVIE DOSE SEND SOME MIX'D
MESSAGES ABOUT MAGIC & THE OCCULT.
BUT THAT'S O.K. I DON'T THINK ONE
SOLID MESSAGE WOULD BE A
GOOD THING.

the
Care Bears
Movie

DIANE LADD
CARNOSAUR
Driven to extinction.
Back for revenge.
RAPHAEL SBARGE · JENNIFER RUNYON · HARRISON PAGE · NED BELLAMY
& CLINT HOWARD
WRITTEN & DIRECTED BY ADAM SIMON

CHICKEN FARM EXPLOITATION. EVIL SCIENTIST, HIPPYS, DIPSHITZ. NICE 90'Z STYLE ROGER CORMAN PRODUCTION. FUN, SELF AWAIR VIDEO STYLE MOVIE. DIANE LADD. IS HER DAD ALLAN LADD? GOOD FUN. NO C.G. YESSSSS. BUT, IT'S ALL T-REX, TYPICLE. I DON'T HATE ON THE DUDE, BUT MAN! DUDE, GIVE ANOTHER DINOSAUR A CHANCE.

ANY WHO... GOOD PACEING, JOKES. SOME KIND'A ROMANCE THING. REDICULES BUT SMART. MILD POLITICAL STUFF. GOOD DEAL.

STUART GORDON'S

CASTLE FREAK

THE FIRST TIME I SAW THIS I THOUGHT IT WAS ALLRIGHT. I WAS A BIT UNDERWHELMED BY THE ENDING. SECOND TIME I HAD MY EXPECTATIONS IN ORDER & I WAS REALLY INTO IT, ENJOIED THE PACE & TONE A LOT. COMBS IS SO CAPTIVATING AT ALL TIMES. I DIG IT WHEN MOVIES DO COCKSHOTS BECAUSE THE REACTION IT GETS IS VERY TELLING OF PEOPLES SOCIAL & MENTEL LIMITATIONS. AND SO... CASTLE FREAK HAS A NICE CLOSE UP OF A MUTALA-TED DONG WHICH IS MAYBE LESS BUT POSSABLY MORE PROVOCATIVE. NOW I LOVE IT.

JEFFREY COMBS BARBARA CRAMPTON
JONATHAN FULLER JESSICA DOLLARHIDE

ORIGINAL IDEA BY CHARLES BAND
STUART GORDON & DENNIS PAOLI
SCREENPLAY BY
DENNIS PAOLI
DIRECTED BY
STUART GORDON 1995

MOON

RATING PENDING

AMAZING FANTASY HOME VIDEO

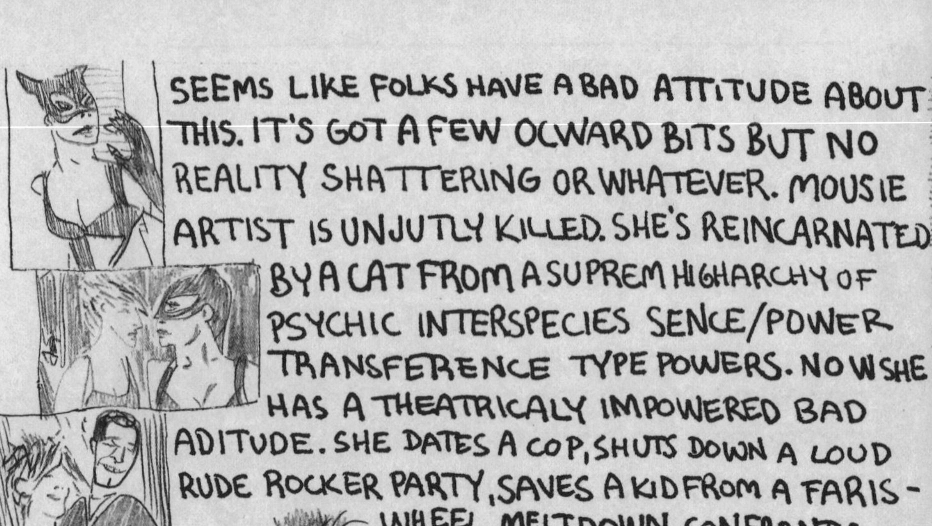

SEEMS LIKE FOLKS HAVE A BAD ATTITUDE ABOUT THIS. IT'S GOT A FEW OCWARD BITS BUT NO REALITY SHATTERING OR WHATEVER. MOUSIE ARTIST IS UNJUTLY KILLED. SHE'S REINCARNATED BY A CAT FROM A SUPREM HIGHARCHY OF PSYCHIC INTERSPECIES SENCE/POWER TRANSFERENCE TYPE POWERS. NOW SHE HAS A THEATRICALY IMPOWERED BAD ADITUDE. SHE DATES A COP, SHUTS DOWN A LOUD RUDE ROCKER PARTY, SAVES A KID FROM A FARIS-WHEEL MELTDOWN, CONFRONTS SOUL LESS CORPRATE VANITY ABUSE PSYCHOPATHS, STEEL JEWELRY {WHICH IF YOU THINK ABOUT IT IS PUNISHING THE MERCHENTS OF THOSE WHO EXPLOITE AND SLAVE PEOPLE FOR THEY'R OWN PERSONA FAULTS AND HANG UPS. SO IT'S O.K.} I COULD LIVE WITHOUT THE C.G. WALL RUNNING & HALLE IS SOMETIMES SO SILLY THAT YOU CAN LET IT BOUNCE AROUND W/ IT. THIS SHOULD BE PG. IT'S A COOL, GOOD IMPOWER-MENT MOVIE FOR TWEENS & GOOFBALLSWEETY PIES.

HALLE BERRY BENJAMIN BRATT

LAMBERT WILSON FRANCES CONROY SHARON STONE

SCREENPLAY BY

JOHN BRANCATO, MICHAEL FERRIS & JOHN ROGERS

DIRECTED BY PITOF

DVD [PG-13] COLOR 104 MINS. 2004 DOLBY DIGITAL

WIDE SCREEN EDITION

MAN I WANT
TO LIKE THIS BUT
ITS A LOT OF WURK
FOR NORMAL TWIST
TYPE PAYOFF. I THINK
IT SPENDS TOO MUCH TIME
ING STORY WHEN IT WOULD
BEEN COOL TO JUST RIDE A
WITH SNIPES & STATHAM
JUST BEING. OH WELL.
THERES VERY LITTLE
WESLEY.

BUMMER.
I GUESS WITH BOTH OF THESE DUDES IN A MOVIE I JUS
WANT TO HAVE FUN BECAUSE THAT'S WHAT THAT SOUN
LIKE WHAT WILL HAPPEN WHEN YOU DO BUT IT IS'NT.
WELL ITS NOT THAT BAD. I WATCHED IT TWICE, BUT
THRICE? NOT A GO TO, MORE LIKE A CHORES WILDCARD.
TO MUCH MOVIE? NOT ENOUGH TIME? I DONT KNOW

JASON STATHAM RYAN PHILLIPPE WESLEY SNIPES
JUSTINE WADDELL W/HENRY CZERNY

WRITTEN & DIRECTED by TONY GIGLIO

R VIOLENCE & LANGUAGE | CC |   CAPITOL

2005 COLOR FEATURE RUN TIME APPROX. 106 minutes

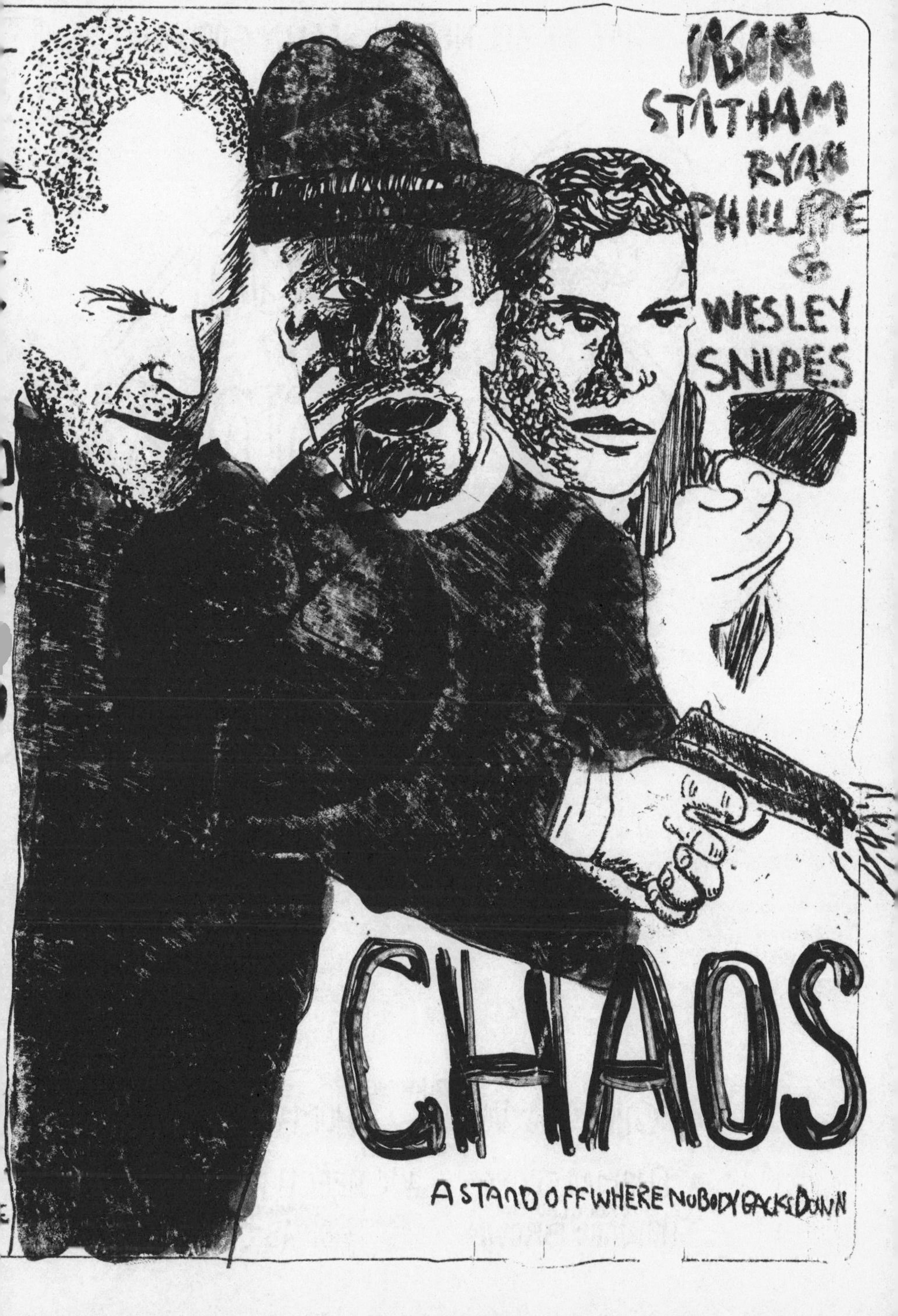

JASON
STATHAM
RYAN
PHILLIPE
&
WESLEY
SNIPES

CHAOS

A STAND OFF WHERE NOBODY BACKS DOWN

STARRING
CHEECH MARIN and THOMAS CHONG

WRITTEN BY
THOMAS CHONG and CHEECH MARIN

PRODUCED BY
HOWARD BROWN

DIRECTED BY
THOMAS CHONG

DUDE, HAVE YOU EVER SEE'N A CHEECH & CHONG FILM? FUUUUUUUUUUUUCKK'N A DUDE!! EVERY ONE NEEDS TO SEE EVERY MOVIE THEY MAKE. I DID'NT KNOW HOW GRASS LOOK'D WHEN FIRST SAW A C&C FILM AND WHEN IT WAS OVER I STILL DID'NT. BUT I DID KNOW THAT SHIT WAS FUNNY. BELIEVE. SO... IN THIS ONE THEY STEAL GAS, SMOKE GRASS, GET BUSY AT THE WELFARE OFFICE, PISS OFF PEE-WEE {TWICE} STEAL A DOPE ASS CAR EMBARAS A RICH ASSHOLE. CHEECH PLAYS HIM SELF & HIS COUSIN. CHONG HAS HIS CHOPPER IN THE DINING ROOM & THE EXH IN THE NEIGHBORS ROSES. PLUS HE PACKS A REAL COCKAROACH IN HIS PIPE & TOKES IT DOWN TILL HE COUGHS IT UP.

UHM. WHAT SHOULD TELL YOU ABOUT THIS. THIS... OH HELL.

CHRIS SARANDON {RAD} IS A COP CHASE'N BRAD DOURIF {RAD'ST} A KILLER OR SOMETHING. DOURIF GETS SHOT & DIES IN THE 1st SCEEN BUT NOT BEFORE HE BUSTS OUT A SPELL THAT HAS HIM LIVE IN A NEARBY DOLL. IF YOU DON'T KNOW IF YOU WANT TO SEE THIS BY NOW I GUESS I'LL TELL YOU THAT HE CONTINUES KILLING & SWEARING AS A DOLL. IN OTHER WORDS... AWESOME. I DON'T HAVE A SINGLE COMPLAINT. TOM HOLLAND IS A RAD DIRECTOR, I WISH HE MADE MOVIES MORE, WHAT A NICE CHILL STYLE, GOOD SHIT. SORT'A H.G. LEWIS, TWILITE ZONE STYLE. THE COLOR REMINDS ME OF THE FIRST CREEPSHOW. FUNNY TOO.

CHILD'S PLAY

CATHERINE HICKS CHRIS SARANDON BRAD DOURIF
SCREENPLAY
DON MANCINI AND JOHN LAFIA AND TOM HOLLAND
DIRECTED BY
TOM HOLLAND

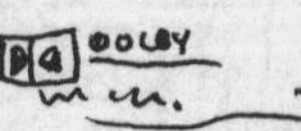

UNITED ARTISTS

FEATURE RUNTIME: 1 hour 27 minutes COLOR 1988

CATHERINE HICKS
CHRIS SARANDON
CHILD'S
PLAY

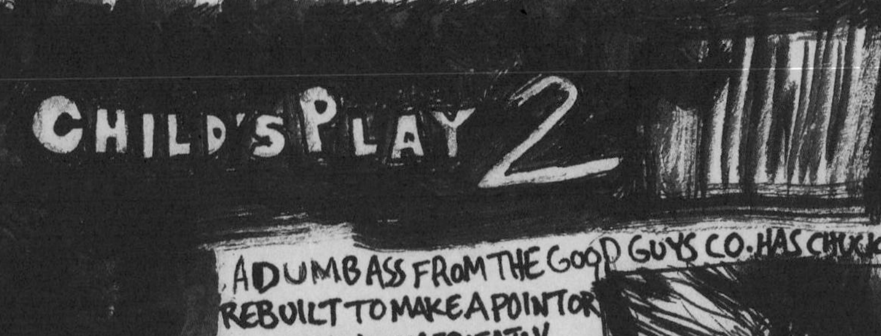

CHILD'S PLAY 2

A DUMBASS FROM THE GOOD GUYS CO. HAS CHUCKY REBUILT TO MAKE A POINT OR SOMETHING. IMEDIEATLY CHUCKY KILLS THE DUDES WHO FIX HIM HE GO'S FULL TILT BACK TO THE KID & IT CONTINUES. THE OPENING SHOT IS GREAT CHUCKYS METAL SKULL ALL SHREDD'D & RAW WHICH WOULD HAVE BEEN

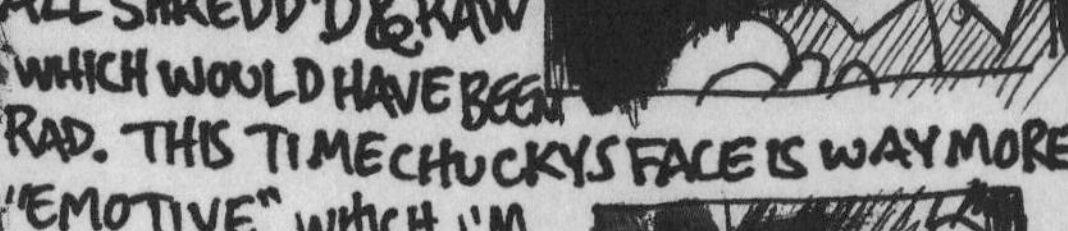

RAD. THIS TIME CHUCKYS FACE IS WAY MORE "EMOTIVE" WHICH I'M LESS INTO BUT IT MAKES SENCE SINCE THE MORE TIME HE'S IN THE DOLL THE MORE HUMAN HE GETS, BUT WHAT EVER. I THINK I SAW THIS AS A YOUTH. I REMEMBERED THE LIQUER STORE FOR SOME REASON... IT MUST HAVE BEEN THE SUSPENCE. CHUCKY MORE THAN ONCE TIES PEOPLE UP WITH FULL BONDAGE EXACUTION, AMAZING. USE'N JUMPROPES NO LESS. WOW

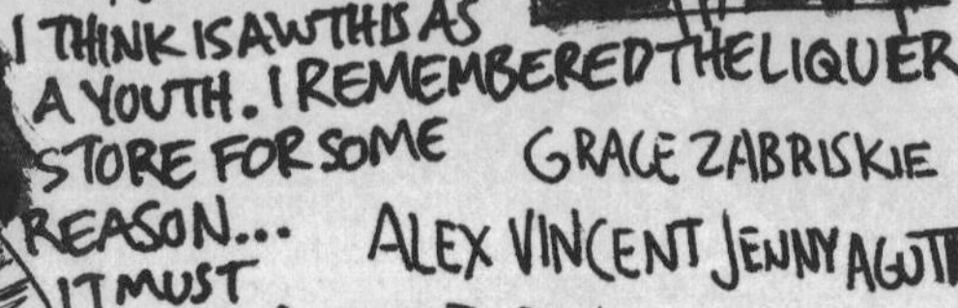

GRACE ZABRISKIE
ALEX VINCENT JENNY AGUTTER
GERRIT GRAHAM CHRISTINE ELISE

R ALEX VINCENT JENNY AGUTTER GERRIT GRAHAM
CHRISTINE ELISE GRACE ZABRISKIE
WRITTEN BY DON MANCINI
DIRECTED BY JOHN LAFIA
1 HOUR 24 MINUTES
COLOR
1990

WIDE SCREEN... THAAT S XTRA
CHILD'S PLAY 2

CHUCKYS BODY & BLOOD IS MINGELED WITH THE MOULTIN VINYL & SO HE IS REBORN. IT'S BEEN 10 YEARS & THERES SOME ONE ELSE POURTRAING THE KID WHO IS NOW IN MILLITARY SCHOOL. CHUCKY MAILS HIM SELF TO THE SCHOOL. THERES ALL KINDS OF JERKS, WHIMPS, MEATHEADS, THERE, CHUCKY LATCHES ONTO A YOUNG'STR, SO HE CAN FINALLY ESCAPE HIS DOLL INCARNATION. CHUCKY IS MORE OF A PUNKASS THIS TIME. THE SUPPORTING CHARACTERS ARE ALLRIGHT BUT I WANT TO FOLLOW CHUCKY MORE THAN THEM. THE SCHOOL BARBER IS RAD, I WOULD LIKE THERE TO BE MORE OF HIM. THE MOVIE WRAPS UP INSIDE OF A CARNIVAL RIDE FULL OF MOUNTAINS OF SKULLS, REAPERS & DEAMONS. TOP IT OFF WITH A FULL DISMEMBERMENT. SWEET.

JUSTIN WHALIN PERREY REEVES JEREMY SYLVERS

R HORROR VIOLENCE LANGUAGE

WRITTEN BY DON MANCINI DIRECTED BY JACK BENDER

ENGLISH COLOR 1 HOUR 30 MINUTES 1991 ANAMORPHIC WIDESCREEN

WIDE SCREEN
CHILD'S PLAY 3
THERE COMES A TIME TO PUT AWAY CHILDHOOD THINGS
BUT SOME THINGS WON'T STAY PUT

JENNIFER TILLY

BRIDE OF CHUCKY

CHUCKY DRINKS A FISHBOWL IN THIS ONE. CHARLES LEE RAY'S OLD FLAME CON'S A COP INTO BRING'N HER THE PIECES OF CHUCKY FROM THE EVIDENCE LOCK'R WHICH ALSO HAS A VARIETY OF TRINKETS FROM OTHER CLASSIC SERIES.' & THERE'S A PINHEAD JOKE LATER. SO... SHE FRANKESTEINS HIM TOGETHER &... ← WELL YOU CAN SEE FOR YOURSELF. BUT THEY HAVE SOME DISAGREEMENTS & CHUCKY WINDS UP KILLING HER & PUTTING HER SOUL IN A DOLL. THIS INSTALLMENT IS MORE COMEDY THAN THE OTHERS HAVE BEEN, NERDY'R TOO WITH MORE OF A GENERAL FANTISY WORLD APPROCH. I WISH IT HAD A SCORE INSTEED OF A SOUND TRACK BUT I'M REALLY INTO THIS ONE. THE SENCE OF HUMER HERE IS GREAT, CHUCKY IS FULL TILT AGAIN BUT NOW HE'S MORE COMPLEX. HE IS ANTOMICLY CORRECT. THE KILLINGS ARE MORE COMPLEX TOO. I LOVE CHUCKYS TEETH, MORE BUCK'T OUT HERE.

JENNIFER TILLY BRAD DOURIF KATHERINE HEIGL
NICK STABILE & JOHN RITTER

WRITTEN BY DON MANCINI DIRECTED BY RONNY YU

1.85:1

COLOR

1 HOUR 29 Minutes

1998

WIDESCREEN DUDE

JENNIFER TILLY

BRIDE OF
CHUCKY

Chucky Gets Lucky.

IN THE LAST SHOT OF BRIDE OF CHUCKY THEY'R BABY IS BORN & FATALY ASSULTS A COP. HERE THE CHILD HAS GROWN UP AS A BRITISH SIDESHOW FREAK. HOLLYWOOD IS MAKING A MOVIE ABOUT ALL THE EVENTS FROM THE OTHER MOVIES & IN DOINGSO MAKE THE DOLLS & CAST THE SPELL, BOOYEA. THEY START KILL'N AGAIN, TRACK DOWN THE KID.. FAMILY REUNION. BUT THE KID HAS NO SEX JUNK HE SAYS BOY, SHE SAYS GIRL HE SAYS GLEN, SHE SAYS GLENDA. THERE'S A TON OF MOVIE NERD JOKES IN THIS ONE. INFACT THIS IS JUST A FLATOUT COMEDY WITH CHUCKY & FAMILY AS THE FOCUS AS THEY KILL HOLLYWOOD TROPES. JOHN WATERS PLAYS A SLEEZ-O SKEEZ POPARATZI PHOTOGRAPHER WHO PHOTOGRAPHS CHUCKY BEAT'N OFF TO A FANGORIA MAG. BECAUSE YOU SEE, THEY NEED THE JIZZ TO IMPREGNATE ACTOR JENNIFER TILLY WHO IS PORTRAING HER CHARACTER FROM BRIDE. REDMAN IS DIRECTING A MOVIE AND IS IN NEGOTIATIONS WITH TILLY. BUT NO WEED IS TOKE'D, HUNH? WELL CHUCKY DRINKS AT LEAST. I THINK THIS IS THE FIRST TIME IN THE SERIES THAT THEY SHOW A TOPLESS WOMAN "BUT IT'S IN THE CONTEXT OF A HOLLYWOOD JOKE". AFTER CREATING & SCRIPTING THE WHOLE SERIES DON MANCINI DIRECTS THIS ONE. PRETTY GOOD, TOO. THE LIGHTING IS A LITTLE OVER DONE THOUGH.

JENNIFER TILLY REDMAN HANNAH SPEARRITT BILLY BOYD AND JOHN WATERS

WRITTEN & DIRECTED BY DON MANCINI

NOTRATED 2004 1 HOUR 24 MINUTES

WIDESCREEN

JOHN WATERS JENNIFER TILLY REDMAN

SEED OF CHUCKY

A DUDE ASK'T ME WHICH ONE OF THESE WAS THE BEST. TRIPPY QUESTION, BUT NOT SUPRISE'N. IF YOU WERE GOING TO WATCH ONLY ONE YOU'D BE MAKING A MISTAKE, BUT I'D SAY THE FIRST {CP1} IS THE MOST WHOLE & IN CONTRAST TO THE OTHERS IT'S GOT MORE GAME, DUE TO THE OTHERS RELIANG ON IT & MOVING FORWARD. CP2 PICKS UP WHERE CP1 ENDS AND WATCHED BACK TO BACK IS BEST. NOT MUCH GROUND IS COVERED IN CP2 BUT IT'S GOTA LOT INVESTED IN THE KID WITH NOT ENOUGH CHUCKY. BUT, IN CP2 THE STAGE IS SET FOR CHUCKYS FULL TILT KILLING. IN CP1 CHUCKYS KILLS SEEM PREMEDITATED MORE FOR KEEP'N HIS COVER, BUT CP2 HAS HIM JUST ENJOY'N SOME MURDER. SO... CP3. LOVE IT OR HATE IT {I DIGIT} CP3 IS THE END OF THE KID STORY. IT'S LIKE 1Ø YEARS LATER OR SOMETHING LIKE THAT AND THEY KIND FOCUS ON ANOTHER KID BUT IT'S STILL IT'S FULLY IN THE VAIN OF FOCUS FROM CP1 & CP2 WHICH IS PUSHING IT TO THE BREAKING POINT <u>BUT</u> CHUCKY IS SUCH A FUCK'N PUNK ASS JERK & STILL LOVEABLE A.K.A. BRAD DOURIF MAKES THIS A MUST SEE. CHUCKYS "DEATH" IS BETTER THAN IT WAS IN CP2. THE "DEATH" IN CP2 IS O.K. BUT IT'S MORE LITTER'AIRË YOU KNOW. ALTHOUGH CP2 HAS THAT KILL OPEN'N WITH THE ODD'LY DOPE METAL SKULL. OKAY, O.K. THEN BC. BC IS WAY DIFFFF. NO KID. NERD HAT TIPP'N ALL OVER. CHUCKY-CENTRIC. I WISH IT WERE A LITTLE MORE LOCKHORNS & A TADBIT LESS SCREAM, BUTT FUCK'IT DUDE; STILL ILL. <u>A POINT</u>: I DIG MANCINI, SAY'N THAT I DO WISH HIS STUFF WAS A BIT LESS STRUCTUR'D HE'S MANACURED BUT I THINK HE LET'S HOLLYWOOD TYPES GET TOO MUCH OF HIS EAR. HIS WEIRDNESS IS ENTERTAINING BUT IT DON'T FEEL LIKE IT'S HIS "WEIRD THING". WHATEVER, I'M A DOPE. BC IS COOL AS ▇ BUT IT'S TOO HUNG UP ON SOME STORY THATS NOT IMPORTANT. KILL THOSE TEENYBOPPRS & GET INTO... OH FUCK IT I CAN'T COMPLAINE. LET'S MOVE ON. SC IS MORE JABBERY, MORE JAM'N. DUDE'S JUST CRUISE'N <DUDE BEING MANCINI>. THE TONES ARE GREAT HOMAGE/LAMPOON ALL THE TIME. YOU CAN ACTUALLY SMELL HIS PENTUP DIRECTOR JUICES HIT'N THE SCREEN. COOL. IT HAS THIS FUNNY NEW BURTON/MID-SERIES ELM ST. FLAVOR {1990'S?} BUT SO MUCH MANIA ENERGY. RAD. WELL IT'S SAID THAT THERE MAYBE A REMAKE OF CP1 {?} SOUND LIKE A WASTE OF THE GREAT MOMENTUM THE SERIES HAS. LIKE ANY DOPE MONSTER IT'S NOT WHERE YOUR FROM. IT'S WHERE YOUR AT. BRAD DOURIF RULES SHEA BROUGHT ALL THESE VIDS TO OUR HOME BECAUSE SHES THE BEST EVER ♡

VIDEO TONFA

presents

THE CHARLES LEE RAY FILM COLLECTION

HI MY NAMES CHUCKY WANNA PLAAAAAAAA

CHOPPER

FUNNY / BRUTAL / FAST / AMAZING INSPIRATIONAL / PSYCHO / LITE & HEAVY. I DIG IT. I PUT IT ON FAIRLY OFTEN, IT JUST FLYS BY & THERES A NICE FEELING HAVING IT ON WHILE I TRY TO SETTLE DOWN. DUDES GOT A LOT OF CHARISMA. IT COVERS A LOT OF GROUND AND TIME VERY SLICKLY. IT'S TOLD IN A TONE THAT KEEPS ME CURIOUS EVEN THOW I'V SEEN IT A BUNCH OF TIMES. IT'S FUN & EASY TO APPRECIEATE MENY OF CHOPPERS CHOICES & ACTIONS. HE'S COMPULSIVE & FUNNY & SMART & FOOLISH & ROMANTIC & DANGERIS. IT COULD BE A SAD STORY BUT HE HAS A PERSIVERIENCE & LAYED BACK STYLE COMBO THATS SO POSI. WHILE STABBING, SLICING, SHOOTING, ROBBING & BASHING PEOPLE CONSTANTLY. NICE.

ERIC BANA SIMON LYNDON
DAVID FIELD DAN WYLLIE BILL YOUNG
VINCE COLOSIMO KENNY GRAHAM KATE BEAHAN

WRITTEN & DIRECTED by ANDREW DOMINIK
R RUNNING TIME APPROX 93 MINUTES

DO YOU WANNA THINK ABOUT STUFF? WHAT KINDA STUFF BUMPY OILY PEOPLE & STUFF? COOL, THIS IS ONE FOR YOU. UNLESS YOU WANT ALL KIND'A STORY & GOOD TALK'N THEN MAYBE NOT. I DIG IT. TAKE YOUR BRAIN OUT, KICK BACK. THIS DIRECTOR IS COOL. HIS STUFF IS A NICE CLEAN POP W/A BROMANTIC SENSE OF HUMOR. THIS IS'NT MY FAVORITE OF HIS BUT IT'S STILL A CUT ABOVE A LOT OF IT'S CONTEMPORARIES. THIS FEELS MORE LIKE A STUDIO TYPE THING THEN HIS OTHERS. THERE ARE GIANT CRABS & SQUORPION & MENY OF THE CLASSICS FROM THE ORIGINAL. NO ONE COULD REPLICATE THE CHARISMA OF THO O.G. SO I THINK THIS NEEDS TO BE SEEN W/NO EXPECTATIONS.

SAM WORTHINGTON GEMMA ARTERTON MADS MIKKELSEN

ALEXA DAVALOS RALPH FIENNES LIAM NEESON

SCREEN PLAY BY

TRAVIS BEACHAM AND PHIL HAY & MATT MANFREDI

DIRECTED BY

LOUIS LETERRIER

DOLBY

2010

DVD PG-13 COLOR 106 minutes

CLASH OF THE TITANS

TROMA

VIDEO UNIVERSE

CLASS OF NUKE'EM HIGH

A mind is
a terrible thing
to nuclear waste.

WOW. I COULD SERIOUSLY FILL PAGES JACK'N OFF ON THIS ONE. NO SHIT. WHEN I SAW THIS I COULD'NT BELIEVE IT. THIS IS THE MOVIE I WISH I HAD SEEN WHEN I WAS 15. IT TOTALY GIVES TROMA THE CRED THAT THEY HAVE BUILT AN EMPIRE FROM. SO LETS GET BIZ'Y. ALL THE KIDS ARE GETTING HIGH ON TOXIC WASTE WEED. THE JOINTS ARE NEON GREEN. SLUDGE COMES OUT OF THE WATER FAUCITS. MOTORCYCLES IN THE HALLWAY. SUPER HUGE BONERS. MONSTER SPERM VOMIT, LAZERS, SEX, SUICIDE, AMAZING HAIR, SUPER NEW JERSEY VOICE, ABBUSE OF THE ELDERLY, ABUSE OF THE NATIONAL ANTHEM. THE MANAGER OF THE NUCLEAR POWER PLANT IS RAD. LLOYD KAUFMAN CO-DIRECTED THIS ONE UNDER THE NAME OF SAMUEL WEIL. THE DOPE SLINGING GANG ARE "THE CREATONS" WHO WERE AT ONE TIME THE HONOR SOCIETY. THE SOUNDTRACK RULES, IT WAS STUCK IN MY HEAD FOR DAYS. ONE OF THE MOST AMAZING SPOOFS OF HIGH-SCHOOL MOVIES EVER. IF YOU LIKE THIS I RECOMEND YOU CHECKOUT "MONSTER HIGH", THERES LESS CARNAGE; BUT MORE ALIENS & TOPLESS GIRLS. NUKE'EM HIGH IS A TOP CONTENDER IN THE SILLY-GROSS ARENA. TRUST.

Screenplay
Richard W. Haines, Mark Rudnitsky, Lloyd Kaufman
Directed by
Richard W. Haines & Samuel Weil
95 MIN (R) Restricted
©TROMA, INC.

TROMA

STALLONE
COBRA

SEEING THIS POSTER AT THE VIDEO STORE WAS EPIC FOR ME. IS THAT A FLAMETHROWER ON TOP OF HIS FUCK'N MACHINE GUN? HIS NAME IS PART OF THE TITLE? IN RECENT YEARS I'VE BECOME RE-OBSESSED BUT NOW BY THE MOVIE IT SELF. AMAZINGLY BEAUTIFUL POLISHED SHINEY COCAINE PHOTOGRAPHY, A SCRIPT THAT MAY ONLY BE TWENTY PAGES LONG. DREAMY, ARROGENT, NEON, PSYCHO COWBOY COP WITH A CHIP ON BOTHSHOLDERS

WHEN COPS CAN'T GET THE JOB DONE CORRECTLY THEY HAVE STALLONE COBRA DRIVE HIS AWESOME 50 DOWN & VIOLENTLY DOMINATE. THERE IS A CULT THAT IS INTO KIDNAPPING & BLADE CENTRIC MURDERS. THATS ABOUT ALL THE PLOT WE GET/NEED. WITHOUT COSMATOS THIS PROBABLY WOULD'NT BE WORTH A DAMN. ALL THOUGH IF STALLONE DIRECTED THAT COULD HAVE BEEN GOOD. COSMATOS GIVES ONE OF MY FAVORITE TYPES OF COMMENTERY ON THIS. HE JUST DISCRIBES TO US WHAT WE ARE SEEING. HE TELLS LITTLE STORIES BUT MOSTLY JUST THE LEADING THE BLIND/PULL YOUR HEAD FROM YOUR ASS SHOT LISTINGS. A TRUE ART FILM. NO SHIT. MUCHO. MACHO.

BRIGITTE NEILSEN AND RENI STANTONI

SCREENPLAY by SYLVESTER STALLONE

DIRECTED by GEORGE PAN COSMATOS

DVD R DOLBY 87 MINUTES 1986 COLOR WB

WARREN OATES
AS THE
COCKFIGHTER
DIRT-VIOLENT
& OUTSIDE the LAWS
COCKFIGHTER
HARRY DEAN STANTON RICHARD B. SHULL
PATRICIA PEARCY MILLIE PERKINS

WILLIFORD, HELLMAN, OATES, STANTON... HOLEY SHIT. PERFECTION. I DON'T USUALY DIG IT WHEN MOVIES USE REAL ANIMAL DEATHS BUT HERE ITS DIFFERENT FOR ME. OBVIOUSLY IT'S IN, HELL; IT IS THE TITLE. COCK ON COCK VIOLENCE. IN SOME WAYS IT'S A MISTAKE FOR ME TO DO THIS TONFA BECAUSE IT'S TRUELY A PERFECT MOVIE, I DON'T WANT TO SOIL IT FOR ME OR YOU. IT'S A MEDITATION & LESSON ON BEING TRUE, DISPITE ALL OF OUR DECEPTIONS AND MISTAKES. OATES MAKES THE SAME MISTAKE TIME & AGAIN, SO HE HAS TO GIVE UP A PIECE OF HIMSELF TO PROVE HIS METTLE. THERE IS NO HALF STEPPING. IN A WORLD OF LIES, SCAMS & EVERY OTHER BRANDS OF BULLSHIT WE HAVE TO CUT OUR OWN PATH. STAY TRUE TO OURSELF, & FOR ME THIS IS A GEM OF A REMINDER.

83 MINUTES
SCREENPLAY BY CHARLES WILLIEFORD
DIRECTED BY MONTE HELLMAN COLOR 1974

COHEN&TA
ROY SCHEIDER ADAM BALDWIN HARLEY CROSS
WRITTEN & DIRECTED by ERIC RED

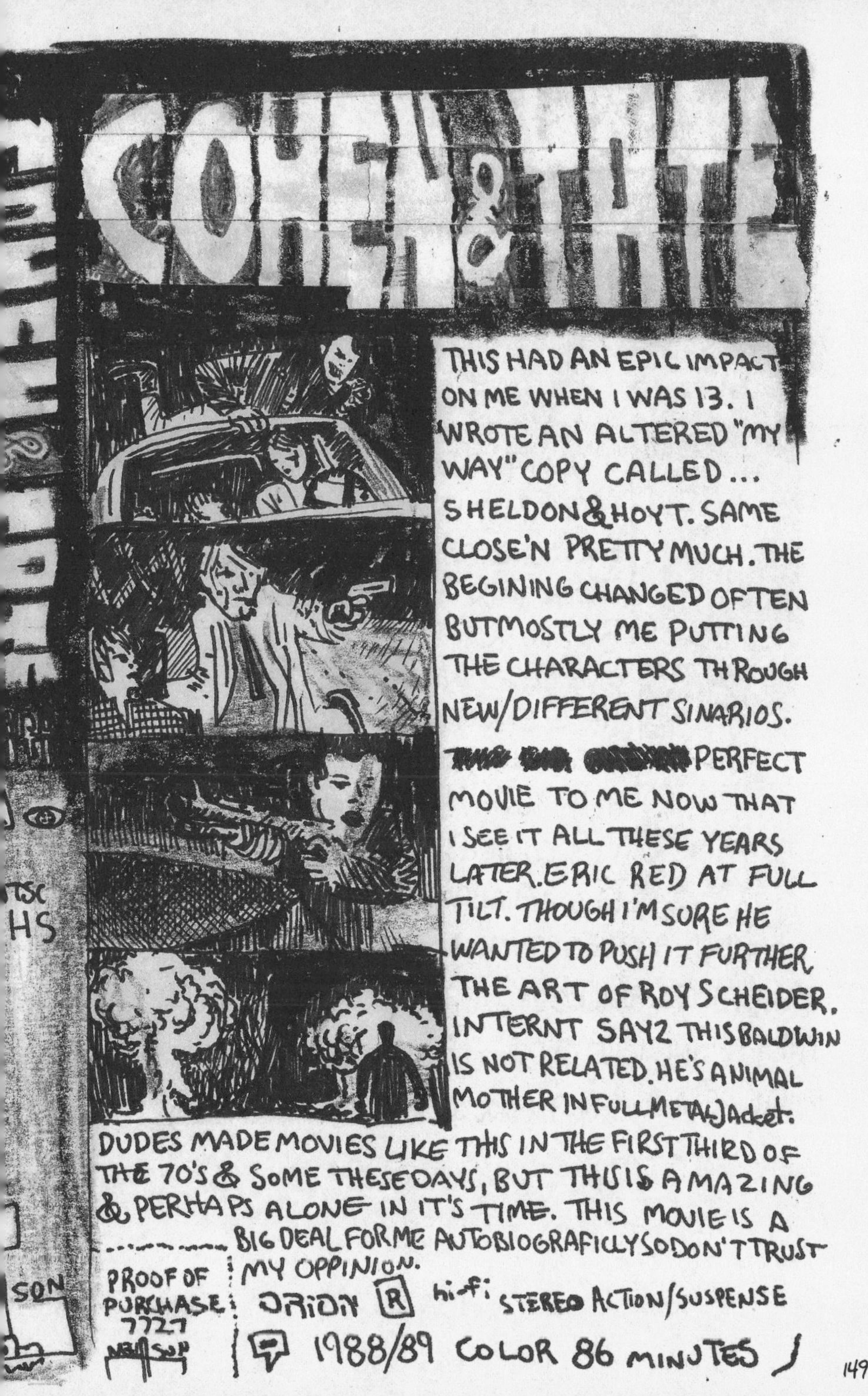
COHEN & TATE
THIS HAD AN EPIC IMPACT ON ME WHEN I WAS 13. I WROTE AN ALTERED "MY WAY" COPY CALLED... SHELDON & HOYT. SAME CLOSE'N PRETTY MUCH. THE BEGINING CHANGED OFTEN BUT MOSTLY ME PUTTING THE CHARACTERS THROUGH NEW/DIFFERENT SINARIOS.
PERFECT MOVIE TO ME NOW THAT I SEE IT ALL THESE YEARS LATER. ERIC RED AT FULL TILT. THOUGH I'M SURE HE WANTED TO PUSH IT FURTHER. THE ART OF ROY SCHEIDER. INTERNT SAYZ THIS BALDWIN IS NOT RELATED. HE'S ANIMAL MOTHER IN FULL METAL JACKET.
DUDES MADE MOVIES LIKE THIS IN THE FIRST THIRD OF THE 70'S & SOME THESE DAYS, BUT THIS IS AMAZING & PERHAPS ALONE IN IT'S TIME. THIS MOVIE IS A BIG DEAL FOR ME AUTOBIOGRAFICLY SO DON'T TRUST MY OPPINION.
PROOF OF PURCHASE 7727
NELSON
ORION
R
hi-fi
STEREO ACTION/SUSPENSE
1988/89 COLOR 86 MINUTES

I DON'T KNOW HOW THIS WAS MADE. BUT IT SEEMS LIKE EVERYONE ON THIS MOVIE IS TRY'N TO DO THEY'R JOB WELL BUT IS TRY'N TO RUIN EVERY-ONE ELSES WERK. WITH ALL THE ELEMENTS SEPERATED THIS WOULD PROBABLY SEEM LIKE A GOOD BET. BUT EVERYTHING WERKS AGAINST IT'S COUNTERPART. THIS BOX IS A TRIP. IT'S A BIGBOX BOOTLEG WITH A COLORCOPY OF A DVD BOOTLEG STUCK IN. YOU CAN SEE THEY USED A MARKER TO BLACKOUT PARTS OF THE ORIGINAL BOXART. I'M FEELING LIKE THESE FOLKS SPEND TOO MUCH TIME WITH MOVIE PEOPLE & NOT ENOUGH TIME WITH MOVIES.

the CONVENT

JOANNA CANTON
COOLIO
JASON DAX MILLER
ADRIENNE BARBEAU

SCREENPLAY BY
CHATON ANDE'SOMETHING'R-OTHER
DIRECTED BY
MIKE MENDEZ

COSMIC
SLOP

BAIRLY HOSTED BY GEORGE CLINTON. HE SHOULD BE A MUCH BIGGER PART OF THIS MOVIE/SHOW.

SPACE TRADERS: DIRECTED BY REGINALD HUDLIN
A TREY ELLIS TELEPLAY FROM DERRICK BELL'S SHORT STORY
THIS ① IS THE LONGEST & IT'S TOO LONG. IT'S ABOUT U.S.A. SELLING OUT, BUT MOSTLY A POLITICIAN NOT? BE A SELL OUT. THERE ISN'T A PAY OFF AS MUCH AS A REAFRIMATION THAT GREED DOMINATES. I WISH THE HAIRCUT ON THE LAWN SCEEN TOOK UP MORE TIME THEN THE FAMILY WATCHING T.V. PARTS.

THE FIRST COMMANDMENT:
WRITTEN & DIRECTED BY WARRINGTON HUDLIN
A PREACHER CONTENDS W/ SELLING OUT HIS LINIAGE OR HIS RELIGION. I LIKE THE ARTY ENDING THOUGH IT IS A BIT FLIP FOR THE BUILD UP WHICH MAKES IT ABSURD, WHICH WAS FUNNY BUT NOT LIKE A SHOWSTOPPER FUNNY. STILL, GOOD.

TANG DIRECTED BY KEVIN RODNEY SULLIVAN
A KYLE BAKER TELEPLAY FROM CHESTER HIMES SHORT STORY
THIS IS ABOUT SELLING YOURSELF OUT. IT'S THE BEST OF THE THREE. A COUPLE TARE AT THEMSELVES & EACH OTHER & THEN AN ETHERIAL DUDE GIVES THEM A LOADED RIFEL. FITTINGLY, AS THE LAST PIECE THIS IS THE ONE W/ THE SOLID ENDING. CLASSIC.

R 1994 HIFI COLOR RUNNING TIME 86 MINUTES

THE MASTERS of TERROR & MACABRE
GEORGE A. ROMERO STEPHEN KING
CREEPSHOW
ADMISSON
· ADULTS
· CHILDREN

THIS MY ARGUMENT FOR EVERYTHING. ALL THE OLD WAYS WITH THE COLORS MELTIN THE EYES OUT OF MY SKULL. INSANELY REWATCHABLE. THERES A COMICBOOK ADAPT- THAT ALSO KILL, WRIGHTSON. THIS IS THE PITCH PERFECT BLUEPRINT OF FILM SPEAKIN PULP SERIEL HORROR COMICS. EVERYTHING RIGHT ON, KING & ROMERO SPAWN THE FINEST FILMS OF THEIR & OUR LIVES.

SO BRIGHT SO GRIM & POETIC & GARISH. PUSHING ALL THE BUTTONS & MAKING IT COME OUT SILK SMOOTH. ALLWAYS A WELCOME ADDITION TO ANY EVENINGS SELECTIONS. IT WILL WASH AWAY THE STAINS & SINS OF ANOTHER MOVIE MAY INFLICT UPON OUR PERSONAGE. A CINIMATIC BALM IF YOU WILL, I WILL. WHAT THE FUCK IS HE TALKING ABOUT? I WILL TELL BUT JUST IN THE VAGUE FOR THE UNINITIEATED. A FRAME OF ANTI COMIC BOOK CHILD ABUSE. THE TALES OF THE ABUSED COMIC UNFOLD OVER ITS JOURNEY FROM A BOYS EYES TO THE TRASH & ON. BETRAIL, TORTURE, MALACE, IGNORENCE, PARANOIA, REVENGE, AROGENCE, ISOLATION, TABOOS, SINS, ALL OUR FAV PERSONAL FAILINGS DRIPPING, CRUSHING, TEARING, SMOTHERING, CREEPING. POUR IT ON, I WOULD LOVE TO SEE IT ON THE SILVERSCREEN.

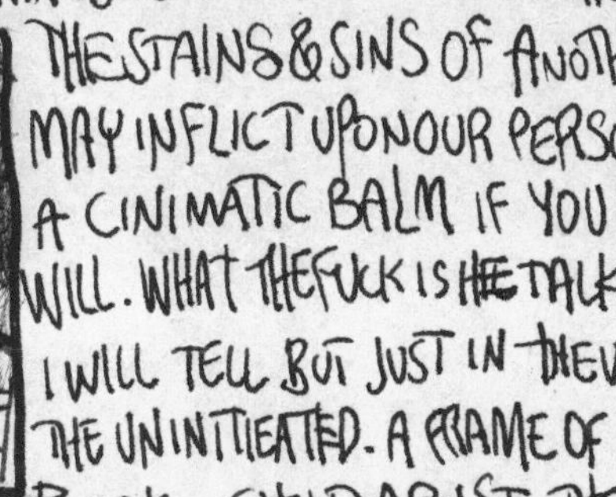

HAL HOLBROOK · ADRIENNE BARBEAU · FRITZ WEAVER
TED DANSON · STEPHEN KING · LESLIE NIELSEN
CARRIE NYE · E.G. MARSHALL · VIVECA LINDFORS

ORIGINAL SCREENPLAY by STEPHEN KING
DIRECTED by GEORGE A. ROMERO

1982

R COLOR 120 MINUTES

Collector's

Edition

STEPHEN KING and GEORGE A. ROMERO
WELCOME YOU TO

CREEPSHOW 2

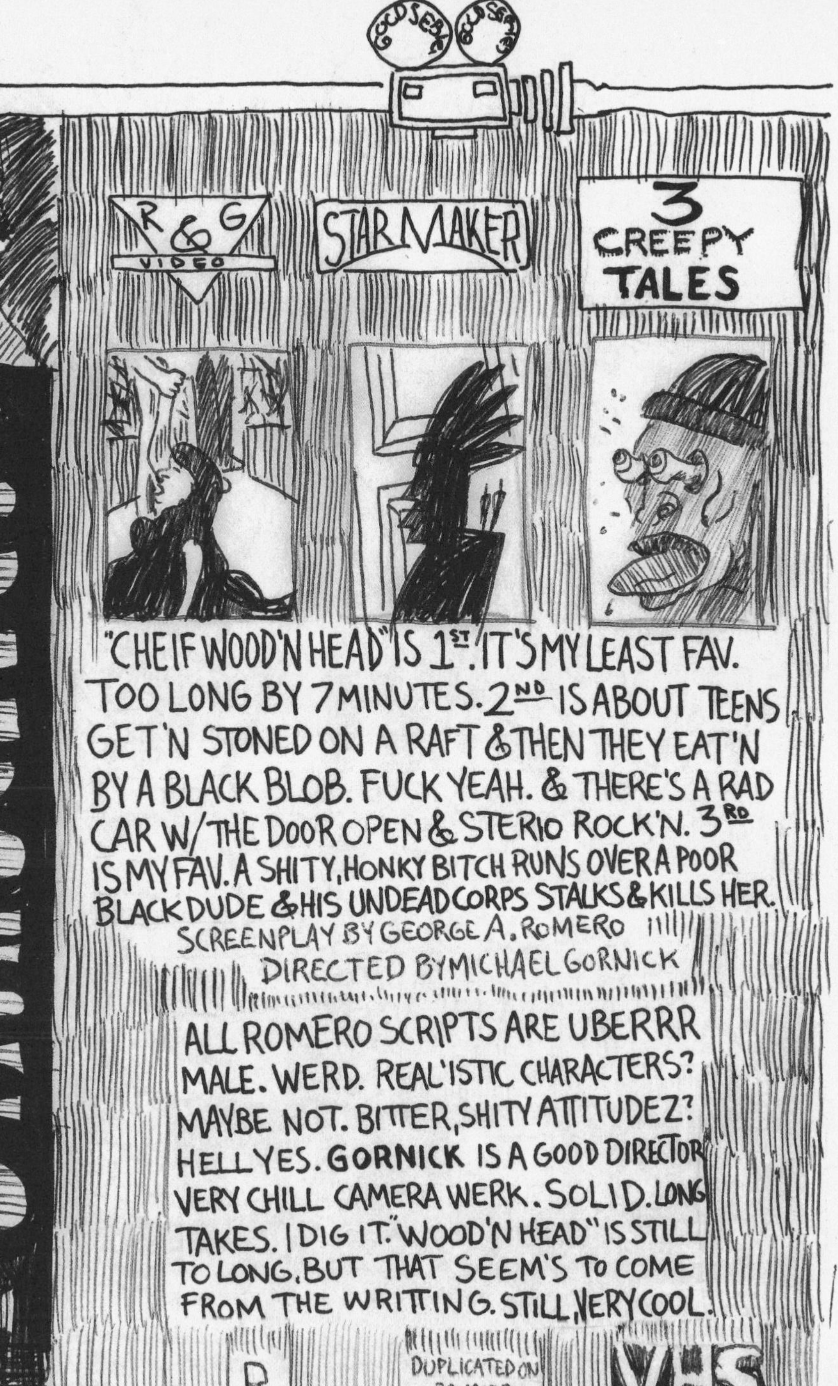
GOOD SEAL
GOOD SEAL
R & G VIDEO
STAR MAKER
3 CREEPY TALES
"CHEIF WOOD'N HEAD" IS 1ST. IT'S MY LEAST FAV. TOO LONG BY 7 MINUTES. 2ND IS ABOUT TEENS GET'N STONED ON A RAFT & THEN THEY EAT'N BY A BLACK BLOB. FUCK YEAH. & THERE'S A RAD CAR W/ THE DOOR OPEN & STERIO ROCK'N. 3RD IS MY FAV. A SHITY, HONKY BITCH RUNS OVER A POOR BLACK DUDE & HIS UNDEAD CORPS STALKS & KILLS HER.
SCREENPLAY BY GEORGE A. ROMERO
DIRECTED BY MICHAEL GORNICK
ALL ROMERO SCRIPTS ARE UBERRR MALE. WERD. REAL'ISTIC CHARACTERS? MAYBE NOT. BITTER, SHITY ATTITUDEZ? HELL YES. GORNICK IS A GOOD DIRECTOR VERY CHILL CAMERA WERK. SOLID. LONG TAKES. I DIG IT. "WOOD'N HEAD" IS STILL TO LONG. BUT THAT SEEM'S TO COME FROM THE WRITTING. STILL, VERY COOL.
R
DUPLICATED ON EP MODE
VHS

CRIMEWAVE

FULL SLAPSTICK. 50'S/80'S MOTIEF. FUCK'N BONKERS. MAYBE YOU CAN TRACK THE STORY BUT MAYBE THERES A LITTLE TOO MUCH STORY? THE COHESION IS SORTA NOT TIGHTENED UP TO TASHLIN LEVEL WHERE IT SEEMS TO BE AIMING. OR THATS WHERE I'D BE AIMING. BRION JAMES FULLY RULES. HE'S MINDBLOWINGLY AMAZING. 100% RAT MODE. IT'S ABOUT A NITWIT WHO GETS IT ALL WRONG AND GETS SHIT FOR IT & WINDS UP ON DEATHROW.

BRION JAMES

LOUISE LASSER, PAUL L. SMITH, SHEREE J. WILSON
EDWARD R. PRESSMAN, BRUCE CAMPBELL, REED BIRNEY

WRITTEN by JOEL COEN & ETHAN COEN & SAM RAIMI
DIRECTED by SAM RAIMI

THEY'RE INVADING YOUR SPACE

I HAVE NOT SEE'N ANY OF THE OTHER CRITTERS MOVIES. AT THE BEGINING THIS DUDE PUTS TWO FUNKY EGGS IN SOME TIN CANS & PLACES 'EM IN SOME SCI-FI CUBBYHOLES, A DOOR LOCKS & THEN THEY'R FLY'N THROUGH SPACE. THEN IT GET'S PICK'T UP BY A SALVAGE SHIP. SO THAT'S THE FIRST 8 MINUTES. THEN IT'S PRETTY MUCH A TRAPPED IN A SPACESHIP WITH AN ALIEN{S} MOVIE. IT WOULD BE HO-HUM IF NOT FOR THE CAST. LEO FROM TWIN PEAKS IS A CREEP, HE STEELS A BUNCH OF DRUGS. ANGELA BASSETT IS TOTALY BUFF AND TAKING NO SHIT. RAD. BUT, AS IF THAT WER'NT ENOUGH... WE GET BRAD DOURIF. FUCK YEAH. BRAD DOURIF IS TOP OF THE LINE FOR ME. ENTERTAINING ENOUGH FOR A LITE MOVIE CHILL OUT, BUT NOTHING SPECIAL OUTSIDE THE CAST, WITH A POSSIBLE EXCEPTION IF IT ADVANCES THE CRITTERS SERIES IN A GOOD DIRECTION, BUT I KIND OF DOUBT IT.

DON OPPER PAUL WHITTHORNE ANGELA BASSETT & BRAD DOURIF

STORY BY RUPERT HARVEY & BARRY OPPER
SCREENPLAY BY JOSEPH LYLE AND DAVID J. SCHOW
DIRECTED BY RUPERT HARVEY

DVD APPROX 94 MINS. PG-13 COLOR 2003

CRITTERS 4
IN SPACE... THEY LOVE to HEAR YOU SCREAM

A JOHN WATERSFILM

JOHNNY DEPP

He's a doll
He's a dreamboat
He's a delinquent.

Cry-Baby

JOHNNY DEPP AMY LOCANE
SUSAN TYRRELL IGGY POP
RICKI LAKE TRACI LORDS
POLLY BERGEN

WRITTEN & DIRECTED
BY
JOHN WATERS

STEBEO
PG-13

WOWWWEE! YOU CAUGHT ME IN MY BIRTHDAYSUIT BUCK NEKKED!

FULL DISCLOSURE: I'M PRETTY OBSESED WITH THIS MOVIE I'V SEEN IT SO MENY TIMES, BOTH CUTS; THAT I HAVE NO IDEA WHICH ONE THIS WAS. THIS IS MY FAVORITE WATERS MOVIE. BUT I THINK I MIGHT ARGUE THAT OTHERS MAY BE HIS BEST. WHAT CAN YOU DO? FOR ME, THERE IS NO BAD WATERS MOVIE. & ALSO MY FAV. DEPP MOVIE TOO. HONESTLY I DON'T WANT TO ANALIZE THE MOVIE TOO MUCH. I HAVE A 50'S ART THING SO I'M A PUSH OVER FOR A COMBO LIKE THIS. THE ENTIRE CAST IS SOLID GOLD. WHAT WITH WW2 MAKE'N ORPHANS A BUSINESS, IT'S A NO SHIT ON THE TEEN SCEEN OF THE 50'S. THE WATERS COMMENTARIE IS GREAT TOO. I LOVE 1950/80'S MOVIES, THEY ARE JUST MY WEIRD THING; AS A TEEN DINGDONG I WATCHED A MOVIE "BOOK OF LOVE" WAY TOO HARD & WHEN I REVISITED IT I WAS STUNNED BY ITS DRAB CALOUSNESS. I STILL HAVE IT THOUGH. BUT CRYBABY IS THE ONE THAT HAS THE RING FOR ME. ITS SO DIALED & PERSONAL, THE CHRYSTALISATION. LIKE THE FIRST MAD MAGAZINES. DIALED IN OBSESSION AT A LEVEL WHERE IT JOINS THE RANKS OF IT'S SOURCES PERFECTLY, LIKE IN "YOUNG FRANKENSTEIN". PERHAPS PUT THE CREDITS ON SLOW-MO. BUT THEN/ALSO THE SOUNDTRACK IS NOT TO BE TAMPERED WITH. IT'S KILLER. SHIT, WHAT AM I SAY'N? JUST BLATHER'N ON & ON. DON'T MESS WITH THE SOUND OR SPEED. PUMP IT UP, THEN KICK BACK W/A DATE AND ENJOY THE SHOW. I LOVE THE DANCING AND MAKE OUT SCENE. IGGY'S THE BEST DANCER DUDE. THE CARS, THE MUSIC, THE TALKING. IT'S PERFECTION. DIG IT.

CRYBABY
Wed Sep 16 09 9:35pm 1
Laur R 275
1 Adult
Redeem free cup of
Stumptown drip coffee at
New Deal Cafe
5250 NE Halsey

CRYBABY
0916 9:35p
275-01
1Ad2

MGM/UA

MOVIE TIME

VAN DAMME

AWWH DUDE, I LOVE THIS MOVIE SO HARD. IT STARTS OFF POSTAPPOCOLIPSE WITH A VOICE OVER FROM THE VILLEN THEN KILLING, CHASE'N, FIGHTING

THE CYBORG SHOWS VANDAMME HER ROBOT SKULL & SAYS SHE HAS THE CURE FOR THE NEW PLAGUE. MOSTLY THIS MOVIE IS ALL FIGHTING & CHASE'N WITH THE CYBORG AS A MᶜGUFF'N. VANDAMME HAS SOME FLASHBACK, BACKSTORY. MOST OF <IF NOT ALL> CHARACTERS ARE NAMED AFTER GUITARS. PYUN IS AT FULL ON RAD POWERS HERE WITH THE FIGHTS AND CAMERA WERK. RAD POWER CREEP VILLENS. THERES NOT MUCH OF SEX STUFF HE'LL TYPICALLY GO FOR, WHICH MAY COME FROM THE SCRIPT. THERE IS A REOCCURRING THEAM OF WHAT IS OBVIOUSLY A RELATIONSHIP OF PHYSICAL ABUSE. CYBORG OR NEMISIS WAS MY FIRST PYUN MOVIE BUT I CAN'T RECALL WHICH I SAW WHEN. GOOD USE OF VANDAMMES REQUISITE SPLITS SHOT, WITH HIM STUFF'N A SWORD DOWN A DUDES THROUGHT. I THINK THE FIGHTS IN HERE ARE PRETTY RAD ON THE JCVD METER BUT I'M NOT REALLY INTO THE FINAL SHOWDOWN FIGHT. AFTER ALL THE RAMPING UP OF EACH FIGHT IT ALL WRAPS UP IN A MILD RAIN CONFRONTATION. FUCK IT, LET'S REWINDE IT & WATCH IT AGAIN.

JEAN-CLAUDE VAN DAMME VINCENT KLYN
DEBORAH RICHTER DAYLE HADDON

WRITTEN BY KITTY CHALMERS
DIRECTED BY ALBERT PYUN

Ⓡ 1 HOUR 26 minutes 1989 COLOR

THIS THE "RENEGADE DIRECTORS CUT" AS OF THAY PYUN WAS FIRED. THE VOICES ARE INCONSISTANT & THE SOUND TOO. BUT AS FAR AS THE MOVE GO'S THIS VERSION HAS MORE TO OFFER IN TERMS OF STORY, PACE, TONE, & THE END IS ABOUT THE SAME BUT ACTUALLY HAS WEIGHT & A MORE NILISTIC IMPLICATIONS WHICH WORKS SO MUCH BETTER. THE POP "FIGHT/CHASE" PACING IS THERE AS MUCH BECAUSE THE STORY IS STRUCTURED INTELIGIBLY. I STILL LOVE THE THEATRICAL CUT BECAUSE OF THESE THINGS. BUT THAT IS BECAUSE

ALBERT PYUN'S CYBORG

IT HAS A MIND NUMBING MEATHEAD NIGHTMARE QUALITY TO IT THAT IS REALLY FRIGHTENING & BEAUTIFUL. IN PYUN'S CUT THINGS ARE CLEARER & SO WE DON'T GET THE SAME CRUSHING HORROR. BUT UNLIKE THE THEATRICAL, PYUN'S HAS AN ENDING THAT MATCHES THE QUALITY OF THE REST OF THE MOVIE.

UNRELEASED DIRECTORS EDITION
ALBERT PYUN'S
CYBORG
ORIGINALLY CONCEIVED AS "SLINGER"

UAV
CARTOON
CLASSICS
COLLECTION
DAFFY
DUCK
VOLUME 8

DAFFY DUCK IS A GOD
I HAVE WATCHED THIS &
MENY OTHERS OF THESE. I
GOT SO MENY DOUBLES
THE PACKAGING ALONE CAN LURE ME IN.
IT'S THE BEST WHEN PORKY PIG IS IN
THERE TOO. I LOVE THOSE TWO SO MUCH.

CARTOON CLASSICS COLLECTION

FEATURING

YANKEE DOODLE DAFFY

STARRING DAFFY DUCK

DAFFY THE COMMANDO

STARRING DAFFY DUCK

DAFFY AND THE DINOSAUR

STARRING DAFFY DUCK

RUNNING TIME

APPROX. 30 Minutes/In Color

GUARANTEED SUPERIOR
QUALITY VIDEO TAPE & RECORDING

UNITED AMERICAN VIDEO CORP
UAV SPECIAL PROMOTIONS

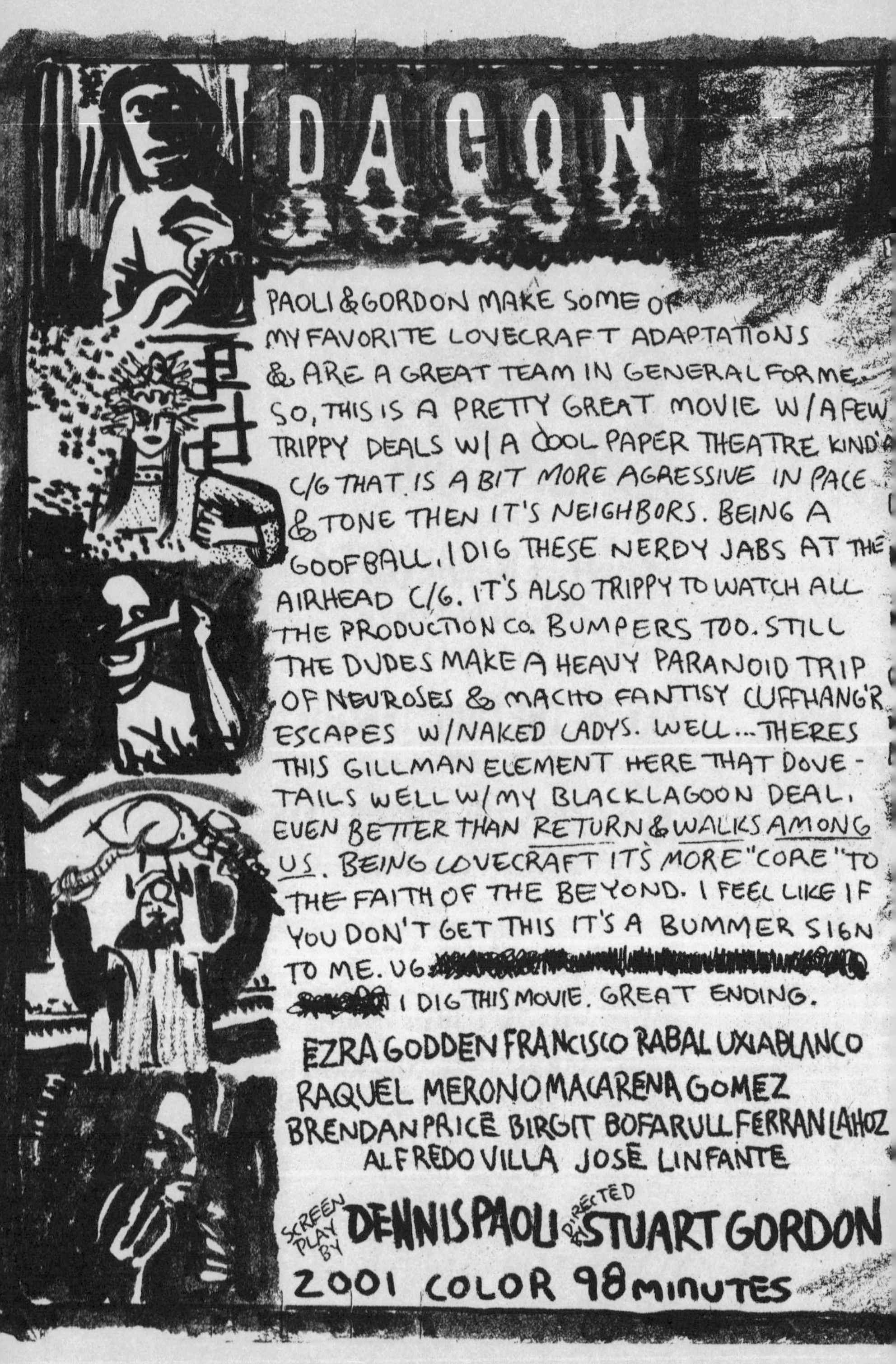
DAGON
PAOLI & GORDON MAKE SOME OF
MY FAVORITE LOVECRAFT ADAPTATIONS
& ARE A GREAT TEAM IN GENERAL FOR ME.
SO, THIS IS A PRETTY GREAT MOVIE W/A FEW
TRIPPY DEALS W/ A COOL PAPER THEATRE KIND'A
C/G THAT IS A BIT MORE AGRESSIVE IN PACE
& TONE THEN IT'S NEIGHBORS. BEING A
GOOFBALL, I DIG THESE NERDY JABS AT THE
AIRHEAD C/G. IT'S ALSO TRIPPY TO WATCH ALL
THE PRODUCTION CO. BUMPERS TOO. STILL
THE DUDES MAKE A HEAVY PARANOID TRIP
OF NEUROSES & MACHO FANTISY CLIFFHANG'R
ESCAPES W/NAKED LADYS. WELL... THERES
THIS GILLMAN ELEMENT HERE THAT DOVE-
TAILS WELL W/MY BLACKLAGOON DEAL.
EVEN BETTER THAN RETURN & WALKS AMONG
US. BEING LOVECRAFT ITS MORE "CORE" TO
THE FAITH OF THE BEYOND. I FEEL LIKE IF
YOU DON'T GET THIS IT'S A BUMMER SIGN
TO ME. UG.
I DIG THIS MOVIE. GREAT ENDING.
EZRA GODDEN FRANCISCO RABAL UXIA BLANCO
RAQUEL MERONO MACARENA GOMEZ
BRENDAN PRICE BIRGIT BOFARULL FERRAN LAHOZ
ALFREDO VILLA JOSE LINFANTE
SCREEN PLAY BY DENNIS PAOLI DIRECTED BY STUART GORDON
2001 COLOR 98 MINUTES

H.P. LOVECRAFT'S
DAGON

IT'S A GOOD PLACE FOR A BAD TIME...

I THINK HE'S UNDER COVER OR INFILTRATING ON THE BIKERS. HE DOSENT LIKE IT WHEN THE GIRLS ARE ABUSED. HE WANTS TO & DOSE ENJOY HAVING "RELATIONS" WITH THEM. KIDNAPPING. MAN I HAVE A LOT OR RESPECT FOR FOLK WHO CAN DRAW MOTORCYCLES COOL. I'M SURE IT WORKS OUT. I FORGET.

1987 COLOR R
90 MINUTE THRILLE

ROBERT CANADA JASON WILLIAMS CYNTHIA GRAY R.A. MIAHAILOFF JUANITA RANNEY SUZANNE TARA MIKE WILES

FBI

WRITTEN BY JASON WILLIAMS
DIRECTED BY
HENRY VERNON

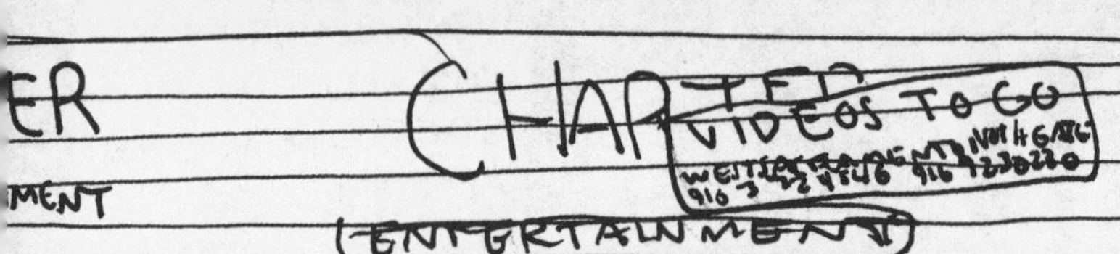

THE DANGER ZONE

HE RIDE THROUGH THE FIRES OF HELL!

HI-FI MONO

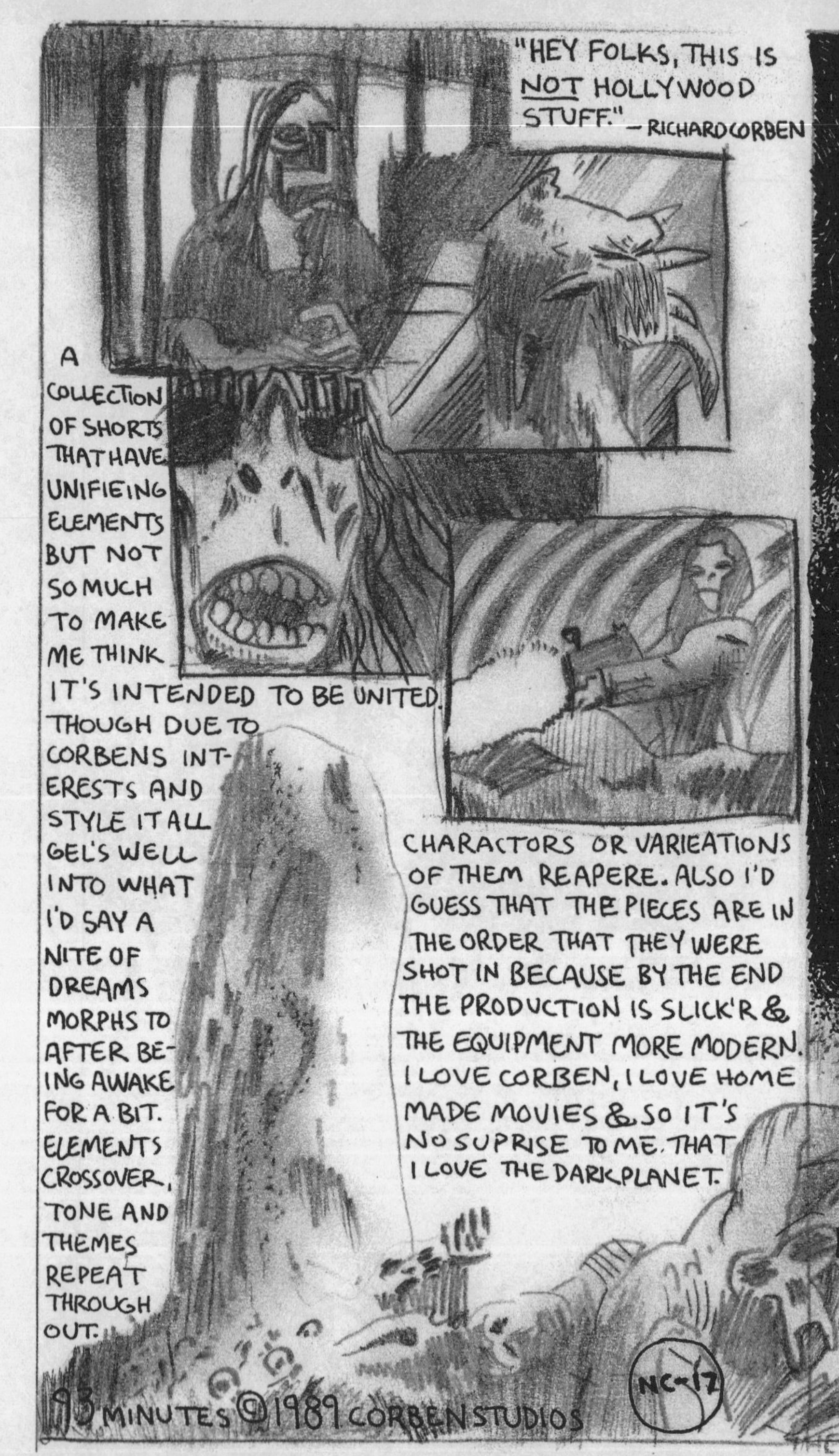
"HEY FOLKS, THIS IS NOT HOLLYWOOD STUFF." — RICHARD CORBEN
A COLLECTION OF SHORTS THAT HAVE UNIFIEING ELEMENTS BUT NOT SO MUCH TO MAKE ME THINK IT'S INTENDED TO BE UNITED. THOUGH DUE TO CORBENS INTERESTS AND STYLE IT ALL GEL'S WELL INTO WHAT I'D SAY A NITE OF DREAMS MORPHS TO AFTER BEING AWAKE FOR A BIT. ELEMENTS CROSSOVER, TONE AND THEMES REPEAT THROUGH OUT.
CHARACTORS OR VARIEATIONS OF THEM REAPERE. ALSO I'D GUESS THAT THE PIECES ARE IN THE ORDER THAT THEY WERE SHOT IN BECAUSE BY THE END THE PRODUCTION IS SLICK'R & THE EQUIPMENT MORE MODERN. I LOVE CORBEN, I LOVE HOME MADE MOVIES & SO IT'S NO SUPRISE TO ME THAT I LOVE THE DARK PLANET.
93 MINUTES ©1989 CORBEN STUDIOS
NC-17

UNEARTHLY TERROR STALKS THE CREATURES OF

THE DARK PLANET

BRUCE JONES KAREN GILBERTSON RICHARD CORBEN

HERB ARNOLD SIMON RIVERSTROKE SAUNDRA MARKS

MUSIC BY PHILIP DEWALT

WRITTEN, PRODUCED & DIRECTED BY RICHARD CORBEN

DARKMAN
SCREENPLAY by
CHUCK PFARRER &
SAM RAIMI &
IVAN RAIMI &
DANIEL GOLDIN &
JOSHUA GOLDIN.
STEREO
COLOR
1 HOUR 36 MINUTES
LIAM NEESON
FRANCES McDORMAND
COLIN FRIELS LARRY DRAKE
STORY & DIRECTED by SAM RAIMI
CC
R
1990

LOVE IT DUDE. I FEEL IT'S ONE OF RAIMIS TOP 3 BEST. DEFINATLY THE LIAM NEESON MOVIE I'M MOST LIKELY TO WATCH. I DIG THE HOLE CAST. FUN AND WILD PULP HERO UNIVERSAL MONSTERS STYLE STRUCTURE. SLAPSTICK NIGHTMARE GANGSTER, MILD SCI-FI/FANTASY/SUPERNATURAL RETROBUTION
DOCTOR WESTLAKE IS A SCIENTIST DEVELOPING A SKINCLONE'N SYSTEM BUT IT'S NOT RIGHT YET. THE SKIN FALLS APART IN A SHORT TIME. HIS GIRLFRIED IS A LAWYER WHOS CLIENT IS A CREEPY BUSINESSMAN. SHE FINDS DOCUMENTATION OF HIS DIRTYNESS. HE TRYS TO SEDUCE HER THINGS GO BAD HE HAS HIS MAFIA DUDES GO TRASH EVERYTHING LOOK'N FOR THE PAPER. THEY BLOW UP DR. WESTLAKE & HIS LAB, BUT HE LIVES... NOW USING HIS SKIN RECIPE HE'S TRIPPLE DOUBLE CROSSING ALL THESES CREEPS & TAKING THEM APART AT THE SEEMS. NOW HE'S TRY'N TO GET BACK W/ HIS OLDLADY BUT HIS FACE KEEPS MELTING OFF. MY FAVE LOOK OF HIS IS AS NORMAL DARKMAN, WITH THE BANDAGES, HAT, & TRENCH COAT. THIS IS A TOTAL "YOU FUCK'D W/ THE WRONG GUY" MOVIE. SAM & IVAN ARE A GREAT TEAM. IT'S FUNNY THAT THERES 5 SCREENWRITERS CUZ IT'S SO MUCH A RAIMI THING. MY HIGHIST RECOMENDATION!

THE ORIGINAL BBC adaptation of John Wyndham's classic story of post-apocalyptic survival

POST APPOCOLIPSE IS PROBABLY MY NO. 1 GENRE. SO SO THIS IS TOTALY ON MY TOO COOL LIST. IT'S A BBC SERIEL SHOW <DUH>. THERE IS A MOVIE TOO, BUT I HAVE'NT SEEN IT.

SO, THERE ARE THESE BIG PLANTS THAT CAN WALK SLOWLY & THEY WILL KILL/MAIM PEOPLE. THEN, ALLMOST EVERYONE GETS BLINDED. AWESOME. WE FOLLOW SOME FOLKS WHO CAN STILL SEE. THEY GET NO END OF SHIT FROM THE BLIND MASS'. KIND OF CHILL & SPACE'Y PACEING, WITH SOME CLIFFHANGERS. SORT OF REINFOURCES THE IDEA THAT MOST PEOPLE ARE SHIT WITH A FEW GOOD PEOPLE, THEN GIVES US A BIT OF SOMEONE WHO, SUBJECTIVLY, CAN BE BOTH. SOME HEAVY STUFF PLAY'D PRETTY DRY.

DVD VIDEO

PG

BBC DVD
Flesh-eating plants go on the rampage in the acclaimed BBC Scifi thriller
THE DAY OF THE
TRIFFIDS
PG
DVD
VIDEO

AS A MOVIE WITH A STORY & A POINT THIS IS AN IFFY CONTENDER. THIS IS MORE OF A COLLECTION OF THEMED SKITS TIED TOGETTHE W/ TIME & CAST ELIMINATION, ALONG WITH A LIVING DEAD STORY. FUNNY THOUGH. AND GOOD ENOUGH TASTE NERD REFRENCES. I MAYBE MISTAKEN BUT I RECALL BEING TOLD THIS WAS A WEEKENDS PROJECT THAT HAS A NICE PRODUCTION VALUE. IT MAKES SENCE TO ME WHAT W/ THE SKIT ELEMENT. A SORT OF ADVANCED BACKYARD MOVIE TASTE WHICH IS A BIG PART OF THE CHARM. THERES A HEAVY EVIL DEAD INFLUENCE {ALL 3}. THE NAZI PART IS THE MOST CARTOONISH ELEMENT BUT THE WHOLE THING IS VERY CARTOONY. I THINK THIS TEAM WILL DO SOME GOOD & MORE COHESIVE MOVIES DOWN THE LINE. IF YOU'D LIKE TO WATCH A GOOFY GORE COMEDY THEN THIS IS A FUN CHOICE.

VEGARD HOEL STIG FRODE HENRIKSEN CHARLOTTE FROGNER LASSE VALDAL
EVY KASSETH RØSTEN JEPPE BECK LAURSEN JENNY SKAVLAN ANE DAHL TORP
BJØRN SUNDQUIST ØRJAN GAMST
WRITTEN BY STIG FRODE HENRIKSEN & TOMMY WIRKOLA
DIRECTED BY TOMMY WIRKOLA

MULTNOMACOUNTY
LIBRARY

DAVID CRONENBERG
& Stephen King's

DEAD ZONE

DEa

WHAT? WHAT AM I SUPOSSED TO SAY? CRONENBERG & WALKEN DEBRA HILL, TOM SKERRITT; GOOD LORD WHAT MORE DO YOU WANT? SERIOUSLY WORTH A MINNIMUM OF THREE VIEWINGS. FOR SURE.

I DON'T READ KING BOOKS, BUT I TEND TO DIG MOVIES THAT ARE ASSOCIEATED WITH DUDE. THE STORY IS'NT TOO MANIA BUT THE TONE IS AMAZING. LIKE A CRAZY SMELL THAT YOU HAVE TO RELAX TO CATCH BUT IF YOU HUFF IT YOU'LL BURRY THE GOLD.

IF YOU HAVE ANY PRE-CONCIEVED SHIT ABOUT THIS MOVIE I RECOMEND YOU MEDITATE HARD BEFORE YOU PEEP THIS.

TOP NOTCH.

CHRISTOPHER WALKEN BROOKE ADAMS
TOM SKERRITT HERBERT LOM ANTHONY ZERBE
COLLEEN DEWHURST NICHOLAS CAMPBELL MARTIN SHEEN
SCREENPLAY JEFFREY BOAM
PRODUCED BY DEBRA HILL DIRECTED BY DAVID CRONENBERG

HOLY SHIT. THIS IS SUCH AN INSPARATIONAL FILM. THE STORY IS CLASSIC. JUST READ THE POSTER. IT'S FULLY THE DUDE THAT MADE IT, THAT MAKES IT. HIS STYLE & CHARISMA ARE EPIC. HE OVERCOMES CLASSIC OBSTICALS AND FAILINGS W/ INSPIRED INGENUITY. THE VIOLENCE & GRAPHIC FX ARE FULL TILT. HE'S "LIKE" A STUNTMAN, COWBOY, ANTIHERO POWERHOUSE. & SUICIDAL ON DRUGS. CEMETARY GANG WAR. POP & BRUTAL. HE DEFINATLY KNOWS THE POWER OF THE HAND. GRAFITTI MOTORCYCLE, TRASH COMPACTER, MURDERS. STRONGARM DRUG DEALER WITH A HEART OF GOLD. OR AT LEAST, SUPER HURT FEELINGS. ROMANTIC FOR HEAVY REACTIONARY DUDES LIKE MYSELF. VAN BEBBER FUCK! I FEEL LIKE I HAVE WOUND DOWN FROM MY POIINT. , PEEP THIS, TRUST

PAUL HARPER JIM VAN BEBBER
MEGAN MURPHY RIC WALKER
MARC PITMAN MAUREEN GENTNER

MUSIC by A-OK and NED FOLKERTH
PRODUCED & PHOTOGRAPHED by MICHAEL KING
WRITTEN & DIRECTED by JIM VAN BEBBER
RUNNING TIME: 81 MINUTES

ASMODEUS PRODUCTIONS INCORPORATED

YOU SUCK

AMY GIVES GOODHEAD

HE QUIT THE GANGS

THEY KILLED HIS GIRL

HE BECAME...

DEADBEAT AT DAWN

DIRECTED & STARRING JIM VAN BEBBER

1988 UR 1 HOUR AND 20 MINUTES

WARNERHOME VIDEO

"IN THE FUTURE" THE GOVERNMENT ARE ASSHOLES. EVERY YEAR THEY HAVE A CROSS COUNTRY NO HOLDS BARRED RACE WITH POINTS EARNED BY RUNNING PEOPLE OVER. WITH A CAST THAT RULES AND PAUL BARTEL DIRECTING, THIS MOVIE IS A DREAM COME TRUE FOR ME, EXPECIALLY AS A TEENAGER WHEN I FIRST SAW IT. IT'S FUNNY... THIS IS BARTELS MOST FAMOUSE MOVIE BUT IS RAIRLY IDENTIFIED AS ONE OF HIS. SO MUCH FUN. AMERIKKKA'S DANGER DIABOLIK.

DEATHRACE 2000

CAST

Frankenstein................ DAVID Carradine
Annie........................ Simone Griffeth
Machine Gun Joe Viterbo... Sylvester Stallone
Calamity Jane............... Mary Woronov
Mathilda the Hun........... Roberta Collins
Nero the Hero............... Martin Kove
Myra......................... Louisa Moritz
Junior Bruce....... "THE REAL" Don Steele

COLOR

VIDEO CASSETTE SCREENING TIME APPROX. 80 MINS.

1975

STORY BY Ib MELCHIOR

SCREENPLAY

ROBERT THOM & CHARLES B. GRIFFITH

DIRECTED by PAUL BARTEL

WARNER HOME VIDEO
A NEW WORLD PICTURE
DAVID CARRADINE IN
DEATH RACE 2000
DAVID CARRADINE

EXPLOSIVE RENTALS
A SLICK, ENTERTAINING ACTION FILM!
DEMO TAPE
VIDEO BOX ART MAY VARY
50 DAY PPV WINDOW
DEEP RISING
FULL-LENGTH SCREENER FOR VIDEO RETAILERS ONLY

SURFIRE PROFITS!

- ACTION-THRILLERS RENT!

ANACONDA	18
THE RELIC	15
ALIEN³	13
SPECIES	14
DEEP RISING	ORDER DEEP

- $11 MILLION BOX OFFICE

- Trailered On JACKIE BROWN

PULSE POUNDING!

FUN-FACTS

DUDES! I KNEW THIS WAS FOR ME WHEN I SEE'N THE PREVIEW. I WENT ON THE FIRST DAY. MY EXPECTATIONS WERE HIGH, &... I WAS NOT BUMMED. I WAS STOKED. IF YOU DIG UN-STUCK UP ADVENTURE THIS IS **THE JAM!** SO SOME BADASS' GIVE SOME ASS HOLES A BOAT RIDE TO FUCK OVER SOME RICH SHITS, BUT THING GO WRONKIGZ... A SEA BEING HAS FULLY TURNED MOST OF THE RICHSHITS INTO BUFFET. AND THE ASS' HAVE LINED THEM SELF'S UP. PERFECTION. JUST GO SEE IT. IF YOU DON'T LIKE IT DON'T TELL ME

R

WHITE TEE CREW
Written & Directed by MAX MARGULIES
ABSURD, AVANTARD. YOUNG MAX HAS AN EYE FOR IT TOO. & AN EAR FOR TASTY DIALOGUE. THIS IS THE SAMPLE PLATTER OF ONE AMERIKKKA'S MOST STUNNING SATIRESTS. ARE WE NOT BEASTS? WE ARE BEASTLIEST AND BEYOND THAT WE ARE FOOLS, BENT ON SELF DESTRUCTION. THIS SHIT IS FUCKING FUNNY AS SHIT TOO.
HE'S GOT HIS NEIGHBOR IN IT & THAT DUDE IS AWESOME. THIS DVD IS HAND MADE SO MAYBE ITS EASIER TO PEEP ON LINE. MAX MARGULIES
MOET

WTC PRESENTS...
The Demolition
Vol. 1

SCREENPLAY BY NEIL BLOMKAMP & TERRI TATCHELL
DIRECTED BY NEIL BLOMKAMP

I MIGHT HAVE BEEN A BIT SICK {FOOD POISONING?} WHEN I SAW THIS. STARTS WITH DOCUMENTRY STYLE CAMERA & KEEPS IT UP FOR QUITE A WHILE BUT DOSE DROP IT AFTER A WHILE WHICH IS TOO BAD. SO ABOUT THIS TIME THE MOVIE GETS PRETTY INTENCE & THEN IT TURNS INTO AN ACTION MOVIE. WHICH IS O.K. BUT IT'S SORT'A A WASTE OF IT'S CONSEPTUAL MOMENTUM. SO THE BACK ½ OF IT IS A BIT OF AN ANIME STEAMPUNK MELLOWDRAMA. NOT AN UNINTELIGENT MOVIE BUT IT FAILS TO SPARK MUCH ACTUAL THOUGHT. SORT'A TOUCHS ON SOCIAL CLASS ISSUES BUT HAS'NT GOT MUCH OF AN OPPINION OF WHAT IT WANTS OUTSIDE OF THE IDEA OF CONSIDERING IT A HEAVY TOPIC. THERES ONE OR TWO INTERESTING CHARACTERS BUT MOST OF THEM ARE SO-SO. IT'S VERY SPECIAL EFFECTS OBSESSED, VERY MUCH SO. BLOMKAMP COULD BE GOOD BUT I'LL WAIT TO SEE SOME MORE BEFOR I MAKE UP MY MIND. MAN, I REALLY DIG WHEN MOVIE THEATRES HAVE THAT NEUTRITIONAL YEAST FOR THE POPCORN. THIS PLACE DID'NT HAVE ANY SO WAS'NT TOO INTO THE CORN. SORT'A DRY'LY STAIL. BUT I DO DIG THE THEATRE. THEATRE IS MY FAVORITE WAY TO [illegible] OUT A MOVIE I THINK IT'S THE PROJECTION THAT DOES IT FOR ME. WITH A TV YOUR LOOKING AT A LITE BUT WITH PROJECTION YOUR LOOKING AT LITE SHINING ON TO A SERFACE WHICH IS MORE CHILL ON MY EYES AND INVITES ME INTO IT RATHER THAN BLASTING OUT INTO MY FACE.

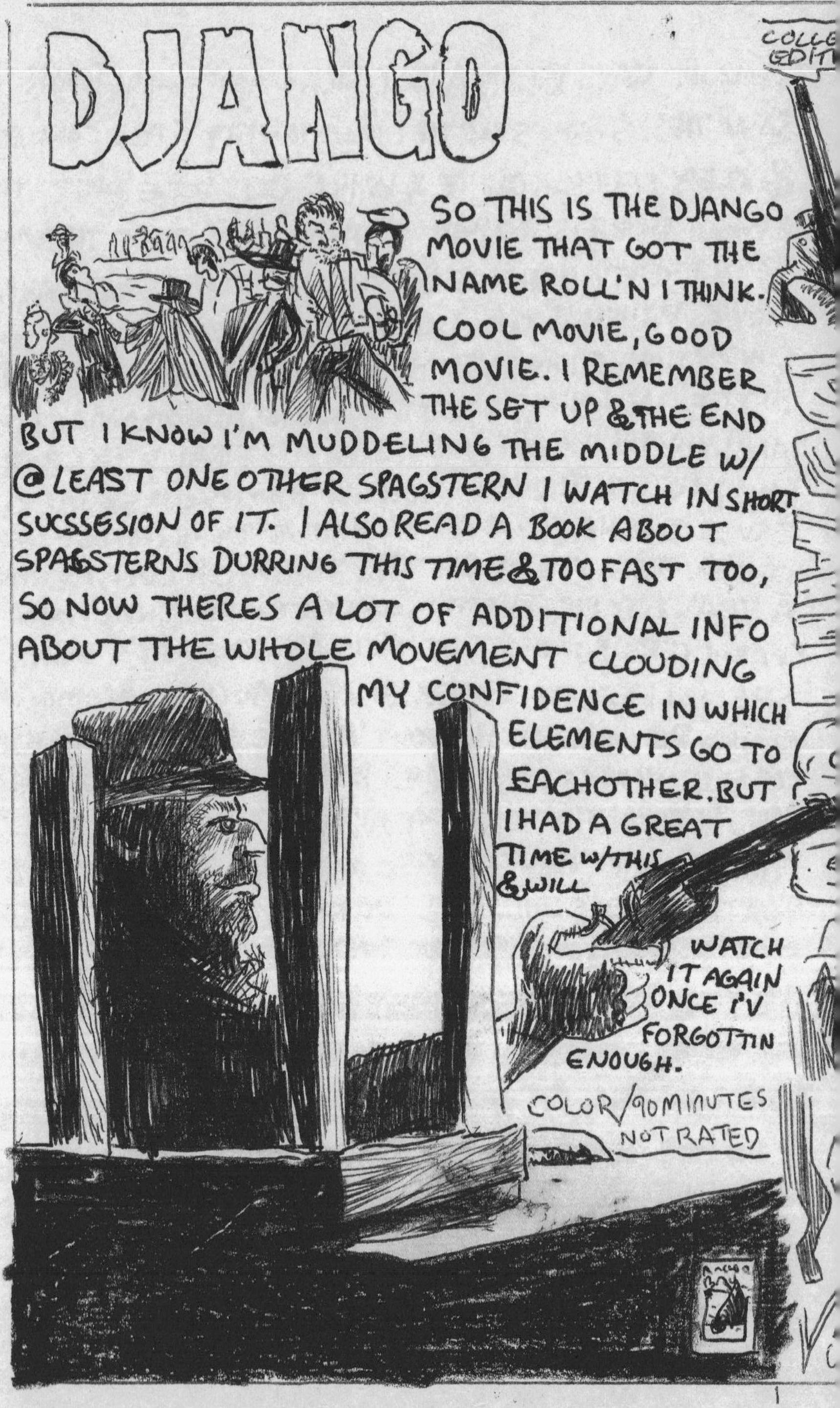

SO THIS IS THE DJANGO MOVIE THAT GOT THE NAME ROLL'N I THINK. COOL MOVIE, GOOD MOVIE. I REMEMBER THE SET UP & THE END BUT I KNOW I'M MUDDELING THE MIDDLE W/ @ LEAST ONE OTHER SPAGSTERN I WATCH IN SHORT SUCSSESION OF IT. I ALSO READ A BOOK ABOUT SPAGSTERNS DURRING THIS TIME & TOO FAST TOO, SO NOW THERES A LOT OF ADDITIONAL INFO ABOUT THE WHOLE MOVEMENT CLOUDING MY CONFIDENCE IN WHICH ELEMENTS GO TO EACHOTHER. BUT I HAD A GREAT TIME W/THIS & WILL WATCH IT AGAIN ONCE I'V FORGOTTIN ENOUGH.

COLOR/90 MINUTES
NOT RATED

COLLECTOR'S EDITION

Franco Nero

DJANGO

GOOD LORD, THIS IS A REALLY MINDBLOWINGLY GREAT MOVIE. I DON'T REALLY SEE MENY MOVIES THIS KIND OF GOOD. I CAN'T THINK OF HOW THIS COMPAIRS WITH ANYTHING. IT IS BEYOND BEING ANY SORT OF GENRE OUT SIDE OF WINDOW DRESSING. PLEASE PARDON MY TRIVIA BUT I THINK THIS WAS NOT AT ALL A DJANGO MOVIE BUT GOT THE NEW NAME FOR TRENDY DISTRIBUTERS. I'M NOT GO'N TO TRY TELL YOU WHAT THIS MOVIE IS ABOUT... CHECK OUT THAT CREDITS. THE DIRECTOR & THE EDITOR ARE THE WRITTERS. IT MAY HAPPEN SOMETIMES BUT I FEEL IT'S AN EXAMPLE OF THE AMAZING INTECITY & POLITICLLY SALAC-IOUS BRUTALITY... UMMM, I GUESS IF YOUR FEELING GENTIL OR SENCITIVE IT MAYBE A SKIP FOR YOU. I BELIEVE THERE'R A NUMBER OF DIFFRENT CUTTS OF THIS, 117 MINUTES BEING ONE OF THE LONGER CUTS. BLUE UNDERGROUND IS USUALLY ON THERE GAME SO I TRUST 'M TO HAVE PROVIDED THE BEST POSSIBLE VERSION. LOOK FOR IT. HIGHLY RECOMEN-DED.

TOMAS MILIAN MARILU' TOLO ROBERTO CAMARDIEL PEIRO LULLI
MILO QUESADA PACO SANS RAYMOND LOVELOCK

WRITTEN BY

FRANCO ARCALLI (EDITOR) & GUILIO QUESTI (DIRECTOR)

COLOR 1967 117 mins.

WIDESCREEN NOT RATED

BLUE UNDERGROUND

TOMAS MILIAN
DJANGO
KILL
...if you live, SHOOT!
BLUE UNDERGROUND
DVD

THE ONLY DOC SAVAGE MOVIE. WERD? I BELIEVE THERES SOME FILM SERIELS BUT I HAVE'NT SEE'N'EM... YET. TRIPPY MOVIE. VERY STILL WITH A DRY JACKHAMMER RAPIDITY. CAN YOU DIG IT? IT'S LIKE A PLAY WITH AN EPIC TON OF SET'S. IT ALSO HAS A SORT'A BRITISH, FLIP EDITING OF TONE. VERY CAPTIVATING.

RON ELY

SCREENPLAY BY GEORGE PAL & JOSEPH MORHAIM

BASED ON THE NOVEL BY KENNETH ROBESON

DIRECTOR MICHAEL ANDERSON

THIS IS A REAL TREAT FOR ME, I'V KNOWN A FEW DUDES WHO WOUL WAX ON EMPHATICLY ABOUT DOC. DUDE CAN SMELL SMELLS THAT NO ONE ELSE COULD SMELL. HE MAY KILL YOU OR DECIDE TO REPROGRAM YOUR CRIMINAL MIND. THE HUMAN MIND IS A ROLLER CO

MOD DISC

COLOR 101 minutes 1975

DOC SAVAGE

THE MAN of BRONZE

KATHY BATES JENNIFER JASON LEIGH
Dolores Claiborne

A STRAIT NONSUPERNATURAL KING, THERE IS A POETIC COSMIC FRAIMING DEVICE BUT ITS A FAMILY DRAMA CRIME HEAVYTRIP DEAL. ITS GREAT, IT DEFIES & ALSO APITIMISES ALL THE THINGS FOLKS CONNECT WITH KINGNESS.
ABUSIVE DRUNK FATHER MYSTERIOUS, OCCWARD SOCIAL
DISADENCE. HAUNTED & RETURNING TO THE OLD HOUSE TO LIVE IT ALL AGAIN & HAVE A BIG FIGHT WITH. KATHY BATES ON A KING IS A GOOD SIGN THAT I'LL DIG IT. THIS WHOLE CAST IS GREAT & I THINK I USUALLY LIKE HACKFORD MOVIES. BLOOD IN BLOOD OUT WAS GREAT.
KATHY BATES
JENIFER JASON LEIGH DAVID STRATHAIRN
JUDY PARFITT JOHN C. RILLY
ERIC BOGOSIAN CHRISTOPHER PLUMMER
SCREENPLAY BY TONY GILROY
DIRECTED BY TAYLOR HACKFORD
R COLOR CC 1995 131 MINUTES

SHAWN
WAYANS
MARLON
WAYANS
DON'T BE A
MENACE
to South Central while drinking your JUICE in the HOOD

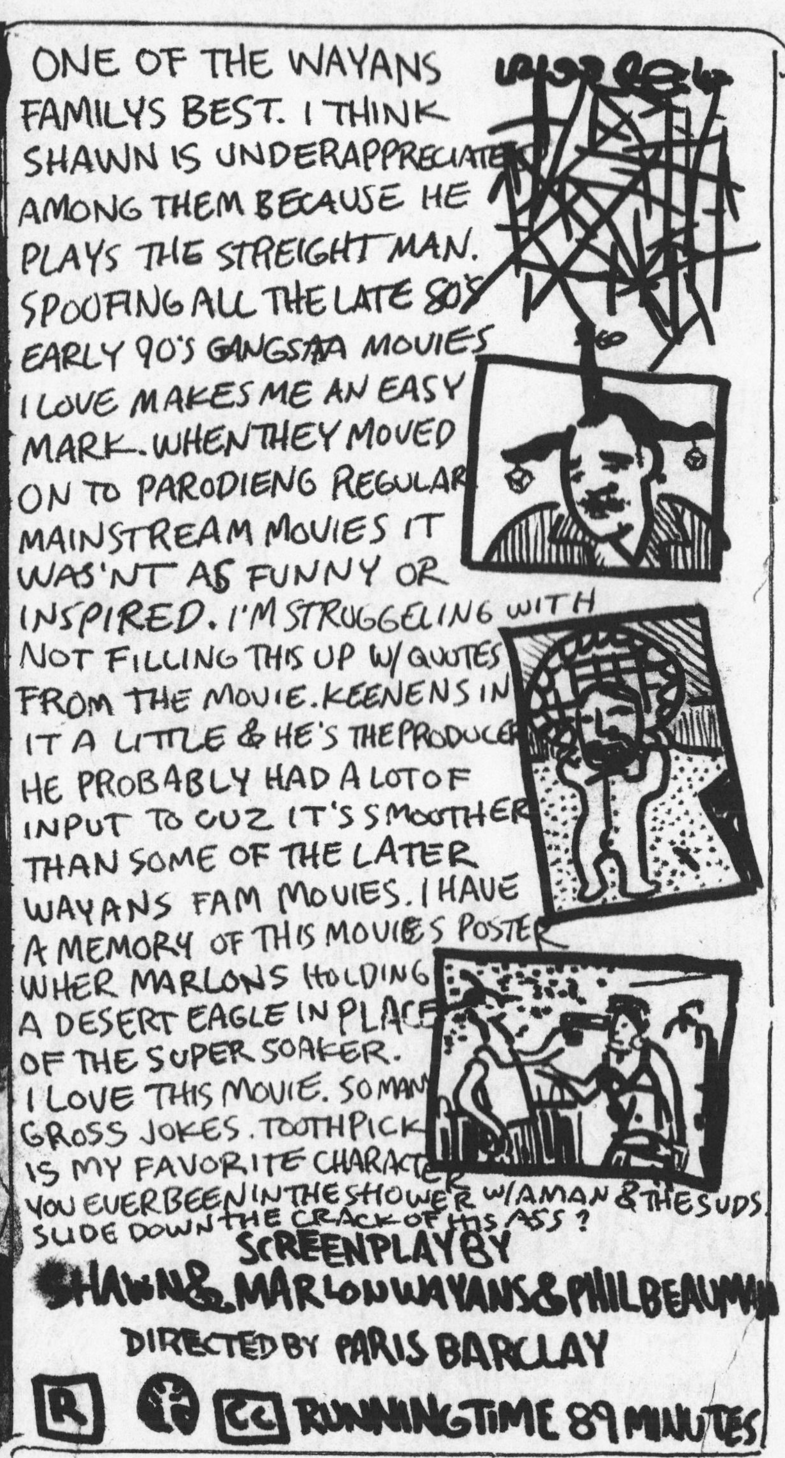
ONE OF THE WAYANS FAMILYS BEST. I THINK SHAWN IS UNDERAPPRECIATED AMONG THEM BECAUSE HE PLAYS THE STREIGHT MAN. SPOOFING ALL THE LATE 80'S EARLY 90'S GANGSTA MOVIES I LOVE MAKES ME AN EASY MARK. WHEN THEY MOVED ON TO PARODIENG REGULAR MAINSTREAM MOVIES IT WAS'NT AS FUNNY OR INSPIRED. I'M STRUGGELING WITH NOT FILLING THIS UP W/ QUOTES FROM THE MOVIE. KEENENS IN IT A LITTLE & HE'S THE PRODUCER HE PROBABLY HAD A LOT OF INPUT TO CUZ IT'S SMOOTHER THAN SOME OF THE LATER WAYANS FAM MOVIES. I HAVE A MEMORY OF THIS MOVIE'S POSTER WHER MARLONS HOLDING A DESERT EAGLE IN PLACE OF THE SUPER SOAKER.
I LOVE THIS MOVIE. SO MANY GROSS JOKES. TOOTHPICK IS MY FAVORITE CHARACTER
YOU EVER BEEN IN THE SHOWER W/ A MAN & THE SUDS SLIDE DOWN THE CRACK OF HIS ASS?
SCREENPLAY BY
SHAWN & MARLON WAYANS & PHIL BEAUMAN
DIRECTED BY PARIS BARCLAY
R
CC
RUNNING TIME 89 MINUTES

CHRISTINE BROWN HAS A GOOD JOB,
A GREAT BOYFRIEND, AND A BRIGHT FUTURE
BUT IN THREE DAYS
SHE'S GOING TO HELL.
DRAG ME TO HELL
ALISON LOHMAN
LORNA RAVER
DILEEP RAO
JUSTIN LONG
SCREENPLAY BY IVAN RAIMI & SAM RAIMI
DIRECTED BY SAM RAIMI

YES DUDE, I'M THANKFUL FOR A RETURN TO PURE RAIMI OR WHATEVER CALL IT. I LOVED IT SITTING IN A THEATRE. C.G. BLA ETC. I KNOW, I WOULD PRE-FUR CLAYMATION TOO. IT'S STILL DOPE. KINDA SCARY BUT MORE CREEPY BUT MOSTLY GROSS. I LIKE THE COMBO OF THEM HERE. I WANT MORE OFF THE CHAIN FROM DUDE. BASEBALL & SPIDERMAN ARE COOL BUT NOT THE GROSS FREAKOUTS COOL. I DON'T KNOW ANY OF THE ACTORS EXCEPT THE EYE GUY FROM JEEPERS CREEPERS BUT · IT'S ALL PRETTY GOOD. 1 HOUR 39 MINS.

PG-13 2009

SAW THIS AT THE THEATRE

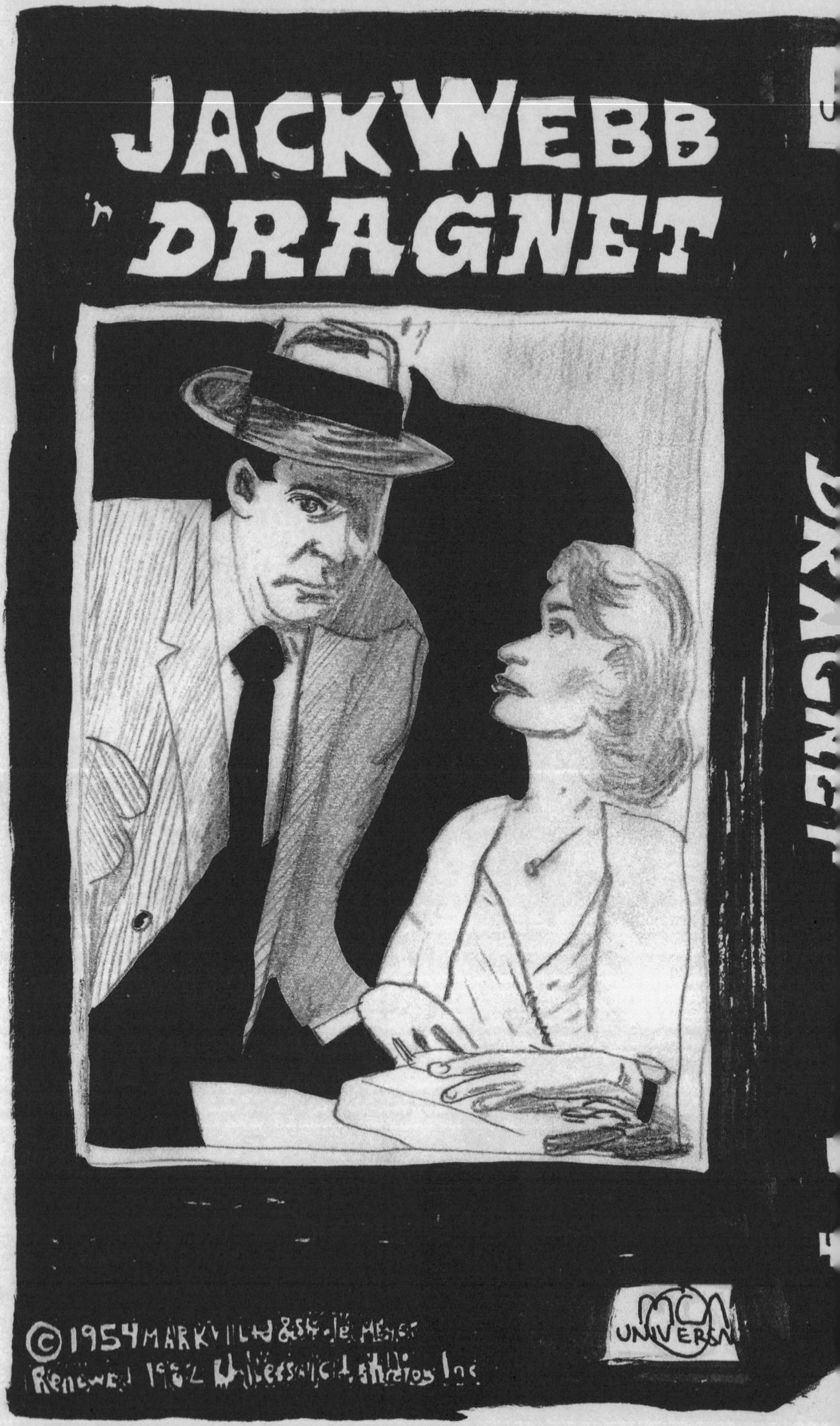
JACK WEBB
in
DRAGNET
DRAGNET

JACK WEBB in DRAGNET

SIMPLY PERFECT. JUST SO AMAZING. WOW. BEAUTIFULLY DRY, TIGHT, QUICK, SMART, FUNNY BRUTAL. JACK WEBB CAPTURES SO MANY OF LIFES TRUTHS WITH WHAT FEELS LIKE VERY LITTLE EFFORT. MASTERFULL. IF COPS WERE LIKE THIS I THINK THEY'D HAVE A BETTER REPUTATION THESE DAYS. COME TO THINK OF IT IF MOVIEMAKERS WERE MORE LIKE THIS THEY'D ALSO HAVE A BETTER REPUTATION. SO PRETTY MUCH THIS IS SO GOOD IT MAKES EVERYONE ELSE LOOK BAD. NO WONDER IT'S MARGINALIZED.

JACK WEBB as Sergeant Joe Friday

BEN ALEXANDER as Officer Frank Smith

WITH RICHARD BOONE & ANN ROBINSON

SCREENPLAY RICHARD L. BREEN

DIRECTOR JACK WEBB

"DUCK SOUP"

THE FOUR MARX BROS.
MARGARET DUMONT LOUIS CALHERN
RAQUEL TORRES EDGAR KENNEDY
SCREENPLAY by BERT KALMAR & HARRY RUBY
ADDITIONAL DIALOGUE ARTHUR SHEEKMAN & NAT PERRIN
DIRECTED BY LEO McCAREY

DUCK SOUP

B&W/ 70 Min.

CHICO & HARPO ARE FULLY SHRED'N IN THIS. I KNOW IT'S A BIG CLASSIC, SO I'LL SKIP THE PITCH. I CAN & DO PUT THIS ON @ ANYTIME, LOOP IT. IT'S SO ON I CAN REINTURPRIT TIME FROM IT. I WISH I HAD MORE TIME TO WARP WITH IT. SOME MOVIES JUST WERK FOR ME THIS WAY. MAYBE IT'S THE UNRELENTING PACE OF THIS TYPE OF MOVIE THAT LET'S ME DO IT. THE DON'T CURE DEPRESION BUT, THEY DO HELP ME EXTEND A THOUGHT OR FEELING FOR A WHILE.

AMAZING HAIR

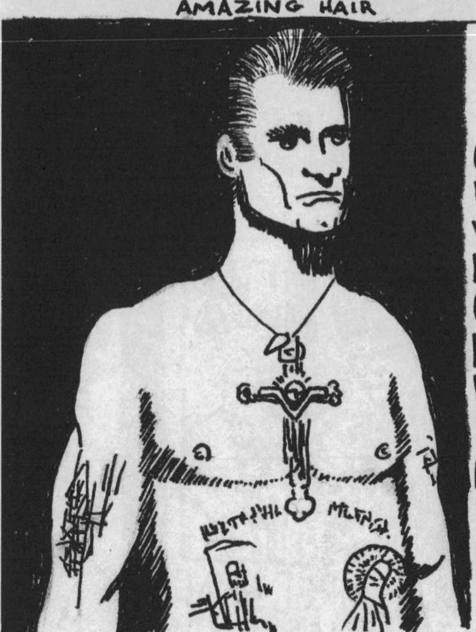

ONLY CRONENBERG.
IF ANYONE ELSE MADE THIS, IT PROBABLY WOULD HAVE BEEN O.K. BUT INSTED HE DID, & IT FULLY DOMINATES. PEEP THIS OUT SUPER HARD Y'ALL. I LIKE THIS EVEN MORE THEN HISTORY OF VIOLENCE. VINCENT CASSEL HAS ONE OF THE BEST NOSES IN MOVIE HISTORY. NAOMI WATTS IS SO-SO FOR ME, BUT FITS WELL HERE. VIGGO AS ALLWAYS IS THE BOMB. IF YOU HAVE NOT SEEN THIS I RECOMEND YOU DO SO TONITE, DUDE. SO FRESH. TRUST.

VIGGO MORTENSEN NAOMI WATTS AND
VINCENT CASSEL
SCREENPLAY BY STEVE KNIGHT
DIRECTED BY DAVID CRONENBERG
R

UNIVERSAL 1 Hr. 41 Mins. WIDESCREEN 2007

FROM THE DIRECTOR OF SCANNERS & EXESTENZ

VIGGO MORTENSEN, NAOMI WATTS VINCENT CASSEL

EASTERN PROMISES

JOE PESCI GERALDINE FITZGERALD
CANDY AZZARA JENNIFER JASON LEIGH
& TAYLOR NEGRON
WRITTEN by
RODNEY DANGERFIELD MICHAEL ENDLER
P.J. O'ROURKE DENNIS BLAIR
DIRECTED by JAMES SIGNORELLI

I DON'T KNOW HOW TO SLEEP... I KNOW HOW TO PASS OUT

SIGNOELLI ONLY MADE 1 OTHER MOVIE WHICH IS ELVIRA MISTRESS O' THE DARK THATS A PERFECT RECORD IN MY BOOK. TOP DOG.

SO... THIS IS ONE OF THE PURIST & BEST RODNEY MOVIES. ALSO THIS IS MY FAVORITE JOE PESCI MOVIE NOW CUZ IT'S FUN W/O THE GANGSTER CHARACTER. RODNEY IS A HAPPY GO LUCKY GUY WORKIN HIS

TRADE, BUT EVERYONE ELSE WANTS HIM TO DO OTHERWISE FOR XYZ. HE TRIES BUT YOU CAN'T BE WHAT YA AINT. RODNEY S FOR SURE WHO HE IS & IT'S AN INSPRATIONAL MOVIE AS SUCH.

THE CAST IS SOLID GOLD. TAYLOR NEGRON AT HIS YOUNG WEIRD PHASE, KINDA. NO ONE IS REALLY YOUNG IN THIS MOVIE. ANYONE UNDER 40 IS A TEENAGER & UNDER TWENTY IS A KID. THERE IS NOT A WASTED SECOND IN THIS MOVIE, IT IS PERFECT. THAT BEING SAID, IT'S FULLY A DUDES MOVIE & MAY NOT BE NON-DUDES'S BAG. FUCK IT. I'LL DROP THIS ONE ON AT A MOMENTS NOTICE. IF YOU DONT DIG IT, I CAN'T TELL YOU ANYTHING.

1983 APPROX. 95 MINUTES Ⓡ COLOR ~~ORION~~

AWESOME. THE STORY MOVES FAST BUT THE SCENES ARE PACT. IT REMINDS ME OF AN UNDERGROUND COMIC. MARY & PAUL HAVE SHIT JOBS & WANT TO OPEN A RESTAURANT. THEY ARE PLAGUED BY SWINGERS & RAPISTS. SO THEY KILL A FEW. THEN RAOUL GETS INVOLVED, THEN THINGS GET COMPLICATED. SUPER COOL. HIGHLY RECOMENDED.

MARY WORONOV PAUL BARTEL ROBERT BELTRAN
ED BEGLEY, JR. BUCK HENRY SUSAN SAIGER
SCREENPLAY BY RICHARD BLACKBURN & PAUL BARTEL
DIRECTED BY PAUL BARTEL

LANGUAGE	ENGLISH<STEREO>			1.85:1
SUBTITLES	ENGLISH, FRENCH			
	CC		APPROX 83 mins	COLOR

A tasty comedy of bad manners

EATING RAOUL

Elephant

a film by

GUS VANSANT

CAT
RUNTIME: 80 minutes
COLOR

R RESTRICTED

CC

DOLBY SURROUND

FIRST TIME I SAW THIS I FELT SICK AFTER & STAYED BUMMED OUT FOR A FEW DAYS. BUT NOT SO WHEN I CAME BACK TO IT. STILL A HEAVY MEDITATIVE BUMMER. SORTOF A SEQUAL OR COVER OR COUSIN OF THE '89 MOVIE. ALSO A BEAUTIFUL BUMMER. HOMESCHOOL PROPAGANDA? ITS GOT THIS MIRROR PUZZLE LYNCHPIN MURDER STROLL THING THATS NICE FOR A BUMMER.

D.O.P. Harris Savides
WRITTEN & DIRECTED by GUS VAN SANT

HBO FILMS

2003

I'V BEEN BURN'T OUT ON EASTWOOD RECENTLY. BUT SHEA GAVE THIS TO MY POP HIS LAST B'DAY & WE ALL WATCHED IT. I GUESS I FORGOT HOW GREAT THIS IS. IT'S CLASSIC LIKE IN A BOB CLARK WAY. THIS IS THE CLINT THAT I WISH MADE MOVIES. IS THAT JAMES FARGO? WHO'S FARGO? I'LL LOOK INTO IT. BUT DUDE, WATCH THIS... LIKE **EVERY** JULY 5th WHEN YOU GET UP. SMOKE A FEW BEERS, KILL THE LEFTOVERS; STRETCH OUT & LET IT PLAY. WAIT. IS THIS SOME RACIST SHIT? IT COULD BE. I HATE TO SEE IT, BUT MY DIG'N OF THE APE FAM. IS SOMETHING THAT HAS BEEN CORRUPTED BY RACISTS AS A CLASS-

SYSTEM TRIP. DON'T BE MEAN OR RUDE DUDE. THAT'S NOT COOL. O.K. SO IT'S SORT'A OLD HONKY TYPY OLD TIME CHILL ALMOST POLITICLY "NICE".

CLINT EASTWOOD SONDRA LOCKE

GEOFFREY LEWIS BEVERLY D'ANGELO RUTH GORDON

WRITTEN BY

JEREMY JOE KRONSBERG

DIRECTED BY

JAMES FARGO

COLOR 114 MINS CC

CLINT EASTWOOD COLLECTION

I WAS'NT PAYING FULL ATTENTION, MORE DEPENDING ON WHO WAS POPPING IN. NOT ENOUGH TOMMY CHONG. SOME WAY OR ANOTHER IT HAS A MOMENTUM BUT NEVER GETS INTERESTING AS A MOVIE. TOO BAD WITH A CAMEO SET LIKE THIS AND AN EVIL BONG. WHAT DO I KNOW? THEY MADE A PART TWO, SO IT MUST BE GOOD? LESS CAST MORE CHARACT-ERS.

SPECIAL APPEARENCES: BILL MOSELEY TIM THOMERSON PHIL FONDACARO & TOMMY CHONG AS JIMBO

SCREENPLAY BY AUGUST WHITE

Produced & Directed by CHARLES BAND & STORY TOO.

©2006 35MM WIDESCREN 86 minut's COLORZ

BARLES CHAND'Z

w/ tommy chong

DUDE, IZ IT A SCARY TRIP?...

NOT TOO MUCH.

JENNIFER JASON LEIGH

JUDE LAW

IAN HOLM

DON McKELLAR

CALLUM KEITH RENNIE

SARAH POLLEY

CHRISTOPHER ECCLESTON

WILLEM DAFOE

eXistenZ

WHY DID'NT/DON'T VIDEOGAMEMOVIES EXPLORE THE WAY THIS DOSE? TO A LARGE DEGREE IF YOUR FAMILURE W/CRONENBERG THIS IS MORE OF A RE-CHRYSTELIZATION OF HIS LARGER TRIP/THEMES. HE'S CREATED A NEW "SPLACE" IN THEMIND & RUNS YOU AROUND & THROUGH IT IN A PERSPECTIVE FLIPPING PARANOID TONE'L "GAME". IT'S CRONENBERG IF YOU KNOW... THEN I DON'T NEED TO SELL YOU ON IT. IF YOU DON'T KNOW THEN GET YOUR WITS ABOUT YOU. MAYBE YOU OUGHT TO EASE IN ON SOME EASTERNPROMISES. THIS IS A FULL SKULLCUSIFAC-ATORIEL BEATATHON. SORRY YALL... EXPLAINING A CRONENBERG IS JUST A FOOLS ERRAND. HOW ABOUT THIS... I LOVE CRONENBERG MOVIES. EXPECIALLY EXISTENZ.

JENNIFER JASON LEIGH JUDE LAW IAN HOLM
DON MC KELLER CALLUM KEITH RENNIE SARAH POLLEY
ROBERT A. SILVERMAN CHRISTOPHER ECCLESTON WILLIEM DAFOE
WRITTEN & DIRECTED by DAVID CRONENBERG

RUNNING TIME: APPROX 97 minutes

DIMENSION HOME VIDEO

COLOR

THE
FACULTY

PROBABLY RODRIGUEZ'S LEAST GOOD MOVIE BECAUSES OF THE SCRIPT I'D GUESS. I'M NO FAN OF K. WILLIAMSON. GOOD DIRECTOR ESSENTIALLY REMAKING ONE OF HIS FAV. MOVIES W/A GOOD CAST. BUT IT FARTS. THE TALKING IS DUMB. THE BIG MONSTER REVIEL IS A WEAK C.G. TROPE & TO A LARGE DEGREE POISONS THE LAST QUARTER OF THE MOVIE. RODRIGUEZ COVERS ALL THE POINTS HE'S DONE HERE IN MOST OF HIS OTHER MOVIES & TO GREATER EFFECT TOO. BUT AS FAR AS A CHEESEBALL SUMMER TEEN HORROR GRINDER IT'S BETTER THEN AVERAGE AND HAS SOME REALLY FUN MOMENTS WHICH I ATTRIBUTE TO RODRIGUEZ UMMM... ITS "BODYSNATCHERS/ PUPPETMASTERS" BAISED AROUND HIGHSCHOOL CULTURE SO A BIT "INVADERS FROM MARS" TOO. PERHAPS WILLIAMSOM IS NOT COMPLETLY AT FAULT. IT IS A BIG ENOUGH FART TO INVOLVE MOREN ONE SOURCE YA KNOW?

JORDANA BREWSTER CLEA DUVALL LAURA HARRIS
JOSH HARTNETT SHAWN HATOSY FAMKE JANSSEN
PIPER LAURIE BEBE NEUWIRTH ROBERT PATRICK
USHER RAYMOND JON STEWART ELIJAH WOOD
STORY BY DAVID WECHTER & BRUCE KIMMEL
SCREENPLAY BY KEVIN WILLIAMSON
DIRECTED BY ROBERT RODRIGUEZ

LOS HOOLIGANS PRODUCTION  CC COLOR 104 minutes

FANGORIA'S

Weekend of HORRORS

SO MENY GREAT MOMENTS & FOLKS ERNESTLY LOVING IT. FANS, ACT'RS, EFFECTS MANIACS AMAZING LINEUP. I WISH THIS WAS ONE IN A BOX SET OF 12. I'M SUPPER JELOUSE OF SHEA CUZ SHE WENT TO THE SHOW THIS YEAR. LOTS OF CLIPS SUPPORTING THE INTERVIEWS WITH THE GUESTS A COOL BEHIND THE SCEENS ON INVADERS FROM MARS THERES A LOT OF POSITIVITY & I THINK THIS IS A GOOD INSPIRATIONAL VIDE FOR CREATIVE FOLKS, EXPECIALLY IF YOUR A HORROR NERD. I LOVE DAN O'BANNON & TOBE HOOPER, AND THEY BOTH GET A PREMIUM PLACE HERE, THOUGH AS I SAID BEFORE I COULD USE A FEW MORE HOURS OF EACH. SOME AMAZING FANS & UP'N COMMERS, EXPECIALY IN THE SFX FIELD. AWESOME.

A PRESENTATION OF O'QUINN PRODUCTIONS & STARLOG VIDEO
EVENT STAGED BY CREATION CONVENTIONS & FANGORIA MAGAZINE
MUSIC BY DAN LESSNER PRODUCER: REX PIANO DIRECTORS: KERRY O'QUINN & MIKE HADLEY

COLOR • 60 MINUTES

MEDIA

MEDIA HOME ENTERTAINMENT 1989

APPEARANCES BY

FORREST J. ACKERMAN, RICK BAKER, JOHN CARL BUECHLER
WES CRAVEN, ELVIRA, ROBERT ENGLUND, ALEX GORDON
ALBERT GLASSER, CLU GULAGER, TOBE HOOPER
WILLIAN KATT, DICK MILLER, STEVE MINER, DAN O'BANNON
CRAIG REARDON

FANGORIA'S...

Weekend OF HORRORS

MEDIA

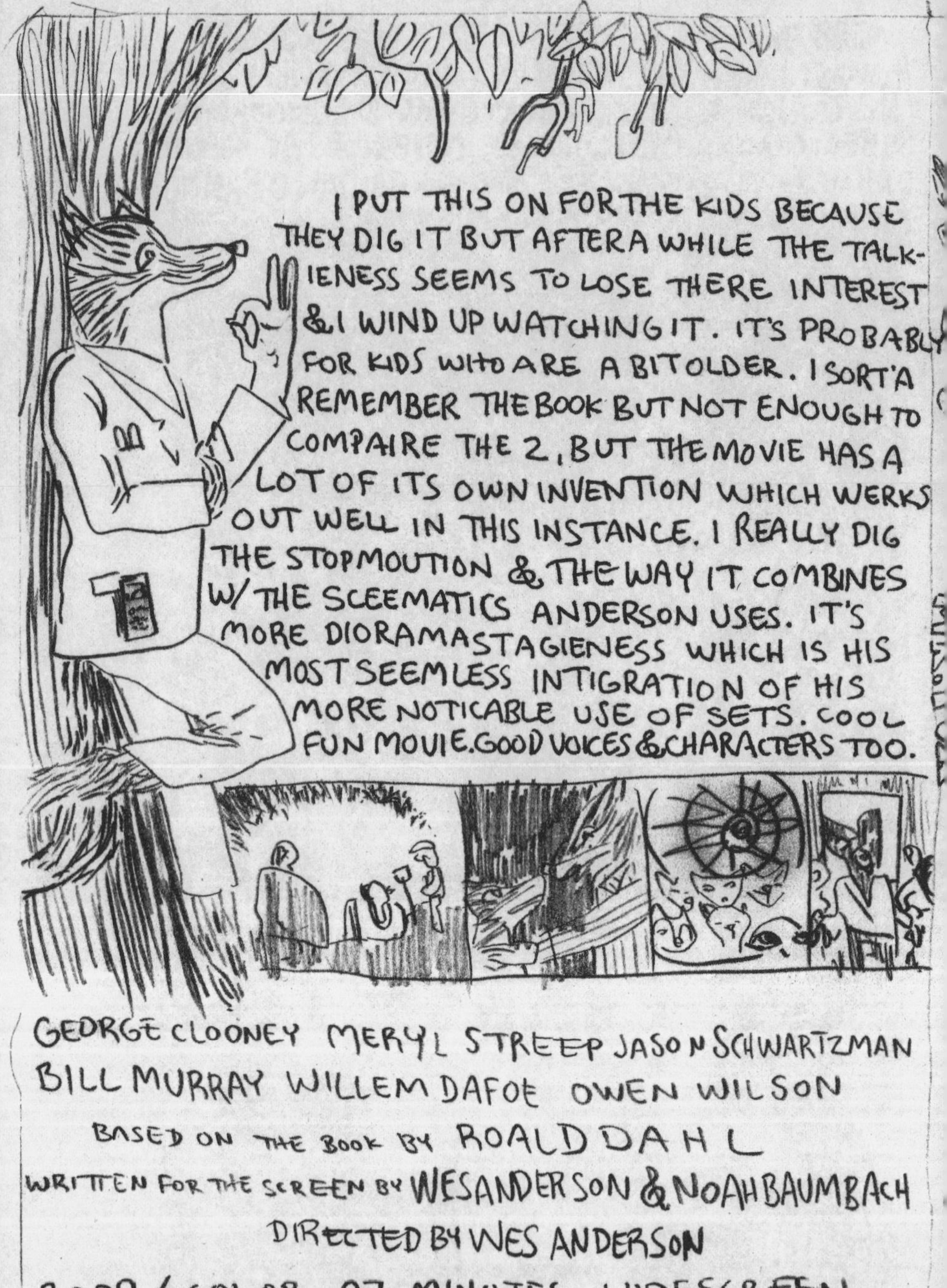
I PUT THIS ON FOR THE KIDS BECAUSE THEY DIG IT BUT AFTER A WHILE THE TALK-IENESS SEEMS TO LOSE THERE INTEREST & I WIND UP WATCHING IT. IT'S PROBABLY FOR KIDS WHO ARE A BIT OLDER. I SORT'A REMEMBER THE BOOK BUT NOT ENOUGH TO COMPAIRE THE 2, BUT THE MOVIE HAS A LOT OF ITS OWN INVENTION WHICH WERKS OUT WELL IN THIS INSTANCE. I REALLY DIG THE STOPMOUTION & THE WAY IT COMBINES W/ THE SCEEMATICS ANDERSON USES. IT'S MORE DIORAMASTAGIENESS WHICH IS HIS MOST SEEMLESS INTIGRATION OF HIS MORE NOTICABLE USE OF SETS. COOL FUN MOVIE. GOOD VOICES & CHARACTERS TOO.
GEORGE CLOONEY MERYL STREEP JASON SCHWARTZMAN
BILL MURRAY WILLEM DAFOE OWEN WILSON
BASED ON THE BOOK BY ROALD DAHL
WRITTEN FOR THE SCREEN BY WES ANDERSON & NOAH BAUMBACH
DIRECTED BY WES ANDERSON
2009 / COLOR 87 MINUTES WIDESCREEN
DVD
PG

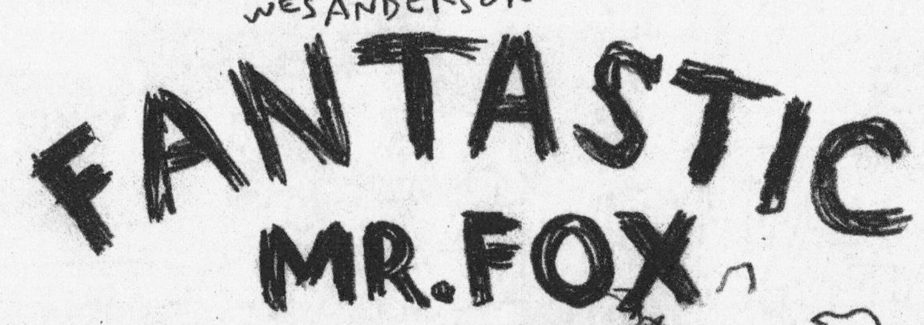
GEORGE MERYL JASON BILL OWEN
CLOONEY STREEP SCHWARTZMAN MURRY WILSON
A FILM BY WES ANDERSON
FANTASTIC
MR. FOX

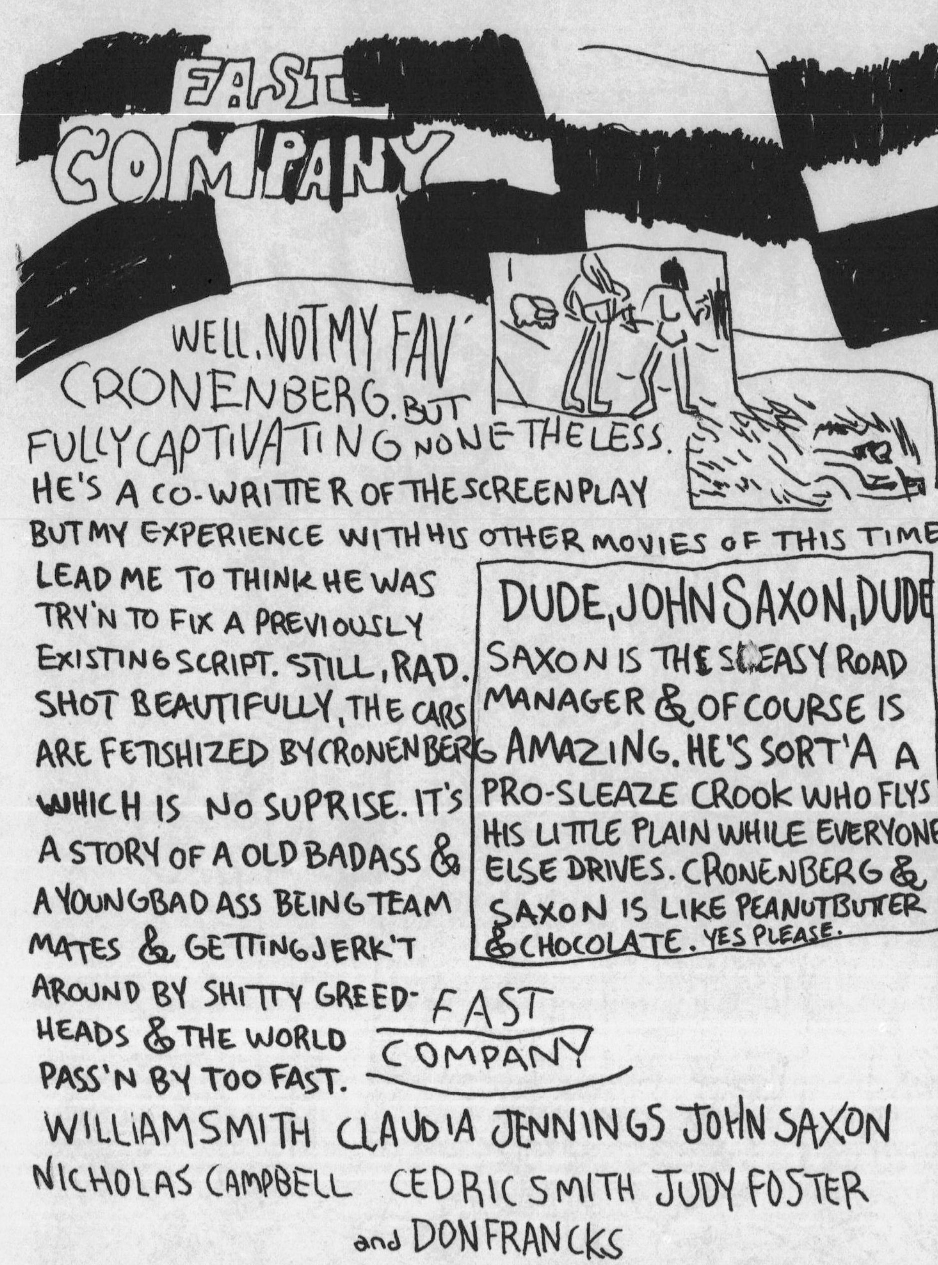
FAST COMPANY
WELL, NOT MY FAV CRONENBERG. BUT FULLY CAPTIVATING NONETHELESS.
HE'S A CO-WRITTER OF THE SCREENPLAY BUT MY EXPERIENCE WITH HIS OTHER MOVIES OF THIS TIME LEAD ME TO THINK HE WAS TRY'N TO FIX A PREVIOUSLY EXISTING SCRIPT. STILL, RAD. SHOT BEAUTIFULLY, THE CARS ARE FETISHIZED BY CRONENBERG WHICH IS NO SUPRISE. IT'S A STORY OF A OLD BADASS & A YOUNG BADASS BEING TEAM MATES & GETTING JERK'T AROUND BY SHITTY GREED-HEADS & THE WORLD PASS'N BY TOO FAST.
DUDE, JOHN SAXON, DUDE
SAXON IS THE SLEASY ROAD MANAGER & OF COURSE IS AMAZING. HE'S SORT'A A PRO-SLEAZE CROOK WHO FLYS HIS LITTLE PLAIN WHILE EVERYONE ELSE DRIVES. CRONENBERG & SAXON IS LIKE PEANUTBUTTER & CHOCOLATE. YES PLEASE.
FAST COMPANY
WILLIAM SMITH CLAUDIA JENNINGS JOHN SAXON
NICHOLAS CAMPBELL CEDRIC SMITH JUDY FOSTER
and DON FRANCKS
CO-WRITTER & DIRECTED BY DAVID CRONENBERG

WILLIAM SMITH
CLAUDIA JENNINGS
and JOHN SAXON

FAST TIMES
AT RIDGEMONT HIGH
SPECIAL EDITION
1 HR 30 MINS. 1982
R
COLOR
I THINK I TRY TO ACTUALLY NOT LIKE THIS FOR A WHILE, BUT THEN DOUBLE CHECK & I DO STILL LIKE IT. IF YOU THINK ABOUT IT, AT THE END OF "ALMOST FAMOUS" THAT KID IS HIM. WHO THEN GO'S & MAKES THIS MOVIE. THIS MOVIE STAYS FUN
I DIG IT.
PE
SEAN PENN JENNIFER JASON LEIGH
JUDGE REINHOLD PHOEBE CATES BRIAN BACKER
ROBERT ROMANUS RAY WALSTON
BOOK & SCREENPLAY BY CAMERON CROWE
DIRECTED BY AMY HECKERLING

HIGH SCHOOL REUNION COLLECTION

ROBERT SHAW MALCOLM McDOWELL

FIGURES IN A LANDSCAPE

SCREENPLAY BY
ROBERT SHAW

DIRECTED BY
JOSEPH LOSEY

GP ALL AGES ADMITTED 1970 110 MINUTES

IF YOU ARE IN TO VERBAL ABUSE THEN THIS IS YOUR MOVIE. ROBERTSHAW HITS THE GROUND RUNNING. EVENTUALY MALCOLM McDOWELL STARTS LAYING BACK INTO HIM ONCE HE STARTS SCREWING UP.

A MOVIE ABOUT TWO MEN BEING STALKED BY A HELICOPTER. ONE IS CLEVER ABOUT DEALING WITH SURVIVAL SKILLS IN THE NATURAL WORLD, WHILE THE OTHER IS CLEVER ABOUT PEOPLE. SHAW & LOSEY WERE BROUGT IN AS REPLACEMENTS & SEEM TO JUST MAKE THEIR OWN BEAUTIFULLY AMAZING MOVIE. THE NAME IS THE STORY AS IS THE POSTER. THERE ARE A LOT OF GREAT "WHYS" AND NO ATTEMPT TO TELL YOU THAT OF THE CHASING. I HAVE'NT SEEN ALL OF LOSEYS MOVIES BUT WHAT I HAVE SEEN IS FANTASTC. SHAW IS THE LYNCHPIN OF THE MOVIE. McDOWELL IS MORE OF THE AUDIENCE STAND IN, THOUGH I DO THINK HE DOSE A GREAT JOB {PRE-CLOCKWORK}. THE CINIMATOGRAPHY IS PERFECT EVEN THOUGH I'M WATCHING IT ON A DEGENERATED VHS. IT'S BASED OFF A NOVEL I HAVE'NT READ SO IT'S HARD TO CREDIT <FOR ME> WITH THE KILLER DIALOGUE, BUT IT'S GREAT, EXPECIALY ROBERTSHAWS LINES. LOOKS LIKE IT WAS ALLAGES IN THE U.K. AND RATED [R] IN THE AMERICAN RELEASE, WHICH I BELIEVE ARE THE SAME CUT. NO CUSSING. EXCEPT POCKET BILLIARDS.

I DON'T KNOW WHAT TO SAY ABOUT THIS MOVIE. I REALLY DIG IT. IT FITS WELL WITH THE THEATRICAL SCI-FI MOVIES OF THE LATE 1960'S & 1970'S. BEAUTIFUL EYECANDY COLORS. GREAT CASTING I WISH THEY'D MADE A FULL LENGTH SERIAL OUT OF THIS. DO I EVEN HAVE TO MENTION THE SOUNDTRACK? DO I? I DO? O.K. THE SOUNDTRACK IS FULLY SHREDDING. QUEEN DUDE! DEFINATLY ONE OF THE BEST COMIC TO MOVIE ADAPTATIONS. WE HAVE A COPY OF FLESH GORDON AND ITS ENTERTAINING BUT ITS NOWHERE NEAR AS SEXY AS THIS ONE. ON TOP OF ALL THAT ITS SUPER CLEAN. WELL NOT SUPER BUT ITS... FUCK I DON'T KNOW. HAVE YOU NOT SEEN THIS? IF NOT THEN ITS TIME TO POP YOUR HEAD OUT OF YOUR ASS & INTO THE DAMN T.V. ITS IN THE LIST OF PERFECT COMICS MOVIES NEXT TO DANGER DIABOLIK AND THE ROCKETEER. I PREFER THE VHS BOX / MOVIE POSTER OVER THIS ROSS PAINTING. REDRAWING OTHER PEOPLES ART USUALLY BUMMS ME OUT BUT NOT THIS TIME. I JUST CRUISED IT OUT. MAN, I CAN'T GET OVER THE CAST HERE. SUCH A PERFECT BLEND. LIKE A ROOTBEER FLOAT ON A SATURDAY AFTERNOON. CORN DOGS WITH MUSTARD, A NAP, & FLASH GORDON. LETS DO IT!

A DINO DE LAURENTIIS *Production*

SAM J. JONES MELODY ANDERSON ORNELLA MUTI

MAX VON SYDOW TOPOL TIMOTHY DALTON

MARIANGELA MELATO BRIAN BLESSED **PETER WYNGARDE**

SCREENPLAY BY LORENZO SEMPLE, JR.

DIRECTED BY MIKE HODGES

FLASH GORDON

Hi-Fi
STEREO
VIDEO
THE FLY
JEFF GOLDBLUM GEENA DAVIS JOHN GETZ
SCREENPLAY BY
CHARLES EDWARD POGUE & DAVID CRONENBERG
DIRECTED BY
DAVID CRONENBERG

CLAUSTERPHOBIC SELF DESTRUTIVEEGOMANIA DEVOLOUTIONARY MELTDOWN. GOLDBLUM IS A SCIENTIST. CRONENBERGS TRIP DOVE-TALES PRETTY APROPRIETLY W/THE BALLSY IDEA OF RECREATING THE FLY. HE FOLLOWS THE NEUROCISE PATH &, SLOW BURNS IT. GEENA DAVIS IS TRIPPY BUT HAS A GOOD CHEMISTRY, SO GO'S THE WAY OF A CRONENBERG. DOPE EFFECTS. SHIT... I HATE TRY'N TO DO A REVIEW OF MOVIES MOST FOLKS ALLREADY KNOW ARE GREAT. I GUESS MAYBE YOU DON'T HAVE ANY HISTORY W/IT, IT'S ABOUT A DUDE DOING TELEPORTATION EXPERIMENTS & IT GO'S BAD CUZ' HE GETS MIXED W/A FLY & IT'S A BAD TRIP FOR EVERYONE. HEAVY/BEAUTIFUL WEIRD BODY CON-TROLE & THE PRICE OF VANITY ELEMENTS LOOM.

1987 or 1986   96 MINUTES

CHILL, SMOOTH, A BIT ITALIAN? SURE. NOT A GORE SLASH'R. THIS ONE'S HELLZA TONE'LL. THIS MOVIE GIVE'S YOU SOME STORY, BUT IS NOT REAL'Y NESSICERY. IT IS THE FOG, AND; SO IT'S KIND'A... FOGGY & DREAMY. DERRR. IF YOU WANT'UH GET ACCADEMIC THIS IS THE ARTY SHIT YOU PROBABLY WONT GET. TO BAD FOOL. A GIANT SIZE POPCORN DREAM COME TRUE.

ADRIENNE BARBEAU JAMIE LEE CURTIS JANET LEIGH
JOHN HOUSEMAN & HAL HOLBROOK
PRODUCED + CO WRITTEN BY DEBRA HILL
MUSIC + DIRECTION + CO WRITTEN BY JOHN CARPENTER

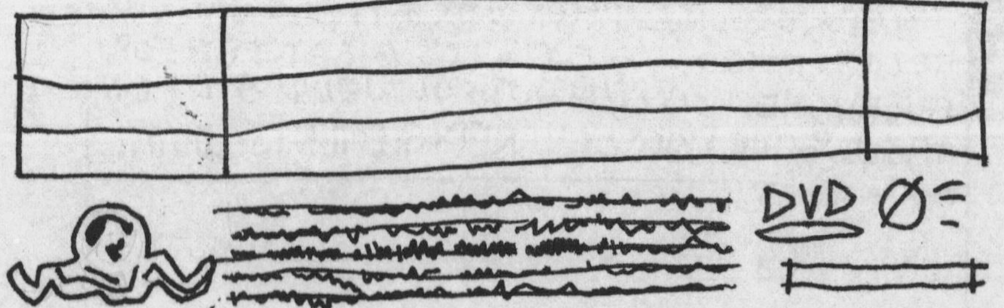

SPECIAL  EDITION

JOHN CARPENTER'S

THE

FOG

A DEBRA HILL PRODUCTION

CHRISTOPHER LAMBERT
FORTRESS

FORTRESS

I LOVE IT. I SAW THIS IN THE THEARE. MUST HAVE BEEN MY FIRST STUART GORDON. LAMBERT IN HIS PRIME. IT'S A SCI-FI PRISON MOVIE. SIIICK. KURTWOOD SMITH IS THE WARDEN. & HE MACKS ON LAMBERTS OLDLADY. SO... JAIL BREAK. CYBORG MACHINEGUN ARM. OH, YEAH. THEY HAVE BOMBS IN THEIR STOMACHS. YES, TNT ON P.M.S.

"WANNA DATE?"

JAMES LORINZ PATTY MULLEN

CHARLOTTE HELMKAMP LOUISE LASSER

WRITTEN BY ROBERT MARTIN & FRANK HENENLOTTER

DIRECTED BY FRANK HENENLOTTER

BIRTHDAY PARTY FATALITY. MAN I THINK SHE ATE POTATO CHIPS LAST. THATS A NICE TREAT ON YOUR JOURNEY TO THE PROMISE LAND. WELL I GUESS IT IS'NT CUZ HER

BOYFRIEND BRINGS HER BACK. BUT NOT HER STOMACH, IT'S COMPLICATED. DUDE REPLACES HER MISSING BITS W/A POTPORIE OF SEX WORKERS DISMEMBERMENTS. HE MAKES A LOT OF POOR CHOICES FOR A SMART FELLA. GUESS THATS CLASSIC FRANKENSTEIN

STUFF. YOU KNOW I WAS VERY IMPATIENT FOR HIM TO LIGHT HER UP, BUT THE EPICLY BUFF PIMP HELD ME THROUGH. I THINK THIS IS ONE OF THOSE "BE CAREFULL WHAT YOU ASK FOR" TYPE DEALS. POTATOCHIPS!

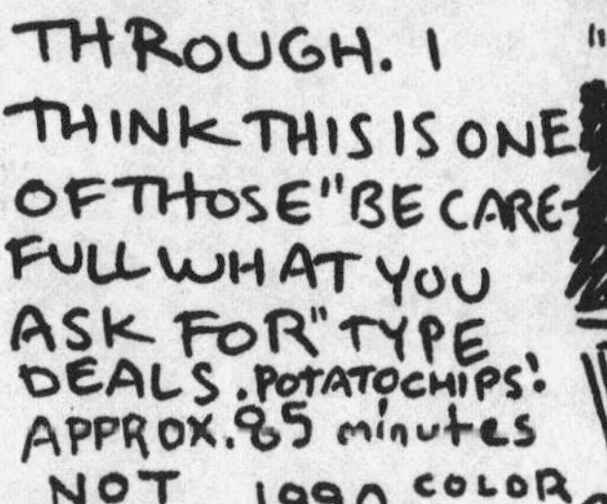

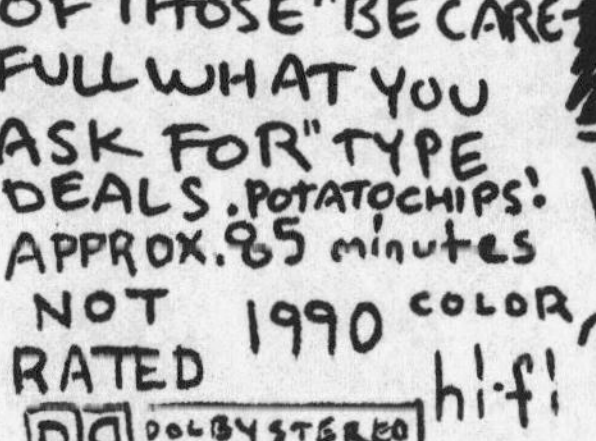

APPROX. 85 minutes

NOT RATED 1990 COLOR

DOLBY STEREO hi-fi STEREO

PREVIEW
VIDEOCASSETTE
FEBRUARY 21 1991

FRANKENSTEIN
UNBOUND

FULL LENGTH FEATURE FILM

Includes preview of
William Peter Blatty's
EXORCIST III

which is totaly rule'n and I recomend you
watch it. Blatty directs and is awesome.

PREVIEW

VIDEOCASSETTE

FEBRUARY 21 1991

FUCK FILMSCHOOL THIS VIDEO HAS EVERY TRICK IN THE BOOK. ROGER CORMAN HITS THE GROUND RUNNING. IN THE FUTURE A SCIENTIST FUCKS UP & RIPS A HOLE IN TIME. POETICLY HE'S SUCK'T IN & WINDS UP IN THE TIME & PLACE OF HIS FAVORITE BOOK... FRANKENSTEIN<DER> SO HE HANGS OUT WITH PERCEY SHELLY, LORD BYRON, DR. FRANKENSTEIN, THE MONSTER AND THEN MAKES OUT WITH MARY SHELLY. THIS IS PURE NERD PORNO. REALLY. IF YOU SAY THIS MOVIE IS BOARING YOUR AN UPTIGHT SQUARE. IT IS AMAZINGLY REDICULES. IT'S A LITTLE MORE BELIEVEABLE THEN MANGA, AND ACTUALL STORY TAKES PLACE. COOL POSTER TOO. THE CAST IS PRETTY TRIPPY. JOHN HURT, JASON PATRICK, RAUL JULIA, & BRIDGET FONDA. WHAT? NO BEN KINGSLEY. SURELY THEY COULD'A MADE SPACE FOR PETER WELLER. OH, WELL. STILL A RULE'N REDICULESS MASH OF POP VIDEO. CAN YOU BELIEVE I WAS ACTUALLY TAKING NOTES FOR THIS? I WOULD NEVER BOTHER TO DEBATE THE MERITS OF THIS VIDEO BECAUSE IT WOULD CHEAP'N THE INTELECT OF THE AUDIENCE. I WISH I COULD SEE THIS AT A DRIVE IN.

CANNON
THE
FREEWAY
MANIAC
THERES
NO EXIT...
FROM THE
TERROR
LOREN HUNTER
JAMES COURTNEY

FREEWAY MANIAC

PSYCHO
ROADKILLER
BLACKCOMEDY
PARODY
SEX

BREAZY PARODY, BLACK COMEDY. DUDE SYSTIMATICLY KILLS EVERYONE HE MEETS EXCEPT HER. SHE GETS AWAY IN HIGHHEELS & NO BRA. SCORES A BIG ROLE, FREEWAY MANIAC SLOWLY/QUICKLY STALKS WHILE KILLING EVERYONE. I FEEL GAHAN SET IT UP AND DEVISED THE KILLS. ITS THAT MOVIE YOU WISH THEY MADE WHEN THEYMAKEAMOVIEIN AMOVIE. WHICH THEY ALSO DO.

LOREN WINTERS, JAMES COURTNEY, SHEPARD SANDERS, DONALD HOTTON, JEFF MORRIS, ROBERT BRUCE

WRITTEN by Gahan Wilson & PAUL WINTERS

DIRECTED by PAUL WINTERS

R MEDIA Hi-Fi COLOR VHS  CANNON 1988

ICE CUBE
Chris Tucker
Friday

MUCH LIKE "UP IN SMOKE" IN THAT YOU DON'T EVEN NEED TO SMOKE OR UNDERSTAND WEED TO ENJOY WATCH'N. CLEVER, FUNNY, CHARMING, CRASS, & UPLIFTING ALL ALONG. THE CAST IS PERFECT, NO ONE'S OUT OF PLACE. I DIG F. GARY GRAY. THIS WILL MOST LIKELY BE HIS LONGIST LASTING LEGACY AMONG

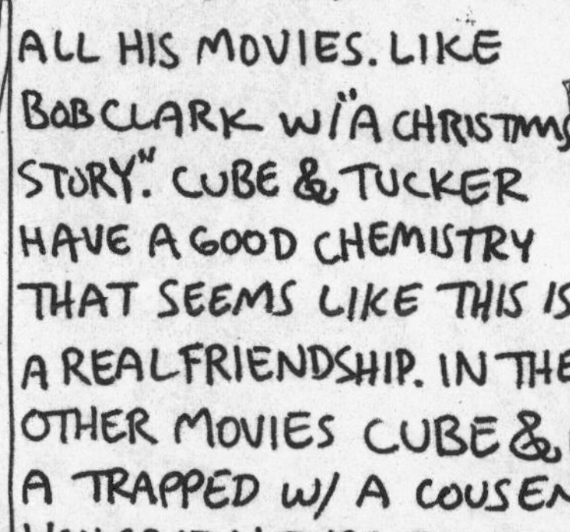

ALL HIS MOVIES. LIKE BOB CLARK W/ "A CHRISTMAS STORY". CUBE & TUCKER HAVE A GOOD CHEMISTRY THAT SEEMS LIKE THIS IS A REAL FRIENDSHIP. IN THE OTHER MOVIES CUBE & EPPS HAVE A TRAPPED W/ A COUSEN WHO MAKES YOU CRAZY TYPE THING THAT MAKES THEM MORE STRESSY WHILE THIS ONE IS MORE CHARMING & INDEERING. PERFECT.

ICE CUBE · CHRIS TUCKER NIA LONG TINY "ZEUS" LISTER REGINA KING ANNA MARIA HORSFORD BERNIE MAC AND JOHN WITHERSPOON

WRITTEN BY ICE CUBE & DJ POOH

DIRECTED BY F. Gary GRAY

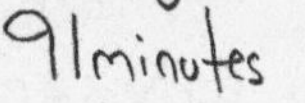

JEFFREY COMBS BARBARA CRAMPTON
KEN FOREE TED SOREL
CAROLYN PURDY-GORDON

ADAPTATION by STUART GORDON, BRIAN YUZNA, DENNIS PAOLI
SCREENPLAY by DENNIS PAOLI | DIRECTED by STUART GORDON

THATS HOW YOU START A MOVIE. I GET HYPNOTIZED EVERY TIME. AFTER A SHOW THIS SUMMER I WAS BURNT & FELL ASLEEP ON THE COUCH W/ THE DOOR OPEN ALL NITE WITH THIS ON AUTO REPEAT. I WAS WAKING UP ON & OFF THROUGH THE NITE TO SEQUENCES NOW OUT OF ORDER IN MY MIND. NO

PROBLEM. A DREAM WITHIN A DREAM. IT GETS MY BRAIN SUPER BUSY. THIS TAPE IS THE HEAVYIST DRUG TO ME THESE DAYS. I'M OUT, I'M GONE; WHEN I EMERGE IT'S GRASPING AT BURNING STRAWS. THERE IT IS, WHAT IS IT, IT WHAT? YES. WAIT. THEN I'M OUT AGAIN. DUDE ITS LESS THAN 90 MINUTES HOW IS IT POSSABLE? SHITS FROM BEYOND IS HOW. DUDES MAKE A THING THAT OPENS THE DOOR TO A PLACE WHICH HYPER JAZZ'S UP YOUR PINIEL GLAND TURNING YOU INTO A FREAK FOR THE BEYOND TYPES TO COME AND DINE ON. THE CAST IS PERFECT, ITS ALL PERFECT FOR ME.

H.P. LOVECRAFT'S **From BEYOND**

© 1986 R 1 HOUR 26 MINUTES

THE FUNHOUSE

PAY TO GET IN.
PRAY TO GET OUT!

FUNHOUSE
USELESS PARENTS, MASKED KIDS WITH NO SOCIAL BOUNDRIES, ASSHOLE DATES W/A TRAMPY FRIEND. STONED IN A MUSCLE CAR, TEASING CARNIES, CUTTING PEEPHOLES IN A PEEPSHOW TENT. THE OLD SLEEPOVER SWITCH SCAM W/ YER FRIEND SO YOU CAN GET YER CHERRY POPPED IN... THE FUNHOUSE. CLASSIC DUMB-ASS MOVE. DISPITE THIS SEEMING LIKE A NORMAL SET UP IT'S HANDELED IN SUCH A WAY THAT YOU DON'T KNOW WHATS GOING TO HAPPEN NEXT. HOOPERS DREAMIEST MOVIE & SOME HOW VERY CLEAR TOO. ONE OF HIS FINEST! ♡ IT. FRANKENSTEINS ALL OVER THE PLACE. INCEST WEIRDNESS, & PRETTY MUCH EVERYONES A FULL ON CREEP. PERFECT. YES, PERFECT.
ELIZABETH BERRIDGE • COOPER HUCKABEE
MILES CHAPIN • SYLVIA MILES
WILLIAM FINLEY • KEVIN CONWAY
WRITTEN by LARRY BLOCK
DIRECTED by TOBE HOOPER
GOODTIMES HOME VIDEO
R COLOR 1981
APPROXIMATELY 96 MINUTES

MAN. FIRST THING FIRST. THANK YOU TOM, FOR GIFTING ME THIS. SO... I FELL IN LOVE WITH ALI GATOR. ALL OF THEM RULE BUT HE'S AWESOME THIS A FAIRLY UNIQUE MOVIE, PRETTY ADULT FOR A KIDS MOVIE. ALI EATS EYEBALLS, TOES, FINGERS. THEY GET DRUNK, STEAL ATV'S, PUMP RAW SEWAGE INTO A HOTTUB. ALL THE HUMAN PARTS ARE DRIPPING IN TEEN BOY SEXUAL FRUSTRATION. MOSTLY THE HUMAN PART IS PRETTY USELESS TO ME. BUT THE G.P. KIDS ARE GREAT. I'D LIKE TO SEE MORE GROSS'NESS THERE'S ONLY ONE PUKE JOKE. BUTT THERE'S PLENTY OF FART JOKES. A TRUE TRIPPY MOVIE.

the

GARBAGE PAIL KIDS {THE BEST}

MOVIE

GATE II
Return to the nightmare

SATANISM IS FOR PUSSYS

GATE II
RETURN TO THE NIGHTMARE

PRETTY O.K. I HAVE'NT SEEN PART ONE. THERE'S SOME COOL CLAYMATION EXPECIALY AT THE END. THE DUDE CONJOURS UP A DEMON W/A PENTAGRAM MADE OUT OF STERIOS & STUFF. THERE'S 2 MEATHEAD ROCKERS WHO HOTBOX THE DEMON IN A PILLOWCASE IN THE BACK OF THEIR MUSCLE CAR. HONESTLY I WISH THE WHOLE MOVIE WAS BASED ON THIS PART. THIS IS TAME FOR A HORROR FLICK. KIND'A PG-13 STUFF. BUT NOT BAD. A CORVETTE TURNS INTO A PILE OF SHIT. THERE'S AN ALCHOHOLIC PILOT. MOST OF THE MAGIC DOES'NT WERK OUT TOO WELL. BUT IT'S NOT ANTI-MAGIC. THE QUESTION IS PUT FORTH, "WHO NEEDS DEAMONS WHEN YOU'V GOT CHICKS?" INDEED, WHO DOES? YOUR GIRLFRIEND IS WHO. SO GET WITH IT KID. I'D BE DOWN TO WATCH THIS AGAIN SOMEDAY. BUT I WOULD'NT MAKE ANYONE WATCH IT.

DIRECTED: Tibor Takacs

SVS TRIUMPH Vision

90 MIN

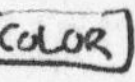

UNTAMED & DEADLY
She ruled the swamp with a BLAZING GUN and a LUSCIOUS SMILE.
'GATOR BAIT
HALF ANIMAL... ALL WOMAN
R
WRITTEN, PRODUCED, DIRECTED: Ferd & Beverly Sebastian

INCEST IS BEST

IF YOU CAN'T KEEP IT IN YOUR PANTS, KEEP IT IN YOUR FAMILY.

I WENT TO THE CLINTON ST. TO SEE THE HICKSPLOITATION TOUR. WELL, THIS WAS FIRST. I CONSIDER RAPE TO BE A LAME TRICK FOR MOST MOVIES IT'S WORTHY OF CONSIDERATION, & EXPLOITATION; BUT USUALLY MADE WITH TOO MANY BONERS. NOT SO WITH THIS ONE. THE MOVIE REVOLVES AROUND THE THEME, WHERE RAPE IS A MUNDANE OFFENCE TO THESE GREASY HICKS; FOR SOME CORRUPT POACHERS IT SEEMS LIKE A REGULAR HOLLIDAY DINNER. SO A COUPLE OF THESE GUYS TRY TO BLACKMALE/RAPE OUR HERO. BUT SHE'S TOTALLY SICK & FUCKS THEM UP FULLY. ONE OF THEM DIES & SO HIS DAD & BROTHERS HEAD OUT TO MURDER/RAPE HER. DUDE. BOAT CHASES, LEATHEL GENITAL MUTALATION. JESUS WEPT. IT'S A TOUGH MOVIE TO PULL OFF WELL, BUT FERD & BEVERLY DOMINATE IT. SOMEONE TOLD ME IT WAS BOARING. WERD? WOW, TOO COOL. GREAT FUCK'T UP ENDING.

SO... BEFORE THE MOVIE THERE WERE A FEW "PREVIEWS". THE FIRST WAS SHADOW OF THE HAWK. WHICH I MUST SEE. IT LOOKS AS THOUGH JAN MICHAEL VINCENT IS ON A CASTANEDA STYLE ADVENTURE. NEXT WAS DEATH HUNT WHICH IS ANOTHER I MUST SEE. I THINK IT HAS CHARLES BRONSON & LEE MARVIN. I THINK. BAD ASS DUDES IN THE SNOW TYPE STUFF. LAST WAS GROUP MARAGE WHICH LOOKS LIKE SOFT SOFT CORE + COMMUNE DRAMA.

THE CLINTON ST. THEATRE IS ONE OF MY FAVORITES. IT'S AN OLD ONE & PRETTY BEAT TOO. THE SCREEN HAS HOLES, ONE TOILET BATHROOMS, INTERIOR DOOR TO A BAR WITH NO T.V. & RAINER ON TAP. THE SEATS CAN BE LOUD THE PICTURES OFTEN UNCROPED, & CRAZY GREAT MOVIES.

CHARTER
ENTERTAINMENT

SHERMAN HEMSLEY • LUIS AVALOS
in

GHOST Fever

WEIRD. AN OLD TIME WACKY GHOST STORY W/ OLD MEN TELLING TIRED OLD MAN JOKES, AS A FAMILY MOVIE. WITH NO KIDS OR ANIMALS & VERY MILD FRISKY JOKES.

I THINK THESE GUYS GOT TOGETHER ONCE THEIR CARRIERS COOLED OFF & DECIDED TO DO ONE LIKE THEY DID BACK IN THE DAY. MAYBE A KID WATCHIN THIS COULD SEE (THAT IT'S O.K. TO STAY SILLY. IF YOU DIG CORNY OLD MAN JOKES LIKE ME IT'S A GOOF.

1987 COLOR
86 MINUTES
FAMILY/COMEDY.

hifi MONO

PG

SHERMAN HELMSLEY & LUIS AVALOS PEPPER MARTIN JENNIFER RHODES, DEBORAH BENSON, DIANA BROOKES MYRON HEALEY, JOE FRAZIER, WRITTEN by RON RICH, OSCAR BRODNEY & RICHARD EGAN

SEE IT BEFORE
IT SEES YOU!
THE
GHOUL
VCL
STARRING JOHN HURT, PETER CUSHING

THE

GHOUL

1920'S YOUNGE RICH PARTYERS RACE TO THE BEACH THROUGH THE MOORS, GET STUCK, RUN ACROSS THE LOCALS & GET

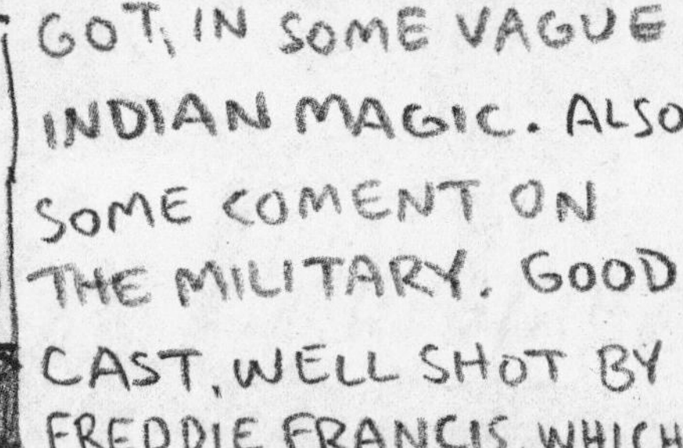

GOT, IN SOME VAGUE INDIAN MAGIC. ALSO SOME COMENT ON THE MILITARY. GOOD CAST, WELL SHOT BY FREDDIE FRANCIS, WHICH ARE THE KEY ELEMENTS OF MY OWN INTEREST IN IT. JOHN HURT & FREDDIE FRANCIS ALSO WORKED ON ELEPHANT MAN WHICH I DID'NT KNOW WHEN I CHOSE THIS. THERES A NO SUPRISE, SUPRISE ENDING. ALSO A FAIRLY STANDARD USE OF XENOPHOBIA OF INDIA BY THE BRITS IN MOVIES OF THE 1970'S.

90 MINUTES COLOR
1975
DIRECTED by
FREDDIE FRANCIS
PRODUCED by
KEVIN FRANCIS

HURT IS THE CREEPY DIM FLUNKY OF THE FOOLISH BIGSHOT TRAUMADEMET-ED CUSHING WHO'S COOL AS USUAL.

IONE SKYE ANNE HECHE
GIRLS IN PRISON

DEMO TAPE
VIDEO BOX ART MAY VARY

They were rebels w/out a clue

IF MEMORY SERVES ME CORRECT{HAHA}FULLER HAD A SCRIPT, THAT WHEN HE WAS DOING IT GOT AXED OR GUTTED & HE GOT THAT MATERIAL IN HERE. NOT CERTINE BUT THIS MAY HAVE BEEN A CABEL MOVIE. I THINK IT'S GREAT. McNAUGHTON... I LOVE HIS MOVIES! THIS A MOVIE OUT OF IT'S TIME. AND STILL YOU{ME} CAN SEE A FEW PUNCHES THAT WERE LITENED FOR WHAT REASON... WHO KNOWS. BUT NOTHING LOST FOR ME. SO IT'S A PATSY DOUBLE CROSS ALA RECORD BIZ BACK STABBING. DISALUSIONMENT, THEN HELL. BUT HELL IS FULL OF RITCHOSE FOLKS TOO. NON STOP PERIL, ALMOST SERIAL STYLE (FULLER & McNAUGHTON). PLUS IF I'M RITE ABOUT THE T.V. THING IT BECOMES THE OBVIOUSE APPROCH. I HOPE THAT TAGLINE DIDN'T GET ONTO THE FINAL BOX. W/ A NAME LIKE "GIRLS IN PRISON" YOU SHOULD'NT HAVE TO TRY. ALSO THERES NOT A LOT OF CLUELESSNESS. I GUESS THEY ARE TRYING TO SPEAK TO THE CLASSICS CROWD DUE TO THE PERIOD PIECE THING. CHECK IT OUT ITS PRETTY GREAT.

IONE SKYE, ANNE HECHE MISSY CRIDER NICOLETTE SCORSESE TOM TOWLES JON POLITO MIGUEL SANDOVAL MYCHELLE DANGERFIELD

SCREENPLAY by SAMUEL FULLER & CHRISTA LANG

DIRECTED BY JOHN McNAUGHTON

1994 [R] 1 HOUR 23 MINUTES [COLOR]

THE GLADIATOR

A HARDMETAL VIGILANTE ON A VENDETTA!

STARRING:

KEN WAHL & NANCY ALLEN

DIRECTED BY ABEL FERRARA
WRITTEN BY WILLIAM BLEICH
PRODUCED BY ROBERT LOVENHEIM

KEN WAHL IS A MECHANIC WHO, WHILE TEACHING HIS LITTLE BROTHER TO DRIVE; GETS ATTACKED BY A MYSTERIOUS ROAD PSYCHO WHO KILLS DRIVERS FOR ANY INFRACTION OR RUDENESS. KEN SURVIVES BUT HIS BROTHER DIES. KEN HAS LOST EVERY LAST PART OF HIS FAMILY. HIS FRIEND REBUILDS KENS TOTALED TRUCK. AT A VICTIMS OF DRUNK DRIVING MEETING KEN ATTENDS AGAINST HIS WISHS. SOMEONE ANGRILY SUGGESTS THAT THEY "DO SOMETHING" ABOUT DUI'S TONITE. KEN SECRETLY BUILDS AN ARMORED HARPOON TRUCK & STARTS HUNTING THE ROAD PSYCHO & ANY DUI'S HE COMES ACROSS. ALL ALONG ALSO KIND'A OCWARDLY FLIRTING W/ NANCY ALLEN. ALL THE CARS ARE COOL & SO IS KEN OF COURSE. THIS IS A T.V. MOVIE DIRECTED BY ABEL FERRARA & IT'S GREAT. T.V. ART MOVIE ABOUT CARS AND REVENGE W/ ROBERT CULP AS THE COP WHOS SEEN IT ALL. NO NONSENSE ENDING TOO WHICH GO'S GREAT. FAIRLY 1950'S.

1991 COLOR · FOR GENERAL AUDIENCES
104 MINUTES

"KILL" IS NOT IN THE TITLE. IT'S A DESIGN ELEMENT THAT HIJACKS THE TITLE. AND WISELY SO, BECAUSE WITHOUT THE "KILL" THE TITLE S JUST MILD.

GOD TOLD ME TO

ITS A LARRY COHEN MOVIE SO IT OUGHT TO HAVE SOME, TOOTH OR BALLS. THIS ONES FUN BECAUSE HE FLIPS IT A FEW EXTRA TIMES WHICH I DIG, CUZ IT WORKS. I DREW THIS SO LONG AGO I CAN'T REMEMBER WHAT THE LAST FLIP EVEN IS ANYMORE. THE DRAMAS PRETTY SOAP BOXY & FEELS LIKE PADDING BUDGET W/ACTING BUT ITS NOT PAD ITS JUST GOT THIS CURT CUTS IN W/70'S PONDERING. SO UNCERTIN AND IMPATIENT. HE PAYS SOME LIP-SERVICE STRUCTURALLY TO MAIN STREAM FORMULA STORYTELLING BUT SHOE-HORNS IN SOCIAL COMMENTERY AND ALL KINDA TRIPS ABOUT OUR NEW WAYS BEING OUR OLD WAYS

TONY LOBIANCO - SANDY DENNIS - SYLVIA SIDNEY - SAM LEVENE
ROBERT DRIVAS - MIKE KELLIN RICHARD LYNCH, DEBORAH RAFFIN
WRITTEN PRODUCED & DIRECTED BY LARRY COHEN
COLOR - 1976 - 92 mins.

WIDESCREEN 

GOD TOLD ME TO KILL

A LARRY COHEN FIL

BLUE UNDERGROUND

GOODBYE PORKPIE

OK, SO; THIS BOX WAS VERY UPFRONT WITH TELLING ME WHAT AN IMPORTANT & INFLUENTIAL MOVIE IT IS. SO, O.K. DISPITE THAT I LIKE'D THIS. QUITE A BIT ACTUALLY. A GOOD ROAD/CHASE, PETTY THEIF, SEXED UP, COP DISS'N, BUDDYS MOVIE. IT'S GOT A HEAVY/SWEET ENDING. SOLID FUN THE WHOLE TIME. A COMMON FOLK INSPIRATIONAL ADVENTURE WITH A MILD'LY CRASS SENCE OF HUMOR. MAYBE SOMETHING LIKE BONNIE & CLYDE MEETS SMOKY & THE BANDIT WITH SOME EXTRA SEX JOKES TYPE OF DEAL. LONG, AWESOME STUNT DRIVING CHASE SEQUENCES FRAIM THE MAJORITY OF THE OTHER SCEENS IN WITCH ONE DUDE'S TRY'N TO GO GET HIS OLD LADY TO COME BACK HOME & THE OTHER GUY IS A PRETTY AIMLESS FLY BY THE SEAT OF HIS PANTS THEIF WHOS JUST CRUISE'N FOR TROUBLE DIPPED ACTION. HE'S A CHARMING JACKASS, AS IS THE OTHER DUDE WHO'S JUST A LITTLE MORE CHILL/WORNDOWN BY LIFE, PROBABLLY BECAUSE HE'S OLD'R. NOW THAT I THINK OF IT, IT'S SORT'A MAYBE A BIT OF DUKES OF HAZARD MEETS TWO LANE BLACKTOP DIRECTED BY BOB CLARK SORT'A TYPE DEALY'O. WELL, MAYBE NOT. ANYWAY'Z, I DIG IT & I FIGURE A LOT OF FOLKS WILL TOO. UNLESS THEY'R SQUARES OR FULL ON FREAKS. BEER.

STARRING TONY BARRY KELLY JOHNSON CLAIREO BERMAN

DIRECTED BY GEOFF MURPHY

HALLOWEEN II

THE Nightmare Is'nt Over!

STEREO

MCA UNIVERSAL
1981
VHS
DONALD PLEASENCE IS SO COOL. THIS WHOLE MOVIE IS SO COOL. IT LITERALLY HITS THE GROUND RUNNING. THE STORY HAS A STALKER PORN QUALITY MORE THAN AN A-B-C STYLE, WHICH I'V HEAR'D FOLKS CRY ABOUT AS DRAG'N BUT TO ME IT'S MORE OF A HYPNO-TIC DRONE MIX'D WITH A CAPPRA LIKE INTREST IN THE VICTIMS. TASTY DUDE. I LOVE THE ENDING MOMENTS OF THIS MOVIE WITHOUT REALLY TRY'N TO UNDERSTAND WHY & THAT IS A GREAT FEEL'N WHENEVER I SEE IT.
JAMIE LEE CURTIS DONALD PLEASENCE
PRODUCED & WRITTEN by
DEBRA HILL & JOHN CARPENTER
DIRECTED by
RICK ROSENTHAL
1981
DINO DeLaurentis corporation

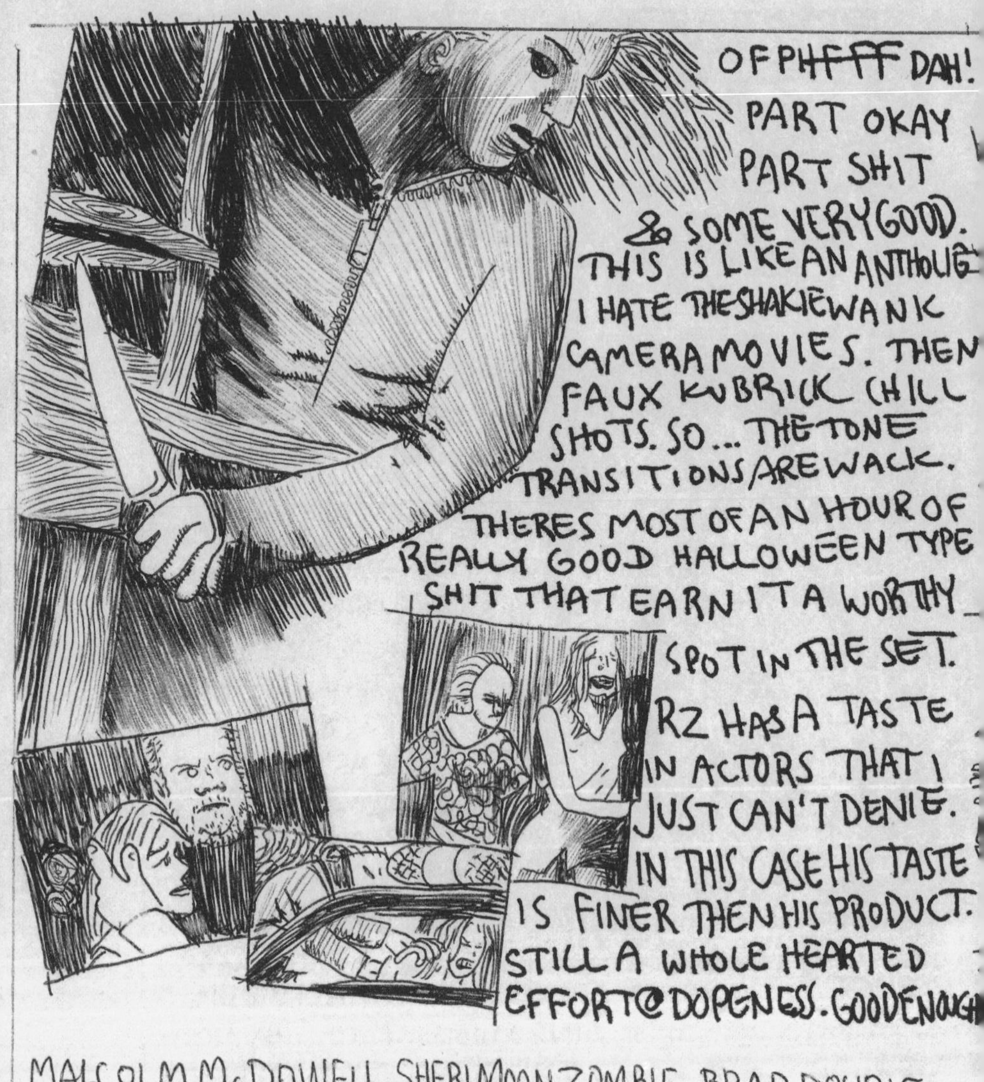

MALCOLM McDOWELL SHERI MOON ZOMBIE BRAD DOURIF
TYLER MANE SCOUT TAYLOR COMPTON DANIELLE HARRIS
WILLIAM FORSYTHE

WRITTEN & DIRECTED by
ROB ZOMBIE

2007 WIDESCREEN 121 MINUTES NOT RATED

TWO DISC SPECIAL EDITION
A ROB ZOMBIE
HALLOWEEN
UNRATED
DIRECTORS CUT

I THINK THIS MAYBE THE BEST OF THE RECENT WAVE OF HORROR REMAKES. AT LEAST I CAN'T THINK OF ONE IN A WHILE.

MALCOLM McDOWELL TYLERMANE SHERI MOON ZOMBIE
BRAD DOURIF DANIELLE HARRIS SCOUT TAYLOR-COMPTO

WRITTEN & DIRECTED
BY
ROB ZOMBIE

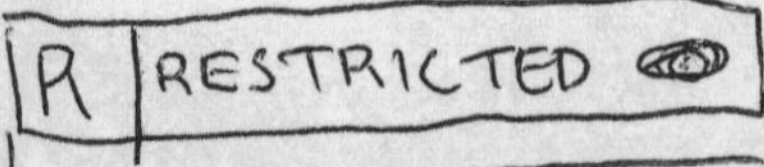

2010

COLOR

APPROX 105 minutes

THEATRICAL EDITION

ROB ZOMBIE MOVIE

HALLOWEEN II

FAMILY IS FOREVER

DANIEL GREEN JANET AGREN CLAUDIO CASSINELLI
GEORGE EASTMAN ROBERT BEN PAT MONTI DONALD O'BRIEN
FRANK WALDEN AMY WERBA AND JOHN SAXON
DIRECT EDY BY MARTIN DOLMAN (FAKE NAME)

FEEL THE GRIP OF FUTUREWORLD ACTION:

I THINK THIS IS ITALIAN BUT IT'S ABOUT STUFF GO'N DOWN IN THE AMERICAN SOUTH. OUR HERO REMINDS ME OF CILLA IN A FEW SHOTS. JOHN SAXON IS THE ONLY DUDE THAT SEEMS AMERICAN BUT WHO CARES. LOTS OF NICE INVIRONMENTS, I DIG THE SET UPS FOR THE ACTION SCEENS. I PUT OFF THIS REVIEW FOR TOO LONG & NOW HAVE FORGOTTEN WHAT THE SETUP IS, BUT IT'S A: BAD ASS LONER W/MYSTERIOUS PAST THATS HOT ON HIS INHANCED ASS, AS HE MEETS A NICE PRETTY WOMAN. HE PROTECTS HER BUT THEN SHE'S IN HARMS WAY BECAUSE SAXON IS ON DUDES ASS W/ A CHOPPER. DUDE IS INHANCED BUT I THINK HE'S GOT A MEMORY PROBLEM OR WAKES UP W/ MORALS OR SOMETHING. IT'S GOOD FUN & I LIKED IT. 1986

1/89

R

VAN DAMME
A JOHN WOO FILM
HARD TARGET
DON'T HUNT
WHAT YOU
CAN'T KILL.
JEAN-CLAUDE VAN DAMME
LANCE HENRIKSEN YANCY BUTLER
WILFORD BRIMLEY
SCREENPLAY CHUCK PFARRER
DIRECTED BY JOHN WOO
MCA
UNIVERSAL
STEREO
SURROUND

JOHN WOO CAN'T DO THIS EVERYTIME, BUT SOMETIMES HE CAN TAKE ONE THAT WOULD USUALLY BLOW & RULE IT INTO AN AWESOME MOVIE. JUST A STREIGHT UP GREAT ACTION MOVIE.

JEAN-CLAUDE HAS WHAT I BELIEVE TO BE THE BEST MULLET IN ACTION HISTORY. I DIG THE SLOWMOUTION & MUSIC. THERE'Z A SLO-MO SHOT OF WILFORD BRIMLEY ON HORSEBACK W/ A BOW & THERES A WALL OF FIRE BEHIND HIM. THAT IS WHAT I WANT TO HAVE BLOW'N UP & PASTED ACROSS THE BIG WALL IN MY HOME.

JOHN WOO'S BEST AMERICAN MOVIE, BEATING FACE OFF. LANCE HENRIKSEN IS PERFECT AS ALLWAYS.

BAREKNUCKLE BRONSON.
COBURN DOSE THE TALKING.
GREAT DEPRESSION ERA
BRONSON IS WANDERING
AND
WINDS UP BAREKNUCKEL'N
FOR $ & HE'S DOPE AT IT.
I THINK THIS IS WALTER HILLS
FIRST TIME DIRECTING &
MY PERSONAL FAV. OF HIS MOVIES, & W/A PG TOO.
HE'S GOT THE SIMPLISITY DIALED SO WELL. SO
SMOOTH. VERY MATTER OF FACT, MEDITATING
ON BRONSON. IT ALL LOOKS SO EASY. MAKES
KUNG FU MOVIES OF IT'S TIME LOOK COMPLEX
BRONSON KEEPS HIS WORD & HE ONLY USES
A FEW. COBURNS THE MOUTH. HE'S GOT THE
CONECTS, BUT MOSTLY SHOOTS HIMSELF IN
THE FOOT: THEY WORK WITH OPIUM HEAD
WHO HALF DOCTOR & RECITES E.A. POE TO
WOMEN. BRONSON GETS A CAT AND A LADY
FRIEND. THE CAT PLAYS ITS CARDS RIGHT &
STAYS IN HIS GOOD GRACES. HILLS CURT
EDITING WORKS NICE & SMOOTH HERE. I DIG IT.

WRITTEN by BRYAN GINDOFF, BRUCE HENSTELL, WALTER HILL

DIRECTED by WALTER HILL

PG APPROX. 94 MINUTES 1975 COLOR DVD CC

CHARLES
BRONSON
JAMES
COBURN
HARD
TIMES

A FILM by RICHARD STANLEY
HARDWARE
IN THE 21ST CENTURY THERE WILL
BE A NEW ENDANGERED SPECIES... YOU DUDE

RUNNING TIME
94 MINUTES
COLOR R
1990

STANLEY ADDAPTS A SHORT COMIC FROM AN ISSUE OF 2000 AD & FULLY ROCKS IT FOR REAL

HARDWARE

DYLAN McDERMOTT STACEY TRAVIS
JOHN LYNCH WILLIAM HOOTKINS
& IGGY POP AS ANGRY BOB
WRITTEN & DIRECTED BY RICHARD STANLEY

POST APOCALIPTIC DUMPSTERDIVER BRINGS HIS ARTY OLD LADY A ROBOT SKULL THAT AINT DEAD. IT GRABS WEIRD ODD'S & ENDS FROM HER RAW MATERIALS & ART TO BUILD IT SELF BACK UP TO KILLING MODE. EVEN THOUGH IT'S A 1990 MOVIE IT STILL HAS THE COOL 50'S/80'S DUDE CHARACTER DROPPIN BEAT GEN SPIRITUALITY. THERE'S ALSO A VOYER DICKBEATER NEIGHBOR WHO TALKS PERV'O TRASH WHILE TELESCOPING ON THE BONE SESSION. LEMMY POP'S UP TO CAPTAIN A TAXI BOAT & LISTEN TO HIS OWN JAMS HOSTED BY IGGY. I DIG IT. DOPESHIT, PEEP IT OUT.

DYLAN McDERMOTT STACEY TRAVIS JOHN LYNCH
WILLIAM HOOTKINS & IGGY POP's VOICE
WRITTEN & DIRECTED BY RICHARD STANLEY

MILLIMETER FILMS

HBO VIDEO

SPOOFY/PARODY'ISH IN A WAY THAT DOSE'NT LEAD TO ANYTHING BUT THE TYPICAL CRED HOMAGE WINK WINK "I LIKE "OLDE SKOOL" HORROR TOO". THERES SOME GOOD/FUN STUFF, I DON'T HATE IT. IT SEEMS THAT DOING PARODY OF THE STERIOTYPE GROUP OF DICKHEADS & FOOLS IS A REDUNDANT AND NEUTRALIZING MOVE. MAYBE LIKE, DOING A PARODY OF SOUTH PARK. BUT IT WAS NICE TO WATCH THEM DIE IN A SFX VARIETY PACK ROLL OUT. I THINK THE DUDE IS WEARING A SHIRT OF A COMICS SHOPPE. I THINK THIS MOVIE WOULD WORK BETTER IF YOU TURN DOWN THE SOUND, PLAY SOME RECORDS W/ THE LITES LOW EAT SOME SNACKS & STUFF

JOEL DAVID MOORE TAMARA FELDMAN DEON RICHMOND MERCEDES McNAB PARRY SHEN JOLEIGH FIOREAVANTI JOEL MURRAY RICHARD RIEHLE PATRIKA DARBO JOSHUA LEONARD TONY TODD ROBERT ENGLUND KANE HODDER

WRITTEN & DIRECTED by ADAM GREEN

83 MINUTES 1.78:1

STARZ ©2007 WIDESCREEN CC COLOR R DVD

HATCHET

IMITATION MID/LATE 80'S HORROR

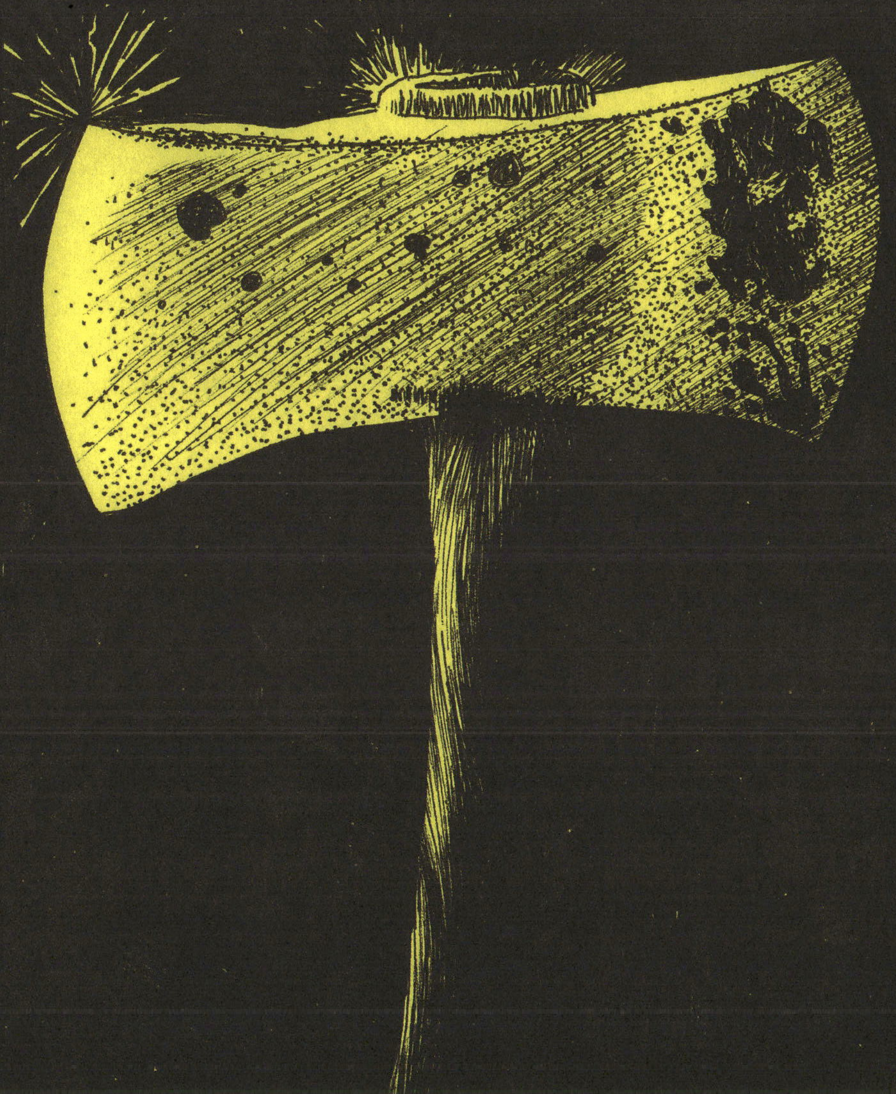

CHRIS ROCK IS PROBABLY MY FAVORITE COMEDY'N WHEN HE'S ON STAGE. SO I'M ALLREADY INTO THIS PLUS HE CO-WROTE & DIRECTED IT. WELL, IT'S O.K. NOT GREAT BUT ENJOYABLE IN A CHILL WAY. ONE OF THE THINGS I DIG ABOUT ROCK IS HIS UPFRONT IN YOUR FACE CONTRIVERCIAL TOPICS & TONE, BUT THATS REALLY PLAY'D DOWN HERE

SO IT FEELS KIND'A TOOTHLESS BY COMPAIRISON. SO, ROCK IS A LOCAL POLITICIAN, WITH A CHARMING ALMOST SILENT FILM QUALITY TO HIS INVENTIVE FORM OF COPE'N W/A TON OF PROBLEMS. SOME SHIT'Y BIG POLITICIANS TRY USE'N HIM TO GET CRED. BUT HE FULLY BLOWS UP & HE WINS & IS RAD AT HIS JOB DISPITE BEING SURROUND'D BY EVIL SHITS. JIMMY STEWERT TYPE SHIT. BERNIE MAC IS HIS BROTHER & IS PROBABLY MY FAVORITE PART OF THE MOVIE. KIND'A WISH HIS CHARACTER WAS MORE PROMINENT. IT WOULD'A BEEN MORE MY JAM IF IT WAS A DUO PIC. ROCK HAS A CHILL SOLID DIRECTING STYLE.

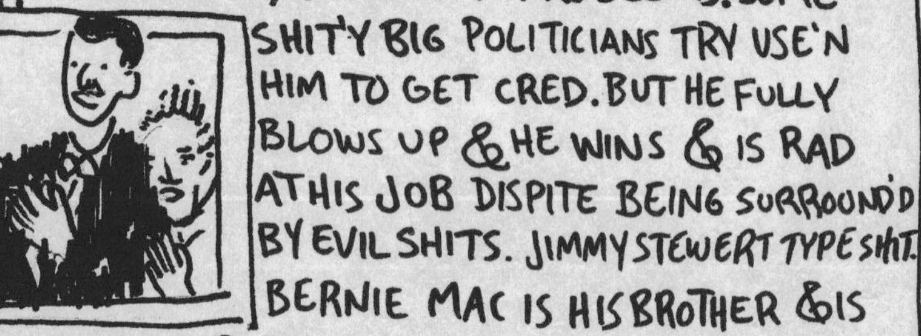

CHRIS ROCK BERNIE MAC DYLAN BAKER
NICK SEARCY ROBIN GIVENS LYNN WHITFIELD
TAMALA JONES JAMES REBHORN

WRITTEN BY ALI LEROI AND CHRIS ROCK
DIRECTED BY CHRIS ROCK

CHECK OUT THE ARM HAIR CLOSE UP IN THE BREAKUP SCEEN.

1 HOUR & 35 MIN. ©2003 COLOR PG-13

CHRIS ROCK BERNIE MAC

HEAD of STATE

W I D E S C R E E N

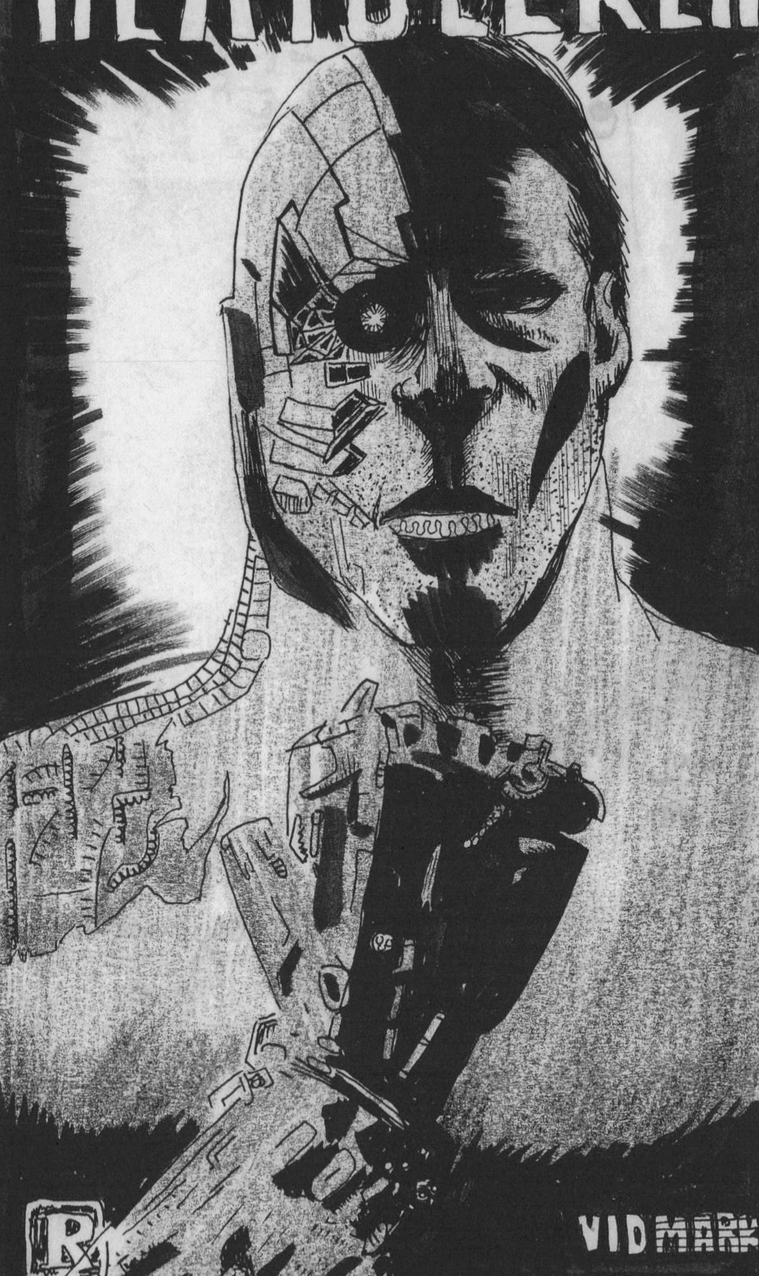

VI

S
A

RE
ULT

HEATSEEKER

THIS IS A GREAT ONE IN THE PYUN CANNON FOR ME. I LIKE THE PAIRING DOWN & THE SUBTILITY OF TONE AMONG INTENSE VIOLENCE THIS IS ONE OF THE MORE STURDY SET-UPS OF THIS FORM OF PYUN, WHICH I LIKE BECAUSE HE CAN/ DOSE USE IT TO GO BEYOND THE CURTIN OF DOGMATIC FIGHT MOVIE STUFF. MY ONLY UN-FUFILLED WISH IS THAT GARY DANIELS IS'NT THE STAR. I CAN WATCH THAT GUY & NEVER GET BOARD. HE'S AMAZING. GEEZ I DON'T KNOW WHAT ELSE TO SAY... I LOVE THIS MOVIE. ESENTIALY IT'S A PURITY REINFORCEMENT DEAL. SOME EXTRA TIME SPENT DEALING W/ REASONS BUT THATS FINE. TRIPPYNESS 4 HEAVY HEADS.

KEITH COOKE THOM MATHEWS NORBERT WEISSER
TINA COTE & GARY DANIELS

COLOR 91 MINUTES 1995 ©

SCREENPLAY BY ALBERT PYUN & CHRISTOPHER BORKGREN
DIRECTED BY ALBERT PYUN

VIDMARK ENTERTAINMENT

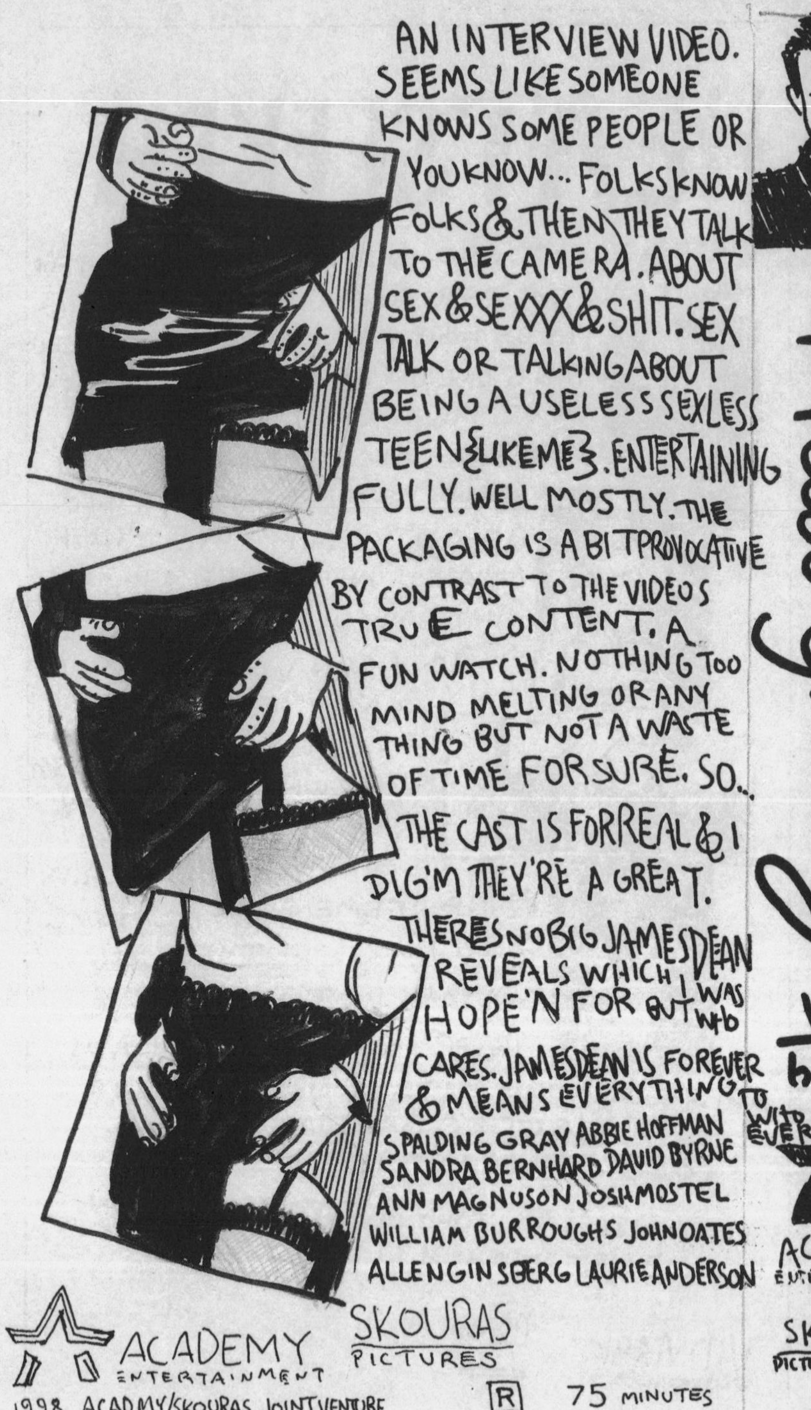
AN INTERVIEW VIDEO.
SEEMS LIKE SOMEONE
KNOWS SOME PEOPLE OR
YOU KNOW... FOLKS KNOW
FOLKS & THEN THEY TALK
TO THE CAMERA. ABOUT
SEX & SEXXX & SHIT. SEX
TALK OR TALKING ABOUT
BEING A USELESS SEXLESS
TEEN {LIKE ME}. ENTERTAINING
FULLY. WELL MOSTLY. THE
PACKAGING IS A BIT PROVOCATIVE
BY CONTRAST TO THE VIDEOS
TRUE CONTENT. A
FUN WATCH. NOTHING TOO
MIND MELTING OR ANY
THING BUT NOT A WASTE
OF TIME FOR SURE. SO...
THE CAST IS FOR REAL & I
DIG'M THEY'RE A GREAT.
THERES NO BIG JAMES DEAN
REVEALS WHICH I WAS
HOPE'N FOR BUT WHO
CARES. JAMES DEAN IS FOREVER
& MEANS EVERYTHING TO WHO EVER
SPALDING GRAY ABBIE HOFFMAN
SANDRA BERNHARD DAVID BYRNE
ANN MAGNUSON JOSH MOSTEL
WILLIAM BURROUGHS JOHN OATES
ALLEN GINSBERG LAURIE ANDERSON
ACADEMY ENTERTAINMENT
SKOURAS PICTURES
1998 ACADMY/SKOURAS JOINT VENTURE
R
75 MINUTES

A FILM BY
OBIE BENZ

Heavy Petting

RODDY PIPER

HELL COMES TO FROGTOWN

IN THE POST APOCALIPSE EVERYONE NEEDS RODDY PIPERS JIZZ. BECAUSE HIS SEED IS RICH. ALL OTHERS FAIL. YET HIS TALENT IS SHACKELED & HE IS... THE UNLAID STUD. AND OF CORSE THERES MUTATED ASSHOLE FROG DUDES. FOLKS DIS ON THIS OFTEN BUT I LOVE IT. YOUNG PIPER IN A ROAD WARRIER-~~BOY~~ & HIS DOG TYPE SEX ACTION COMEDY.

RODDY PIPER
SANDAHL BERGMAN CEC VERRELL

STORY by DONALD G. JACKSON & RANDALL FRAKES
SCREENPLAY by RANDALL FRAKES
DIRECTED by R. J. KIZER & DONALD G. JACKSON

COLOR - RUNNING TIME 88 MINUTES

REALLY VERY AMAZING BELIEVE

STEVE RAILSBACK IS SO RULE'N. THIS MOVIE IS RULE'N TOO. BUT WITHOUT RAILSBACK IT WOULD BE "JUST" REALLY GOOD. TO BE FAIR THIS VERY WELL MADE, IF IT WERE A THEATRICAL RELEASE IT WOULD HAVE HAD BLOOD, SWEARS, NAKEDNESS BUT WOULD NOT LIKELY HAVE HAD THE SEVIERITY OF INTENCENESS THAT WE GET HERE. THE REST OF THE CAST IS ALSO RITE ON. NO DOUBT KILLZVILL REALDEAL. I LOVE CRAZY-ASS WEIRD MANIACS BUT REAL CHEES ASS MIND FUCK POWER TRIPPERS JUST BUMMOUT MY THING. STILL, DUDE IS SUCHA TRIP. AND STEVE IS THE FULL BULL, CHARLES' JOHNSON IS MADE OF KINGLY DEVELS FOOD WHICH IS NOT SO HOT FOR HIS LOVERS BUT MAKES YOU COME TO TERMS WITH THE FACT THAT THE LIFE YOU LIVE IS NOTHING BUT A WAVE OF HYSTERICAL DOUBT & FEAR.

SUBTITLES: ENGLISH FRANCAIS & ESPANOL

STEVE RAILSBACK & GEORGE DICENZO

BOOK BY BUGLIOSI TELEPLAY BY JP MILLER

DIRECTED & PRODUCED BY TOM GRIES

NOT RATED COLOR 184 MINUTES

HELTERSKELT

HELTER SKELTER

SELLING
MURDER TRIAL

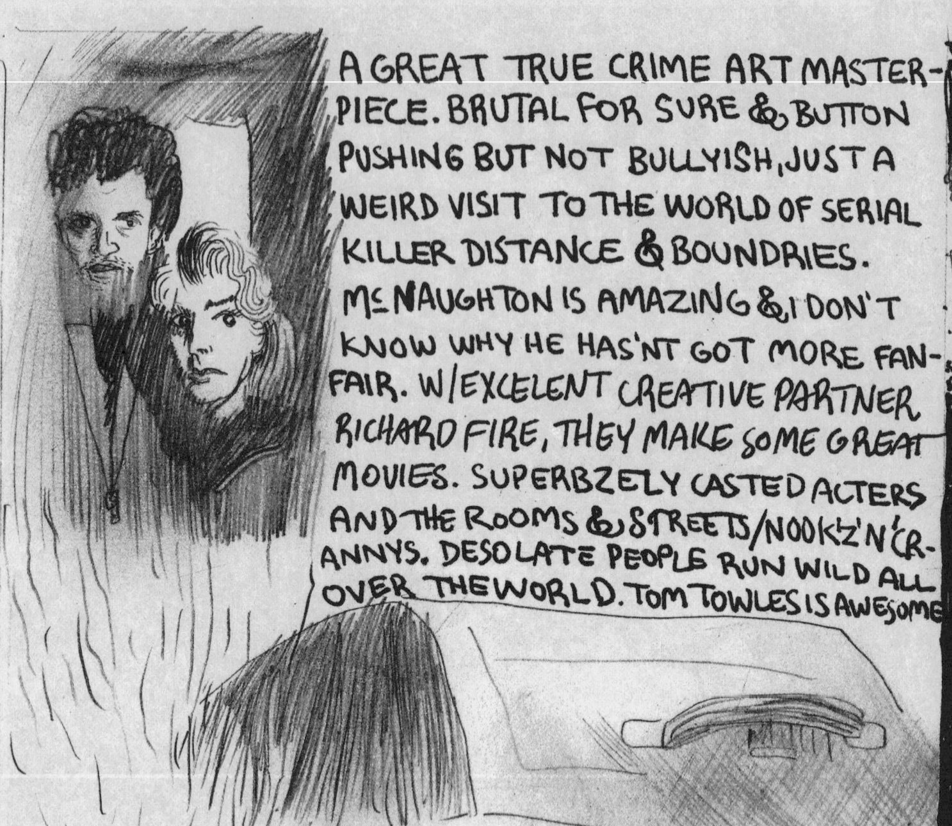

A GREAT TRUE CRIME ART MASTERPIECE. BRUTAL FOR SURE & BUTTON PUSHING BUT NOT BULLYISH, JUST A WEIRD VISIT TO THE WORLD OF SERIAL KILLER DISTANCE & BOUNDRIES. McNAUGHTON IS AMAZING & I DON'T KNOW WHY HE HAS'NT GOT MORE FANFAIR. W/EXCELENT CREATIVE PARTNER RICHARD FIRE, THEY MAKE SOME GREAT MOVIES. SUPERBZELY CASTED ACTERS AND THE ROOMS & STREETS/NOOKZ'N'CRANNYS. DESOLATE PEOPLE RUN WILD ALL OVER THE WORLD. TOM TOWLES IS AWESOME

MICHAEL ROOKER TOM TOWLES TRACY ARNOLD
WRITTEN BY
RICHARD FIRE & JOHN McNAUGHTON
DIRECTED BY
JOHN McNAUGHTON

DVD7700 · COLOR · Runtime approx 83 mins · NR
1986?

2 DISC SET

20th ANNIVERSARY SPECIAL EDITION

HENRY

PORTRAIT OF A SERIAL KILLER

A FILM BY JOHN McNAUGHTON

DVD

AMALIE + PSYCHO + TEXASCHAINSAW = 100%
POSERCRAP.
WHAT A TURD. WELL SHOT, GREAT FX
BUT WHO CARES WHEN THE STORY IS
SO TIRED & WEAK. DON'T WASTE MY
TIME W/ HEARTLESS WINDOWDRESSING.
IT'S FAKE & VAPID. JUST WATCH
THE MOVIES ON EVERY FILMSKOUL
SYLABUS. THESE GUYS DID. THEY
MADE A LIST OF THEY'R FAV. SHOTS
& THEN "PUT THEY'R OWN TWIST"
ON'EM. YOU CAN'T PLOW A
FIELD BY READING A BOOK.
THIS IS A SPOILED BRAT
W/TOO MUCH MAKE-UP.
CICILE DEFRANCE MAIWENN PHILIPPE NAHON
DIRECTOR OF PHOTOGRAPHY MAXIME ALEXANDRE
ALEXANDRE AJA DIRECTED & CO-WROTE
WITH GREGORY LEVASSEUR
WHO DID THE SPECIAL EFFECTS
UNRATED
CC
DVD

WIDESCREEN

HIGH TENSION

ALEX COX'S HIGHWAY PATROLMAN

EL PATRULLERO

EXCELENT. IT'S BEEN YEARS SINCE I'D SEEN THIS. I DIG IT EVEN MORE NOW. TOP 3 FOR COX, FOR ME. SO SMOOTH/SO RUGGED. NATURAL, FRANK, CHARMING, SAD, WARM, ALARMING, HUMAN. FUNNY TOO, YES. BRUTAL. BUT NOT TOO GRIM. HONESTLY IF I WERE PUT ONE COX MOVIE AS HIS BEST THIS IS IT. THOUGH I'M MORE PRONE TO REVISIT THE FUNNY'R STUFF. NO JUDGEMENT IN THAT JUST MY SHOT AT

SANITY MANAGEMENT. COX PULLS OFF AMAZING OFF THE CUFF STYLE & ALSO HAS SO MUCH PERCISION OF TIMING & CHARACTER IN THESE BEAUTIFUL SHOTS ITS SO GOOD. REALY INSPIRING. NICE LAYERS IT UNFOLDS SIMPLEY. MY HIGHEST RECOMENDATION. I WAS'NT GONNA BE A COP ANYWAY BUT THIS WOULD BE A MUST FOR FOLK WHO THINK ABOUT THAT KIND OF LIFE.

ROBERTO SOSA BRUNO BICHIR VANESSA BAUCHE ZAIDE SILVIA GUTIERREZ PEDRO ARMENDARIZ JR. JORGE RUSSEK ERNESTO GOMEZ CRUZ EDUARDO LOPEZ ROJAS

WRITTEN & PRODUCED by LORENZO O'BRIEN
MUSIC by ZANDER SCHLOSS
DIRECTED by ALEX COX

MICROCINEMA.COM ALEXCOX.COM 1991 

R

ALEX COX'S
HIGHWAY
PATROLMAN
EL PATRULLERO
'UG

XENOPHOBIC CITY FOLK NIGHTMARE BUTTON PUSHER. IT'S ALLRIGHT... I GREW UP W/MOVIES INFLUENCED BY THIS SO THERE WAS NO "OH SHIT" MOMENT FOR ME. PROBABLY A BRUTAL SALATIOUS MOVIE AT THE TIME, IS NOW NOT VERY HEAVY IN TODAYS BRO'D OUT BULLY HUSTLER JOCK HORROR THING. AS FAR AS STORY IT'S AN INSIDEOUT WESTERN THING. MAYBE NOT IN-SIDEOUT BUT LIKE A TIMEBENDING MIRROR. ANNALOGUE? IS THAT RIGHT? JEEZ, I DON'T KNOW.

IF YOU WANTO SEE A FAMILY GO OUT TO THE STICKS & GET TORN TO BITS W/A MACHO OPTIMISTIC END THEN HERE IT IS. THIS IS ALSO MOST FOLKS MAIN REFRENCING FOR MICHAEL BERRYMAN. FOR A LOT OF YEARS I BELIEVED I'D SEEN THIS ON T.V. BUT IF I HAD THEN I MUST HAVE COMPRE-SED IT W/ ANOTHER MOVIE. THERE WAS A DIRT BIKE RACE IN MY "MEMORY". I LIKE CRAVEN, BUT MY FAV.'S COME AFTER THIS ONE; WHATEVER. STILL... THERES NO FALSE MOVES FOR WHAT HILLS HAVE EYES IS FOR & ABOUT.

SUSAN LANIER ROBERT HOUSTON

DEE WALLACE RUSS GRIEVE JOHN STEADMAN MARTIN SPEER

MICHAEL BERRYMAN VIRGINIA VINCENT JAMES WHITWORTH

DVD

ANCHOR BAY

WRITTEN & DIRECTED BY WES CRAVEN

1977 COLOR 89 minutes   

WES CRAVEN'S
THE HILLS HAVE EYES

WHITEBREAD MILKTOAST KID GETS STOCKED, BULLY'D & SUBJECTED TO OTHER FORMS OF ABUSE BY HAUER AS THE HITCHER. ERIC REDS MOST KNOWN MOVIE & PROBABLY HARMONS BEST, SO FAR AS I'V SEEN. THERES ONLY COMPLAINT ABOUT THIS & IT'S A NERDY WHINE SO REALLY I'V GOT NO COMPLAINT. IF I HAD MY CAKE & ATE IT TOO THERES A SCENE AT THE END WHERE HOWELL "MANS UP" ON THE COOL COP. IT DON'T CUT IT FOR ME. HE'S TOO WHIMP, GO'N NUTS IS THE EDGE HE MIGHT HAVE HAD & THERE A STRUCT-URALL THING W/ AN ABUSIVE/MAKEN YOU A MAN TYPE ABUSE WHERE HOWELLS BECOMING MORE MACHO OR ANIMAL. THE FINALË IS A POWER FANTASY-IMPOWERED VICTIM SO THAT SORT'A WASH'S MOST OF THAT OUT SO NO REAL DEAL BRE-AKER. BUT... IF THE IN CAR FACE OF WERE MORE VAGUE ABREVIEATED TYPE THING. I ♥ IT. SO GOOD.

RUTGER HAUER C. THOMAS HOWELL the III
JEFFREY DEMUNN JENNIFER JASON LEIGH
WRITTEN BY ERIC RED
DIRECTED BY ROBERT HARMON
1984

DVD R COLOR 98 minutes ENGLISH

RUTGER HAUER C. THOMAS HOWELL
JENNIFER JASON LEIGH
JEFFREY DeMUNN
THE
HITCHER

HOLLYWOOD DINOSAURS

Scenes From Classic Dinosaur Movies!

HOLLYWOOD DINOSAURS

"DINOSAURS ARE BACK AND THEY'RE BIGGER THAN EVER!"

VIDEO TREASURES IS A LABEL I PAY ATTENTION TO. THIS IS A VIDEO ZINE, WRITTEN & DIRECTED BY TED NEWSOM. GREAT MOVIE JUST FOR MAKING A "TO WATCH" LIST. DUDE REVIEWS DINOSAUR MOVIES IN VOICE OVER ON "BEST OF MONTAGE" STYLE TEASE SHORTS. NOT THE BEST, BUT I WISH THERE WE'RE MORE OF THESE THINGS. DUDE SHITS ON REPTILICUS, WHICH IS EASY BUT UNNECISERY. MOSTLY HE JUST SHOWS OFF HIS NERD POWERS & MOVIE COLLECTION. COOL

VIDEO TREASURES

VIDEO TREASURES INC.
500 Kirts Boulevard
TROY, Michigan 48084

DUPLICATED EP Mode
NOT RATED

SHAKEY PICTURES
— PRESENTS —
HUMAN HIGHWAY
A FILM by Neil Young.

WHEN LOVE & FATE COLLIDE

A FILM BY NEIL YOUNG.

RUSSEL TAMBLYN - DEAN STOCKWELL · DEVO
NEIL YOUNG - DENNIS HOPPER
SALLY KIRKLAND GERALDINE BARON
CHARLOTTE STEWART
DIRECTED BY BERNARD SHAKEY & DEAN STOCKWELL

CENTERED AROUND AN ATOMIC POWER PLANT & A TRAIN CAR DINER WE FOLLOW THE MID-WEST TYPES WHO WORK & VISIT DURRING WHAT WILL BE THEY'R LAST DAY IN THEIR PRESENT FORM. DEVO ARE HEAD'D OUT TO DUMP SOME NUKE-WASTE DEAN STOCKWELL HAS INHERITED THE DINER WHICH HE PLANS TO RUN INTO THE GROUND. TAMBLYN & YOUNG ARE DING-DONGS W/HEARTS OF GOLD. YOUNG HITS HIS HEAD & SEE'S AN ALTERNATE LIFE AS A ROCKSTAR, SORT'A WIZARD OF OZ TYPE MIRROR CASTING. HIS ACTING REMINDS ME OF STEPHEN KING IN CREEPSHOW. ITS A LOT OF FUN. I LIKE IT ALOT.

I AM MY FILMS

A PORTRAIT OF WERNER HERZOG

DIRECTED BY CHRISTIAN WEISENBORN & ERWIN KEUSCH

THIS IS A COLLECTION OF INTERVIEW & DOCUMENTERY WITH HERZOG IN GERMEN{?} MOST SEEMS TO BE FROM THE VOLCANO PERIOD. GOOD STUFF, SOME OF WHICH MAY BE REDUNDENT IF. YOU'V SEEN OTHER HERZOG DOCUMENTERIES. THERES AN INTERVIEW WITH A DUDE WHO'S SUCH A DICK/BULLY & HE'S JUST FIENDING FOR AN OPPERTUNITY TO DUMP HIS SHIT DOWN HERZOGS THROAT. SOMETIMES THESE GUYS GET AN INTERESTING THING FROM THEY'R SUBJECT BUT CLEARLY DON'T GET IT ON ANY TRUELY RESPECTFULL ARTISTIC LEVEL WHICH MIGHT ACTUALLY PROVOKE SOME THOUGHT FOR THE VIEWER. STILL INTERESTING. I DIG IT.

BOOTLEG.

NTSC GERMAN LANGUAGE W/ENGLISH SUBTITLES

I am my films

A PORTRAIT OF WERNER HERZOG

I am my films

VHS

I'M GONNA
GIT YOU
SUCKA
UA
FUCK THE CUP. POUR IT
IN MYHAND FORA DIME.
MGM/UA

THERE WAS A DRIVE-IN THAT WE WOULD PASS SOMETIMES BUT DIDN'T EVER GO TO & IT HAD THIS & SHOCKER I RECALL. IT WAS SUCH A HEAVY COMBO IN MY MIND. I DID'NT KNOW THIS WAS A COMEDY OR THAT SHOCKER WAS'NT SCARY. FOR ME THIS WAS LIKE THAT MAD MAGAZINE SYNDROME WHERE I LEARNED ALL THE JOKES BEFORE I SAW THE SOURCES. WHICH ALSO MADE IT A DECODER FOR ME TO LOOK FOR THESE DUDES OR THINGS. IT'S CORNY & LOW BUDGET, AND I'M A SUCKER FOR THAT.

THE FIRST TIME, WHEN HIS MOM HAS A MUSTACH WHEN SHE DOSE KUNGFU, MY MIND WAS BLOWN. I GOT DIZZY. STILL, I'LL SEE A MOVIE & THE SPOOF ON IT IS RUNNING IN MY HEAD OFF THIS. THE MORE KEENEN IS INVOLVED THE MORE I DIG IT WAYANS WISE. HE'S GOT MORE OF A STAGE STYLE.

Approx. Time 1 hr 29 min
COLOR 1988

KEENEN IVORY WAYANS BERNIE CASEY
ANTONIO FARGAS ISAAC HAYES JIM BROWN
JA'NET DUBOIS CHRIS ROCK

WRITTEN & DIRECTED by KEENEN IVORY WAYANS

IMMORTAL

FUCK. SERIOUSLY FUCK'N CONFUSING TO ME. I'V WATCHED THIS LIKE 6 TIMES TRY'N TO GET IT. IN THE FUTURE HORUS IS FUCKING W/A DUDE WHO'S LEG GETS TORN OFF IN A HELICOPTER CRASH. HE TAKES CONTROL OF DUDE TO DO RAPES ON A FULLY FORMED SUPER TEST TUBE LADY WHOS 3 DAYS OLD? I THINK. THERE ARE 4 HUMAN ACTORS & EVERYTHING & EVERYBODY ELSE IS C.G. WHICH MAKES IT VERY STRANGE & CONFUSING TO ME. BILAL MADE COMICS OF THIS IN THE 1980's OR SO. THERE ARE A LOT OF BIT'S WHICH REMIND ME OF OTHER MOVIES, BUT PERHAPSE THOSE MOVIES SNAKED STUFF FROM THE COMICS. THERE SEEMS TO BE NO END TO THE PARADOXICAL NATURE OF THIS MOVIE. THERES A SHARK HEADED DUDE TOO, WHO IS RED. THIS IS A PREFTY UNIQUE MOVIE. YOU MAY VERY WELL HATE IT, I'M TOO BAFFELED BY IT TO KNOW HOW I FEEL ABOUT IT. I GUESS I'LL HAVE TO WATCH IT 3 OR 4 MORE TIMES.

LINDA HARDY THOMAS KRETSCHMANN
CHARLOTTE RAMPLING

LOOSELY BASED ON THE COMICSTRIPS BY ENKI BILAL "CARNIVAL OF THE IMMORTALS" & "WOMAN TRAP"

SCREENPLAY BY ENKI BILAL & SERGE LEHMAN

DIRECTED BY ENKI BILAL

APPRX. 102 Minutes [R] COLOR 2004 1.78:1 16×9 ENGLISH

IMMORTAL
A FILM BY ENKI BILAL

LIKE MOST COMICS DOC.'S THIS IS FULL

OF STRANGE SELECTIONS OF GREAT/TERRABLE FOLKS WHY ARE YOU TALKING TO THIS CREEP?. THEN ONE OF MY FAVS FOR 9 SECONDS SAYING SOME OUT OF CONTEXT LINE BUT OF COURSE I WATCH IT OR PARTS OF IT OVER.

ITS REALY GOOD TO HAVE ANY CHRONICALING OF ARTISTS. I JUST WANT HOURS OF INTERVIEWS WITH JUST A FEW OF THESE ARTISTS. WHO CARES WHAT I THINK YOU SHOULD TAKE A LOOK IF YOUR INTRESTED IN SOME SMALL PRESS COMICS.

KEVIN EASTMAN, WENDY PINI, ROBERT WILLIAMS, ERIK LARSON, SCOTT McCLOUD
JIM WOODRING, ERIC POWELL, JESSICA ABEL, TONY MILLIONAIRE, CARLA SPEED McNeil
CRAIG THOMPSON, KEITH KNIGHT, LINDA MEDLEY, SHANNON WHEELER, BATON LASH
SCOTT MILLS, DAN VADO, GARY GROTH, BRETT WARNOCK, SCOTT ALLIE
LANDRY WALKER, ERIC JONES, MIKE WELLMAN, MATT MADDEN
TREVOR ALIXOPULOS, JAMES SLIME

LETTER BOX ALL REGION NTSC 

 APPROX RUNNING TIME: 77 MIN.

INDEPENDENTS
A GUIDE FOR THE CREATIVE SPIRIT

I'M NOT SURE WHY BUT I'V BEEN PUTTING THIS FILTER OF "I MIGHT NOT BE INTO THIS DUDE ANYMORE." WHY? I DON'T KNOW. WELL, THIS IS ACTUALLY PRETTY FUN AND COMPELLING. SODERBERGH BUSTS OUT ON HIS EQUIRMENT NERD EXTRA HARD ON THIS ONE HE MAKES IT FUN SO IT DOES'NT BOTHER ME LIKE SO MANY OTHER DUDES. SORT'A IN A FIELD LIKE "KING OF COMEDY" WHERE IN THE END I FEEL LIKE IT CONDONES BEING A MASSIVELY OUT OF CONTROL EGO-MANIAC WHICH IS REALY INSPIRING IF YOUR THE TYPE WHO MAKES UNCOMMON CHOICES WITH A RUTHLESS SOCIAL STRUCTURE CRUSHING PEOPLE LIKE YOU LEFT & RIGHT. IT ROMANTICIZES THIS WITH NOT MUCH BAD EFFECT TO VERY MENY PEOPLE. LIKE NILEISTIC OPTIMISM. TECHNIQUE & STYLE ASIDE, WHAT THIS IS, IS A THEME THAT IS A BIG PART OF DUDES MOVIES WHICH IS WHY IT WERKS ON ME. I'M NOT EXACTLY THE SAME AS I WAS WHEN I GOT INTO HIS STUFF WHICH IS WHY I PROBABLY PUT THAT PRE-FACE ON HIM WHEN I PEEP OUT HIS NEW JAMS. REAL GOOD, DIG THE CAST WHICH IS A STRONG SUITE OF DUDE ALSO.

MATT DAMON
SCOTT BAKULA
JOEL McHALE
MELANIE LYNSKEY

BASED ON THE BOOK BY KURT EICHENWALD
SCREENPLAY BY SCOTT Z. BURNS
DIRECTED BY STEVEN SODERBERGH

COLOR 108 mins

based on a tattle-tale

RENTAL

INSIDEMAN IS SORT OF LIKE "HISTORY OF VIOLENCE" IN THAT IF ALLMOST ANYONE ELSE DIRECTED IT, IT WOULD BE A FART; BUT SPIKE LEE TOTALY MAKES IT RAD. THIS SCRIPT IS OK BUT NOT A CAST LIKE THIS TYPE OF O.K. LIKE CRONENBERG, LEE CAN SAVE A MOVIE BY SHEER ARTISTRY ALONE. THE STORY IS A NORMAL CLEVER BANKHEIST CHESS GAME DEAL WITH A BUILTIN "OH WOW" ENDING. DENZEL IS A CHARISMATIC BADASS AS USUAL I'D WATCH A COMMERCIAL WITH DUDE IN IT. IN FACT THE CASTING IS GREAT WHICH ALONE COULD SAVE A MOVIE, BUT SPIKE LEE JUST MAKES IT ALL WORK.

LEE PUTS HIS TEETH INTO THIS, BUT IT'S STILL NOT AS HEAVY AS ONE OF HIS ORIGINALS; BUT THAT PROBABLY MAKES THIS MOVIE A BIT EASY'R TO SELL BUT LESS CAPTIVATING. STILL REALLY GOOD.

DENZEL WASHINGTON CLIVE OWEN JODIE FOSTER

CHRISTOPHER PLUMMER WILLEM DAFOE CHIWETEL EJIOFOR

WRITTEN BY RUSSELL GRAZER DIRECTED BY SPIKE LEE

2 HRS 9 MINS ©2006 COLOR ENGLISH

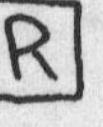

WIDESCREEN

REMASTERED COLLECTOR'S EDITION
A TOBE HOOPER FILM
Invaders from Mars
THERE'S NO PLACE ON EARTH TO HIDE!

Invaders From Mars

TOBE HOOPER & DAN O'BANNON
KAREN BLACK & BUD CORT

THIS MOVIE IS SO TIGHT. BEAUTIFUL, CLASSIC 50'S FLAVE'R W/KILL'R 80'S EFFECTS. IT'S PG, SO IT MAKES A GREAT MOVIE TO START YOUTH DOWN THE PATH OF VIDEOTARDULENCE. IF YOUR EXPECTING HARD SCIFI/HORROR YOU MIGHT WANT PUT THAT ASIDE FOR THIS. O'BANNON & HOOPER ARE MASTERS OF GENRE, BUT THIS IS A LOVE LETTER TO THE MOVIES OF THEY'R YOUTH. AND A LOVELY ONE AT THAT. I'LL WATCH THIS AT THE DROP OF A WERD. YOU COULD SERIOUSLY TAKE ANY FRAIM FROM THIS, BLOW IT UP & COVER A WALL W/ IT. BEST WALL-PAPER IN TOWN. TRUST.

Karen Black Hunter Carson Bud Cort
Timothy Bottoms Laraine Newman James Karen
and Louise Fletcher Invaders created by Stan Winston

Screenplay By
Dan O'Bannon & Don Jakoby

DIRECTED BY
Tobe Hooper

RUNTIME: 102 min. Color Rated PG

VIDEO TREASURES

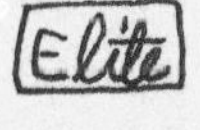

ANCHOR BAY

JACK THE RIPPER
KLAUS KINSKI

DO YOU DIG WOMEN, NAKED, DIE'N; FROM STAB WOUNDS AT HANDS OF KLAUS KINSKI DRESS'D AS JACK THE RIPPER?

A. "No." or B. "YES."

if A: I SUGEST YOU GO AWAY.

if B: O.K. DUDE, PUT ON YOUR MOST BEST SHOES & BOUNCE DOWN TO THE VIDEOSHOP AT THE FAST'ST RATE THAT COOLNESS DICTATES. GET THIS SHIT. GO HOME, GET IN THE GOOD CHAIR; THEN PEEP IT OUT.

KLAUS KINSKI JOSEPHINE CHAPLIN HERBERT FUX ANDREAS MANNKOPFF LINA ROMAY URSULA VON WIESE
SCREENPLAY & DIRECTED BY JESUS FRANCO

SPECIAL FEATURES

ONE SHOULD JUDGE A MAN MAINLY FROM HIS DEPRAVITIES: VIRTUES CAN BE FAKED BUT DEPRAVITIES ARE REAL - KINSKI

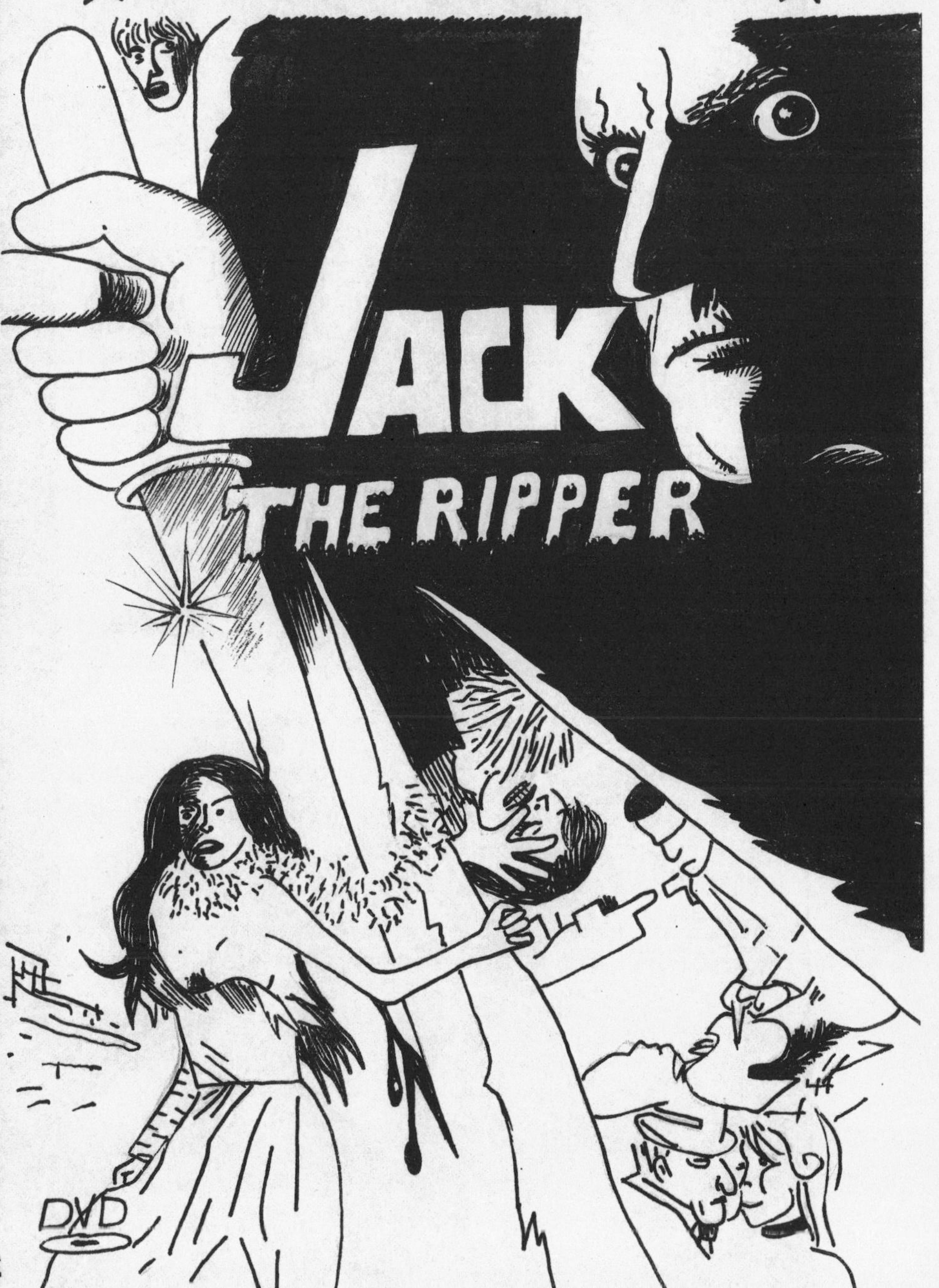
WIDE SCREEN EDITION
JACK
THE RIPPER
DVD

JEEPERS CREEPERS

AMAZING. VERY TRUELY CLASSIC.
WHAT A GREAT MOVIE THIS IS WHAT SO MENY HORROR MOVIES LACK THESE LAST DECADES STYLE, CHARM, MYSTERY.
THE CREEPER HAS A NICE BACKWOODS SOUTHERN TRENCH COAT GOTH PSYCHO QUALITY UNTILL WE FIND OUT WHAT HE IS.
COOL CARS, COOL MONSTERS, COOL STORY. COOL COOL, COOL. PEEP IT OUT.
SISTER & BROTHER RETURNING ON BREAK SEE SOME STRANGENESS & FOOLISHLY INVESTIGATE. THEN THEY ARE PERSUED & TOYED W/ BY THE CREEPER.
ROMANTIC HORROR FILM NERD SALVA CREATES A BEAUTIFUL 1950'S/80's TONE OF CLEAR & STYLISH TALE OF UNBOUNDABLE MONSTER HUNTING PEOPLE WHO ARE THE HUNTED.
GINA PHILIPS · JUSTIN LONG · JONATHAN BRECK · EILEEN BRENNAN
WRITTEN & DIRECTED BY VICTOR SALVA
R RESTRICTED
APPROXIMATE RUNNING TIME 1 HOUR 30 MINUTES COLOR 2001

THE SINNERS OF HELL!

EVEN WEAK MEAK PUSHOVERS GET THEY'R OWN SPECIAL HELL. KIDS WHO DIE BEFORE THEY'R PARENTS DO TOO. IF YOU GIVE IN TO THE TEMPTATIONS OF HELL YOU BECOME HELL VERMIN WHICH I THINK IS LIKE A LOW LEVIL DEAMON. OUR MAIN CHARACTER BUMBELS THROUGH A SERIES OF DEATHS AFTER RIDING IN A CAR WHICH "ACCIDENTELY" {?} RUNS OVER A DRUNK YAKUZA. HE KEEPS HIS MOUTH SHUT WITH A LOT OF CONVINCING & SO IT BEGINS. AFTER A WHILE DUDE DIES & GO'S TO HELL WHERE HE MEETS EVERYONE FROM LIFE AGAIN IN THEY'R OWN CUSTOMIZED SIN REVEALING TORTURE FEST. EXCELENT. ARE YOU INTO HELL? INTERESTED IN HELL? LIVING IN YOUR OWN PERSONAL HELL? WELL I'M NOT SURE IF THERES ANY HELLPFULL HINTS HERE FOR YOU BUT IT'S WELL WORTH FINDING OUT. BACK IN THE DAY DUDES TOOK A DRY'R APPROACH TO GORE & I DIG IT. NOT ALL IN YOUR FACE & STUFF

WIDE SCREEN EDITION

JAPANESE LANGUAGE W/ENGLISH SUBTITLES

NOBUO NAKAGAWA
THE MASTER OF JAPANESE HORROR

JIGOKU

THE SINNERS OF HELL

SOLVING THE FOLLOWING RIDDLE WILL REVEAL THE AWEFULL SECRET BEHIND THE UNIVERSE, ASSUMING YOU DO NOT GO UTTERLY MAD IN THE ATTEMPT.

PERFECT'O! AMAZING! I LOVE IT!! SO, THESE DUDES TAKE THIS DRUG, OR IT TAKES THEM; HARD TO SAY FOR SURE. BUT IT STRIPS AWAY SOME BARRIERS OF PERCEPTION OR ADDS AN AWAIRNESS TO THE WAY THEY {WE} SEE IT. NO MATTER, BECAUSE THINGS ARE GOING BAD P.D.Q. THE TIME LINE IS FULLY WACKED OUT, INTENTIONALLY. DUDES ARE SORT'A PARANORMAL JANITORS OR SOME-THING. I FEEL LIKE IT'S HARD TO EXPLAINE W/OUT BLOWING THE STORIE. THE DOG IS AWESOME. CLANCY BROWN IS SUPERCOOL, DUH. OH! DUDE, IT'S SORT'A LIKE A MIX OF PHILIP K. DICK/BUCKAROO BANZI/WILLIAM S. BURROUGHS & ALL THE OTHER STUFF 90'S COLLAGE WASTE-OIDS ARE INTO. BUT JUST THE GOOD PARTS. NOW, WITH ALL THAT SAID; IT'S PURELY, FULLY A DON COSCARELLI MOVIE. SO THAT MEANS IT'S AMAZING, BEAUTIFUL, FUNNY, SCARY, PSYCHIDELIC, DREAMY, RAZOR SHARP & FUZZED OUT. NICE HOMEMADE WEAPONS. ANGUS BUT NO REGGIE. I HOPE EVERYTHING IS O.K. SO FAR, IN MY EXPERIENCE, I'M THE DUDE WHO LIKES THIS WAY MORE THEN ANYONE I'V SPOKIN W/.

CHASE WILLIAMSON ROB MAYES PAUL GIAMATTI
CLANCEY BROWN GLYNN TURMAN

WRITTEN & DRECTED BY DON COSCARELLI
by DAVID WONG

R 99 MINUTES 2012 COLOR DOPE

KEANU REEVES DOLPH LUNDGREN

JOHNNY MNEMONIC

IT IS SAID THAT THE ORIGINAL CUT OF THIS WAS PERFECT. WELL THIS CUT IS THE ONLY 1
IS THERE A GOOD WILLIAM GIBSON MOVIE? THIS IS AS GOOD AS IT GETS SO FAR AS I'V SEEN. I HEAR ROBERT LONGO IS A SCULPTER.
AVAILABLE TO US REGULAR FOLKS SO WHO CARES? YOU CAN SEE SOME WASTFUL EDITING MOMENTS & THE PACE IS DISCORD-ENT. THERE IS A LOT OF GOOD BITS & INGREDIENTS. BUT IT'S LAID OUT IN A DUMB WAY. IF YOU PUT IN A BIT OF WORK THERES A GOOD QUANTITY OF IDEAS TO FLIP OVER & A CAST THAT IS CLOSE TO WASTE
A KEANU MOVIE YOU DON'T HAVE TO IMAGINE A JOINT IN HIS MOUTH
KEANU REEVES DOLPH LUNDGREN BEAT TAKESHI
ICE-T HENERY ROLLENS
SCRENPLAY by WILLIAM GIBSON
DIRECTED by ROBERT LONGO
TRI STAR
R
CC
COLOR APPROX 98 MIN
1995 USA NTSC

SUBTITLED

THE INTERNATIONAL COLLECTION

hi-fi MONO

HELLLA TIGHT. TRUST.

THIS AINT THE FIRST TATI I'V SEEN BUT IT IS THE FIRST ONE THAT IS TOTTALY "FOR" ME. HIS OTHERS ARE RAD TOO, PLAY TIME WAS THE ONE I DUG MOST UNTILL I SAW THIS. LOT'S OF PHYSICLE COMEDY AS USUAL, BUT TATI'S CHARACTOR IS MUCH MORE BELIEVABLE HERE THAN IN SO MANY OTHERS. THIS' AN EARLY'R MOVIE & SO IT HAS A GRITTY'R FEEL THAN MENY OF HIS LATER, WHICH CAN BE TOO CLEAN SOMETIMES. I LOVE THIS ONE BEST SO FAR. I WATCH IT OFTEN.

BLACK & WHITE, BUT THERE'R A FEW HAND COLOR'D PROP'S LIKE A FLAG OR A BALOON. NICE.

1948 B/W 79 minutes
COMED SUBTITLED NOT RATED RECOMENDED FOR ALL AGES

hi-fi mono

STARING Jacques Tati Guy Decomble Paul Frankeur Santa Relli Maine Vallee
DIRECTED BY JACQUES TATI
SCREENPLAY BY JACQUES TATI. HENRI MARQUET and RENE WHEELER

from the Janus Collection

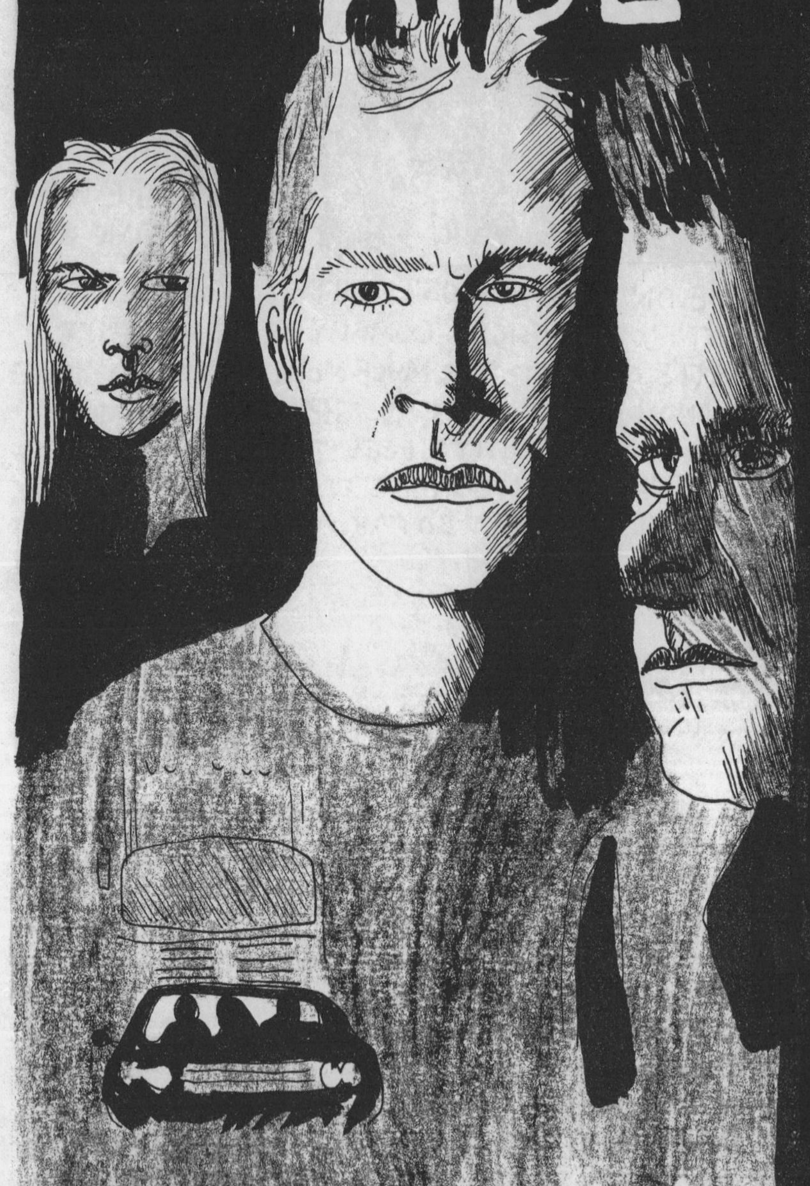
JOY RIDE

THIS IS A GREAT MOVIE. YOU CAN SEE THE T.V. WRITTING IF YOU DON'T LET JOHN DAHL WORK HIS MAGIC. DAHL JUST RULES SO HARD IF SOMEONE ELSE HAD THIS SCRIPT IT'S LIKELY THEY'D HAVE MADE AN O.K.'ISH MEDIOCRE NO THRILL THRILLER. SO, THIS DUDE IS ALL CRUSH'D OUT ON THIS GIRL & BUYS A CAR TO GO PICK HER UP FROM SCHOOL BUT HE STOPS TO BAIL HIS BIG BROTHER OUT OF JAIL. HIS BROTHER PUTS A C.B. RADIO IN THE CAR & HE STARTS FUCK'N W/ TRUCKERS. THINGS GO TOO FAR & NOW THEY HAVE A STOCKER. THEY GET THE GIRL & THINGS GO FROM BAD TO WORSE. PEOPLE DIE, GET KIDNAPPED, PUT IN BOOBY-TRAPS. I THINK PAUL WALKER IS ONE OF MY FAVORITE HIM-BO'S OF THE TIME. STEVE ZAHN IS FUNNY AS EXPECTED LEELEE SOBIESKI IS GOOD BUT PRETTY MUCH HAS NOTHING TO DO & PLAYS THE OBJECT. IF THERES A BAD JOHN DAHL MOVIE I HAVE NOT SEE'N IT. HE'S IN THAT SPIKE LEE/CRONENBERG CATAGORY, BUT SEES TO GET LESS FANFAIR. WHICH IS TOO BAD BECAUSE HE IS FULLY AMAZING.

WRITTEN BY
CLAY TARVER & J.J. ABRAMS
DIRECTED BY JOHN DAHL
R 2001 COLOR APPROX 96 MINUTES

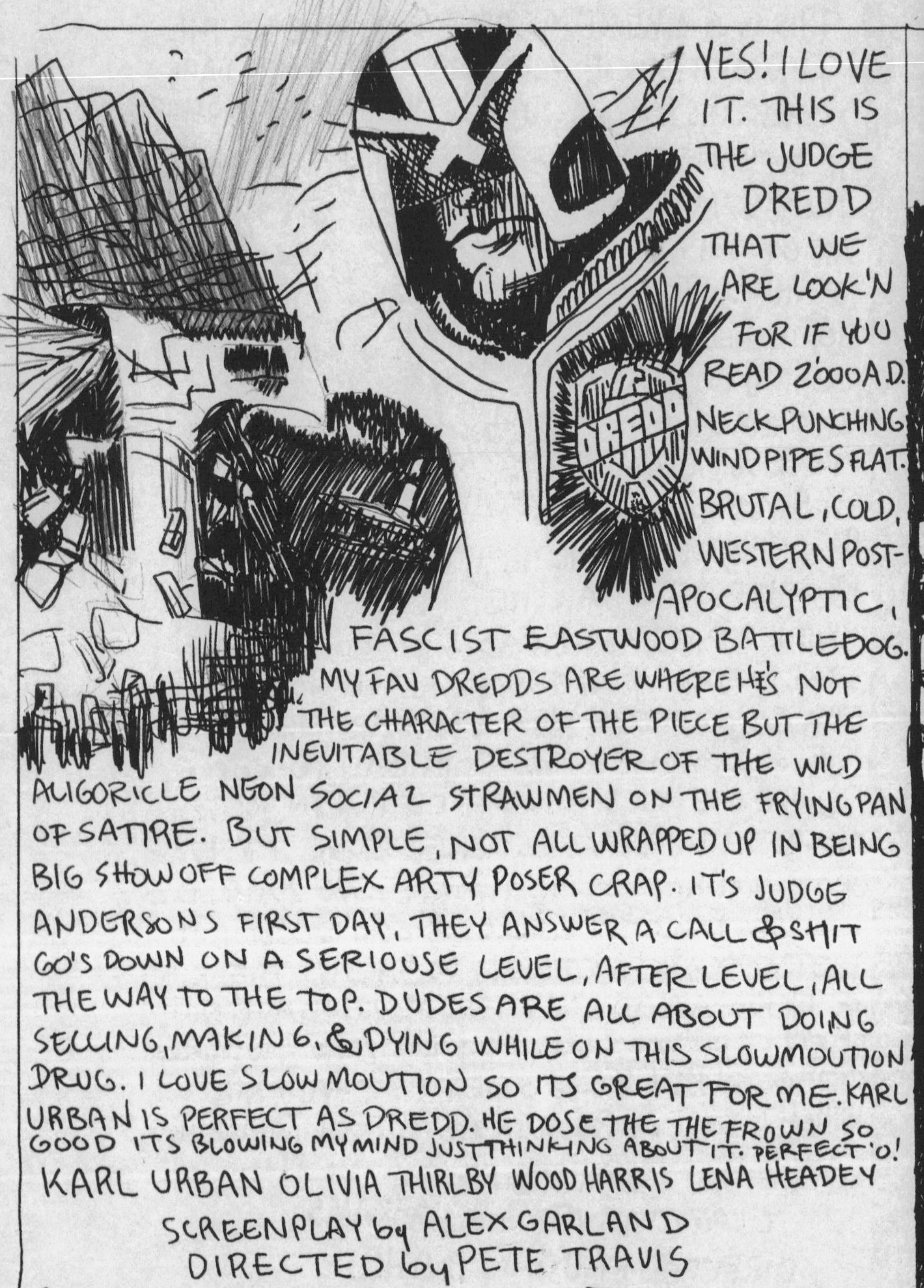

YES! I LOVE IT. THIS IS THE JUDGE DREDD THAT WE ARE LOOK'N FOR IF YOU READ 2000 A.D. NECK PUNCHING WINDPIPES FLAT. BRUTAL, COLD, WESTERN POST-APOCALYPTIC, FASCIST EASTWOOD BATTLEDOG.
DREDD
MY FAV DREDDS ARE WHERE HE'S NOT "THE CHARACTER OF THE PIECE BUT THE INEVITABLE DESTROYER OF THE WILD ALIGORICLE NEON SOCIAL STRAWMEN ON THE FRYING PAN OF SATIRE. BUT SIMPLE, NOT ALL WRAPPED UP IN BEING BIG SHOW OFF COMPLEX ARTY POSER CRAP. IT'S JUDGE ANDERSONS FIRST DAY, THEY ANSWER A CALL & SHIT GO'S DOWN ON A SERIOUSE LEVEL, AFTER LEVEL, ALL THE WAY TO THE TOP. DUDES ARE ALL ABOUT DOING SELLING, MAKING, & DYING WHILE ON THIS SLOWMOUTION DRUG. I LOVE SLOW MOUTION SO ITS GREAT FOR ME. KARL URBAN IS PERFECT AS DREDD. HE DOSE THE THE FROWN SO GOOD ITS BLOWING MY MIND JUST THINKING ABOUT IT. PERFECT 'O!
KARL URBAN OLIVIA THIRLBY WOOD HARRIS LENA HEADEY
SCREENPLAY by ALEX GARLAND
DIRECTED by PETE TRAVIS
2012 COLOR 96 MINUTES R CC WIDESCREEN

DREDD

RODDY
PIPER
IN
JUNGLEGROUND
ONE TOUGH NEIGHBORHOOD

OUR VILLEN IS A 2-FACED GRASS ROOTS TYPE CRIME LORD IN THE BAD PART OF TOWN {JUNGLEGROUND} WHICH IS ONE SIDE OF THE BRIDGE WHICH LEADS TO PIPERS TURF, WHERE HE IS AN HONEST RITCHOUS COP WHO CAME FROM THE STREETS. HIS GIRLFRIEND IS AN UP & COMMING SCULPTER. HE GETS DRAGGED INTO A BULLSHIT ASSIGNMENT BY A FED & IT GO'S BAD, LEADING TO PIPER BEING CAPTURED & SHAIMED BY OUR VILLEN. A "MOST DANGEROUS GAME" SCINARIO IS ACTIVATED WHERE PIPER MUST SURVIVE & REACH HIS OLD LADYS PLACE BY DAWN OR SOME EXTRA BAD SHIT WILL GO DOWN. WITH THE HELP OF A YOUNG EXPERIENCED NIAVE HOOKER HE MAKES HIS WAY THROUGH JUNGLEGROUND THE MOVIE OPENS WITH THE MURDER BOMBING OF A PIZZA BOY. THATS NOT COOL. WHOS RESPONCIBLE? OUR VILLEN. WHOS BETRAIL OF HIS OWN CREW SETS THE SCENE FOR HIS DOWNFALL. FAIRLY COMMON STORY THAT'S SAVED BY PIPERS STYLE & CHARISMA.

AS AN ADD'D TREAT A SLEAZY "UP TOWN" ART DEALER GETS WASTED UNCEREMONIOUSLY WHICH FEELS BETTER THAN THE CLASSIC VILLEN DEFEAT AT THE END.

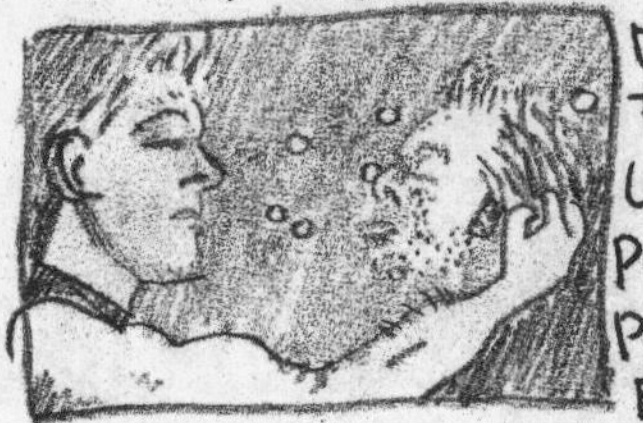

LIGHT, BREEZY POP ACTION THAT PIPER SAVESS FROM COOKIE CUTTERSVILLE. THANK YOU RODDY.

CAT ACTION
APPROX 90 min.
R

RODDY PIPER TORRI HIGGINSON
PETER WILLIAMS & JR. BOURNE
MUSIC BY VAROUJE
WRITER MICHAEL STOKES
DIRECTOR DON ALLAN

VAN DAMME

JEAN-CLAUDE VAN DAMME

KICKBOXER!!!

IF YOUR ENEMY REFUSES TO BE HUMBLED
DESTROY HIM

THIS IS MORE OF A GLOSSY DISTILLATION OF OTHER VANDAMME MOVIES THAN A STORY UNFOLDING OVER THE COURSE OF THE MOVIE. ITS COOL, IT ISN'T AS PERSONAL AS SOME BUT HAS A HAZEY DREAMY SENSE ABOUT IT. MAYBE THATS JUST TIME HAS FIRE WASHED THIS WHOLE MOVIE. ITS THAT PART WITH ALL THE BUSTED UP BEER BOTTLES AND THEY GAUZE UP THEIR FISTS, THEN DIP'M IN SOME HONEYWAX JUICE; NOW CRUNCH THEM INTO THAT TROUGH OF SHATTERED BEER BOTTLES. FIGHT IN TRUNKS AROUND ROPES & TORCHES.

VIDEO

KILLER KLOWNS

from

OUTERSPACE

GRANT CRAMER

SUZANNE SNYDER JOHN ALLEN NELSON

ROYAL DANO JOHN VERNON

WRITTEN BY
CHARLES &
STEVEN CHIODO

MEDIA

DIRECTED BY
STEPHEN CHIODO

DUDE, I'M NOT SCARED OF KLOWNS SO THIS WAS LIKE A ONE OF THE DAY'S I'll SEE IT. BAD CALL. THIS MOVIE SHREDS SO HARD. GO SEE IT NOW IF YOU HAVE NOT ALLREADY. IT'S CANDY ON YOUR BRAIN PAD, DAD.

KILLER KLOWNS from OUTERSPACE

STARRING: GRANT CRAMER SUZANNE SNYDER JOHN VERNON JOHN ALLEN NELSON & ROYAL DANO

SUCH AMAZING SPECIAL EFFECTS THE KLOWNS ARE SO CAPTIVATING I WANT THOSE MASKS IN MY HOUSE SO I CAN STAIR AT THEM ALL DAY. THIS IS PROBABLY THE BEST KLOWN MOVIE I'V SEEN. ACTUALLY IT DEFINATLEY IS. I DON'T KNOW WHY IT'S TAKEN ME SO LONG TO WATCH THIS. IT FULLY RULES.

I'D LOVE TO WATCH THIS IN A DOUBLE FEATURE WITH MONSTER HIGH.

MEDIA

1988 COLOR 90 MINUTES PG-13 CC

AWESOME! TELLY IS SO BOMB. THE GLASS', HAT'S. SUTES, LOLLYPOPS; FUUUCK'N SMOOOOTH... KOJAK IS THE BOSS, HE CALLS THE SHOTS. HOMICIDES. HE SOLVES THEM, & USUALY CAP'S THE PERP' IN ONE SHOT. DUDE TALKS SO DOPE, TOO. DAP? KOJAK'S GOT IT ALL & THEN SOME. A FRIEND LET ME BORROW THIS. I HOPE HE HAS SEASON TWO. IF YOU DIG BADASS' WITH A HEART OF GOLD, GET KOJAK.

ENGLISH FULL FRAME COLOR DOUBLESIDED APPROX. 18 Hrs. 38 min

TELLY SAVALAS

KOJAK

SEASON ONE

DISC 1-3 EPISODES 1-22

AMAZING! INSPIRING... EDUCATIONAL?

LOU ADLER ONLY MADE TWO MOVIES. THIS, & "UP IN SMOKE" WHICH YOU MAY HAVE HEAR'D OF. ROB MORTON IS NANCY DOWD UNDER AN ALIAS. THIS BLEW ME AWAY. I CAN NOT BELIEVE HOW BRILLIANT THIS MOVIE IS. CLEARLY MENY PEOPLE HAVE MADE REFRENCE OR TAKEN FROM THIS BUT STILL THERES VERTUALLY NO MENTION OF IT. THIS IS AN IGNORED CORNERSTONE OF CHILD OF SOLDOUT PUNK ART. WHO KNOWS WHY? FUCK IT. IF YOU HAVE NOT SEEN THIS YOUR SHORTING YOURSELF ON ALOT OF COMODIFIED ART HISTORYS SCREW JOBS. REQUIRED JR. HIGH VIEWING DUDE.

WRITTEN BY ROB MORTON DIRECTED BY LOU ADLER
DIANE LANE RAY WINSTONE JOHN LEHNE
CHRISTINE LAHTI PETER DONAT
MARIN KANTER & LAURA DERN
FEE WAYBILL STEVE JONES PAUL COOK
PAUL SIMON
1982 COLOR 87 minutes R

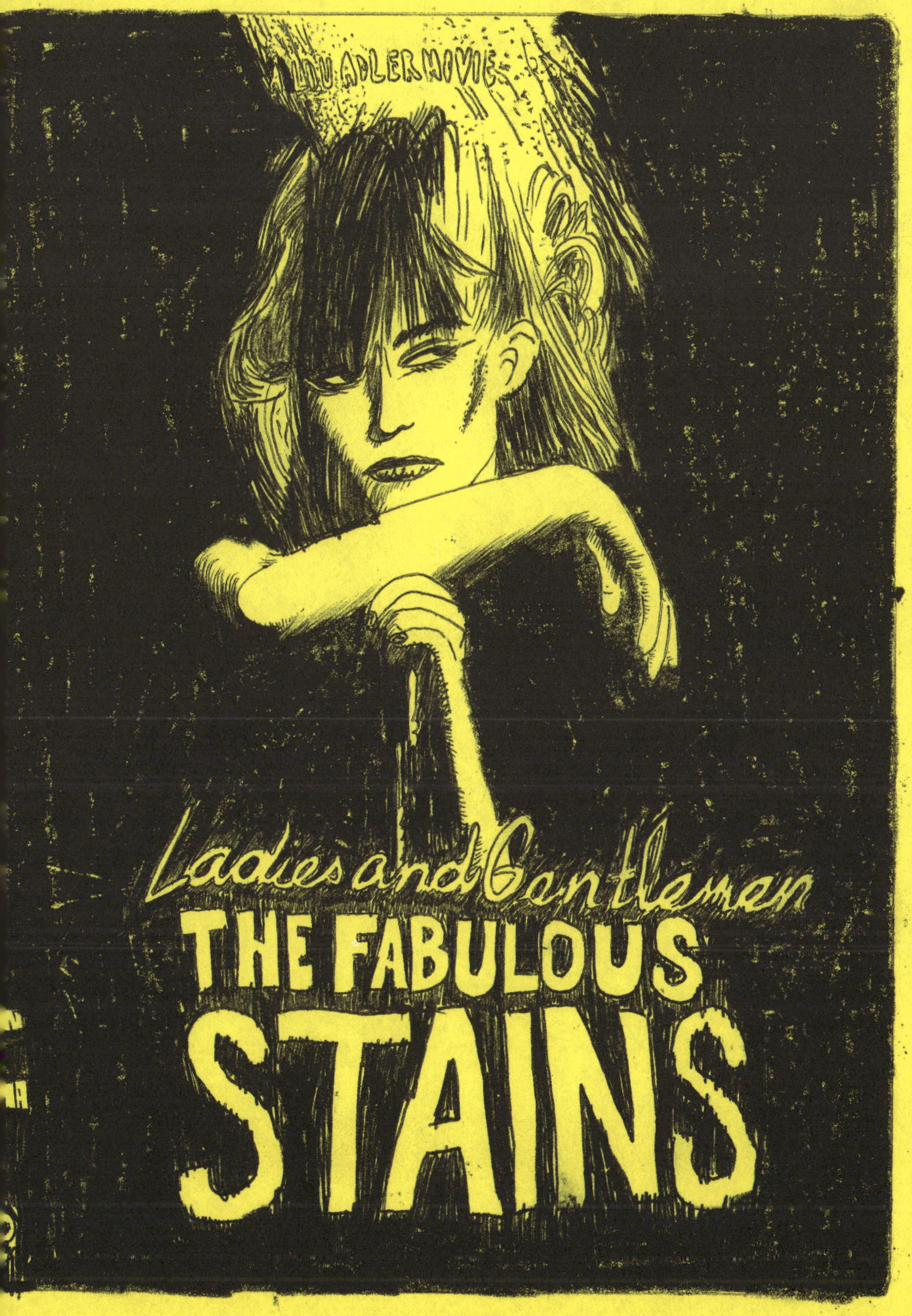

A LOU ADLER MOVIE

Ladies and Gentlemen

THE FABULOUS

STAINS

UNRATED DIRECTOR'S CUT

GEORGE A. ROMERO'S

LAND OF THE DEAD

WIDESCREEN

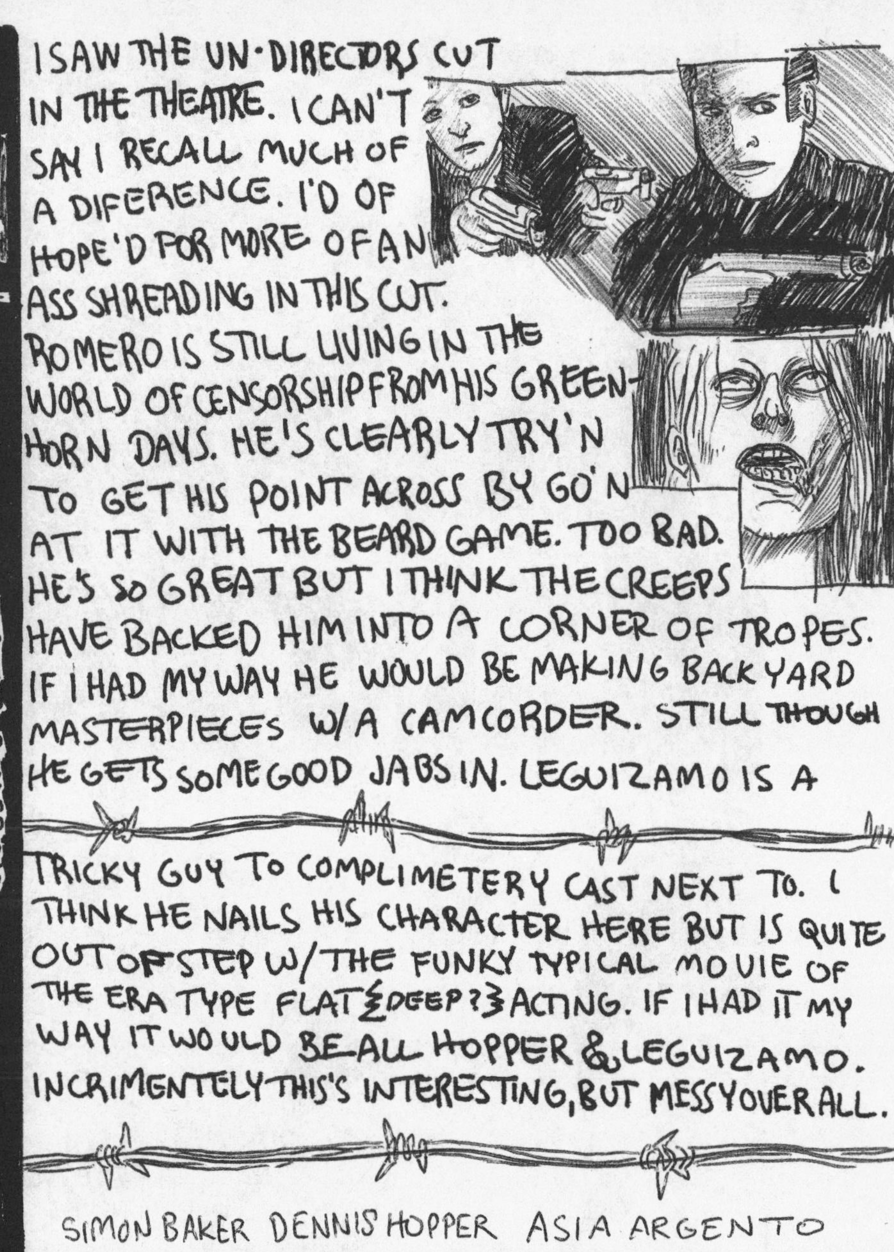

I SAW THE UN-DIRECTORS CUT IN THE THEATRE. I CAN'T SAY I RECALL MUCH OF A DIFERENCE. I'D OF HOPE'D FOR MORE OF AN ASS SHREADING IN THIS CUT. ROMERO IS STILL LIVING IN THE WORLD OF CENSORSHIP FROM HIS GREEN-HORN DAYS. HE'S CLEARLY TRY'N TO GET HIS POINT ACROSS BY GO'N AT IT WITH THE BEARD GAME. TOO BAD. HE'S SO GREAT BUT I THINK THE CREEPS HAVE BACKED HIM INTO A CORNER OF TROPES. IF I HAD MY WAY HE WOULD BE MAKING BACK YARD MASTERPIECES W/A CAMCORDER. STILL THOUGH HE GETS SOME GOOD JABS IN. LEGUIZAMO IS A

TRICKY GUY TO COMPLIMETERY CAST NEXT TO. I THINK HE NAILS HIS CHARACTER HERE BUT IS QUITE OUT OF STEP W/THE FUNKY TYPICAL MOVIE OF THE ERA TYPE FLAT {DEEP?} ACTING. IF I HAD IT MY WAY IT WOULD BE ALL HOPPER & LEGUIZAMO. INCRIMENTELY THIS'S INTERESTING, BUT MESSY OVERALL.

SIMON BAKER DENNIS HOPPER ASIA ARGENTO
ROBERT JOY JOHN LEGUIZAMO

WRITTN & DIRECTED
BY
GEORGE A. ROMERO

NOT RATED

2005

WIDESCREEN 1 hour 37 minutes

THE LAST FRONTIER

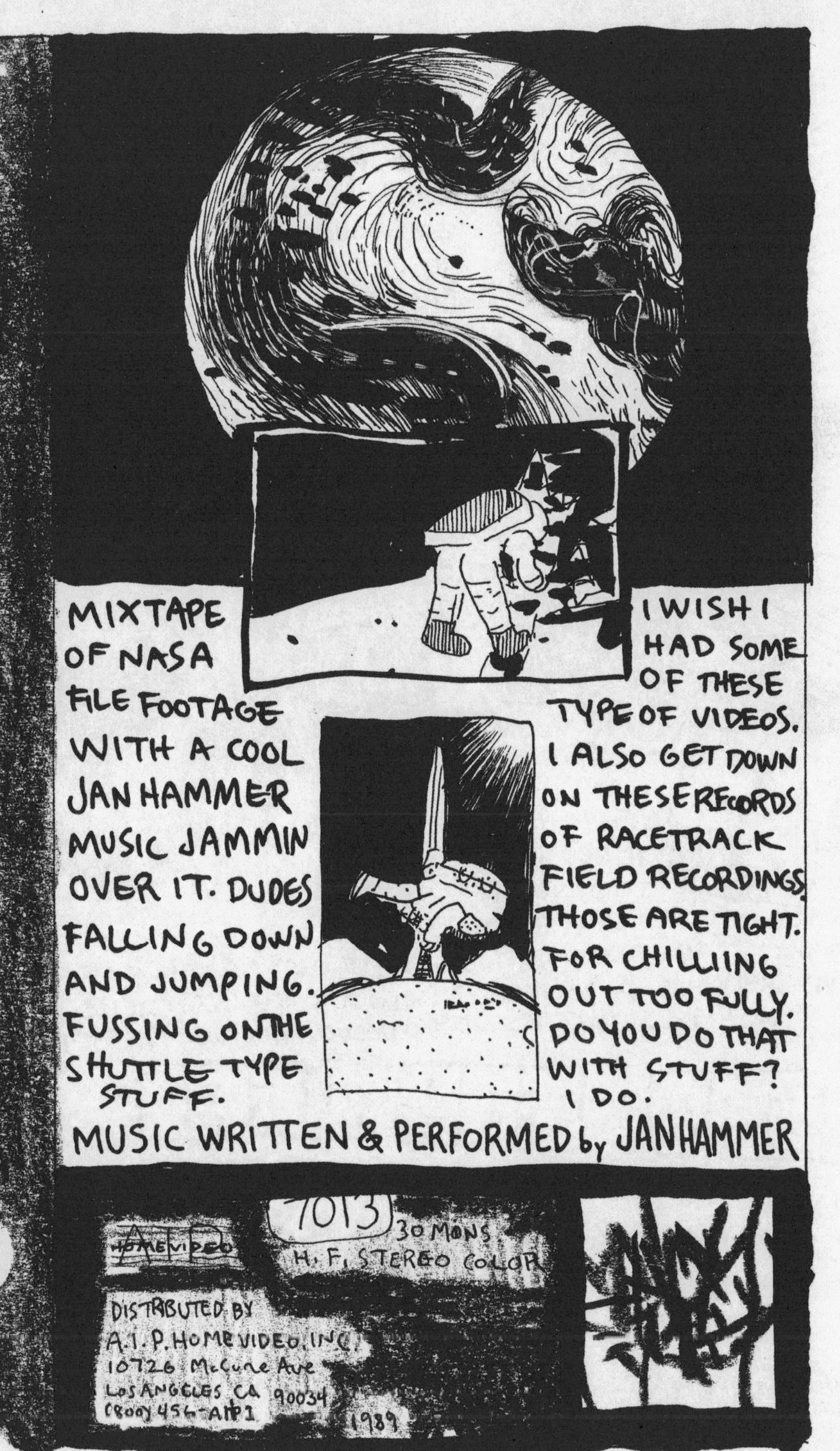
MIXTAPE
OF NASA
FILE FOOTAGE
WITH A COOL
JAN HAMMER
MUSIC JAMMIN
OVER IT. DUDES
FALLING DOWN
AND JUMPING.
FUSSING ON THE
SHUTTLE TYPE
STUFF.
I WISH I
HAD SOME
OF THESE
TYPE OF VIDEOS.
I ALSO GET DOWN
ON THESE RECORDS
OF RACETRACK
FIELD RECORDINGS.
THOSE ARE TIGHT.
FOR CHILLIING
OUT TOO FULLY.
DO YOU DO THAT
WITH STUFF?
I DO.
MUSIC WRITTEN & PERFORMED by JAN HAMMER
7013
30 MINS
H. F. STEREO COLOR
AIP HOME VIDEO
DISTRIBUTED BY
A.I.P. HOME VIDEO, INC.
10726 McCune Ave
LOS ANGELES CA 90034
(800) 456-AIP1
1989

THIS IS LIKE LOOKING INTO A FIRE WHILE TRIPPING OUT DOORS. HYPNOTIC, FREAKY, IMPOWERING, DEPRESSING, UNNERVING, PERPLEXING, UNCONTROLABLE AGRESSIVE BOMBARDMENT IN A SHOCK DREAM WORLD. HARD TO COME DOWN FROM. FULL ON PYUN WEIRDNESS DREAM FACEGRINDER. REVENGE, TRACKER, KILLER, GHOST TOWN MYSTERY AMONG A JUNGLYFOREST. PYUNS DISINTERIST IN TELLING A STORY IS PRETTY WELL ON HERE. SEEMS HE'D RATHER HAVE YOU FEEL THE EVENTS & LET YOU "PUT IT TOGETHER" BUT HE'S SO "IN THE MIND" IT SEEMS
HE'S GOT FOLKS TRY'N TO GET HIM TO HAND YOU AN EXPLENATION. USUALY IT JUST JOLTS ME OUT OF THE ZONE. WHICH PROBABLY HAS A DESIRABLE RESULT FOR FINANCIERS. I THINK PYUN WANTS THAT ZONE TO FOLLOW YOU AWAY AT THE END.
LEFT FOR DEAD
VICTORIA MAURETTE ANDRES BAGG
MUSIC by TONY RIPARETTI EDITED by KEN MORRISEY
WRITTEN by CHAD LESLIE DIRECTED by ALBERT PYUN
FEATURE RUN TIME APPROX. 87 minutes
WIDESCREEN
R
CC
2007 COLOR

LEFT FOR DEAD

The Legend of
HELLHOUSE
"THE LEGEND OF HELL HOUSE"
PAMELA FRANKLIN, RODDY McDOWALL
CLIVE REVILL, GAYLE HUNNICUTT
SCREEN PLAY by RICHARD MATHESON
DIRECTED by JOHN HOUGH
20 FOX

IS PERFECTION THE WRONG WORD TO USE FOR THIS MOVIE? NO WAY. I LOVE IT. WAS THIS REALLY MADE IN 1985? IF SO, EXTRA WOW! A SELECT GROUP SIMULAR BUT VERY DIFFERENT OCCULT'ISH FOLKS ARE BROUGT TO "THE MT. EVEREST OF HAUNTED HOUSES" IN AN EFFORT TO SORT IT OUT. THEN YOU KNOW WHAT HAPPENS. BUT IT'S SO GREAT, DIALED IN WITH PERFECTION. RICHARD MATHESON SR. IS JUST AMAZING AS EXPECTED. SOME HOW THIS KIND OF STORY IS USED OFTEN & WITH OUT ANY TEETH OR PUREITY. MATHESON SR. IS THE MAN WHO CAN SHARPIN THIS BLADE TO COMPLETE PERFECTION.

RECORDED IN HI-FI

1985 94 Minutes

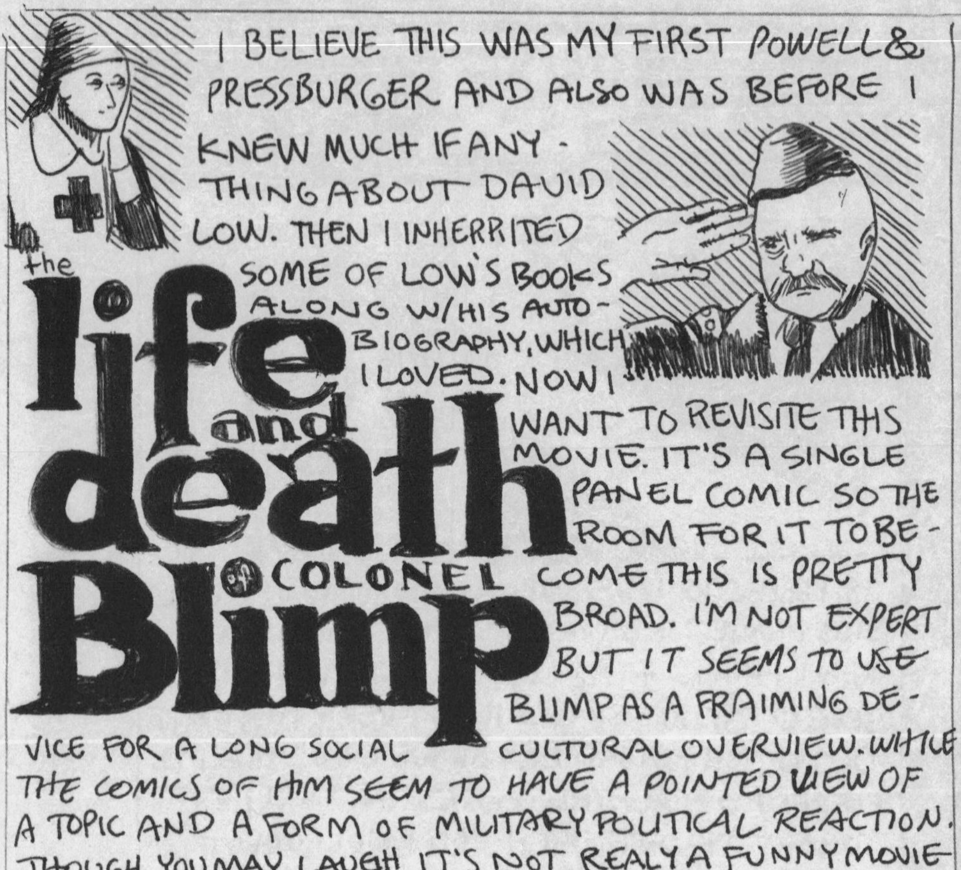

the life and death of Colonel Blimp

I BELIEVE THIS WAS MY FIRST POWELL & PRESSBURGER AND ALSO WAS BEFORE I KNEW MUCH IF ANY-THING ABOUT DAVID LOW. THEN I INHERRITED SOME OF LOW'S BOOKS ALONG W/HIS AUTO-BIOGRAPHY, WHICH I LOVED. NOW I WANT TO REVISITE THIS MOVIE. IT'S A SINGLE PANEL COMIC SO THE ROOM FOR IT TO BE-COME THIS IS PRETTY BROAD. I'M NOT EXPERT BUT IT SEEMS TO USE BLIMP AS A FRAIMING DE-VICE FOR A LONG SOCIAL CULTURAL OVERVIEW. WHILE THE COMICS OF HIM SEEM TO HAVE A POINTED VIEW OF A TOPIC AND A FORM OF MILITARY POLITICAL REACTION. THOUGH YOU MAY LAUGH IT'S NOT REALY A FUNNY MOVIE OR COMIC {AGAIN, AN EDUCATED TYPE MIGHT SEE JOKES I DON'T} BUT I'D SAY IT FEELS GOOD TO WATCH. THE COMIC IS BEAUTIFUL, LOW IS SO CLEAN & MEASURED BUT LOOSE & VITAL TOO. A REAL NATURAL. EVEN WITH THESE REFRENCE POINTS ITS AN ARTY FILM. AND I DIG IT. AND ITS A COMICS MOVIE & IT'S DOPE. SO MANY COMICS MOVIES ARE SLAVES TO FORMULA & THIS IS SCISSORS IN THE WIND.

1943 163 MINUTES · COLOR · MONAURAL

Powell and Pressburger's

the life and death of COLONEL Blimp

STANLEY KUBRICK COLLECTION

STANLEY KUBRICK'S

Lolita

LOLITA

STANLEY KUBRICK COLLECTION

KUBRICK & NABOKOV, WHAT DO YOU THINK IS GONNA HAPPEN? IT TOOK ME A FEW VIEWS TO GET IT ENOUGH. TYPICAL OF BOTH THESE DUDES. THIS IS ONE KILLER MOVIE, TRUST. REPEAT VIEWINGS ARE VERY REWARDING. SHELLEY WINTERS MAKES THE WHOLE THING PERFECT. SHE JUST MAKES IT ALL CLICK. THEY COULD RENAME THIS ONE "HOW TO NOT FUCK UP A BOOK TO MOVIE ADAPTATION". WHENEVER I SEE THIS MY ENTIRE WORLD IS RESET, I'M CALM, HAPPY, OPPTIMISTIC, READY TO GET DOWN & BUST OUT SOME ART. KUBRICK IS INSPIRING TO ME LIKE VERY FEW FOLKS COULD EVER BE. HE KNOWS HOW TO PUT TOGETHER AMAZING PEOPLE ON A PROJECT IN THE MOST COMPLIMENTRY WAY.

I HAD COMPANY OVER, AND THEY PICK'D THIS AS OUR EVENINGS CHOICE. I'D WATCHED IT JUST A FEW MONTHS BACK, BECAUSE DAVID LYNCH HAD MENTIONED IT IN AN INTERVIEW. I DON'T RECALL WHAT HE SAID BUT THAT REMINDED ME THAT IT HAD BEEN A LONGTIME SINCE I'D LAST SEEN IT. <7 YEARS'ISH>

A BOOK IS NOT A MOVIE & LIKEWISE. BUT THIS IS A CASE WHERE I RECOMEND BOTH.

JAMES MASON SUE LYON
SHELLEY WINTERS PETER SELLERS

SCREENPLAY
VLADIMIR NABOKOV
DIRECTOR
STANLEY KUBRICK

NOT RATED B&W/Feature: 152 Mins.

India 1965
Bengali with English Subtitles
BLACK and White
67 minutes approximately

Artificiel Eye

Mahapurush

<The Holy Man>

Starring
Charuprakash Ghosh
Rabi Ghosh
Gitali Roy

I THOUGHT THIS WAS GOING TO BE A SUPER SERIOUS "ART" MOVIE. INSTED IT'S A FUN, COOL, SHORT, DETECTIVE, SCIENCE/MYSTIC TYPE MOVIE. COOL. I THINK IT IS PART OF A SERIES. IF SO I'LL KEEP AN EYE OUT FOR THE OTHERS. I REALLY ENJOYED DRAW'N THIS BOX. SOME MOVIE BOXS ARE JUST SO GROSS TO DRAW. THIS ONE WAS NICE. SO... GOOD MOVIE, NICE BOX NO COMPLAINTS FROM ME. GET DOWN ON THIS, UNLESS YOU HATE BLACK & WHITE, SUBTITLE MOVIES. FOOL.

DIRECTION Screenplay & Composer — Satyajit Ray

Producer — R.D. Bansal, RDB & Co.

Satyajit Ray
Mahapurush

<The Holy Man>

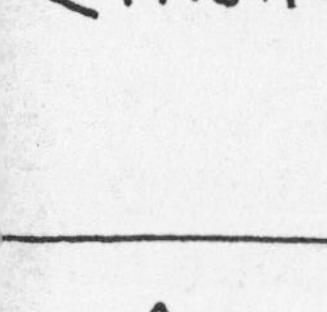

DREAMS IN THE WITCH-HOUSE

STARRING EZRA GODDEN MUSIC RICHARD BAND

TELEPLAY by DENNIS PAOLI & STUART GORDON BASED ON A SHORT STORY BY H.P. LOVECRAFT

DIRECTED BY STUART GORDON COLOR 55 MINUTES NOT RATED

I REALLY LIKE THE PAOLI/GORDON COMBO, & I MOSTLY LIKE THIS PICTURE BUT IT HAS THAT "NEW HORROR" ELEMENT THAT SEEMS TO CREEP INTO THIS SERIES. THE STORY IS WITH IT BUT AT THE END IT JUST GO'S W/ THE CHEAPSHOT & LEAVES YOU W/ NO STIMULIS OF CONTEMPLATION; WHICH IS ONE OF MY FAORITE ELEMENTS OF MOST OF THEY'RE OTHER PROJECTS. THIS IS'NT A QUESTION OF BRUTALITY, I THINK DAGON IS WAY MORE BRUTAL BUT STILL HAS THAT STING OF PRIMAL ESSENCE W/OUT JUST THOWING DINNER ON THE FLOOR & WALKING OUT. STILL, GOOD

CIGARETTE BURNS

STARRING NORMAN REEDUS & UDO KIER

DIRECTED BY JOHN CARPENTER 59 MINUTES

MUSIC by CODY CARPENTER WRITTEN by DREW McWEENY & SCOTT SWAN NOT RATED

THIS STORY IS O.K. BUT CARPENTER MAKES IT HIS OWN & KEEPS W/ THE PRESUMADLY PREREQUISET TORTURER GORE IN A WAY THAT HIGHLITES HIS POINT ABOUT THE PATH OF THE BULLY PORN INSATABLE TASTE THING. WERE HAS THE CHARM & WIT & POPCORN'N FUN BEEN GO'N? WELL... ER. UM, THIS IS MORE A CAUTIONARY TALE ABOUT NOT KNOWING WHEN TO SAY WHEN. ASKING FOR IT, AS I OFTEN CALL IT. GOOD CAST MOSTLY TOO. I LIKE REEDUS BUT HAD A WERD NITE WHERE I SAW BLADE 2 & JOE DIRT & NOW DUDE IS 1/2 KID ROCK TO ME WHICH IS PROBABLY RACIST OF ME.

ANCHOR BAY

CC DD DOLBY

2005

2 FILMS FROM THE MASTERS OF HORROR
STUART GORDON
JOHN CARPENTER
HORROR
DREAMS IN THE WITCH HOUSE
CIGARETTE BURNS

SO "IF "GUYS GET "EXCITED" THEY KILL ALL THE LADIES. IT'S A NEW JAM THATS SWEEP'N THE GLOBE. I'M A DANTE FAN SO I CHECKED IT OUT & DUDE WANTED TO DO THIS AS A FEATURE FROM LONG AGO. MAN... I WISH THIS WAS A 12 HOUR SERIES. SO MENY GOOD IDEAS TO GO INTO, IT COULD GO FOR AGES. BUT IT'S QUICK, SUPER CONDENCED. THE END IS GOOD BUT COULD HAVE USED SOME MORE TIME FOR ME. SEEM'D RUSH'T TO ME. BUT STILL REALLY GOOD. MASTERS OF HORROR IS A SERIES I LIKE. THERES A WIDE VARIETY OF QUALITY IN IT & THIS IS ONE OF THE BETTER ONES I'V SEE'N YET. SOME OF THE SHOWS ARE CLEARLY MOVIE IDEAS TRUNKATED TO THE HOUR LONG SHOW & OTHERS ARE BUILT FOR IT SO IT SEEMS. FROM WHAT I'V SEE'N THE SHRUNK'N MOVIE TYPES HAVE BOLD'R IDEAS BUT THE AMPUTATIONS ARE OBVIOUS ENOUGH. STILL I'M GLAD THEY'R DO'N THESE BECAUSE IT KEEPS SOME GREAT FOLKS DO'N THERE THING.

KERRY NORTON
JASON PRIESTLEY
ELLIOTT GOULD
TELEPLAY BY SAMM HAMMMMMM
DIRECTED BY JOE DANTE
COLOR / 60 MINS. / NOT RATED
2007

BASED ON THE SHORT STORY BY JAMES TIPTREE JR WHO'S SOMEONE ELSE WITH A COUPLE OTHER NAMES TOO

MASTERS OF HORROR

THE SCREWFLY SOLUTION

THE ORIGINAL STORY

MAX HEADROOM

YES IT'Z DA 'BIZ' NAM

FROM ENGLAND WITH LOVE

THIS IS THE TV MOVIE
NOT THE SHOW. THIS IS FIRST & I LIKE
IT MORE THAN I RECALL DIGGING THE SHOW
NEWS REPORTER GETS IN OVER THEIR
HEAD WINDS UP SORTA DYING. I BORROWED
THIS OFF OF TONY & I MIGHT HAVE FORGOT
TO GET THE STATS OFF IT BEFOR I RETURNED
IT, BUT I THINK THERE WAS JUST NO INFO
ON IT. MATT FREWERS IN IT & I DIG HIM
HE'S HIMSELF FOR A GOOD WHILE BEFORE
HIS TRANSFORMATION. I WISH WHEN I
LOOK FOR THINGS ONLINE THAT MAX HEAD-
ROOM WOULD HOST ALL THE RESULTS
TO ME. FORTUNE TELLER/PSYCHO ANALYSIST
PERSONAL PROGRAMABLBE BOSS &
MANAGER. TECHO-RAIDER EGGTIMER.

BY ANNABEL JANKEL & ROCKY MORTON & COLIN WILSON
1985 COLOR 57 MINUTES

TOO MUCH'
OF A NOT ENOUGH STORY OFF A GAME
THERES A LOT OF GOOD STUFF AS ELEMENTS
BUT THE CO-HESION IS WONKY
& MELLOWDRAMATICLY OVER
DRAWN. NEUROSIS W/ OUT TEETH
BUT THERES SOME COOL EMO/BRO
ELEMENTS. NOT AS A PUTDOWN TO THE WHOLE MOVIE
BUT AS A MEANS TO ENJOY SOME OF THE MODERN
SENSE JAMMING SOUND ISSUES SO MENY MOVIES HAVE.
JUST TURN THE SOUND OFF. YOU HAVE THE POWER TO
ALTER YOUR INJESTION OF ART. DO IT ON YOUR OWN
TERMS. I SAY I'D HAVE LIKED IT A BIT SHORTER & SILENT
OR MAYBE A HOMEMADE SOUNDTRACK. I LIKE & WATCH MOST
MARK WALBERG MOVIES THIS IS ONE OF MY LEAST FAVORITES.

MARK WAHLBERG MILA KUNIS
BEAU BRIDGES CHRIS "LUDACRIS" BRIDGES & OLGA KURYLENKO
SCREENPLAY BY BEAU THORNE
DIRECTED BY JOHN MOORE
2008 COLOR UNRATED 103 MINUTES

NTSC DVD

20th FOX

MARK WALBERG
MAX PAYNE
UNRATED

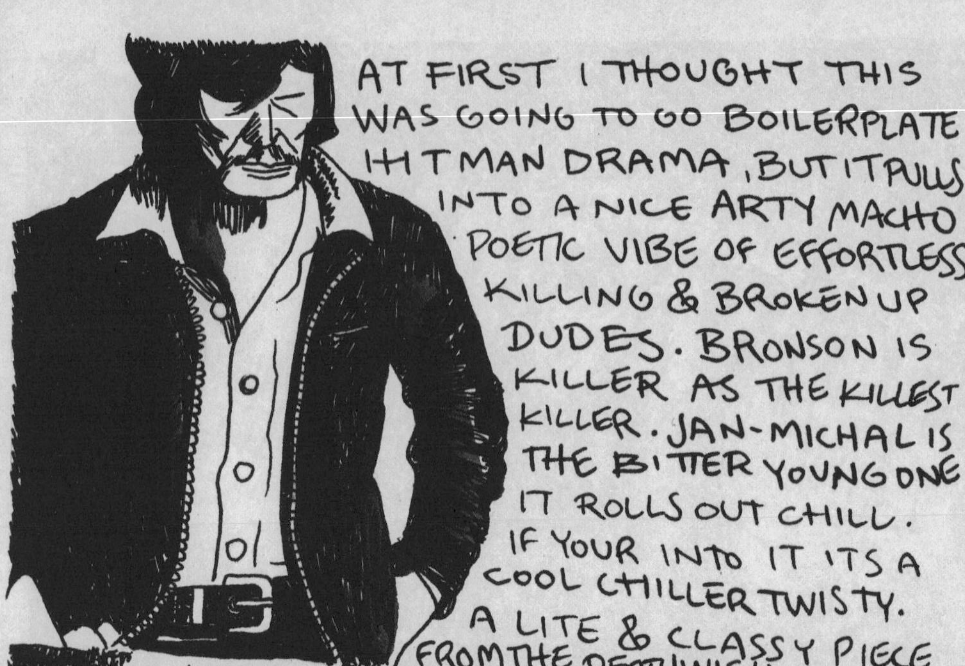

LEASURE Action.

BRONSON IS SO COOL YOU CAN'T EVEN TELL IF THE MOVIE COULD EXIST W/O HIM. BUT OF COURSE... IT COULD'NT.

CHARLES BRONSON

JAN-MICHAL VINCENT KEENAN WYNN JILL IRELAND

WRITTEN by LEWIS JOHN CARLINO

DIRECTED MICHAEL WINNER

PG 1972 COLOR 1 HOUR 39 MINUTES DVD

THE MECHANIC

Charles Bronson

CLEAN. FAST,
PROFESSIONAL

THE MIDNIGHT HOUR
VIDEO MOVIE GUIDE
GOOD LORD, WHAT A FUN BOX TO DRAW. A WEIRD COMBO OF PHOTO, SKULL ART, WITH CHILL PHOTOSHOP. USUALY I DON'T DIG THESE COMBOS, BUT THIS ONE I DO DIG. SO... THE MOVIE, IT'S O.K., FUN, CHILL, SORT OF A PG-13 TYPE STARTER HORROR MOVIE. IT'S GOT 50'S NOSTALGIA, COOL GOULZ, LE VAR BURTON. NOT GREAT, BUT PRETTY COOL.
THE MIDNIGHT HOUR
SHARI BELAFONTE-HARPER
LE VAR BURTON · LEE MONTGOMERY
DICK VAN PATTEN · KEVIN McCARTHY
WRITTEN BY BILL BLEICH
DIRECTED BY JACK BENDER
ANCHOR BAY

COLLECTORS EDITION

SHARI BELAFONTE HARPER

LE VAR BURTON

DICK VAN PATTEN

THE MIDNIGHT HOUR

DIGITALLY MASTERED

TYPICAL SIMPLE STORY, COULD BE THE PLOT OF A KIDS MOVIE. BUT ITS NOT. ALL THE ®RATED CLASSICS EXCEPT GORE. THE RADNESS STEMS FROM THE REVELING IN AWESOME DUDE LIFE STYLE IN EVERY SCENE {& ALMOST EVERY SHOT} HOTDOGS, SPRINTCARS, BIKINIS, DONUTS, FARTS, SMASH UPS, MASONIC CREEPS, LOVE, REVENGE, CROOK'D COPS, AMAZING JACKETS, ELECTRIFIED PISS.

TEAM RAT
15" OF HEAVEN
MIDNITE
SPARES
M 15 + RECOMMENDED FOR MATURE AUDIENCES 15 YEARS AND OVER

THE IMAGE ON THIS DVD WAS SO WRONG THAT I LOOKED UP THE POSTER WHICH IS STILL PRETTY UNHELPFULL & MISLEADING. THE EXCUSE/McGUFFIN FOR THIS IS, THERE IS AN ULTIMATE WEAPON {IT LOOKS LIKA FLYING BASKETBALL} & IT'S FUMBELING ABOUT WITH ASSHOLES/DIPSHITS/TEENS. WHATEVER. ITS LIKE A STREAMLINED TROMA THING. JUST TRIPPY SETUPS TO JOKES, MONSTERS, TOPLESS GIRLS {IN BOTH SENCES}. WE WATCHED THIS W/CLASS OF NUKEM HIGH AT THE BAD APPLE WHICH I LIKED BUT MIGHT HAVE BEEN A BIT MUCH FOR SOME. THERES VOICE OVER WHICH IS FINE IN THIS MOVIE W/ITS VAUDVILLE SPEED ACTS. THE PAST FEW HALLOWEENS THIS DVD HAS POPPED UP ON THE CHEAP'O HORROR VIDEO DUMPS FOR A COUPLE BUCKS WHICH IS PROBABLY PART OF WHY THE BOX ART IS SO WHACK. THESE TWO DINGDONGS RELEASE MR. ARMAGEDON FROM THE BASKETBALL THING I THINK. THERES A LOT OF EXPLAINING THATS MOSTLY JUST SET UPS OR PADDING, WHICH ALL ARE MESHING IN MY

HEAD. , RAPPING ALIENS A TON OF CORNY JOKES FUCK IT. IF YOU WANT A FUN BRAIN DRAIN PEEP THIS. I DIG IT. GOOD STUPID FUN. HEAD LOPPER TITTY POPPER KITCHEN SINK COLLAGE BOY THING.

DEAN IANDOLI DIANA FRANK DAVID MARRIOTT
DJ KERZNER ROBERT M. LIND SEAN HAINES DAVID FUHRER
WRITTEN BY ROY LANGSDON & JOHN PLATT
DVD VIDEO DIRECTED BY RUDIGER POE
R COLOR APPROX 84 MINUTES 1989

RCA

MONSTER
HIGH

MONSTER
ON THE
CAMPUS

SCIENCE
EXPERIMENT
UNLEASHES
CAMPUS
FRENZY?

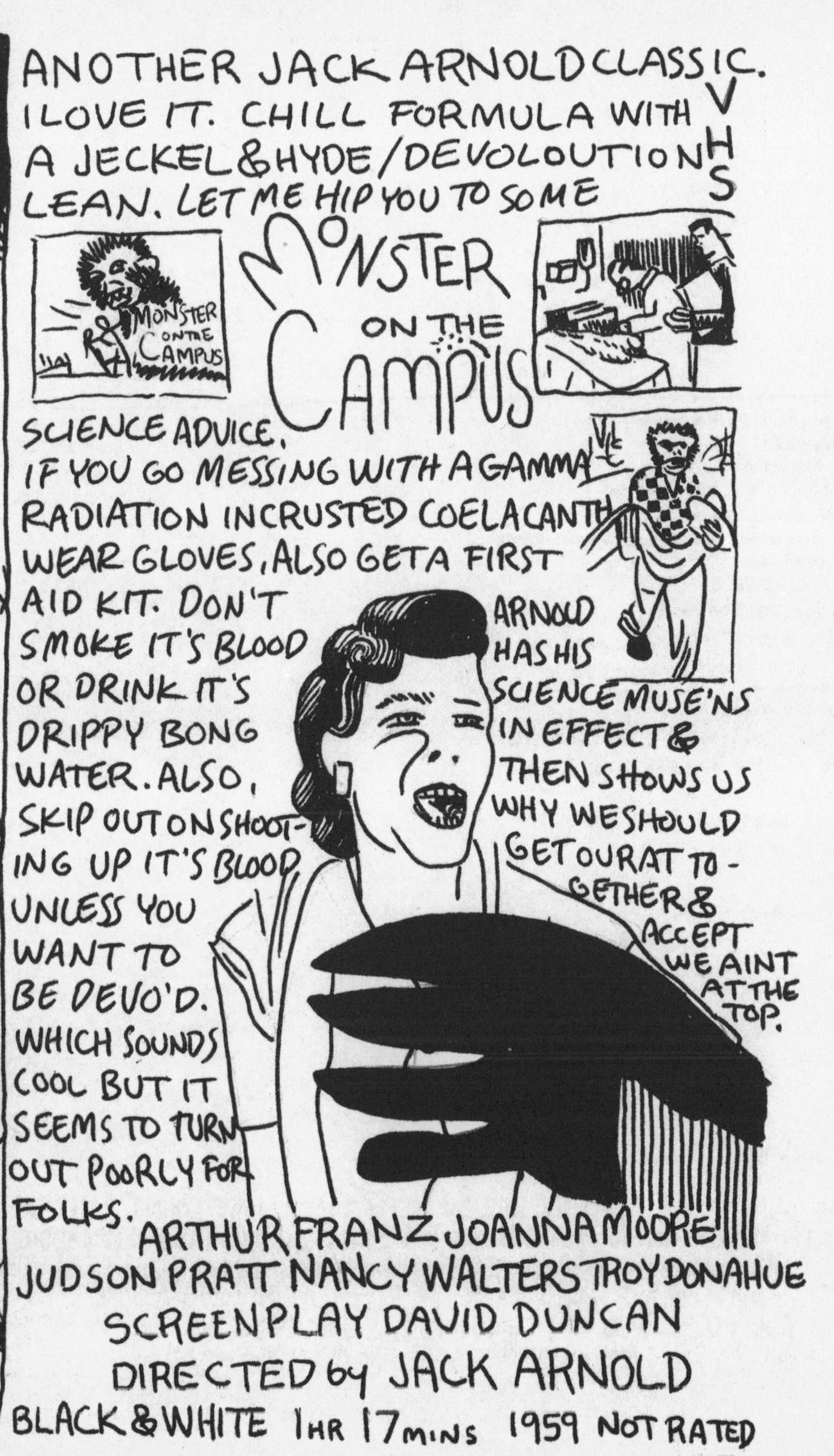
ANOTHER JACK ARNOLD CLASSIC.
I LOVE IT. CHILL FORMULA WITH
A JECKEL & HYDE / DEVOLOUTION
LEAN. LET ME HIP YOU TO SOME
VHS
MONSTER ON THE CAMPUS
SCIENCE ADVICE.
IF YOU GO MESSING WITH A GAMMA
RADIATION INCRUSTED COELACANTH
WEAR GLOVES, ALSO GET A FIRST
AID KIT. DON'T
SMOKE IT'S BLOOD
OR DRINK IT'S
DRIPPY BONG
WATER. ALSO,
SKIP OUT ON SHOOT-
ING UP IT'S BLOOD
UNLESS YOU
WANT TO
BE DEVO'D.
WHICH SOUNDS
COOL BUT IT
SEEMS TO TURN
OUT POORLY FOR
FOLKS.
ARNOLD
HAS HIS
SCIENCE MUSE'NS
IN EFFECT &
THEN SHOWS US
WHY WE SHOULD
GET OUR AT TO-
GETHER &
ACCEPT
WE AINT
AT THE
TOP.
ARTHUR FRANZ JOANNA MOORE
JUDSON PRATT NANCY WALTERS TROY DONAHUE
SCREENPLAY DAVID DUNCAN
DIRECTED by JACK ARNOLD
BLACK & WHITE 1 HR 17 MINS 1959 NOT RATED

1. Everyday Is Like Sunday
2. Suedehead
3. Will Never Marry <live>
4. November Spawned A Monster
5. Interesting Drug
6. The Last of the Famous International Playboys
7. My Love Life
8. Sing Your Life
9. Seaside, Yet Still Docked
10. We Hate It When Our Friends Become Successful
11. Glamorous Glue
12. Tomorrow
13. Your The One For Me, Fatty
14. The More You Ignore Me, The Closer I Get
15. Pregnant For The Last Time
16. Boxers
17. Dagenham Dave
18. The Boy Racer
19. Sunny
20. Credits

Approximate Running Time: 70 Minutes

I LOVE MORRISSEY. I WATCHED THIS SO MENY TIMES I LOST COUNT. SUEDEHEAD WAS MY INTRODUCTION TO MORRISSEY &, THE SMITHS. I WAS INSTANTLLY ADDICTED TO THE SONG & WHEN I LEARNED ABOUT OR SHARED INTEREST BEING JAMES DEAN I FELT LIKE THERE WAS SOMEONE MAKING MUSIC FOR PEOPLE LIKE ME, WHICH ASSURED ME I WAS NOT THE ONLY PERSON WHO SAW THE WORLD THIS WAY. THANK THE STARS FOR MORRISSEY AND IF YOU DON'T LIKE HIM, I DON'T CARE. THANK YOU VERY MUCH.

Morrissey ¡Oye Esteban!

MY DAD SHOWED ME THIS AS A LAD & IT WENT OVER MY HEAD. I WAS EXPECTING PINK PANTHER BUT GOT A DRY YET SILLY POLITICAL SATIRE. THEN YEARS LATER I GET INTO JACK ARNOLD AND I SEE IT AGAIN & IT'S PRETTY GOOD. I HATE POLITICS SO TO ME THIS APPEALS ON A SILLY SELLERS & ARNOLD ANNA-LISIS WAY. PRETTY GOOD MOVIE MADE BY SOME GREAT FOLKS, NONE OF THEY'R BEST BUT STILL WORTH A LAZY AFTERNOON WATCH EVERY NOW & THEN. FOR ARNOLD THIS ONE IS A BIT MORE MUTED IN STYLE & EDITING TOO. STILL, HIS STYLE IS THERE IF YOU LOOK.

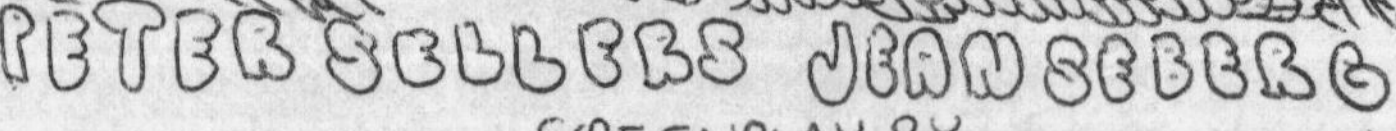

PETER SELLERS JEAN SEBERG

SCREENPLAY BY

ROGER MacDOUGALL & STANLEY MANN

from the novel by

LEONARD WIBBERLEY

PRODUCED BY WALTER SHENSON

DIRECTED by

JACK ARNOLD

NOT RATED 1959 COLOR 83 MINUTES

the Mouse that Roared

Peter Sellers

Peter Sellers

Peter Sellers?

DAVIDLYNCH
MULHOLLAND DR.

SAW THIS AT THE CAMERAONE TOTAL CONFUSION, SERIOUSLY. THEN I PEEP'D IT OVER WEEKEND NITES OF INDULGENCE & JABBER A FEW TIMES WITHOUT COMMING UP WITH ANY CLUE. THE AGAIN I DID IT IN A LYNCH JAG & I KIND'A GOT IT STUCK IN MY THOUGHTS. I PUT IT ON SOME INVISABEL TO STUDY LIST & IT FEEL INTO A WELL IN MY HEAD. THEN... ONE NITE SHEA PUT IT ON & I WAS, TIRED BUT READY FOR A MOVIE. HAVING COME TO TERMS WITH THE TONE I SAW THINGS THAT LIT MY MIND UP & GOT ON ME, FREAKING ME OUT JUST ENOUGH TO GET ME TO WATCH THE HOLE THING. SO... WHATS THE MORAL TO THIS? DON'T BLAME A DUDES ART FOR WHATEVER BAD TRIP YOUR ON. I LOVE IT. LETS WATCH IT. NOW!
JUSTIN THEROUX NAOMI WATTS ANN MILLER
LAURA ELENA HARRING & ROBERT FORSTER
WRITTEN & DIRECTED BY DAVID LYNCH
R
COLOR 2002 2 HRS 27 MINS

I DO NOT KNOW IF THIS T.V. SHOW STILL EXISTS, BUT I HOPE SO. T.V. IS SO UPTIGHT & SELFIMPORTANT THESE DAYS. HERE, WE HAVE A VARIETY SHOW PRODUCED FOR OR BY CHANEL ZERO OF LAS VEGAS. QUINTAS HOSTS & HAS A RUNNING FEUD W/ HIS BROTHER CLONE KALISTO. KIND'A REMINDS ME OF THE ERNIE KOVAKS SHOW W/ A SMALLER CAST & BUDGET. MY FAVORITS ARE THE ZANSKY & EGO BITS. ZANSKY HOSTS VERY SHORT MYSTERIOUS STREIGHT FACED ABSTRACTED OLD MOVIES. EGO HAS THE ABILITY TRAVEL ABOUT THE COSMOS TELEPATHICLY. SO HE WINDS UP RUNNING ERRANDS FOR QUINTAS. WHILE THE TONE AND APPROCH ARE CAMP/SILLY, I FEEL THIS IS MORE SATIRE THEN PARODY. I GOT SOME GOOD LAUGHS OFF EACH EPISODE.

RUNTIME 88 min.

AS A BONUS THIS COMES WITH A COMIC, A GOOD ONE TOO. AS FAR AS COMPANION PIECE COMICS FOR MOVIES THIS IS THE BEST I'V SEEN. OR, AT LEAST MY FAVORITE. THE ROCKETTERS MOVIE ADAPTATION IS A CLOSE COMPETITER FOR ME W/ THE RUSS HEATH ART. BUT HERE WE HAVE A COMPANION PIECE WHICH GROWS & INRICHES THE SOURCE MATERIAL.

STARRING GILBERT HERNANDEZ

WRITTEN & DIRECTED by GILBERT HERNANDEZ

DVD COLOR NTSC ZERO DC DOLBY DIGITAL 2005

BRIGHT RED ROCKET PRESENTS

EXPLORE THE MYSTERIOUS ENDLESS ENIGMA OF MYSTERY

WITH YOUR HOST

QUINTAS

IN

THE NAKED COSMOS

IN CELESTIAL VISION

JOHN BELUSHI

DAN AYKROYD

IN

Neighbors

ARE YOU SMART? DISIPOINTED? DO YOU LIKE ART BUT OFTEN FIND MUCH OF IT WEAK, SHALLOW & VAPID? WELL DUDE, IF YOU SAY YES, THEN THIS JUST MIGHT BE THE MOVIE FOR YOU. THEY FLIP THE STEREOTYPES IN THIS WITH BELUSHI AS THE STREIGHT MAN. IT'S GREAT. TRUST. AYKROYD & MORIARTY MOVE IN TO THE ONLY OTHER HOUSE ON THE COURT. IN THE COARSE OF THE EAVNING THEY MANAGE TO FLIP ALL OF BELUSHIS SWITCHS & EXPOSE ALL HIS & HIS FAMILYS BULLSHIT DELUSIONS. A TENSE & POINT'D COMEDIC MASTERPIECE. IT TOOK A FEW VIEWINGS FOR ME TO COME TO TERMS WITH THE COMBINATION OF VENEMOUS SATIRE & PAN'ISH MIND FUCKS.

JOHN BELUSHI DAN AYKROYD

CATHY MORIARTY KATHRYN WALKER

SCREENPLAY BY

LARRY GELBART

NOVEL BY

THOMAS BERGER

DIRECTED BY

JOHN G. AVILSEN

R COLOR PUMP CITY APPROX 95 min.

THIS IS A DOCUMENTERY ON EACH ELM ST. MOVIE & THE T.V. SHOW. I DID'NT EVEN REMEMBER THERE BEING A TV SHOW "FREDDYS NIGHMARES" SOUNDS LIKE IT DID'NT LAST LONG BUT MOST OF THE DUDES FROM IT WENT ON TO "TALES FROM THE CRYPT." I GOT'A SEE THIS SHOW. SPEAKING OF GOTTA SEE... IF YOU EVEN LIKE ANY OF THE ELM ST. MOVIES YOU OUGHT TO SEE THIS. IT'S 4 HOURS & IT STILL FEELS LIKE THEY COULD HAVE GONE ON A LOT LONGER. THEY TALK TO ALMOST EVERYONE INVOLVED, HONESTLY I COULD WATCH 4 HOURS OF JOHN SAXON ALONE. ENGLUND IS A GREAT INTERVIEW, SO ALL ABOUT IT WITH HIS ARTISTRY. HE'S ON A FEATURE ON "EATEN ALIVE" TOO & HE'S JUST CAPTIVATING. THEY DON'T DO ANYTHING ON THE RE-LAUNCH WHICH MAKES SENCE. IT WOULD HAVE BEEN COOL IF THEY'D SPENT SOMETIME ON THE POSTER ART. REMEMBER WHEN MOVIES HAD COOL POSTERS? IT'S BEEN A WHILE DUDE. NOT THAT I DID IT .01% WORTH OF HONOR W/ THE INTERPRITATION OVER THERE MYSELF. WELL I'M NOT TRY'N TO WHINE, SORRY. THIS IS A TRUELY DOMINANT DOCUMENTATION OF ANY {MOVIE(S)} EXPECIALLY "ONE" THIS COOL. ELM ST. 2 IS DEFINATLLY THE ONE I'LL RE-VISIT NEXT, I CAN'T EVEN REMEMBER THE LAST TIME I SAW THAT ONE. FUCK, WHAT CAN I SAY WITH OUT BLOWING IT. JUST PEEP THIS OUT Y'ALL.

NEVER SLEEP AGAIN: THE ELM STREET LEGACY
NARRATED BY HEATHER LANGENKAMP
WRITTEN BY THOMMY HUTSON
DIRECTED BY
DANIEL FARRANDS & ANDREW KASCH

COLOR NOT RATED 240 Mins. 2010

NEVER SLEEP AGAIN

THE ELM STREET LEGACY

THE ULTIMATE NIGHTMARE DOCUMENTARY

FROM CLIVE BARKER, THE CREATOR OF *HELLRAISER*

NIGHT
BREED

COME MEET THE DEAD OF NIGHT

NIGHT BREED

COLOR/APPRIX. 102 minutes/1990 R

DUDES'LL TELL ABOUT THIS IS CUT & A MESS. PFFFT SWHATEVER DUDE, CREEPY TABOO FOLKS, MAGIC FOLK FUCKED OVER. THE END IS A BIT LOW WOW CURTNESS. CRONENBERG FULLY STEALS THE SHOW AT EVERY APPEARENCE. IF ANYTHING I'D SAY CUT IN ANOTHER DOSE OF HIM ON THAT

CRAIG SHEFFER ANNE BOBBY
DAVID CRONENBERG CHARLES HAID
WRITTEN & DIRECTED BY CLIVE BARKER
BASED ON HIS NOVEL "CABAL"

MEDIA

VIDEO TREASURES

NIGHT SHIFT

WHAT CAN I SAY... I HATE RON HOWARD MOVIES. I LOVE HENERY WINKLER, I HATE SHELLY LONG, I LOVE PIMP'N FROM A MORGUE. SO IT'S A TOUGH CALL. WINKLERS HAIR IS PRETTY BOARING. BUT, MICHAEL KEATON <1st MOVIE> IS TOTALY BONKERS. I THINK I LIKED DRAWING THE BOX MORE THEN WATCHING THE MOVIE. THERE ARE A FEW COOL THINGS TO SPOT IF YOU LOOK CLOSE ① THERES AN AMAZING SIGN THAT SAYS "BLAZELAND USA ② SHELLY LONG HAS "SOMETHING" ON HER LIP ③ THERES A NICE TAHOO CRUISER ④ SCREENWRITTER BABALOO MANDEL I DON'T KNOW WHO THAT IS BUT A NAME LIKE THAT IS VERY REASSURING. SO I DON'T DIG IT WHEN RON HOWARD DIRECTS MOVIES, BUT I LIKE HIS ACTING AND HIS BROTHER CLINT IS SO CHARISMATIC THAT MY HEART MELTS. THIS IS ONE OF RON'S LEAST BAD MOVIES. TOTALY VANILLA. EDDIE MURPHY INTERVIEWED RON ON SNL, AND AFTER HEARING THAT THERE WERE NO BLACK FOLKS IN THE MOVIE EDDYE SAYS "I DON'T KNOW IF I SHOULD HIT YOU OR THANK YOU". NICE. A DUDE TOLD ME "YOU DON'T PAY PROSTITUTES TO BONE YOU, YOU PAY THEM TO LEAVE". SHIT I WOULD PAY SHELLY LONG TO LEAVE BEFORE THE SEX. SO WHY DID I WATCH A RON HOWARD MOVIE? MOSTLY BECAUSE MY FRIEND IS TOTALY INTO IT AND I USUALLY AGREE WITH WHAT HE LIKES. BUT I THINK HE MIGHT HAVE ONE OF THOSE SENTIMENTEL CRUSH'S ON THIS ONE, BY THE WAY THERE IS A BLACK DUDE IN THE MOVIE, BUT THEY KILL HIM IN THE FIRST SCENE. SINCE WATCHING THIS TAPE IT HAS BECOME MY TEST TAPE FOR MY "NEW" VCR'S. IT'S GOT'N MUNCHED A BIT, BUT STILL WERKS.

R

106 min.

AS IF LOOKING AT THE LIST OF SCREENWRITTERS WAS'NT ENOUGH OF A HINT, I'LL TELL YOU; THIS ONE IS KIND OF HERKYJERKY. STILL PRETTY DECENT. JOHN SAXON IS AMAZING AS USUAL. THIS ONE IS STRUGGELING WITH IT'S CHOICES BETWEEN HORROR & COMEDY. I HAVE'NT REVISITED THIS ONE SINCE 1989. I WATCHED IT AT MY BUDDYS HOUSE, & THE SCEEN WHERE Freedy MARIONETTES THE DUDE IN THE HOSPITAL WITH HIS OWN BLOOD VAINS WAS ON AS AN EARTHQUAKE HIT. THE TV WAS SHAKING AROUND AS I JUMP'D IN A DOORFRAME, I JOKED "FREDDYS HERE". AT THAT SAME MOMENT FREEWAYS WERE COLLAPSING ON PEOPLE & THE WORLD SERIES WAS POSTPONED. SO IT SEEM'D A LOT HEAVY'R THEN, THAN IT DOSE NOW.

ROBERT ENGLUND HEATHER LANGENKAMP JOHN SAXON PATRICIA ARQUETTE LAURENCE FISHBURNE CRAIG WASSON PRISCILLA POINTER DICK CAVETT ZSAZSA GABOR & DOKKEN

SCREENPLAY: WES CRAVEN & BRUCE WAGNER & CHUCK RUSSELL & FRANK DARABONT

DIRECTED BY CHUCK RUSSELL

ENGLISH

IF YOU THINK
YOU'LL GET
OUT ALIVE,
YOUR DREAM'N.

STRONG SEQUEL. THIS ONE ACTUALLY HOLDS UP ALONE AS A MOVIE. NO EXPERIENCE REQUIRED. FREDDY IS MORE PAN'ISH THAN IN THE PAST. HE'S ACTUALLY QUITE QUAINT HERE. NOT SO MUCH A DREAM STALKER THAN A SIDESHOW GRIM REAPER. THERE ARE A FEW GREAT CAMIOS THAT FIT WELL, ARE FUN, & DON'T BREAK THE FLOW. TALALAY DOSE A GREAT JOB PLAYING BETWEEN INFLUENCES, SORT'A LYNCH/BURTON/COEN'S STYLE. BUT NOT RIP OFF. SHE PRODUCED ALL THE PREVIOUS SEQUALS I THINK. SHE ALSO PRODUCED A FEW OF JOHN WATERS MOVIES. YAPHET KOTTO IS A DREAM SPECIALIST WHO IS'NT IN THE MOVIE ENOUGH FOR ME, BUMMER. HE'S THE JOHN SAXON OF THIS ONE. TYPICEL ELM ST. BUSINESS TEENS DIE IN PERSONALITY APPROPRIET WAYS. FREDDYS FAILY HISTORY IS EXPLORED. PLUS CAMIOS FROM JOHNNY DEPP & ALICE COOPER.

ROBERT ENGLUND LISA ZANE SIMON GREENBLATT
LEZLIE DEANE YAPHET KOTTO

SCREENPLAY
MICHAEL DE LUCA

STORY & DIRECTION
RACHEL TALALAY

FREDDY'S DEAD

THE FINAL NIGHTMARE

WOW. THIS IS GREAT. YOU MAY WANT TO HAVE A PEN & PAPER HANDY SO YOU CAN MAKE A LIST OF THE MOVIES YOU WANT TO GO CHECK OUT AFTER THIS.

MOSTLY CLIPS & SPOTLIGHTS W/SPECIAL GUESTS TELLING HOW AMAZING THE MOVIE ARE & SO FAR FROM WHAT I'V SEE'N THEY'R RIGHT. UNLESS YOUR NOT INTO SEX, VIOLENCE & CRUDE JOKES I CAN'T SEE ANY REASO WHY THIS WOULD'NT BE A GREAT GUIDE TO A HOME FILM FEST FOR WEEKS ON END. IT SEEM'S LIKE THEY MUST HAVE HOURS OF MATERIAL FOR THI THAT DID'NT MAKE IT IN. I'D LOVE TO SEE IT A

WRITTEN & DIRECTED BY MARK HARTLEY

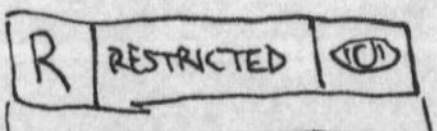

103 Min.
2008 COLOR

WIDESCREEN

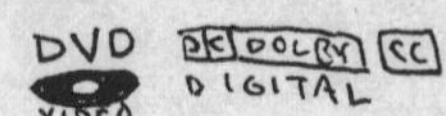

MAGNET

MALCOLM McDOWELL
in
Lindsay Andersons
O LuckyMAN!
music and songs by ALAN PRICE
Smile while you're makin it
Laugh while you're takin it
Even though you're fakin it
Nobody's gonna know...
R
RESTRICTED
MALCOLM McDOWELL
RALPH RICHARDSON RACHEL ROBERTS ARTHUR LOWE
HELEN MIRREN DANDY NICHOLS MONA WASHBOURNE
SCREENPLAY by DAVID SHERWIN
MUSIC & SONGS by ALAN PRICE
DIRECTED by LINDSAY ANDERSON

WAS'NT SURE WHAT TO EXPECT OF A ↑ BY THE WHO DID "IF...". THIS IS A PICARESQUE UPS & DOWNS OF A YOUNG MAN TYPE DEAL. THERES A COURIS STYLE INTERLUDE THING

W/ALAN PRICE & CO. FRAIMING THINGS WITH SONG OVERFLOWING BACK TO OUR LUCKY MAN. WHATS THE POINT? I DON'T KNOW... WHICH ONE DO YOU WANT? IT'S A WEEKEND OR SLOW DAY INDOORS ALONE WITH NO EXCURSIONS OUTSIDE. AT LEAST THATS HOW IT'S BEEN FOR ME. THERES A BIT THE END WHERE THERES A WALL PASTED WITH T.REX POSTERS, FOR WHAT REASON I KNOW NOT; BUT IT STAYS WITH ME. SORTA FUNNY IT'S CALLED A COMEDY, COULD EASIELY BE A MUSICAL OR DRAMA. THE UPS & DOWNS CAN BE A BIT BRUTAL AND GET YOU A BIT MORE WEARY FOR THE FINISH, BUT IT LEAVES OFF WITH AN OPTIMISTIC OPENER FEEL.

1973

DAVID LYNCH AND MARKFROST
PRESENT
ON THE AIR
NATIONAL

YES. WATCH "ON THE AIR". I DREW A MEDIEOKER ART HERE & I KNEW IT. THEN I HANDED IT OVER TO DUNJA & SHE RULED ALL OVER IT. THANKFULLY. I THOUGHT ABOUT WRITTING A REVIEW ON THE PANTS BUT THAT WOULD THROW IT OFF FOR ME. GREAT SHOW. SO FUNNY. WHY ARE'NT THERE MORE OF THESE? BECAUSE FOOLS BE TRIP'N.

HEATH LEDGER
THE ORDER

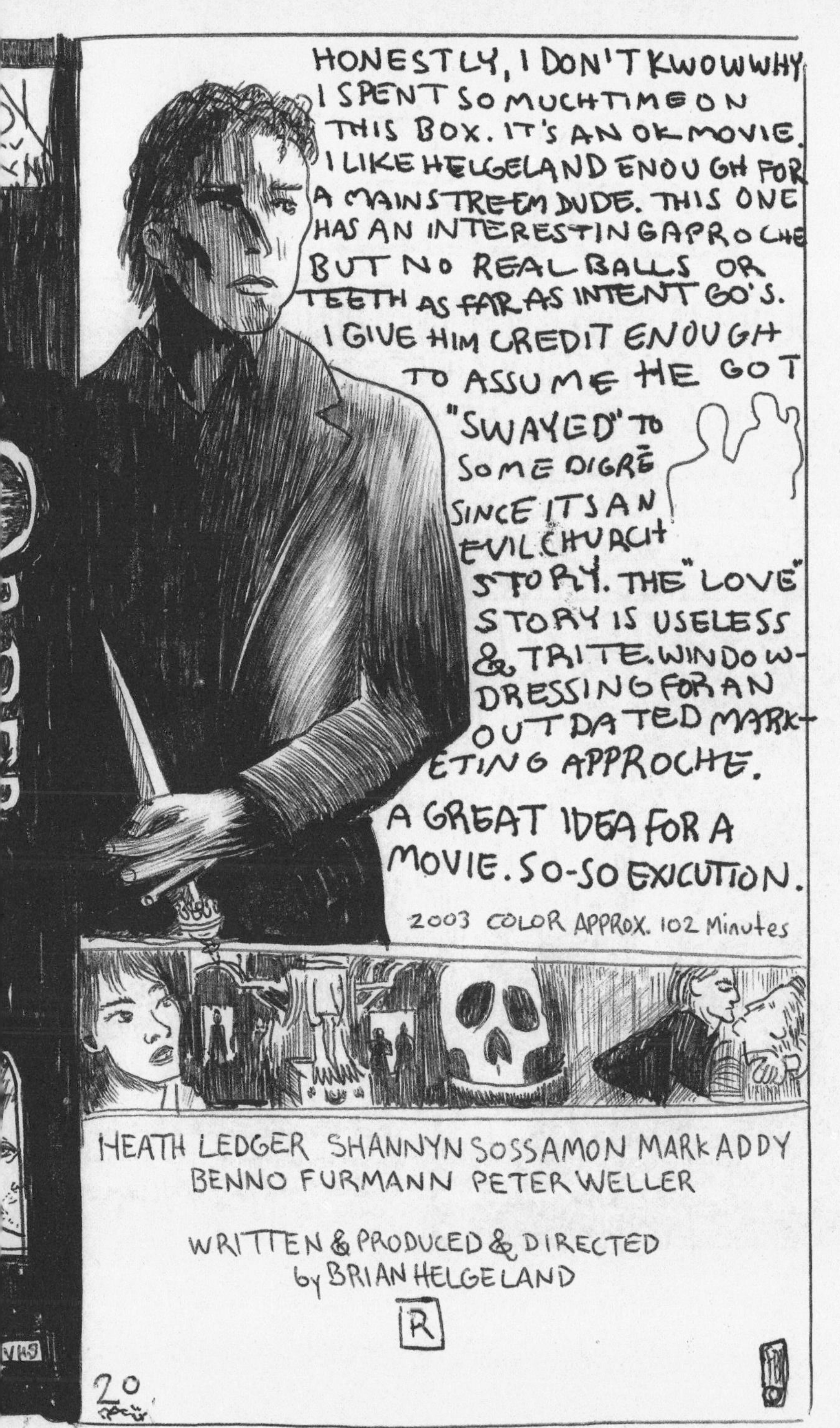
HONESTLY, I DON'T KWOW WHY I SPENT SO MUCH TIME ON THIS BOX. IT'S AN OK MOVIE. I LIKE HELGELAND ENOUGH FOR A MAINSTREEM DUDE. THIS ONE HAS AN INTERESTING APROCHE BUT NO REAL BALLS OR TEETH AS FAR AS INTENT GO'S. I GIVE HIM CREDIT ENOUGH TO ASSUME HE GOT "SWAYED" TO SOME DIGRĒ SINCE ITS AN EVIL CHURCH STORY. THE "LOVE" STORY IS USELESS & TRITE. WINDOW-DRESSING FOR AN OUTDATED MARKETING APPROCHE.
A GREAT IDEA FOR A MOVIE. SO-SO EXICUTION.
2003 COLOR APPROX. 102 Minutes
HEATH LEDGER SHANNYN SOSSAMON MARK ADDY
BENNO FURMANN PETER WELLER
WRITTEN & PRODUCED & DIRECTED
by BRIAN HELGELAND
R
VHS
20

ORDET

HEAVY, BEAUTIFUL, HEAVY. THIS MOVIE COULD SERIOUSLY MESS YOU UP. I DIG IT. FULLY SHREEEED'D'ED ME. BELIEVE. NO ONE MAKES MOVIES LIKE THIS THESE DAYS. TOO BAD. SO THERES THIS FAMILY IN A HOUSE, & ONE SON SAYS HE IS JESUS. ANOTHER WANTS TO MERRY A GIRL WHO'S FAMILY HE'S FORBIDEN TO KNOW. & THE OTHER SON HAS A VERY PREGNENT WIFE WHO IS THE ONLY PERSON WHO DOSE ANY WERK AT ALL.

SPECIAL FEATURES

- IT WILL HAUNT YOU FOR WEEKS. <GOOD VALUE>
- NO UGLY COLORS.
- SUBTITLES
- MAY CURE IGNORENCE <NO PROMISES>

1955 - 125 Minutes - BLACK AND WHITE - Monaural - In Danish with optional English Subtitles - 1.33:1 aspect ratio

THE CRITERION COLLECTION
CARL TH. DREYER'S
ORDET

FRED WILLIAMSON JIM BROWN PAM GRIER
GANGSTAS

IF YOU REMEMBER THE 1970's

ORGINAL GANGSTAS

OF CINIMA AMERICANA THEN THIS IS A SWEET DEAL, BECAUSE WE GET SO MANY OF THE ICONS & COHEN DIRECTS TOO. ITS A FAIRLY CLEAR & EASY SET UP. THINGS HAVE GOTTEN TOO FAR OUT OF HAND IN THE NEIGHBORHOOD & ITS UP TO THE OLD CREW TO COME HOME & CLEAN OUT THE TRASH. I'M A SUCKER FOR ALL ~~THE ELDERS~~PLOITATION TYPE MOVIES. THEY'RE NOT FULLY OLD YET BUT ITS GOT THAT HEY OLD TIMER YER WASHED UP" "OH YEAH KID WELL IM STILL GOING TO KICK YOUR ASS. FEEL GOOD OLD TIMEY MANNERS VIOLENCE. IT DOSENT COME OFF TOO SMOOTH, KINDA MORE GRINDER THAN THAN ONE MIGHT THINK OF FOR A 1996 MOVIE, SO THAT ELEMENT CARRYS OVER WELL TOO. ITS A CORRECT COMBO. FUN.

FRED WILLIAMSON JIM BROWN PAM GRIER PAUL WINFIELD ISABEL SANFORD RON O'NEAL RICHARD ROUNDTREE

WRITTEN BY AUBREY RATTAN
DIRECTED BY LARRY COHEN

R 99 minutes 1996 COLOR HIFI STEREO

SORT'A {OF} A HOW TO START A VIGELANTE SQUADREN
I LIKE THE CAST AND THE IDEA, AND THE DIRECTING SEEMS COMPITENT BUT THIS DIDENT SEAL THE DEAL FOR ME. MAYBE IT'S TRY'N TO BE TOO EPIC. KIND'A LIKE A SCORSSASI FLOP. "EXTREM" BRITISH STYLE MOVIES CAN GO A LITTLE PORNO BROMANCE ON VIOLENCE BUT COME UP SORT'A CHECKLIST VAPID. THERES AN EXCELENT MOVIE IN THIS MOVIE IT JUST NEEDS 15-20 MINUTES TO GO AWAY. IT COULD BE DRY'R, SMOOTHE, ARTY'R. THE [illegible] ARE TIRED & [illegible] FOR ME.

SEAN BEAN DANNY DYER RUPERT FRIEND
SEAN HARRIS LENNIE JAMES BOB HOSKINS

WRITTEN & DIRECTED BY NICK LOVE

| R | RESTRICTED | APPROX 100 MIN | 2007 COLOR |

SEAN BEAN DANNY DYER BOB HOSKINS
A NICK LOVE
OUT LAW

VINTAGE CLASSICS

KIRK DOUGLAS

PATHS OF GLORY

THIS MOVIE IS TOO WORLDLY & EXPANCIVE FOR THE TEENAGE'D MIND I WAS DEAL'N WITH WHEN I FIRST SAW THIS. I DON'T KNOW WHAT I WAS EXPECTING THEN BUT THIS WAS NOT IT. THANKFULLY I GOT A FEW MORE BRAINS SINCE THEN. THIS MOVIE IS GREAT. "DUH" YOU SAY 'CAUSE IT'S KUBRICK. BUT HE'S NOT SO SPOONFEED'N HERE SO FOLKS SEEM TO SKIP ON IT. I CAN SAY I'D LIKE MORE TIMOTHY CARREY CUZ I DO, BUT THATS NOT A COMPLAINT. I THINK I NEED'D TO GO THROUGH MORE BEATINGS FROM THE WORLD TO GET WHAT WAS GO'N ON. NOW DAYS I'M INTO IT BUT IT'S NOT A REAL POSITIVE STORY SO I NEED TO HAVE THE RIGHT MOOD OR MINDSTATE TO PUT IT ON. SORRY IF THIS IS'NT MUCH HELP AS A REVIEW BUT WHO WANTS TO GAZE INTO KUBRICKS NAVEL EVEN MORE THEN WHAT HAS ALLREADY BEEN GAZED. LOOK... JIM THOMPSON CO-WROTE THIS. WHAT SHOULD I SAY? "IT'S GOOD". WHO CARES? CHECK IT OUT IF YOU DIG ANYONE INVOLVED IN THIS. OR NOT.

KIRK DOUGLAS, RALPH MEEKER, ADOLPHE MENJOU
GEORGE MACREADY WAYNE MORRIS RICHARD ANDERSON
TIMOTHY CARREY

SCREENPLAY BY
STANLEY KUBRICK, CALDER WILLINGHAM & JIM THOMPSON
DIRECTED BY STANLEY KUBRICK

1957 APPROXIMATE FEATURE RUNNING TIME: 1 HOUR 27 MINUTES
BLACK & WHITE
NOT RATED

UNITED ARTISTS

WOULD GIVE CARRIE A RON FOR HERMONEY

-SOME DUDE, TV

A CHILL CREEPER. VERY DOPE. DUDE IS PSYCHOKILLER VIA PSYCHIC COMA. HE CAN TYPE, COMMAND HAND JOBS, OPPERATE ELEVATERS; ALL FROM BED.

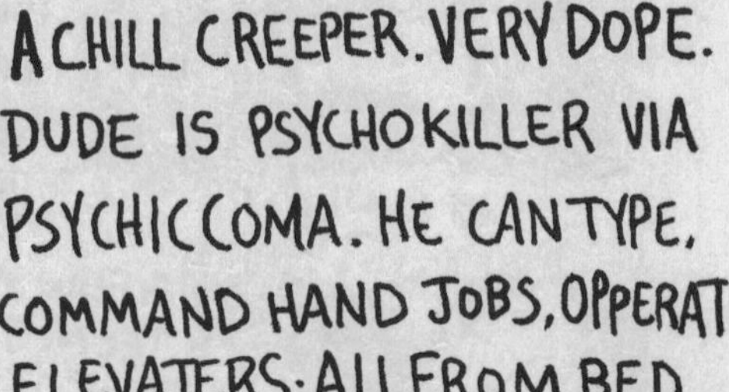

LIVES UP TO IT'S REPUTATION GRIPPING, BRILLINTLY PLAYED

HE'S ALSO A GRUMPY, SELFISH COCKBLOCKER. DAMN, DUDE BEATS MOST MOVIE KILLERS WITH IN AN INCH OF THEIR "LIFES". I THINK THIS IS AUSTRAILIAN. STRONG, STYLISH DIRECTION. NOT SO MUCH A MESSAGE MOVIE, MORE OF A INVALID POWER FANTASY. TOO COOL. IF YOU ARE A PARANOID NURSE, THIS MIGHT FUCK YOU UP.

SUSAN PENHALIGON ROBERT HELPMAN ROD MULLINAR
BRUCE BARRY JULIA BLAKE HELEN HEMINGWAY ROBERT THOMPSON

SCREENPLAY EVERETT DE ROCHE
DIRECTOR RICHARD FRANKLIN

1978 RATED PG COLOR RUNNING TIME APPROX 112 min

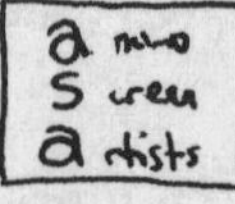

A RICHARD FRANKLIN FILM
PATRICK

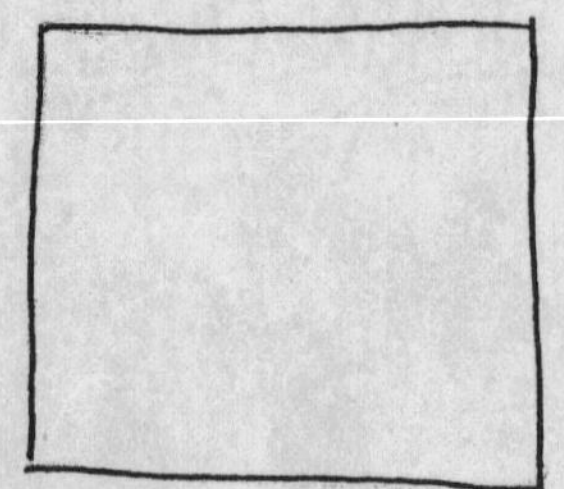

VERY SHORT AND STILL I SAY... WAY TOO LONG. I PUT THIS ON WHILE FOLKS WERE ON A FOOD RUN. THE FEW WHO STAY'D SAW THE BOX AND COLLECTIVELY DESCRIBED WHAT IT WOULD BE LIKE. AND THEN WE WATCHED IT. WE HAD'NT MISSED ANY BAD JOKE, LAME SET UP, TOOTLESS TWIST, THAT CAME ON. WE HAD EVEN BOTHERED TO FOLLOW THROUGH ON IT ALL WITH MORE DEVELOPMENTS NOT USED SAD. IF IT WERE HALF AS LONG IT WOULD BE A BAD S.N.L. SKIT.

STARRING

DAMON JONES BOB KIRSH JANE LEYDEN

WRITTEN BY

DAMON JONES BOB KIRSH and PATTI FRICK

DIRECTED BY

CHARLIE CALL

COLOR

Full Screen

Approx. 9 min.

See what happens when a woman has it her way

RUDY RAY MOORE is

PETEYWHEATSTRAW

THE DEVILS Son IN LAW

RUDY RAY MOORE IS

PETEY WHEATSTRAW

The Devil's Son In Law

ONE OF MY ALL TIME PERSONAL FAVORITES. SO MANY OTHER MOVIES JUST DON'T BRING ANYTHING THIS POWERFULL OR COOL. AN UNRELENTING FOLK HERO. PETEY IS BORN AND PROMPTLY SMACKS THE DOCTOR. PETEY GETS PICKED ON, THEN HE MEETS HIS "MARTIAL ARTS" MASTER, FROM HERE ON OUT PETEY STOMPS ASS. HE BECOMES A HIGHLY SUCESSFULL COMEDIEN, HIS RIVALS CAN NOT CONTROLL HIM SO THEY KILL HIM. PETEYS CHARISMA IS SO BOSS THAT THE DEVIL WANTS HIM TO BE HIS DAUGHTERS OLD-MAN IN EXCHANGE FOR A RETURN TO EARTH FOR VENGENCE. NOW PETEYS STOMPING ASS WITH THE DEVILS MAGIC CANE. THIS MOVIE NEVER GETS OLD FOR ME. RUDY MAKES FULL USE OF HIS HOUSE BRAND SHIT-FU. AND THE SOUNDTRACK JUST WON'T QUITE. I COULD, HAVE, AND WILL AGAIN WATCH THIS MOVIE TWICE IN A ROW.

93 MIN./COLOR RATED **R** HI-FI 1979

RUDY RAY MOORE
LEROY & SKILLET
WILDMAN STEVE

JIMMY LYNCH
EBONY WRYTE
G. TITO SHAW

WRITER * DIRECTOR CLIFF ROQUEMORE

DISTRIBUTED EXCLUSIVELY BY
XENON ENTERTAINMENT GROUP
1440 9th Street
Santa Monica CA 90401

RUDY RAY MOORE IS

DON COSCARELLI IS SO, PERFECT. WHAT CAN I SAY? HE FITS SOME PLACE IN THE MIDST OF O'BANNON ARGENTO & LYNCH. BEAUTIFUL DREAMY FILMS WITH A MACHO GEEK SENCABILITY. I WACHED THIS AT MY BRO'Z & HE'S GOT IT IN A SET THAT IS IN THE BALL I THINK IT'S FROM ENGLAND.

I LOVE THIS MOVIE SOOO HARD. WISH THEY'D GOT'N THE DUDE FROM #One TO BE MIKE, BUT I DIG LEGROS SO IT'S NOT A PROBLEM. THEY WELD 2 DOUBLE BARREL SHOTGUNS TOGETHER.

THIS IS AN ART MOVIE AT FILMS HIGHIST STANDARD.

1988 COLOR R 1 Hour 37 minutes

ANGUS SCRIMM REGGIE BANNISTER

JAMES LE GROS PAULA IRVINE KENNETH TIGAR

WRITTEN & DIRECTED BY DON COSCARELLI

PHANTASM II

THE BALL IS BACK!

FOR TEN YEARS
THE SECRET OF
PERIGORD CEMETERY
HAS REMAINED A
MYSTERY. NOW THE
ULTIMATE EVIL IS
ABOUT TO BE
REVEALED

PHOBOERTCIA

RATED "X"

VIDEO ZINE, GOOD, ARTY, 2 ORIGINAL PIECES 3 LOST GEMS. I HOPE THERE'S MORE TO COME.

- BUMP & GRIND: 90'S FILM AGEING - VIDEO COLAGING - 70'S AVANT-GARDE STYLE ABOUT A DUDE GO'N TO A TRIPPY PORNO ARCADE W/A MEAN/FUNNY END.
- SLEAZE TOUR: A DRIVE BY VIDEO TOUR OF PORTLAND & B.C. ADULT SPOTS W/A VISIT TO A VERY IMPRESSIVLY ORGANIZED & DISPLAYED PONOGRAPHY COLLECTION.
- HOT VIEWS FROM THE HOMEFRONT: 1940'S STAG. LOT'S OF ORAL.
- 70'S PORNO ACTRESS INTERVIEW: TYPICLE BUT LOOKS GREAT. IT'S ALL RED, ORANGE, & PINK. VERY COOL.
- FREAK OUT DIGEST: RANDOM SEQUENCES FROM AN UNFINISHED ADULT FILM. PROBABLY BETTER THEN MANY COMPLETE ADULT FILMS.

RAD, I DIG IT. IAN SUNDAHL PUT THIS ALL TOGETHER. HE'S A RAD ARTIST AND THIS IS JUST A SAMPLE OF HIS DOPE'NESS.

PHOBOEROTICA

Phobos Films

POSITIVELY THE 5 MOST EROTIC FILMS EVER MADE!

EMBASSY HOME ENTERTAINMENT
The Pit

DOWN IN THE PIT THERES SOMETHING ALIVE
HALF-HUMAN, HALF MONSTER, HALF CRAZED
PRAY TO GOD IT ONLY KILLS YOU

THERE IS A PIT W/ HUNGRY KILLER THINGS BUT THATS NOT THE SCARY PART. THE KID IS AMAZING, A SYMPATHETIC PORTRAITE OF A PSYCHOPATIC CHILD, WHO IS SHIT ON BY MOSTEVERYONE. CREEPY. AMAZING. HE CUSTOMIZES HIS OWN PORN COLLAGING HIS TEACHERS HEAD ONTO NUDES FROM LIBRARY ART BOOKS. EXTORTS STRIPPING IN A WINDOW BY TAPE RECORDING ON PHONE. BUT HE'S TRYING TO BE NICE. HE ONLY COXES TOTAL ASSHOLES TO THE PIT. IT TIPS IT'S HAND TO A LOT OF THOUGHTFUL POTENTIALS BUT STAYS ON COURSE. SMART, SIMPLE, TABOO. THIS WOULD SEEM MORE PG-13 BUT THE CREEPY KEEPS IT R MAYBE.

SAMMY SNYDERS JEANNIE ELIAS

SCREENPLAY BY IAN A. STUART

DIRECTED BY LEW LEHMAN

96 MINUTES COLOR ©1981 R

WINNER!
Science Fiction Film Award
ON A DISTANT PLANET...
FAR INTO THE FUTURE...
THE HUNGRIEST JAWS BELONG TO
DINOSAURS!
PLANET OF THE DINOSAURS
21
SCI-FI

ACTIVE H

I LOVE IT!

STEGOSAURIS DUDE! WELL A LITTLE BIT.

IF YOU DIG DINOSAUR'S MOVIES THIS IS A MUST.

PLANET 'O' tha APES STYLE OPEN'R. KILL THA BIMBO. STEGVHSORIZ.

IT SEEM'S ORT'A FOREIGN. I WATCHED IT, LIKE FIVE TIMÈZ.

PRODUCED & DIRECTED by James K. Shea, SPECIAL FX STEPHEN CZERKI

STARRING JAMES WHITWORTH, PAMELA BOTTARO, HARVEY SHAIN

COLOR/85 minutes Science Fiction #A501

MGM/UA HOMEVIDEO
POLTERGEIST
THEYR HERE

THE SPIELBERG SCREENPLAY CREDIT KEPT ME AWAY FROM THIS FOR A LONG TIME. MY MISTAKE. I SHOULD HAVE KNOWN HOOPER WOULD MAKE A GREAT MOVIE OUT OF WHATEVER HE HAD TO DEAL WITH. BUT THIS DOSE SEEM TO BE THE BEGINING OF THE POISONING OF HOOPER. THERES SO MUCH GOOD STUFF IN HERE. I'V SEEN POLTERGEIST SPOOF'D SO MANY TIMES {MAD MAGAZINE SYNDROME} THAT THERE WERE'NT ANY BIG SHOCKERS BUT HOOPER PLAYS IT SO WELL THAT I DID'NT EXPECT'M COMMING. SO TRIPPY & PARANOID W/A TASTY BURN WHICH IS MOSTLY SPIELBERG IT WOULD SEEM. HOOPER HAS A SMOOTH CLASSY'NESS THAT TAKES THE CONARTIST SETUP & TONE OFF OF THE SCRIPT. IT'S TRUELY UNIQUELY AMERICAN IN A WAY THATS INTROSPECTIVE. GREAT MOVIE.

JOBETH WILLIAMS CRAIG T. NELSON BEATRICE STRAIGHT
STORY & SCREENPLAY by STEVEN SPIELBERG
DIRECTED BY TOBE HOOPER
COLOR [PG] 1982
APPROXIMATE SCREENING TIME: 1 hour 55 minutes

JOHN CARPENTERS
PRINCE OF DARKNESS
MCA
HOME VIDEO
STEREO

PRINCE OF DARKNESS

GOBOB 1 HR 42 MINS R

ONE OF CARPENTERS BEST IF NOT THE BEST. OFTEN BLOWN OFF BECAUSE FOLKS ARE TOO OFTEN FOOLISH. WHAT A BEAUTIFUL UN-NERVING PIECE OF ART THIS IS. NIGEL KNEAL WORSHIP TO THE MAX. IT'S SO HYPNOTIC, I COULD <AND HAVE> WATCH IT ON BACK TO BACK REPEAT. PURE UNRELENTING EVIL IS REAL. & A GOOD AND LOVING GOD IS A FAIRYTALE MENT TO COMPFORT THE WEAK FOOLS OF THIS WORLD. NICE BLOWOFF DUDE. ALICE COOPER IS A BUG BUM. YESSSSSS. IF YOU DON'T DIG THIS MOVIE YOU MAY NOT WANT TO TRUST MY TASTE IN MOVIES OR WHATEVER.

DONALD PLEASENCE LISA BLOUNT VICTOR WONG
JAMESON PARKER & ALICE COOPER

SCREENPLAY BY
MARTIN QUATERMASS
DIRECTED BY
JOHN CARPENTER

MCA HOME VIDEO

1987

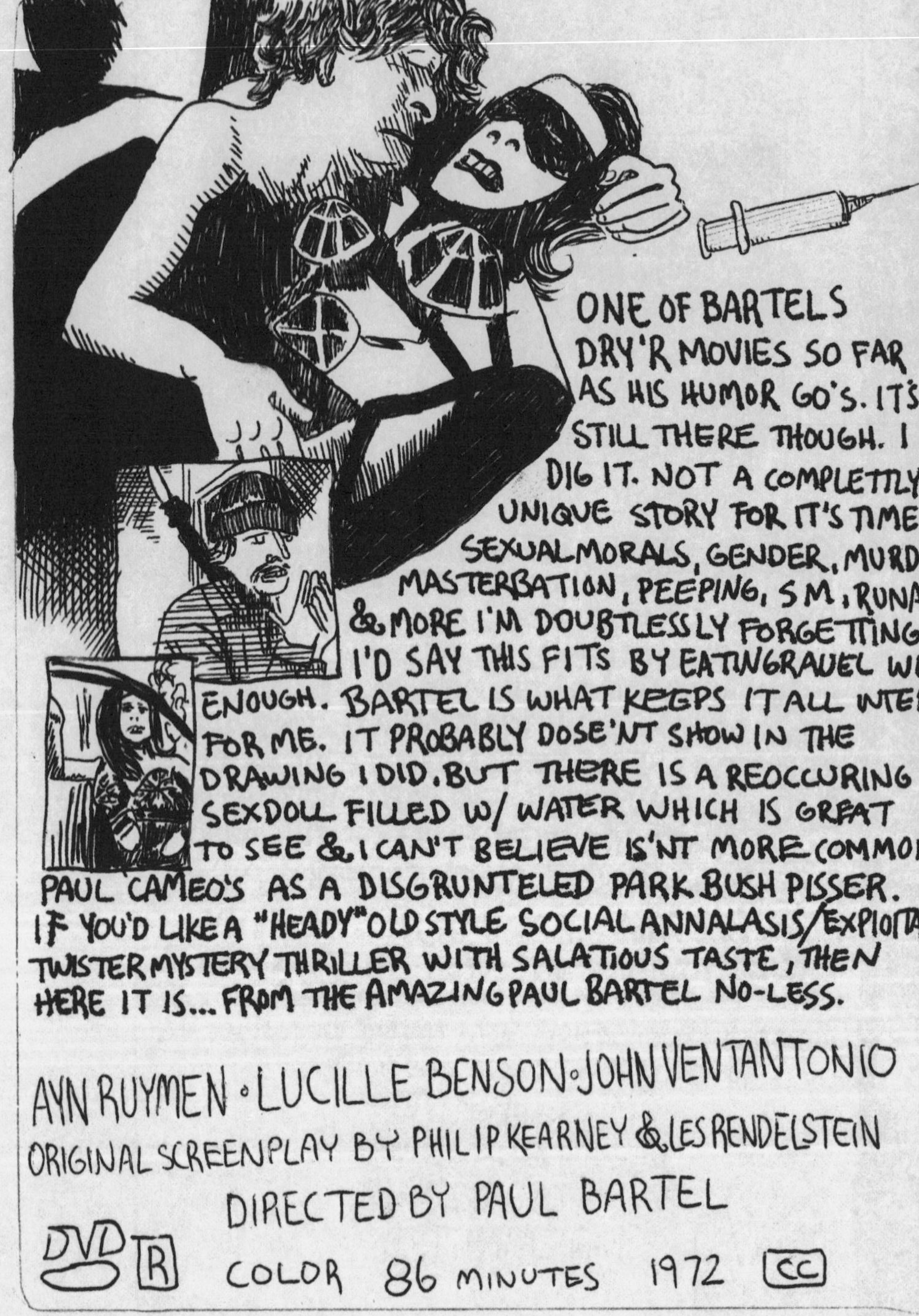
ONE OF BARTELS
DRY'R MOVIES SO FAR
AS HIS HUMOR GO'S. IT'S
STILL THERE THOUGH. I
DIG IT. NOT A COMPLETTLY
UNIQUE STORY FOR IT'S TIME.
SEXUAL MORALS, GENDER, MURDE
MASTERBATION, PEEPING, S M, RUNA
& MORE I'M DOUBTLESSLY FORGETTING.
I'D SAY THIS FITS BY EATING GRAVEL WE
ENOUGH. BARTEL IS WHAT KEEPS IT ALL INTE
FOR ME. IT PROBABLY DOSE'NT SHOW IN THE
DRAWING I DID. BUT THERE IS A REOCCURING
SEXDOLL FILLED W/ WATER WHICH IS GREAT
TO SEE & I CAN'T BELIEVE IS'NT MORE COMMON
PAUL CAMEO'S AS A DISGRUNTELED PARK BUSH PISSER.
IF YOU'D LIKE A "HEADY" OLD STYLE SOCIAL ANNALASIS/EXPLOITA
TWISTER MYSTERY THRILLER WITH SALATIOUS TASTE, THEN
HERE IT IS... FROM THE AMAZING PAUL BARTEL NO-LESS.
AYN RUYMEN • LUCILLE BENSON • JOHN VENTANTONIO
ORIGINAL SCREENPLAY BY PHILIP KEARNEY & LES RENDELSTEIN
DIRECTED BY PAUL BARTEL
DVD R COLOR 86 MINUTES 1972 CC

PRIVATE PARTS

Cheryl is a lovely girl...

But to George, she's a living doll.

PSYCHO
FROM
TEXAS

IF YOU DIG THE COEN BROTHERS I THINK YOU OUGHT'A SEE THIS

SO THIS IS THE SECOND HALF OF THE HICKSPLOITATION TOUR <DOUBLEFEATURE> PREVIEWS: ① SHADOW OF THE HAWK <looks dope> ② DEATH HUNT ③ GROUP MARAGE. NONE OF WHICH I'V SEEN. SOOOO... PSYCHO FROM **TEXA$**. DUDES! I'D LOVE TO SEE IT A FEW MORE TIMES. I WAS DIG'N THE MOVIE, BUT AFTER MY BRAIN SAID "that also happens in ___ COEN BROTHERS MOVIE" A FEW TIMES, I STARTED TRIP'N OUT ON HOW MUCH "IT SEEM'D" LIKE ONE OF THEY'RS. USUALY SOMETHING LIKE THIS COULD RUIN ONE OR BOTH OF THEM BUT. NOT SO IN THIS CASE. THIS DUDE CRUISES AROUND KILL'N, TERRORIZING, HARASS'N, JOKE'N; SOMETIMES IT'S CREEPY, FUNNY, MEAN, BOARING, SHOCKING. IT JUST KEEPS MOVING. THE SORT WHERE YOU DAMN YOURSELF EVERY SECOND YOUR IN THE TOILET <GOLD GLOREY OR GOLD NUGGETS>. ANYWAY. THIS IS A LOT TRASH'YR, RUDE, CRUDE, AND ABRUPT THEN SOME WOULD EXPECT FROM THIS COMPARISON. BUT STILL, GET WITH IT. THIS MOVIE IS HIGHLY WATCHABLE. TRUST. JOHN KING III IS VERY RAD SO MUCH CHARISMA. HE FONDELS THE SCIENERY.

JOHN KING III HERSCHEL MAYS

CANDY DEE JANEL KING

DIRECTED & PRODUCED BY JIM FEAZELL

DOLPH LUNDGREN
LOUIS GOSSETT, JR.
THE PUNISHER
JUDGE. JURY. EXECUTIONER. ALL IN A DAY'S WORK.

DOLPH IS POETRY IN MOUTION, YES.
LIKE A BEAUTIFUL STATUE
COME TO LIFE WITH A
PERMINENT 5 O'CLOCK
SHADOW.

I USED TO BE DOWN ON THIS MOVIE.
I WAS TRIP'N. THIS MOVIE IS VERY RAD. YES, I KNOW; HE'S NOT GOT THE SHIRT. THE PUNISHER SKULL KNIVES ARE AWESOME. LOU GOSSETT, JR HOLDS THE MOVIE TOGETHER WELL. HE'S TOUGH & DEVOTED TO FINDING HIS OLD PARTNER FRANK CASTLE. THERES A SEWER DWELLING DRUNK STAGE ACTOR WHO SPEAKS IN VERSE & INFORMS THE PUNISHER. RIDING HIS MOTORCYCLE THROUGH THE CITYS SEWERS KILLING MAFIA DUDES, BAIRLY TALKING; THATS A GOOD PUNISHER TO ME. SOLID, CLEAN DIRECTING. THE PUNISHER STORY NOT AN UNCOMMON ONE FOR AN ACTION MOVIE, EXPECIALL IN THE 1980'S; BUT WHERE SO MENY OF THOSE MOVIES MESS AROUND WITH TRY'N TO BUILD A SIMPATHETIC HERO, PUNISHER IS FULL TILT WITH SHORT EXPLINATIONS AND UNREPENTENT 'Z. A TRUE ULTRAVIOLENT ART FILM. A GREAT SOLID REVENGE TRIP.

DOLPH LUNDGREN LOUIS GOSSETT, JR JEROEN KRABBE KIM MIYORI

WRITTEN BY BOAZ YAKIN 92 minutes

DIRECTED BY MARK GOLDBLATT 1989 R

NEW WORLD INTERNATIONAL LIVE HOMEVIDEO

JANE IS A COOL LOOK'N TOUGH GUY BUT SOME HOW LACKS THAT PUNISHER QUALITY. I BELIEVE THERES TOO MENY DIFERENT EMOTIONS ON DISPLAY. PUNISHER IS'NT EXACTLY A ONE NOTE CHARACTER BUT HE DOSE HAVE A SINGULAR TONE ABOUT HIM.

FIRST THING FIRST. WHATS UP WITH THE COVER? IS THAT A PUNISHER KEYCHAIN/BOTTLE OPEN'R? THIS IS'NT SO MUCH LIKE THE OTHER PUNISHER MOVIES. IN THIS ONE HE'S DRUNK A LOT OF THE TIME AFTER HIS FAMILY DIES, WHICH; TAKES A LONG TIME. THIS'S THE ONE FOR FOLKS WHO DON'T READ THE COMICS. EPIC TIME SPENT ON THE ORIGIN, KIND OF A CHECKLIST STYLE STORY IN BOGDONIVICH'ESQ MANNER. EVERYTHING IS TIED TOGETHER. SORT'A TOO TOM CLANCY FOR ME. PARTS OF THE STORY & MOST OF THE CHARACTERS FROM THE SECOND HALF OF THE MOVIE ARE FROM THE ENNIS RUN ON THE COMIC. I GET THE FEELING THE "FILMMAKER" HAS A SET OF BOOK SHELVES WITH EXPENCIVE HARD COVER BOOKS ABOUT "ALL THE GREAT/IMPORTANT DIRECTORS" BUT HAS NO PERSONAL ARTISTIC VISION. THE VISUALS ARE AFFECTED OR LIFTED FROM OTHERS MATERIAL. THERE'S NO DAP OR SENCE OF HUMOR. THE CAST IS ACTUALLY PRETTY GOOD. HENSLEIGH IS ACTUALLY PRETTY SUCESSFUL AT KEEP'N TRAVOLTA ON AN EVEN KEIL WITH THE OTHER ACT'ORS TONE. THIS IS THE LEAST PUNISHER'ISH MOVIE TO ME MOSTLY BECAUSE HE'S ACTUALLY PRETTY JUSTIFIED IN HIS ACTIONS. HE ONLY KILLS THE PEOPLE RESPONCIBEL FOR HIS FAMILYS DEATHS. NO WAR ON CRIME. IF THIS HAD NO SHIRT & A DIFFERENT TITLE IT WOULD BE A STANDARD FARE ACTION MOVIE. O.K.'ISH

THOMAS JANE · JOHN TRAVOLTA · WILL PATTON · ROY SCHEIDER · LAURA HARRING
BEN FOSTER · SAMANTHA MATHIS · REBECCA ROMUN STAMOS
SCREENPLAY JONAYHAN HENSLEIGH & MICHAEL FRANCE
DIRECTED BY JONAYHAN HENSLEIGH

R 2004 COLOR 141 Minutes  

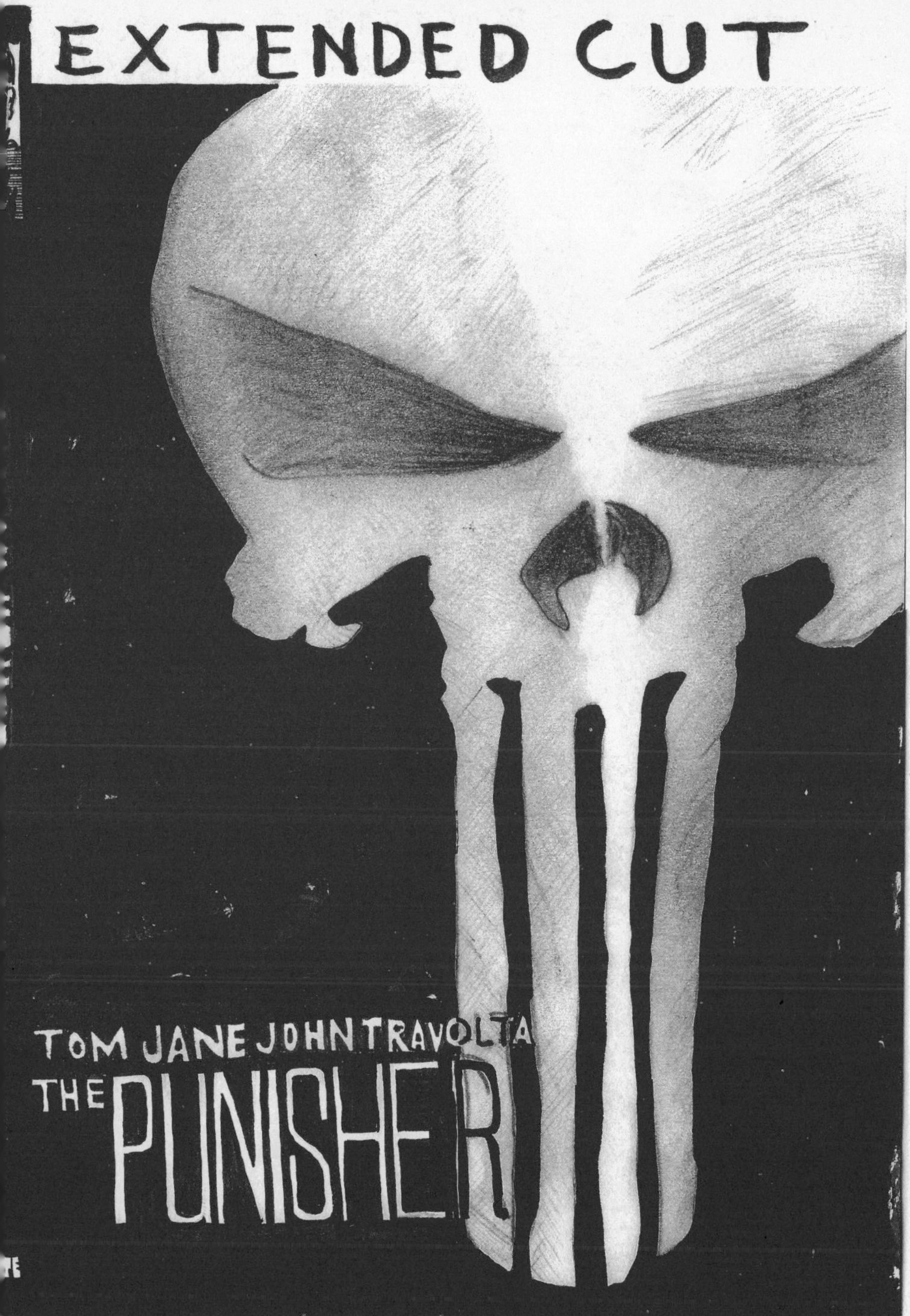

EXTENDED CUT

TOM JANE JOHN TRAVOLTA

THE PUNISHER

STEVENSON IS THE MOST PERFECT PUNISHER. SPOT ON. DRY, BRUTAL, DRIVEN, BENT, HARD AS FUCK. THE ORIGIN IS LAY'D OUT IN QUICK FLASHBACKS, COOL. GOOD MOVIE. IT'S NOT WITHOUT PROBLEMS, BUT VERY RAD. HELLZ' OF RIP'N VIOLENCE, HELLLLLZ'UH. THERE'S A SUBPLOT WITH A WIDOW & ORPHAN THAT'S HO-HUM MICRO IS IN THIS ONE. THERE'R 3 VERY GOOFY SCEANS IN THIS, THE 2nd & 3rd ARE FUNNY; THE FIRST ONE COULD WERK BETTER BUT HAPPENS SO EARLY IT'S MORE OF A STATEMENT OF INTENT. AS FUNNY AS IT SOUNDS THERES OBVIOUSLY A GOOD 5-10 MINUTE GUN BATTLE MISSING. BUT I'M NOT REALLY COMPLAINING. I DIG THIS MOVIE A LOT. BRUTAL FULL ON URBAN COMBAT, WAR ON CRIME. GOOD DIRECTION. NICE COLOR CHOICES. SOLID GORE, VERY CRUNCHED NOSES, NECK BREAK'Y. BEST PUNISHER MOVIE YET. MORE FROM THIS TEAM PLEASE. COOL.
AWESOME OVER THE TOP VILLENS, VERY SERIAL/PULP STYLE. FUNNY, VIOLENT, WELL PLAY'D. LOT'S OF PUNISH'N LOT'S
RAY STEVENSON DOMINIC WEST JULIE BENZ
COLIN SALMON DOUG HUTCHISON DASH MIHOK WAYNE KNIGHT
WRITTEN BY
NICK SANTORA & ART MARCUM & MATT HOLLOWAY
DIRECTED BY
LEXI ALEXANDER
R
CC
MARVEL KNIGHTS
2008 COLOR 103 MINUTES DVD

WIDESCREEN & FULL SCREEN EDITION
WAR ZONE
PUNISHER
VENGEANCE HAS A NAME

MOVIE CHARACTER, BASED ON A COMIC BOOK CHARACTER; BASED ON A MOVIE CLICHE. PUNISHER '89 HAS A SEQUENCE WHICH FEELS LIKE AN OLD FRANK MILLER DAREDEVIL, WHICH COMES OFF PRETTY WELL. PUNISHER '04 HAS A COUPLE SHOTS THAT LOOK JOE QUESADA'ISH, THEN A WHOLE LOCATION & SEQUENCE FROM THE ENNIS/DILLON BOOK; BUT MANAGES TO COME OFF LAME & UN-FUNNY IN THE EXTENDED CUT THERE IS AN BRADSTREET BASED OPENING SEQUENCE IN "COMIC BOOKY" "ANIMATION" "FUMETI" STYLE, WEAK. PUNISHER '08 STREIGHT UP HAS BRADSTREETS NAME ON THE COVER, WHICH IS FROM THE FINAL SHOWDOWN LOCATION; BUT IT'S O.K. I THINK IT'S GOT MORE CHARACTERS FROM THE BOOK THAN PUN. 89 & PUN. 04 PUT TOGETHER. ALL 3 HAVE REFRENCES TO A LOST FAITH IN GOD. IN PUN'89 IS THE FRAIMING SEQUENCES WHERE HE ASKS GOD WHAT TO DO BUT GETS NO ANSWER SO HE STAYS ON HIS PATH. IN PUN'04 THE DUDE WHO SAVES HIS LIFE AFTE THE FAMILY SLAUGHTER SAYS "GOD GO W/ YOU" & CASTLE SAYS "GODS GONNA SIT THIS ONE OUT." & IN PUN'08 AT THE END HE SAVES HIS POLICE INFORMENTS LIFE AS A JESUS SAVES LITESIGN BURNS OUT OVER HIS SHOLDER. PUN'89 IS THE MOST SOLID SINGULAR MOVIE IN THAT IT REQUIRES NO WORLD OUTSIDE IT'S OWN. IT'S SUPER SOLID, NOT PERFECT BUT CONTAINS NO TRUE FLAWS. PUN'04 IS LONG & VAPID WITH LITTLE TRUE PUNISHER'NESS MADE WITH MORE AMBITION THAN INTENT. I'M GLAD THAT THIS TEAM DIDN'T MAKE ANOTHER TOOTHLESS INSTALMENT. PUN'08 IS MY PERSONAL FAVORITE, & IT'S GOT THE MOST PUNISHER'ISH BEHAVIOR & BODY COUNT IT'S GOT TOO MUCH STOREY FOR A MOVIE WITH HALF A PLOT. I HEAR'D THAT STAN LEE SUGUESTED THEY DROP THE SKULL SHIRT IN PUN'89. I'D BELIEVE IT. WHEN PUN'08 GOT GOING JOHN DAHL WAS INVOLVED FOR A MOMENT, DAMN! I WOULD LOVE TO SEE HIS VERSION. THAT DUDE RULES SO HARD. I'V NOTICED THAT THE SKULL LOGO USED ON THE MENU SCREEN FOR PUN'08 IS THE SAME AS THE BOTTLEOPEN'R LOGO ON PUN'04 I GET THE IMPRESION THAT THE TWO ARE NOT BEING CONSIDERED AS A SERIES, BUT THAT PUN'08 HAD TO DEAL WITH THE AFTERMATH OF PUN'04 TRY'N TO GO SEQUAL & NOT GETTING IT TOGETHER.

VIDEO TONFA

THE PUNISHER

$ 1.00

THE FRANK CASTLE FILM COLLECTION

HAMMER FILM

Quatermass 2 Commentery

I DID'NT FULLY WATCH THIS, THIS TIME BECAUSE I WAS PEEP'N OUT THE COMMENTERY WITH NIGEL KNEAL & VAL GUEST. FIRST THING FIRST. THE MOVIE IS RAD. SERIOUSLY AWESOME. BUT THE COMMENTERY IS THE THING HERE. NIGEL KNEAL WROTE ALL THE ORIGINAL QUATERMASS T.V. SHOWS WHICH WERE LATER MADE INTO MOVIES BY HAMMER. IT'S ALL GOOD. VAL GUEST IS COOL. HE MAKES SOME GREAT MOVIES, & THIS IS ONE OF THEM. BUT KNEAL & GUEST DON'T REALLY GET ALONG. SO THE COMMENTERY IS OFTEN ABOUT THERE DISAGREEMENT OVER THE CAST & TREATMENT OF THIS CHAPTER OF THE QUATERMASS STORY. ALL BEEF ASIDE THIS IS A SOLID COMMENTERY BRIAN DONLEVY'S DRINKING & HAIRPIECE ARE COMMON TOPICS. YOU CAN ALMOST HEAR THE SQUEEK OF THE CASTING COUCH WHEN GUEST RECALLS WERKING WITH VERA DAY. I STRONGLY RECOMEND THAT ANYONE INTO CLASSIC SCI-FI OR BRITISH T.V. IN GENERAL CHECK OUT THE WHOLE QUATERMASS SERIES. BUT THE COMMENTERY IS PRETTY MUCH JUST FOR THE HARDCORE HEADS.

united artists presents

A

HAMMER FILM

PRODUCTION

DIGITALLY REMASTERED
SYLVESTER STALLONE. RICHARD CRENNA
WRITTEN BY
SYLVESTER STALLONE & SHELDON LETTICH
PRODUCED BY BUZZ FEITSHANS
DIRECTED BY
PETER MACDONALD
READ THE JOVENOVEL BY DAVID MORRELL
CONTAINS RAMBO TRILOGY DOCUMENTARY

DUDE IS BANG'N OUT NEW ROOF TILES ON THE TEMPEL WHEN CRENNA COMES & LAYS A HEAVY TRIP ON DUDE & HE'S LIKE... I BETTER NOT. BUT YOU KNOW. FOOLS RUSH IN. NOW DUDE HAS TO SAVE HIM. THIS ONES COOL BUT NOT ON PAR W/ 1 & 4 BUT NOT LIKE THATS A REASON TO NOT WATCH THIS ONE. STILL ILL. TANK VS. HELL'ACOPTER. IF MEMORY SERVES ME CORRECTLY THIS WAS THE 1st ONE I EVER SAW.

THE KNIFE RAMBO ROCKS HERE IS FULLY MONDO. DUDE IS SO TAN & TONED HERE & HIS HAIR IS LIKE THE OTHER STAR OF THE SHOW. I DO HAVE TO SAY THAT THE BOE STUFF IN THIS ONE IS LESS VISCEREL THAN IT HAS BEEN IN THE PAST. MAYBE THIS ONES SO ACTION PAK'D THAT THE BOE PORTION IS LOST IN THE MEYLEY.

1988 COLOR 102 MIN

1999 100 MINUTES COLOR (R) WIDESCREEN

GUY PEARCE
ROBERT CARLYLE
DAVID ARQUETTE
RAVENOUS

BRIGITTE NIELSEN & ARNOLD SCHWARZENEGGER
SANDAHL BERGMAN PAUL SMITH ERNIE REYES, JR.
RONALD LACEY. MUSIC BY ENNIO MORRICONE
written by CLIVE EXTON & GEORGE MacDONALD FRASER
DIRECTED BY RICHARD FLEISCHER
COLOR
1985 APPROXIMATE RUNNING TIME 1 HOUR 30 minutes PG-13

AS FAR AS BEING FAMILUR W/ANY SOURCE MATERIAL I'V READ AS MENY OF THE FRANK THORNE COMICS AS POSSIBLE. THIS IS AN O.K. MOVIE BUT I GET THE FEELING ITS A CONAN CASH IN... DUH. SHE HAS REAL COOL HAIR. IT'S A JAMES DEAN MULLET SUPREME.

FAIRLY LITE ADV. FAIR. ERNIE REYES JR. IS SUPER YOUNG & THE COMIC RELIEF OR CUTE/FUNNY CHARACTER.

SHEA SAYS "SWORD & SANDAHL BERGMAN!"

BERGMAN IS THE VILLEN HERE WHICH IS AN INTERESTING TWIST OFF THE MILIAS CONAN WHERE SHES THE ASSKICK'N ROMANTIC INTREST PROTAGONIST. HONESTLY, YOU CAN PROBABLY SEE FROM THE POSTER WHERE THIS MOVIE GO'S OFF COURSE. IF IT HAD NO ARNOLD IT WOULD HAVE BEEN... WELL, WAIT. IT'S EVERY MALE CHARACTER THAT RUINS MOST OF IT. SHOULD'A BEEN ALL NIELSEN & BERGMAN. BUT THIS IS A CASH IN SO IT'S GOT KITCHEN SINK SYNDROME & A TOOTHLESS RATE'N. THERES 30 to 40 MINUTES OF COOL GOOD MOVIE HERE.

TURNER

MGM/UA

PG-13

REPTILICUS

"WE CAN'T LICK REPTILICS WITH OUR SMALL ARMS AND FIELD PIECES." DIALOGUE*

* THE DIALOGUE IS FULL OF SUGGESTIVE PHRASING PRETTY FUNNY. IT'S COOL BECAUSE THEY PLAY IN THE "LOW'NESS" OF THEY'R ART. STREIGHT FACE.

I DON'T KNOW WHAT THE STORY IS ON HOW THIS GOT MADE, BUT IT'S THE CLASSIC CHEAPO BRAIN-SCRAMBELER. THERE ARE 3 PARTS, FIRST: REPTILICUS IN A WORLD OF PRETTY NICE MINIATURES. I REALLY DIG HIS TEETH BY THE WAY. THATS NOT HIM ON THE COVER; IT'S SOME BULLSHIT BY SOMEONE WHO PROBABLY NEVER SAW IT. SECOND: STOCKFOOTAGE MONTAGE'S. WHICH I PERSONALLY DIG. SEAMONAL CINEMA VERTE. THIRD: IS A SMALLCAST WHO ARE CUT IN AMONG THE GOOD STUFF. THEY ARE THE PART THAT MAKE THIS A FAMOUSE CHEESE'MO.

REPTILICUS

STORY, PRODUCTION & DIRECTION
SIDNEY PINK

SCREENPLAY IB MELCHOR & SIDNEY PINK

1962 COLOR 82 MINUTES NOTRATED [RECORDED IN THE EP MODE]

ORION

The
RESURRECTED

WELL, I HAVE NOT READ THE LOVECRAFT SO I DON'T KNOW HOW IT COMPAIRS. I LOVE IT. O'BANNON SAYS HIS CUT WAS SCRAPED & THE PRODUCTION RECUT IT WITH O'BANNONS DISCARDED ELEMENTS, SET NEXT TO OTHER MOVIES OF HIS IT SHOWS THAT HIS FLAVOR &

PACE IS FAIRLY CRUSHED ALONG WITH MUCH OF HIS HUMOR. OH WELL. WHAT WE GET IS STILL GREAT.

THERES SOME POINTLESS OF TOPIC BITS BUT THERES NO BAD STUFF TO DERAIL IT. CHRIS SARANDON IS GREAT. HE'S DOING THREE CHARACTERS BASICLY. HE'S WITH IT THEN LOSES IT & GETS SUPER GROSS AND HE'S HIS OWN 5 TIMES GRANDPA. THE EFFECTS ARE FANTASTIC TOO.

DUDE INHERRITS AN OLD FAMILY BOOBYTRAP THAT WRECKS UP HIS LIFE SO HIS WIFE HIRES A DETECTIVE TO PEEL BACK THE VEIL.

SOMETIMES KNOWN AS SHATTERBRAIN

The RESURRECTED

BASED ON H.P. LOVECRAFTS "CASE OF CHARLES DEXTER WARD"

CHRIS SARANDON

JOHN TERRY JANE SIBBETT

SCREENPLAY BY BRENT V. FRIEDMAN

DIRECTED BY DAN O'BANNON

1991 APPROX. RUNNING TIME: 108 MIN.

REVENGE OF THE NERDS TELIVISION PILOT

I'M A NERD & I'M PROUD OF IT FEATURETTE

DELETED SCENES

THEATRICAL TRAILER

ROBERT CARRADINE ANTHONY EDWARDS
TED McGINLEY BERNIE CASEY
SCREENPLAY BY STEVE ZACHIARAS & JEFF BUHAI
DIRECTED BY JEFF KANEW

R

NO ONES REALLY GOING TO BE FREE UNTILL NERD PERSICUTION ENDS.

REVENGE OF THE NERDS
PANTY RAID EDITION

EVERYONES FAVORITE NERDS ARE BACK!

SWEET MOVIE. THE DUDES GO TO A FRAT CONFRENCE IN FORT LAUDERDALE. JOCKS COCKBLOCK THEM ALLOVER OF COURSE. THEY STAY AT THE HOTE CORAL ESSEX WHERE BOOGER MEETS HIS MASTER... SNOTTY. SNOTTY RULES IT DUDE. SO DOSE THE DEVO SOUNDTRACK & THE NERDS DO A RAP ABOUT NERD RADNESS. THE JOCKS GET OUR DUDES LOCKED UP & LATER THEY KIDNAP THEM, THEN STRAD'M ON A DESERTED ISLAND WHERE BOOGER FINDS A HUGE POT PLANT. I THINK THIS IS THE FIRST NERD MOVIE I SAW BECAUSE PART 1 IS RATED [R] SO MY FOLKS SAID NO. OH WELL I STILL IT & IT'S A GREAT SEQUAL. NO ON 15. YO.

ROBERT CARRADINE ANDREW CASSESE
TIMOTHY BUSFIELD LARRY B. SCOTT CURTIS ARMSTRONG ANTHONY EDW

WRITTEN BY
DAN GUNTZELMAN & STEVE MARSHALL
DIRECTED BY JOE ROTH

PG-13

WIDESCREEN

89 MINUTES

SOUNDTRACK BY DEVO {AKA: BEST BAND EVER}

DVD

20 FOX

1987 COLOR

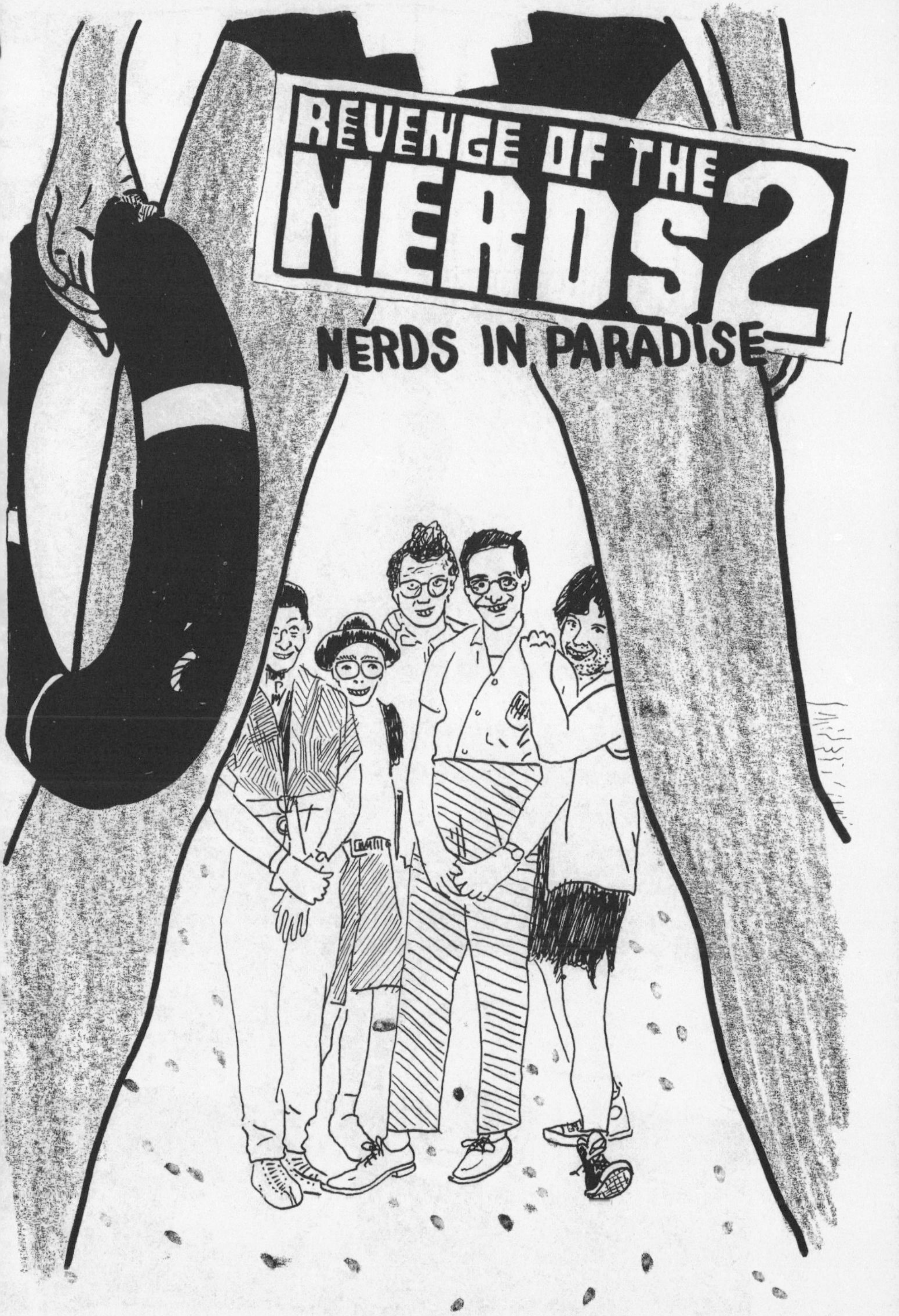

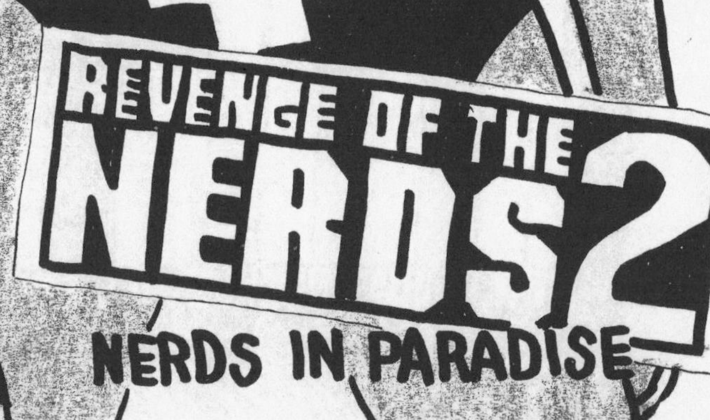
REVENGE OF THE
NERDS 2
NERDS IN PARADISE

THE STORY OF RICKY HO

AKA BLOOD KNUCKLZ ALL STAR BEATDOWN

A'NOTHER BOOTLEG I GOT FROM TOM

SO SOMETIMES THIS IS CALLED "RICKY O", "THE STORY OF RICKY" & "RICKY HO" & A FEW OTHER COMBONATIONS OF THE SAME.

DUDE. DUDE... HEY, dude; PEEP THIS OUT. OVER THE TOP DRAGONBALL ULTRAVIOLENCE AIRPLANE FACE MELTER TEX AVERY FREAKFEST... DUUUUDE. IF THAT SOUNDS LIKE A BAD THING YOU MAY NOT DIG THIS MOVIE, OTHERWISE ... PEEP... THIS... OUT. FOR REAL. I'D SAY THIS IS COMEDY FOR MEATHEADS. SQUARES MIGHT BE INTO IT IF IT WERE IN THE RIGHT CONTEXT. MAYBE NOT. SO WHATS THE STORY? DUDE GO'S TO PRISON, SHIT IS BURLY DUDE STOMPS ASS FULL TILT. WARDEN & HIS SON ARE EVIL SHITS. EVERYONE IN THE PRISON IS EATHER CROOKED OR A USLESS DIPSHIT. RICKY TRYS TO BE COOL BUT NO SLACK IS CUT TO HIM & SO, ASS' ARE STOMP'T INTO MUDHOLES, GUTS POUR OUT ONTO THE YARD, NAILS IN EYEBALLS, OPIUM IS MADE & YOU KNOW SHITS JUST GONNA SNOWBALL. SORT'A SIMULAR TO CYBORG BUT WITHOUT THE STREIGHT FACE. THIS IS SO MUCH FUN TO WATCH, I'LL POP IT IN AFTER A NITE OF DRINK WHEN I WANT ENTERTAINMENT I CAN SPACE IN & OUT ON WITH NO PROBLEMS PLUS IT'S FUNNY AS ALL GETOUT. BASED ON A COMIC & ANIME THAT I'D LIKE TOO PEEP.

FAN SIU WONG MEI SHENGFAN KA-KUI HO
YUKARI OSHIMA FRANKIE CHEN

1991 COLOUR 91 MINUTES SUBTITLED

WRITTEN & DIRECTED BY
LAM NGAI KAI

THE ACTION-PACKED HIT!!!
DAVID ARQUETTE SALMA HAYEK
DEMO TAPE
VIDEO BOX ART WILL VARY
90-DAY
ROADRACERS
FULL-LENGTH SCREENER FOR VIDEO RETAILERS ONLY

HOT-RENTING EXCITEMENT

SIZZLING HOLLYWOOD STARZ!

SEXY SALMA HAYEK

DOPY DAVID ARQUETTE

ACTION DIRECTOR ROBERT RODRIGUEZ

FROMDUSKTILLDAWN 14

DESPERADO 13

ROADRACERS

ORDER DEEP

DAVID ARQUETTE SALMA HAYEK

THIS IS ONE MY FAVORITE ROBERT RODRIGUEZ MOVIES. FAKE 50'S DELINQUENT ROCK'N'ROLL CAR REBEL W/OUT A PLAN LOVELETTER GOOFBALL COMEDY. I GOT THE IMPRESSION THIS WAS AN HBO MOVIE BUT NOW I DON'T KNOW WHERE I GOT THAT FROM. ANYWAY, ARQUETTE IS GREAT HERE. HE FITS THE BILL TO A "T". HE & RODRIGUEZ BOTH HAVE A DAFFY DUCK FLAVOR WHICH MAKES SOME OF THEY'R OTHER MOVIES SORT'A TILT THEY'R HEAD. BUT TOGETHER THESE BIT'S & QUARKS ARE PERFECT FITS. WHERE AS IN A LOT OF THE MOVIES THIS STYLE FROM THEY'R DAY WOULD DEAL W/ RACIST STUFF ON THE MILDSIDE HERE IT'S AN UPFRONT ELEMENT W/ MANY FACITS & HAS VARIOUS RESULTS. PROBABLY MORE INLINE W/ HAIRSPRAY SO FAR AS THAT GO'S. RODRIGUEZ'S BODYSNATCHERS OBSESSION IS PROBABLY AT IT'S MOST NERDY HERE WITH AN OBSESSED DUDE WATCHING THE MOVIE DAILY @ THE THEATR THEN ANNILIZING & DROOLING OVER IT IN SOCIAL CONVERSATION & THEN THERES A GREAT CAMEO TOO. I LOVE THIS. MOST MOVIE DON'T DO THIS & WHEN THEY DO IT TENDS TO BE OBNOXIOUS & HANDJOBY BUT HERE IT'S PERFECT. I GOTTA SAY I DON'T THINK I DIG DUDES OTHER MOVIES AS MUCH AS THIS ONE, THOUGH I DO DIG MOST OF THEM. SO... ANYWHO, THIS IS A SCREENER BOX & THERES ALLWAYS THESE TEMPLATE BACKS TO'M THAT ARE FUNNY FOR A FEW BUT NOW I'M TIRED OF IT. BUT THE COVERS ON THESE ARE SOMETIMES WEIRD/WILD MISC. PHOTOS COLLAGED TOGETHER. NONE OF THESE IMAGES ARE FROM THIS MOVIE. I LIKE THE BOOTLEG'Y-NESS OF IT.

PRETTY RULE'N. IT SEEMS LIKE THERES TWENTY MINUTES MISSING OUT OF THE MOVIE BUT WHATS THERE IS COOL. THE ROBOTS ARE AWESOME. IN THE FUTURE WE HAVE GIANT ROBOT BATTLES INSTED OF GOING TO WAR.
SOUNDS GOOD. JEFFRY COMBS IS IN THE FUTURE BUT HE'S NOT A LEAD CHARACTER. THERES SOME PLOT BUT I WON'T RUIN IT BY TRY'N. STEWERT GORDON MADE IT. I LIKE IT MORE THEN CASTLE FREAK & ABOUT AS MUCH AS SPACE TRUCKERS, EVEN THOUGH I THINK SPACE TRUCKERS HAS BETTER WRITING. IF YOU WANT A "FILM" YOU MIGHT WANT TO PASS. IF YOU WANT TO SEE A DOPE ASS FLICK, THEN I HIGHLY RECOMEND ROBOT JOX.
GARY GRAHAM ANNE-MARIE JOHNSON
PAUL KOSLO ROBERT SAMPSON DANNY KAMEKONA
HILLARY MASON & MICHAEL ALLDREDGE
SCREENPLAY BY JOE HALDEMAN
STORY & DIRECTED BY STUART GORDON
©1990
APPROX. 85 MINUTES
DVD
PG
COLOR

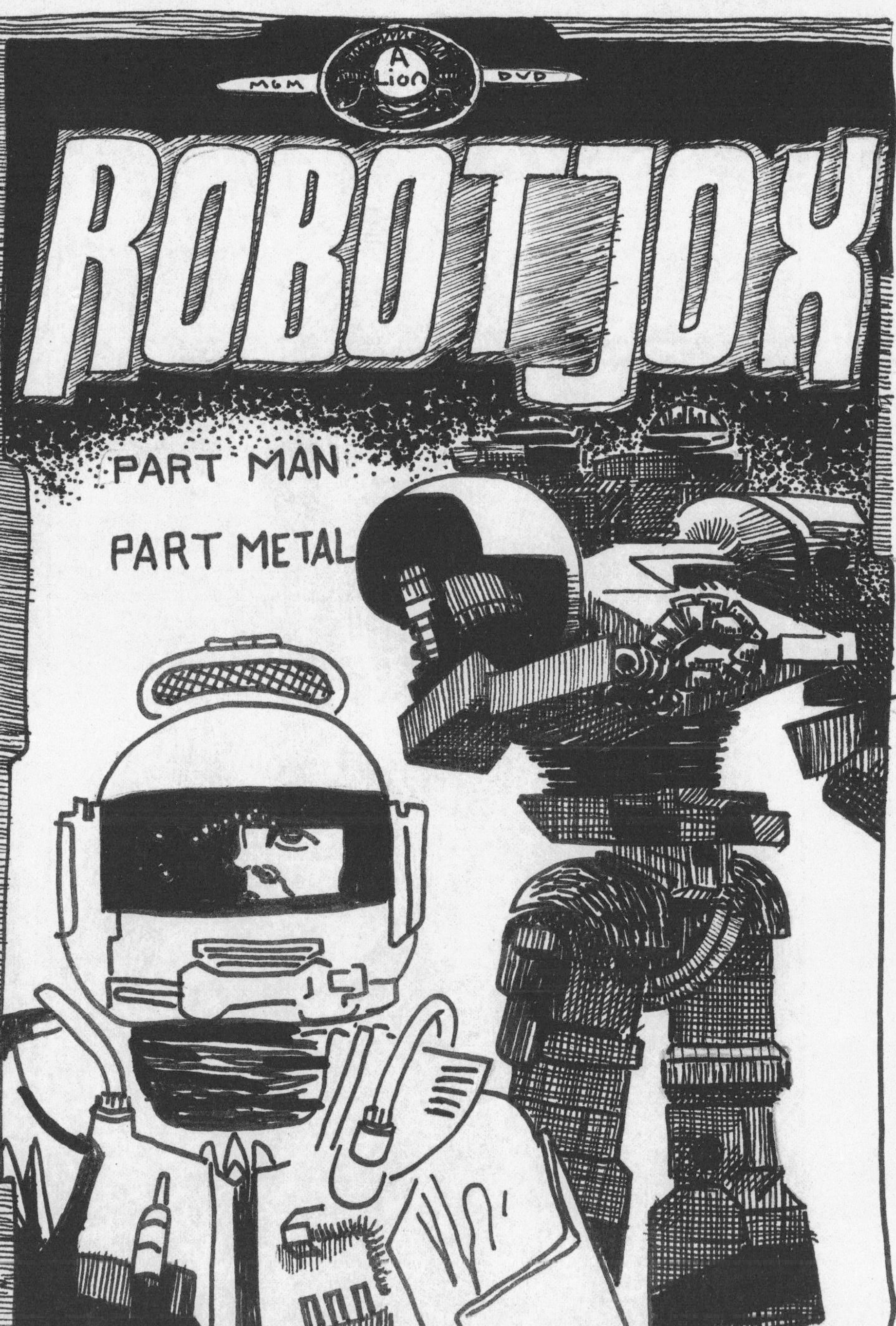
A
MGM
Lion
DVD
ROBOT JOX
PART MAN
PART METAL

THE
ROCKETEER
DIG WOW

IT'S PROBABLY TOO TOUGH FOR ME TO ACURATLY REVIEL MUCH ABOUT THIS MOVIE
I SAW IT IN THE THEATRE & LOVED. STILL DO.
THIS IS IN THE TOPS FOR COMICS ADAPT. FOR ME. LIKE: DANGER DIABOLIQUE; OR WESTWARD BATMAN. TOP BILLING!!!
IT THRLLS ME IN A GOOD COMICS TYPE WAY. SO EARNEST & FUN. PERFECT JOB FOR JOHNSON. HEART, FUN, ADVENTURE, HOPE & HEARTACHE... IN NICE POP-CLASSIC STYLE.
THIS IS ALSO PERFECT DALTON TOO. HE'S WHAT I WISH WE HAD MORE OF.
CONNELLY IS A GREAT FIT FOR THE BETTY THING. SHE IS MORE THAN WE EVEN GET FROM THE COMICS
THE HOLE THING FROM THE GROUND UP IS PERFECT FOR ME.
SO FAR, JOHNSON IS MY FAV. COMIC TO MOVIE ADAPTER. TOO COOL
BILL CAMPBELL ALAN ARKIN
JENNIFER CONNELLY PAUL SORVINO THIMOTHY DALTON
BASED ON THE COMIC BY DAVE STEVENS
SCREENPLAY BY DANNY BILSON & PAUL DE MEO
DIRECTED BY JOE JOHNSON
PG
RUNNING TIME 109 minutes COLOR HIFI STEREO 1991

MORE CLASS THAN
BOND
MORE HIP THAN
POWERS
DUMBER THAN
SMART
ROD STEELE
0014
YOU ONLY LIVE
UNTIL YOU DIE

PRETTY MUCH A BOND SPOOF WHERE ALL THE WOMEN TAKE THEY'R TOPS OFF. PROBABLY SHOWED ON SKINIMAX. MAY PASS AS PORN IF YOUR A LITTLE KID. NOT REALY TOO FUNNY. SO, I GOT THIS BECAUSE IT'S BASED ON AT LEAST ONE MINARA COMIC. SO, AS AN ADAPTATION THIS IS A TAME, HALF ASS. OH, WELL. KIND'A FUNNY JUST FOR EXISTING. UNINSPIRE'N JOKES. THIS PROBABLLY WOULD SERVE BEST AS BACKGROUND FOR A CRAZY STAG PARTY. IF YOUR SAD & LONELY THIS IS WORTH A FEW CHUCKELS. OTHERWISE, WHAT EVER. EASY'R THEN READING A NEW

R APPROXIMATE RUNNING TIME: 75 MINUTES 1997

ROBERT DONAVAN SITA THOMPSON DE'ANN POWER JOHN LAZAR JACQUELINE LOVELL MICHELLE BAUER GABRIELLA HALL SCOTT COPPOLA MARK COLLVER BRIAN KENT DELPHINE PACIFIC KIRA REED STACEY MOBLEY

WRITTEN & DIRECTED by ROLFE KANEFSKY

NED BEATTY IS A FREEWAY VICELORD WHOSGANG OVER THE COURSE OF THE FIRST 2/3'S OF THE MOVIE DISTROY OUR HEROS FAMILY & LIFE. I GOTTA SAY IT TAKES DUDE FOREVER TO GET HIS VENGEANCE ROLLING & EVEN THEN HEMEASURS IT OUT SELECTIVELY. BUT WHEN YOU GET THAT TRUCK ON THE SCREEN IT'S SOLID GOLD. GOOD MOVIE. IF YOU'V SEEN MENY VENGEANCE MOVIES YOU'LL KNOW IT ALL GO'S ALONG A COMMON TRAJECTURIE BUT THE PACING BURN'S YOU UP WHEN SOME OF THE ABUSE COMES. IN CASE YOU DID'NT NOTICE DUDE BUILDS A MONSTER TRUCK W/A GIANT DRILL COMMING OFF THE FRONT. WORTH A FEW VIEWS FOR SURE. THE BUILD UP STILL STRESSED ME OUT. NED BEATTY IS SUCH A CHARMING SHIT, GREAT.

hifi / MONO 1987 COLOR 92 minutes REVENGE R

DON MICHAEL PAUL LAWRENCE DANE NED BEATTY
LISA HOWARD

WRITTEN BY MICHAEL MONTGOMERY
PRODUCED & DIRECTED BY STEVEN H. STERN

CHARTER
ENTERTAINMENT

ALWAYS USE USE RIGHT
TOOL FOR THE JOB

ROLLING VENGEANCE

Judge, Jury, and Executioner

RICHARD GESSWEIN
MARGARET TRIGG
JAYNESMITH
JAMES COLE
CLARKMOORE
CARROL BRANDON BAKER

ROTOR

HOLY SMOKE. JASON SHOWED THIS AT THE COMICSHOP & RAN THE SOUND THROUGH A BASS AMP. IT WAS AMAZING. THE MUSIC AT THAT DEGRE IS SO BOLD IT MATCHS & THEN TRANCENDS YOU{ME} INTO THE WORLD OF IT. THEN LATER I SEE IT W/A RAMBUNCTIOUS BUNCH & IT WAS'NT HAPPENING. THIS IS A VERY FUN MOVIE BUT I GUESS IT MAYBE ONE TO SEE & HEAR IN A CONTROLED ENVIRONMENT. ANYWAY. THROUGH AMBIVALINT ERROR AN EXPIERAMENTLE ROBO-CYBORG-COP-FRANKENSTEIN DUDE IS PRE-MATURIELY AWOKEN & GETS DOWN TO OVERCOMP-ENSATING ON THE JUSTIC ISSUE. SOME BEACHBOYS JOKES. THE SPECIALTY BAD-ASS IS GREAT HER NAME IS DR. STEELE I ♥ THE ROTOR PROFILING.

COLOR/APPROX. 90 min.

SCREENPLAY by BUD LEWIS
DIRECTED by CULLEN BLAINE
Music by DAVID ADAM NEWMAN

IMPERIAL ENTAINMENT CORP

ORIGINAL STORY BY CULLEN BLAINE

CIARA PRODUCTIONS

RUN COYOTE RUN

A BIZARRE MEDLEY. HAZEY & JAGGED. LIKE DREAMING WHILE FITFULLY SLEEPING IN A CAR. EACH STOCK OF FILM APPEARS TO BE PRESENT & VIDEO TOO. ALSO THERES SOME BEAUTIFUL STOCK FOOTAGE, STREETS, TWILIGHT TRAFFIC. BLOW OUT & CONTRASTY DAY FOR NITE STUFF. AT FIRST I HAD SOME ISSUES FOLLOWING ALONG BUT ONCE AN EXPOSITURY OFFICE SCENE CAME ON I KNEW TO LET LOOSE THE SHACKLES OF WHY & RODE ALONG WITH THE WHAT. THE BOOKLET/ZINE TELLS OF THE ORIGIN OF THIS MOVIE. PIECES ASSEMBELED FROM PREVIOUSE FEATURES W/ PLOT BUMPER INCERTS. WHIRLED WORLDS COLIDING & BLEEDING, TIME A FASHONS SLIDE ALONG THIS TARE IN THE KALIDASCOPE OF RENEE HARMON.

BLEEDING SKULL VIDEO

1987/COLOR/72 MINUTES

RUN

COYOTE

RUN

STARRING RENEE HARMON ★
FRANK NEUHAUS
SCREENPLAY by RENEE HARMON
ART DIRECTION by WILLIAM LUCE
PRODUCED by RENEE HARMON
DIRECTED by JAMES BRYAN

AN ABEL FERRARA CXRISTMAS MOVIE. ICE-T. WHAT MORE INCENTIVE DID I NEED? NONE. BUT MAYBE YOU DO. OK PEEP IT... THEY ARE DRUG DEALERS. I DIG IT. PROBABLY WONT WATCH IT ON X-MAS THOUGH. ITS SHORT BUT FITS PERFECT, WITH COOL LONG ARTY CAMERA. I LOVE THE PERSONALIZED PACKAGING THEY DO ON THEIR PRODUCT. THATS A CLASSY DRUG DEALER. SOME DUDES JUST LICK A FOLDING SANDWITCH BAGGY. ICE-T GETS TO LAY IT ON HEAVY WITH THE INTIMIDATION WHICH I LOVE, BECAUSE IT'S MORE ON HIS RAPPING SIDE WHICH REALY OPENS UP THE COMPLEXITY OF HIS CHARACTERS. THIS MOVIE SITS WELL W/ KING OF NEW YORK. IT FEELS SMALLER, MORE INTIMATE AND STRESSY, BUT STILL W/ THE CLARITY, BEAUTY, CURT CUTS & SMALL SPACES. IT'S A LOT OF GAME, CAN YOU GET W/ IT?

DREA DE MATTEO LILLO BRANCATO JR. ICE-T
VICTOR ARGO NAOMI MORALES LISA VALENS
STORY BY
CASSANDREA DE JESUS
SCREENPLAY
SCOTT PARDO & ABEL FERRARA
DIRECTED BY
ABEL FERRARA

R 83 mins

2002 COLOR ARTISAN

DREA DE MATTEO
LILLO BRANCATO JR.
ICE-T
'R XMAS
A FILM BY
ABEL FERRARA

A FOOLISH CRIMINALS COMEDY. AND SILLY. IF YOU DIG THAT THEN THIS IS A GOOD ONE. THERE ARE PLOT LIKE ELEMENTS BUT ITS MORE LIKE CHARACTER DEVELOPMENT. HAMBURG IS GOOD AT LETTING THE CHARACTERS BE THE JOKE THING I REALLY LIKE THIS MOVIE EVEN THOUGH WHAT I JUST WROTE WOULD TALK ME OUT OF WATCHING IT. LIKE A FEEL GOOD MOVIE OR SOME SILLY NOSTAGIA GOOF. WHICH IT IS. I THINK THE VIBES & CHEMISTRY OF THE CAST IS A KEY ELEMENT. A WIDE VARIETY OF DING DONGS. SONG DESICRATION. JEWISH GANGSTERS IN SOME EASTCOAST SWEATER CATALOGUE TOWN. BUT MOSTLY DING DONGS. NOT TOO CRIMEY. I WATCHED THIS PRETTY REGULAR WORK'N AT THE MOTEL 6. PEEP IT. OR DON'T.

SAM ROCKWELL STEVE ZAHN MARK RUFFALO
JOSH PAIS PAUL GIAMATTI HARVEY FIERSTEIN
CHRISTINA KIRK & MICHAEL LERNER

WRITTEN & DIRECTED BY
JOHN HAMBURG

COLOR ENGLISH 1 HR. 28 MINS. 1998

SAM rockwell
STEVE zahn
mark ruffalo
JOSH pais
PAUL giamatti
A JOHN HAMBURG MOVIE
SAFEMEN

RODDY PIPER

SCI-FIGHTERS

TRIB

IN THE YEAR 2009,
THEY'RE YOUR ONLY HOPE.

PIPER IS A SPECIALY LICENCED COP W/ A "BLACK BADGE" WHICH ALLOWS HIM TO PICK HIS CASES & BLOW OFF HIS "BOSS". HE'S ON THE TRAIL OF BILLY DRAGO WHO WAS ON THE MOON IN PRISON BUT DIES & IS REANIMATED AS SOME KILLING, RAPING, INFCTIOUS, DRIPPY, WHISPERING DILDO SWITCHBLADE {GOLD TOO} WEILD-ING "ALIEN" MENACE. RODDY HAS SOME PERSONAL INTERIST & HAS A HOT SCIENTIST LADY HELP HIM & TURN DOWN HIS ADVANCES WHILE THEY CRACK THE CASE. PIPER SWEARS A BIT MORE THAN USUAL & HAS UNIQUE PUT DOWNS SO MAYBE HE HAD A BIT MORE FREE REIGHN IN HIS TAMPON TURTLENECK. DRAGO GETS SLIMY & GROSSER W/TIME BUT KEEPS HIS FISHHOOK SMILE.

SCI-FIGHTERS

RODDY PIPER JAYNE HEITMYER
BILLY DRAGO

WRITTEN BY MARKSEVI
DIRECTED BY PETER SVATEK

THERE ARE A COUPLE BROKEN MIRROR SCEENS.

THE SENTINEL

THE SENTINEL

COLOR/1 Hr. 32 MINS. (R) 1976

IF YOU WANT A SLOW DRY ARTY AMERICAN MODERNLIVING DRAMA HORROR WITH THAT CATHOLIC FLAVOR, THEN THIS IS A GOOD ONE. THE EDITING IS BRASH, WHICH IS TENCE AT FIRST, THEN IRRITATING & IN THE END IT TEASES US PRETTY GOOD. I WISH THAT THERE HAD BEEN LESS BEGINING & MORE ENDING ESPECIALLY WITH THE LAST FEW SHOTS. ITS ALL GOOD WITH A CAST LIKE THIS. THE "SCARY STUFF" IS MORE. POWERLESS TO THE TURNING OF FATE W/ EXISTENTAL DREDD. AND JOHN CARRADINE ROLLING HIS EYES BACK OUT THE WINDOW TO THE WORLD WITH POWDER ON.

CHRIS SARANDON · CRISTINA RAINES
MARTIN BALSAM · JOHN CARRADINE · JOSE FERRER
AVA GARDNER · ARTHUR KENNEDY · BURGESS MEREDITH
SYLVIA MILES · DEBORAH RAFFIN · ELI WALLACH

SCREENPLAY by
MICHAEL WINNER & JEFFREY KONVITZ
DIRECTED by MICHAEL WINNER

sex,

lies,

and

videotape

I REMEMBER FOLKS MAKING A BIG DEAL ABOUT THIS WHEN IT CAME OUT. ANDIE MAC DOWELL BOTHERS ME A LITTLE, BUT LIKE THE REST OF THE CAST. SODERBERGH IS A UNIQUE ARTIST IN MOVIES. I LIKE A FEW OF HIS MOVIES VERY MUCH & THE OTHERS ARE STILL GOOD, BUT NOT WHAT I'M INTO THIS BEING THE SECOND FOR ME. IT FEELS VERY MUCH LIKE A PLAY, WHICH I DIG THESE DAYS. BUT IT FEELS UNNATURALY OVER WRITTEN. IT DOSE'NT FEEL LIKE ANY LIVING GO'S ON OFF CAMERA. A LITTLE TOO PUPPETY FOR THE SUBJECT. NOT BAD, BETTER THEN MOST OF IT'S TYPE FROM IT'S ERA.

james spader andie macdowell
peter gallagher laura san giacomo
written & directed
steven soderbergh

Approx. 99 mins.  COLOR

Bobcat
Goldthwait
Julie
Brown
Shakes the Clown

The Citizen Kane of alcoholic clown movies

SHAKES OPPERATES IN THE WORLD OF MOVIES LIKE BADNEWS BEARS & BARFLY. HAD I NOT SEEN BAD SANTA FIRST I THINK IT WOULD HAVE HAD A MORE PROFOUND EFFECT. NONE THE LESS, THIS IS A GOOD SOLID DRUNK COMEDY. GOOD CAST & SOLID WRITING/DIRECTING FROM BOBCAT. WORTHY OF IT'S CULT STATUS FOR SURE. IF THERE WERE MORE CLOWNS LIKE SHAKES I THINK MORE PEOPLE WOULD LIKE CLOWNS. I KNOW I WOULD.

87 min.
columbia TristAr Home Video

HONESTLY, I WAS DRUNK@FRAIM 1. MY MIND WAS ALL OVER THE PLACE; BUT I FULLY ENJOYED IT. D.W.'S CHOICE. BELIEVE. DO YOU DIG KUNG FU MOVIES? YES? OH, WELL THEN PEEP THIS SHIT. FULLY USELESS REVIEW. 1/2 NAKED DUDES IN FULL EFFECT. TRUE THAT.
ALEXANDER FU SHENG, CHI KUAN CHI
IRENE CHEN L-LING, GORDON LIU CHIA-HUI
DIRECTED BY
CHANG CHEH
DVD
3
NTSC
MONO

SHAOLIN
MARTIAL ARTS
FULLY RESTORED FROM THE ORIGINAL FILM

FUN SNAPY ADVENTURE COMEDY W/STYLISH'LY FRIVELOUS CAMERA PLAY THAT RITCHIE DOSE SO WELL. BUT AS A FAN OF HOLMES & FAKEHOLMES MOVIES I GOTTA SAY... THIS IS NOT A HOLMES MOVIE. OR A FAKEHOLMES EITHER. MORE A CASE OF

WINDOW DRESSING TO GET A MOVIE PROJECT ON IT'S FEET. I'M COOL W/ THAT. DOWNEY'S DO'N HIS CUTE SHIT CHARM'R DRUNK

GENIOUS ACT & LAW'S THE TALENTED YOUNG'R BROTHER W/ HIS SHIT A BIT MORE STREIGHTEN'D OUT BUT W/OUT DIRECTION. WHATEVER. IT'S POP IT'S LITE FUN. I WAS'NT COMPELLED TO KEEP IT BUT I'D WATCH IT AGAIN A FEW YEARS DOWN THE ROAD. THERES A MILD STEAM PUNK ELEMENT BUT NOT A LOT.

ROBERT DOWNEY JR. JUDE LAW
RACHEL McADAMS MARK STRONG
EDDIE MARSAN

SCREENPLAY BY SIMON KINBERG
MICHAE ROBERT JOHNSON ANTHONY PECKHAM
DIRECTED BY GUY RITCHIE

DVD PG-13 COLOR 128 mns

ROBERT
DOWNEY JR.
JUDE
LAW
RACHEL
McADAMS
MARK
STRONG
SHERLOCK
HOLMES

THE SHINING
JACK NICHOLSON SHELLEY DUVALL
SCATMAN CROTHERS DANNY LLOYD
BASED ON THE NOVEL BY STEPHEN KING
SCREENPLAY BY
STANLEY KUBRICK & DIANE JOHNSON
DIRECTED BY STANLEY KUBRICK

I'M NOT GOING TO GET INTO IT WITH THIS MOVIE & ITS CULTURE OF ANALYSIS. IT'S DOPE FUR SHURE, BUT I'M

COOL WITH IT RIGHT THERE. I DIG THAT LOGO. SHELLEY DUVALL IS SUCH A TRIP. SHES GOT SOME HYPNOTIC HEAVY CHARISMA / VIBE. SCULPTURALLY CHARACATURISH. THE PERFECT OLIVE OIL. SO HERE SHE IS FULLY TRIPPED OUT SQUEEKIN & CREEPIN IN A BIG EMPTY PLACE FULL OF TAXING PSYCHIC VAMPIRISM & A WAVE OF PHANTOM GUILT. SCATMAN CROTHERS HAS ONE OF THE COOLEST INTRODUCTIONS IN ANY KUBRICK FLICK. NICHOLSON IS UNTOUCHABLE IN HIS TWISTS OF UNHINGED MADNESS. GOOD FUCKING LUCK FOLLOWING THAT ACT. I GUESS THERE ARE PEOPLE WHO MAY NOT KNOW ABOUT THIS OR KUBRICK, TO WHICH I GUESS I'D SAY GO PEEP'M, THIS IS SORTA ONE OF HIS MORE NORMAL AND EATABLE MOVIES. ONE OF THE ACTUALLY CREEPY UNNERVING FREAKY MOVIES MADE OFF OF A KING BOOK.

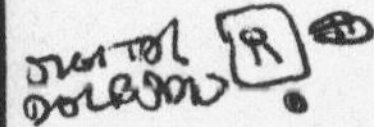

AS A YOUTH I WAS WATCHING THIS PURELY FOR THE SALATIOUS BEAVIOR & PUNK ICONOGRAPHY. I THOUGHT IT WAS OKAY THEN. SINCE THEN I'V READ & LISTENED TO MORE OF SEX PISTOLS & SID... AND AVOIDED THIS MOVIE. BUT THEN I FOUND OUT ABOUT ALEX COX & WATCHED EVERYTHING I COULD OF HIS. EXCEPT SID & NANCY. THEN, LAST YEAR I FOUND THIS, IT WAS A GOOD DEAL SO I GOT IT. OH!... DUH!! THIS ISN'T SOME BEHIND THE MAN EXPOSE POSE AS SO MANY MUSIC BIO DEALS ARE. THIS IS MORE IN LINE W/LYNCH'S DUNE. CONSIDER THE DIRECTOR. DO THEY DO RAZORSHARP ACURATE ADAPTATIONS OF CLINICAL SOURCE MATERIAL? OR ARE THEY WILDLY VISIONARY ARTISTS WHO MIX THEY'R OWN COLORS & CREAT A TRUTH TO THEM SELF'S THROUGH WHAT IS AT HAND? I'LL TAKE DOOR #2, PLEASE. COX HAS A DREAMY ABSTRACT FORM OF PARODY WHICH WILL WINK AT YOU BUT NEVER TIP IT'S WHOLE HAND. JOKE'M IF THEY CAN'T TAKE A FUCK. I WROTE "LOVE KILLS" REAL BIG BECAUSE THATS WHAT THIS WAS SUPPOSED TO BE NAMED BUT BLAH blah BLAH STUDIOSHIT. THIS IS AN ALEX COX MOVIE MORE THAN A SID & NANCY MOVIE. I READ THAT COX ORIGINALL WROTE THIS AS A POST APOCHALIPS FLOOD'D ENGLAND W/ SID AS THE LEAD BUT THAT IT WOULD BE A POLITICAL SATIRE/PARODY TYPE THING. KIND'A MORE DEATH & THE COMPUS STYLE? JUST GUESSING.

FEATURE RUN TIME: 1 hour 51 minutes COLOR

SID & NANCY
LOVEKILS
A FILM BY ALEX COX

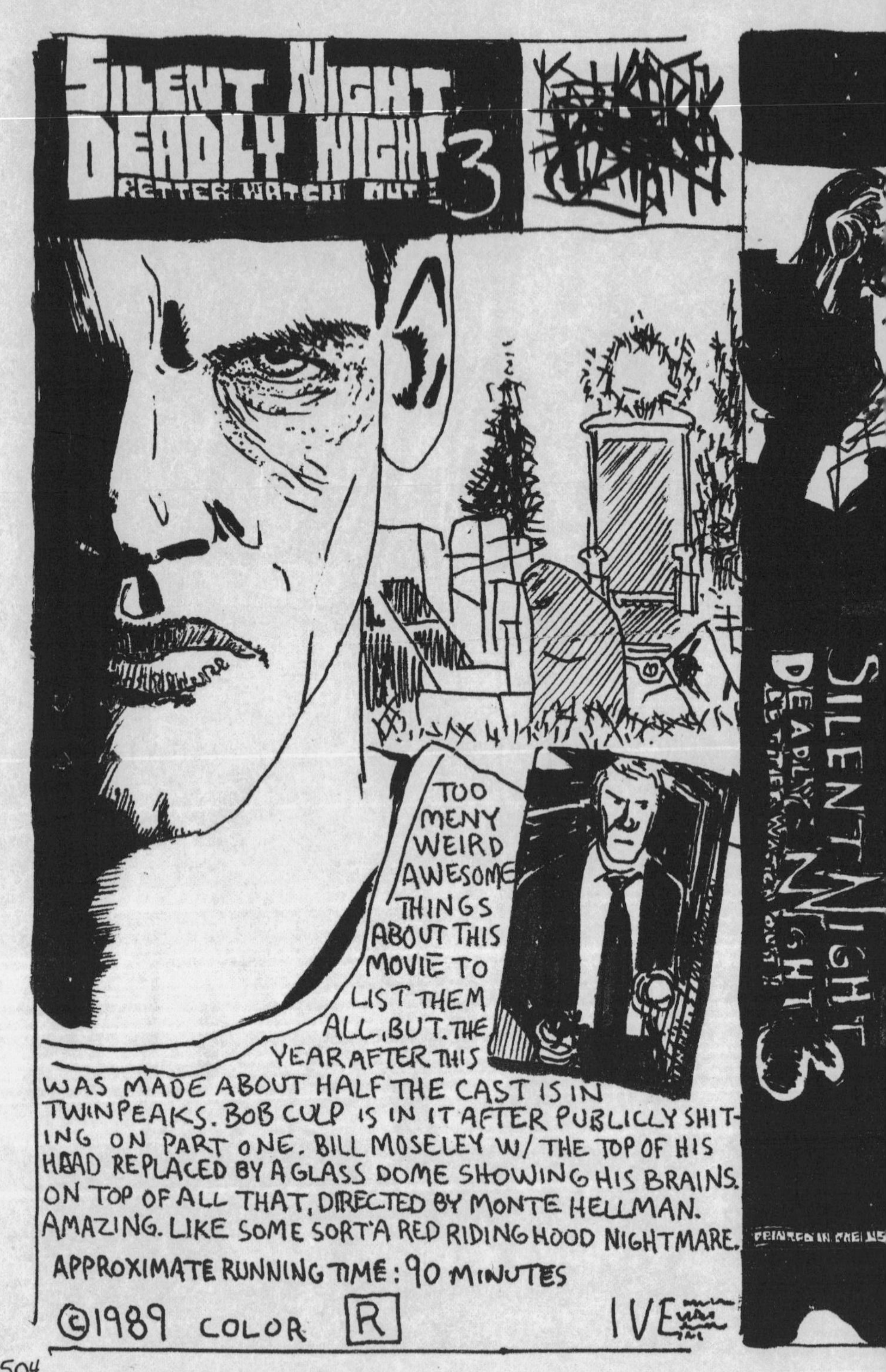
SILENT NIGHT, DEADLY NIGHT 3
BETTER WATCH OUT
TOO MENY WEIRD AWESOME THINGS ABOUT THIS MOVIE TO LIST THEM ALL, BUT. THE YEAR AFTER THIS WAS MADE ABOUT HALF THE CAST IS IN TWINPEAKS. BOB CULP IS IN IT AFTER PUBLICLLY SHITTING ON PART ONE. BILL MOSELEY W/ THE TOP OF HIS HEAD REPLACED BY A GLASS DOME SHOWING HIS BRAINS. ON TOP OF ALL THAT, DIRECTED BY MONTE HELLMAN. AMAZING. LIKE SOME SORT'A RED RIDING HOOD NIGHTMARE.
APPROXIMATE RUNNING TIME: 90 MINUTES
©1989 COLOR
R
IVE
SILENT NIGHT DEADLY NIGHT 3

IVE

SILENT NIGHT,
DEADLY NIGHT 3
BETTER WATCH OUT

VHS
HI-FI

RICHARD BEYMER BILL MOSELEY ERIC DARE
SAMANTHA SCULLY ELIZABETH HOFFMAN ROBERT
DIRECTED BY MONTE HELLMAN CULP

SIMONES SHOE CLOSET

THE ALTERED UNIVERSE

searching for love & meaning in her meaningless life, Simone finds it in the world of heel fetishism.

WRITTEN & DIRECTED by FRAN VICTOR

ORIGINAL MUSIC by KID CRESC

FRAN VICTOR
IAN SUNDAHL
ROLLYN STAFFORD
LILYA ABILDAYEVA
STEPHEN EDLEFSEN
SARAH BROOKE DORSEY
EVA HEIDEMAN
DENA BARSKIN
SHODY RYON
PHILIP O'NEIL
LOREN FELIXKELLY
RICO RIZOLATTI

SIMONE TALKS ABOUT FAIRNESS & EQUALITY BUT DOSE NOT EXHIBIT THE TRAITS IN HER SELF SOCIALY. SHE CHOOSES TO MAKE SOME LIFE CHANGES TO HAVE A RELATIONSHIP W/A COWORKER SHE HAS A CRUSH ON. HE IS ONLY INTER-ESTED IN WOMEN W/ PROPER SHOE FASHION... 4 INCH HEELS, MINIMUM. SHE ENTERS THE TRANSFORMATION AS A FORM OF SUBMISSION. SHE IS INBOLDENED BY A FASHIONABLE HIGHHEELED CO-WORKER WHO SEEMS TO WIN ATTENTION DUE TO HER HEEL FASHIONS. SIMONES PLAN BEGINS TO WORK & SHE STARTS TO FEEL EQUAL OR GOOD ABOUT HER SELF. SHE DEVELOPS A RELATIONSHIP SHE HAD ONLY FANTASIZED ABOUT. HER TASTE IN HEELS GROWS & SO DOSE HER SELFESTIME. THROUGH SUBMISSION SHE HAS METAMORPHOSIZED INTO A STRONGER, TRUER, & MORE DOMINANT PERSON WHO IS NOT ONLY AN EQUAL BUT A MASTER OF HER OWN LIFE & PASSIONS. SIMONE IS SO UNSURE AND MEEK AT THE BEGINING THAT ITS UNCOMPFORTABLE. THEN SHE IS MORE CHARMING AT HOME FANTASIZING, IT IS OCWARD WATCHING HER GROW BUT EMPOWERING TO SEE HER BECOME HER TRUE SELF. ITS SEXUAL BUT THERES NO SEX. I DIG IT. POSITIVITY THROUGH EMPOWERMENT.

FVVPRODUCTIONS 24 MINUTES 31 SECONDS

SIMONE'S
SHOE CLOSET

SLEEPAWAY CAMP

WOW. CLASSIC SLASHER STYLE TEENAGER MURDER CAMP. BUT UNLIKE SO MENY OTHERS THIS ACTUALLY HAS A GREAT FOLLOW THROUGH, WITH ONE OF THE BEST ENDINGS I'VE EVER SEE'N.

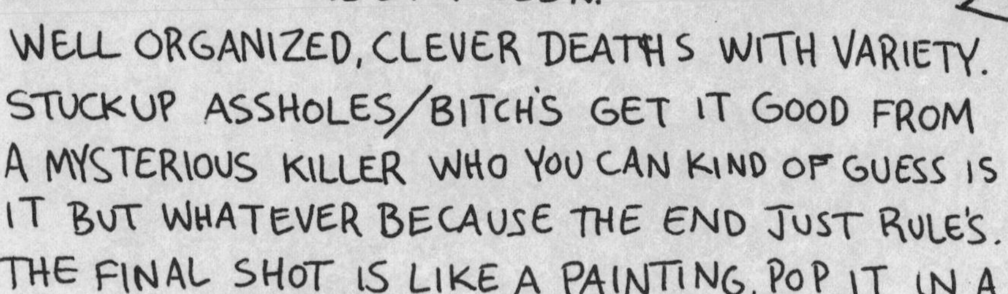

WELL ORGANIZED, CLEVER DEATHS WITH VARIETY. STUCKUP ASSHOLES/BITCH'S GET IT GOOD FROM A MYSTERIOUS KILLER WHO YOU CAN KIND OF GUESS IS IT BUT WHATEVER BECAUSE THE END JUST RULE'S. THE FINAL SHOT IS LIKE A PAINTING, POP IT IN A FRAIM & NAIL IT TO THE WALL.

THE OPEN'N SEE'N IS AWESOME TOO, LIKE A PUBLICSERVICE SHORT IT'S A OVER THE TOP SET UP OF BAD CHOICES; THAT FULLY DE-RAILS INTO TRAGITY. GREAT STUFF.

MIKE KELLIN KATHERINE KAMHI PAUL DEANGELO JONATHAN TIERSTON FELISSA ROSE CHRISTOPHER COLLET KAREN FIELDS

WRITTEN & DIRECTED BY

ROBERT HILTZIK

SLEEPAWAY CAMP

SLEEPAWAY CAMP II

Unhappy Campers

OK, SO... IN THIS ONE THE BOSS' SISTER IS CRUZ'N AROUN AS A CAMP COUNCELER KILLING ALL THE SHITHEADS, SLUTS, DOPE'RS, JOKERS, YOU NAME IT. EVERYONE GET'S A MORE APPROPRIATE/LITTERAL SLAY'NG IN THIS ONE. THIS IS THE CLASSIC STERIOTYPE OF IT'S TIME. START IN KILLING. KEEP KILLING UNTILL THE END WITH LITTLE MORE THAN CHARACTER SET UPS AS "STORY". SEX. DRUGS. RUBE GOLDBERG'ESQUE DEATHS. EXCESSIVE TOPLESS'NESS. HORROR MOVIE NERD'S DEVISE THERE OWN MEANS OF EXICUTION. AN OUT HOUSE DROWNING. TONS OF GRANNIE PANTY SHORT SHORTS. REALLY JUST PLAIN FUN FOR HORROR FREAKS. THE BIG REVIEL FROM PART ONE IS EXPLAINED & ELABORATED ON SO I RECOMEND YOU SEE IT FIRST.

PAMELA SPRINGSTEEN RENÉE ESTEVEZ

BRIAN PATRICK CLARKE WALTER GOTELL

WRITTEN BY

FRITZ GORDON

DIRECTED BY

MICHAEL A. SIMPSON

Cult Director Michael A Simpson's
SLEEPAWAY CAMP II
Unhappy Campers

WOODY GOES TO THE HOSPITAL IN THE 70'S & WAKES UP 200 YEARS LATER. A PERFECT SCI-FI MOVIE. HARD TO PLACE, BUT SORT'A ALPHAVILLE & MARX BROTHERS 'ISH. PROBABLY MY #1 WOODY MOVIE FOR INTRODUCING FOLKS TO HIM. KIDS COULD WATCH THIS & DIG IT. WELL, KIDS WHO LIKE BENNY HILL COULD. IT WOULD PROBABLY BE A GREAT CLOSER IN A DOUBLE FEATURE WITH THX1138. SOME TIMES I HEAR A FOOL SAY SOME TRASH ABOUT THERE BEING BAD WOODY MOVIES... I SAY BULLSHIT. I WILL STREIGHT UP STREET FIGHT {& WIN} ANY ONE OVER THIS. WOODY IS RULE'N ALL OVER YOUR SAD ASS TOP 10 DIRECTORS, WAY OVER YOUR HITCHCOCK.

WOODY ALLEN AND DIANE KEATON

SCREENPLAY

WOODY ALLEN & MARSHALL BRICKMAN

DIRECTOR

WOODY ALLEN

UNITED ARTISTS

PG DVD

FEATURE RUNTIME 1 HOUR 27 minutes COLOR 1973

MGM
DVD
WOODY ALLEN
DIANE KEATON
SLEEPER

A DARIO ARGENTO FILM
SLEEPLESS

NON HO SONNO. YOU DON'T SAY?
OR MAYBE LE SANG DES INNOCENTS.

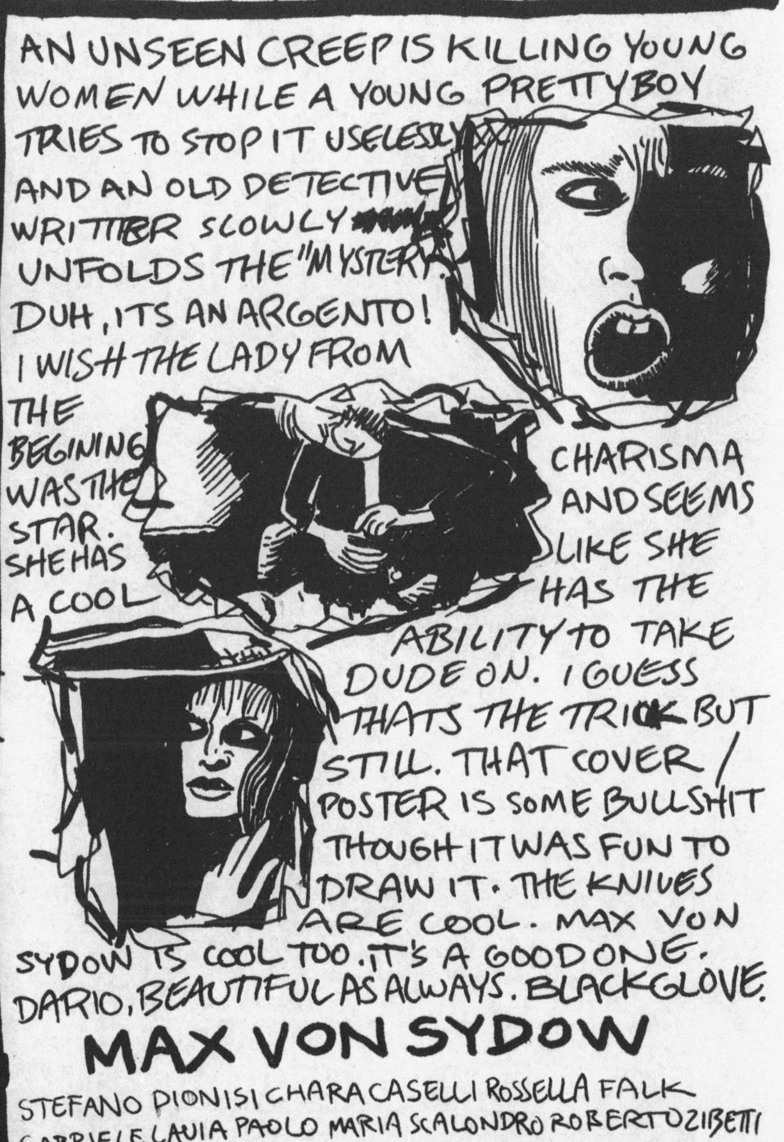

AN UNSEEN CREEP IS KILLING YOUNG WOMEN WHILE A YOUNG PRETTYBOY TRIES TO STOP IT USELESSLY AND AN OLD DETECTIVE WRITTER SLOWLY UNFOLDS THE "MYSTERY". DUH, ITS AN ARGENTO! I WISH THE LADY FROM THE BEGINING WAS THE STAR. SHE HAS A COOL CHARISMA AND SEEMS LIKE SHE HAS THE ABILITY TO TAKE DUDE ON. I GUESS THATS THE TRICK BUT STILL. THAT COVER / POSTER IS SOME BULLSHIT THOUGH IT WAS FUN TO DRAW IT. THE KNIVES ARE COOL. MAX VON SYDOW IS COOL TOO. IT'S A GOOD ONE. DARIO, BEAUTIFUL AS ALWAYS. BLACKGLOVE.

MAX VON SYDOW

STEFANO DIONISI CHARA CASELLI ROSSELLA FALK
GABRIELE LAVIA PAOLO MARIA SCALONDRO ROBERTO ZIBETTI
SCREENPLAY by DARIO ARGENTO & FRANCO FERRINI

DIRECTED by DARIO ARGENTO

R 2001 COLOR 116 MINUTES CC

SLEEPWALKER

SLEEP WALKERS noun Nomd..
SHAPSHIFTING CREATURES W/ HUMAN & FELINE
ORIGINS. VULNERABLE TO DEADLY CAT SCRATCHES
SLEEPWALKER FEEDS UPON LIFE FOURCE OF
VIRGINAL HUMAN FEMAILS. VAMPIRE LEGEND
1884

I FEEL LIKE THIS MOVIE HAS A LOT OF GOOD ELEMENTS, IDEAS, CAST, BUT THEY ALL SEEM TO EXIST SEPERATLY FROM EACH OTHER. THIS IS NOTED AS KINGS 1ST ORIGINAL SCREENPLAY? HMMM O.K. WELL I FEEL THIS COULD USE A RE-EDITING. PERHAPS. THEY BUILD UP A NICE TONE BUT DASH IT EVERY 5 minutes OR SO. LIKE A TV MOVIE JOG OR DOUBLE TAKE. MAYBE IT WORKED BETTER IN ~~THE~~ THEATRE. AMONG THE OTHER KING MOVIES THIS IS ON THE MORE HO-HUM SIDE FOR ME. STILL IT HAS A LOT OF WORTHWILE STUFF & PROBABLY WORTH A LOW-KEY VIEWING w/ FRIENDS OR A DATE.

BRIAN KRAUSE MÄDCHEN AMICK
ALICE KRIGE
WRITTEN BY STEPHEN KING
DIRECTED BY MICK GARRIS

1992 CC R COLOR APPROX. 89 MINS.

THIS CHARMING MAN 1
WHAT DIFFERENCE DOES IT MAKE? 2
PANIC 3
HEAVEN KNOWS I'M MISERABLE NOW 4
ASK 5
THE BOY WITH THE THORN IN HIS SIDE 6
HOW SOON IS NOW 7
SHOPLIFTERS OF THE WORLD UNITE 8
GIRLFRIEND IN A COMA 9
SHEILA TAKE A BOW 10
STOP ME IF YOU THINK 11
YOU'VE HEARD THIS ONE BEORE
THE QUEEN IS DEAD A FILM BY DEREK JARMAN 12
Includes THE QUEEN IS DEAD,
THERE IS A LIGHT THAT NEVER GOES OUT and PANIC

DIRECTED BY:
3, 5 & 12 Derek Jarman
7 Paula Grief and Richard Levine.
9 & 11 Tim Broad
1 Tyne Tees
2 4 6 8 & 10 BBC

Executive Producer Ray Still

Approximate Running Time 50 minutes

GEE WHIZ... WHAT CAN I SAY. I LOVE THE SMITHS. I WATCHED THIS VIDEO AT LEAST THREE TIMES THIS TIME. I DON'T EVEN KNOW WHAT I CAN SAY ABOUT THIS VIDEO. I LOVE IT. IF YOU HAVE NOT HEAR'D THE SMITHS I RECCOMMEND THEM TO EVERYONE. TO ANY SMITHS FAN WHO HAS NOT GOT THIS, I SAY YOU SHOULD LOOK INTO GETTING ONE FOR YOUR HOME COLLECTION. EVEN THE PACKAGING IS PERFECT.

THE SMITHS
THE COMPLETE PICTURE

SO, I'V SEEN THIS STREIGHT. & M.S.T. 3K STYLE. THIS TIME M.S.T. STYLE. SO... I NOTICED THEY FULLY DROPPED THE COKE DEALING ANGLE. OH WELL. SOUL TAKER IS PRETTY ENTERTAINING ON IT'S OWN - Z'DAR IS FULLY CAPTIVATING AS ALLWAYS. YES! COOL BOX TO DRAW TOO. REAL NICE SOCIAL SPACE OUT

FIREPLACE, ROOM; TONE SETTER. FUN ACTING THE STAR WROTE THE SCREEN-PLAY; SO THAT'S A GOOD SIGN.

A NICE BRAIN DRAIN FRIDAY NITE. PEEP THIS, GOOD FUN, NO HASSEL VIDEO FUN. SORRY ABOUT THE MESS, BUT I WROTE THIS ON THE BUS AT 1:49 AM ♡ tim

WRITTEN BY VIVIAN SCHILLING

SOULTAKER

THE
SOULTANGLER

1987/COLOR/90 MINUTES

AMBITIOUS INDEPENDENT MADSCIENTIST KIDNAPPING DRUG PSYCHO 1960/80'S GORE INTENTS DRY PSYCHIDELIA. DUMB COP/NOSIE YOUNG LADY REPORTER. THIS IS NON STOP. THE MAD SCIENTIST HAS MADE A DRUG THAT LETS HIM TRAVEL THROUGH YOUNGE LADYS EYES & BE IN THEM BUT IT FORCES THEIR SOULS OUT. BUMMER. SPREY BLOOD EVERYWHERE. IT'S GREAT. IT CAME WITH A ZINE TOO WHICH IS ALSO GREAT. SOLID GOLD

STARRING
JAMIE KINSER PIERRE DEVEAUX TOM BAWNA LOUISE MILLMAN

SPECIAL EFFECTS GEORGE HIGHAM MIKE LACKEY

WRITERS PAT BISHOW LANCE LAURIE

DIRECTED BY PAT BISHOW

BLEEDING SKULL! VIDEO

DENNIS HOPPER

STEPHEN DORFF

DEBI MAZAR

SPACE TRUCKERS

HOLY SMOKE SON-BING! DUDES... WHAT PERFECT MOVY. THE PACE IS AWE INSPIRING TO ME. I USED TO BE SO-SO ON STEPHEN DORFF, BUT THIS TURNED ME AROUND. DENNIS HOPPER IS AS IS NO SUPRISE THE BEST & GET'S TO BE OUR PROTAG. STUART GORDON IS JUST SO GREAT FOR ME & I MUST SAY I THINK THIS DEFINATLY ONE OF MY MOST FAVORITES OF HIS CATALOGUE. THIS ONE JUST JAMS & WONT WASTE A SECOND ON SIDE TRACKS OF FOOLISHNESS. SO MUCH FUN. PURE ADVENTURE CLASSIC. DEBI MAZAR GETS TO ACTUALLY DO A TON OF ACTING WHICH I'M SAD TO SAY IS NOTE-WORTHY BECAUSE SHE USUALLY GETTS SHORTED ON SCREEN TIME. SHES ALSO ONE OF THE COHESIVFIENG ELEMENTS OF THE WHOLE PICTURE.

THE PACE IS WHAT I CALL "RPG". SORT'A "& THEN & THEN & THEN etc." JUST NO END OF FRESH OBSTICALS. SO MUCH FUN. I LOVE IT.

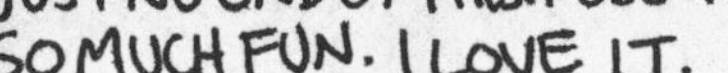

DENNIS HOPPER STEPHEN DORFF DEBI MAZAR
& CHARLES DANCE

STORY BY STUART GORDON & TED MANN
SCREENPLAY BY TED MANN
DIRECTED BY STUART GORDON

PG-13 COLOR

1998 APPROX. 96 minutes

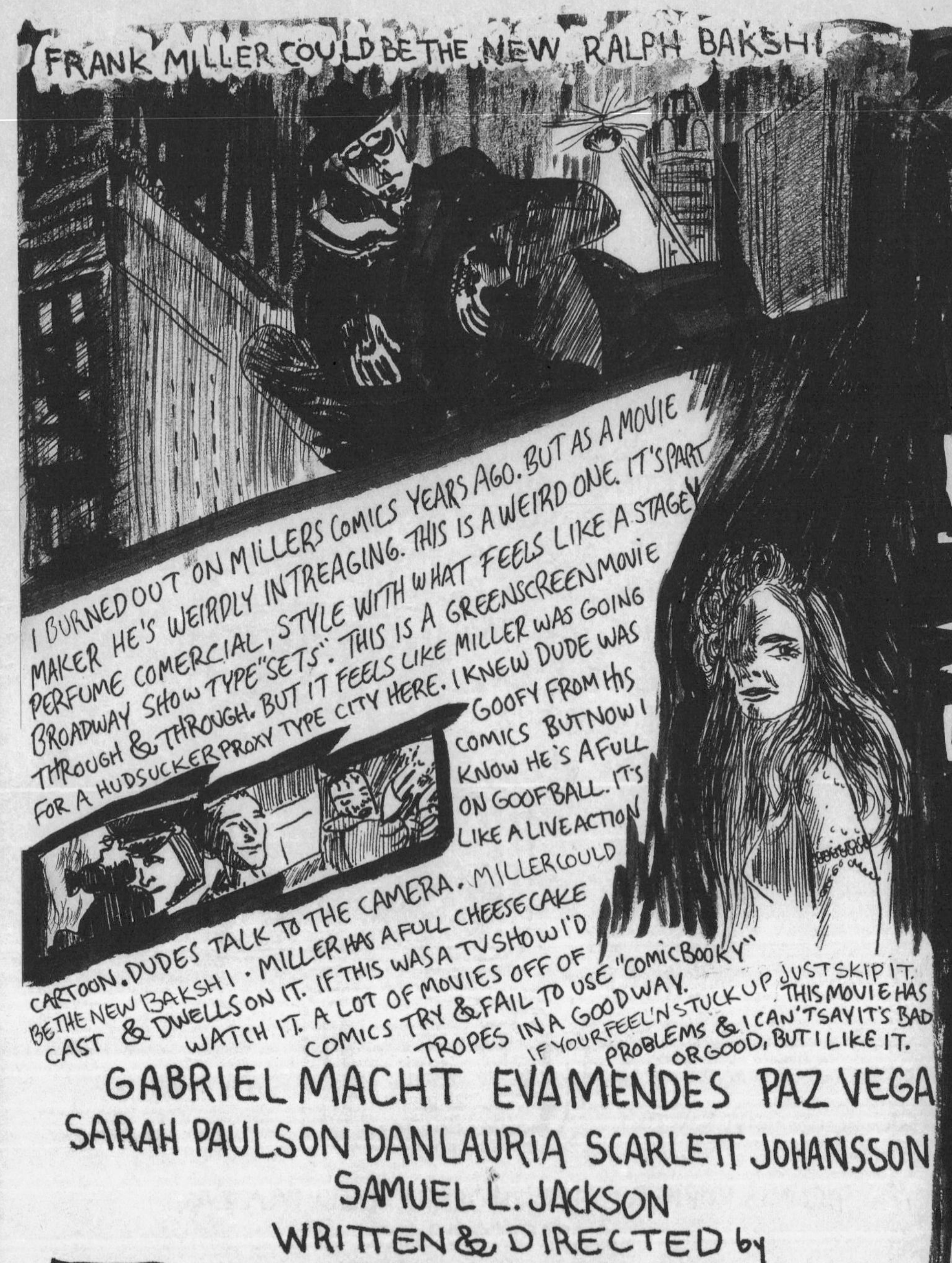

2008 COLOR FEATURE RUN TIME APPROX. 108 minutes

I DID'NT DIG THE "DRY FOR WET" SCEEN NEXT TO THE SLO-MO WATER PORN SHOTS.

GABRIEL MACHT
EVA MENDES
SARAH PAULSON
SCARLETT JOHANSSON
SAMUEL L. JACKSON
THE
SPIRIT
A FRANK MILLER CARTOON MADE SPYKIDS STYLE.

FROM THE DIRECTOR OF LIFEFORCE

SPONTANEOUS COMBUSTION

BRAD DOURIF CYNTHIA BAIN JON CYPHER
& MELINDA DILLON

SCREENPLAY by TOBE HOOPER & HOWARD GOLDBERG
DIRECTED by TOBE HOOPER *

SPONTANEOUS COMBUSTION
I RENT THIS EVERY FEW YEARS. IT'S GOT SO MENY FANTASTIC INGREDIENTS BUT THE RESULT IS OCWARD. THE 1950/80'S MOTIEF IS A PERSONAL FAV OF MINE & SO ARE HOOPER & BRAD DOURIF. AND IT FULLY DELIVERS ON THE TITLE PROMISE. GOV. CONSPIRISY PLOT HAS A KINDERED THING W/THE "TONE" IN A TV MOVIE WAY. IT IS SAID THAT PRODUCERS TOOK THIS MOVIE & MADE THIS FORM OF THE MOVIE W/ UNUSED TAKES AGAINST HOOPERS WISHS. SEEMS LIKELY.
IF YOU ARE'NT ALL-READY A HOOPER FAN, DON'T START HERE
1990 COLOR 97 MINUTES R

I DIG TOM JANE. HE'S OFTEN THE BEST THING IN HIS MOVIES. HE'S MY FAV. FRANK CASTLE BUT THAT MOVIE SUCKS. SO, TOM JANE'S COOL BUT THE MOVIES HE'S IN ARE TOO OFTEN NOT. BUT THIS ONE IS COOL & PRETTY GOOD TOO.
HE'S A COP IN AFRICA & SEE'S THAT THAT'S NOT COOL. BUT WHAT CAN HE DO ABOUT IT? HE'S A WELL TRAINED INTITELED WHITE MAN WITH SHAME ISSUES TO VENT. WELL? WHAT WOULD YOU DO? ROB BANKS? WITH A BIG MOUSTACH & AVIATOR GLASS'? BUR-DOY! SEEMS LIKE THAT WOULD STREIGHTEN OUT ALL YOUR PROBLEMS DOSE'NT IT? UT-OH DUDE, MAYBE NOT. THIS IS BASED ON SOME TRUE STORY SO IT HAS THAT CHOPPY TIME LAPSE EDITING AND MELLOW DRAMATIC CELIBRATIONS, MELTDOWNS, & VIOLENCE. JANES BEST.
TOM JANE
DAVID PATRICK O'HARA
DEXTER FLETCHER
DEBORAH KARA UNGER MARIUS WEYERS ASHLEY TAYLOR
WRITTEN BY BIMA STAGG DIRECTOR BRONWEN HUGHES
R1
CC
APPROX 112 minutes COLOR 2004

TOM JANE IS

STANDER

GOOD COP. GREAT CRIMINAL!

Jamie Fox Sam Shepard
Jessica Biel Josh Lucas

WRITTEN BY
W.D. RICHTER
DIRECTED BY
ROB COHEN

©2005

PG-13 COLOR APPROX. 121 minutes

WIDESCREEN SPECIAL EDITION

JOSH LUCAS JESSICA BIEL JAMIE FOXX

STEALTH

STORYTELLING
a film by
TODD SOLONDZ

HAVE YOU EVER SEE'N A TODD SOLONDZ MOVIE? IF NOT, YOU OUGHT. JUST SO YOU KNOW. FOR ME, HE IS A BIG INSPIRATION. HE'S MORE BRUTAL & AS GOOD AS [illegible]. SO, I HEAR'D THAT THERE WAS AN ADDITIONAL CHAPTER TO THIS MOVIE, THAT THE "STAR" OF SAID CHAPTER ACTUALL SUE'D OUT OF THE MOVIE. I DON'T KNOW IF IT'S TRUE, BUT A WIMP MIGHT NOT DIG BEING AS COOL AS THIS MOVIE IS, REGUARDLESS OF THEIR PRESENCE. IF YOU HAVE SEE'N A T. SOLONDZ MOVIE BEFORE, THEN YOU CAN EXPECT ANOTHER SUCH CLASSIC.

SELMA BLAIR PAUL GIAMATTI
ROBERT WISDOM JOHN GOODMAN
LUPE ONTIVEROS JONATHAN OSSER
MARK WEBBER MUSIC BY BELLE & SEBASTIAN AND
NATHAN LARSON WRITTEN & DIRECTED BY TODD SOLONDZ

COLOR

APPROX. 87 min.

R RESTRICTED

RICHARD FARNSWORTH · SISSY SPACEK

IMOUTIONALY AGRESSIVENESS
WITHOUT BULLY'N ME. THANKS
DUDE. THIS RULES. ALVIN IS A
CHILL'D OUT COMPLEX GUY. HE'S A
HARD ASS WHO STAYS ON TOP OF IT. NO B.S.
TYPE TALK. IF YOU DON'T LOOK YOU MAY JUST
GET THESE ELEMENTS BUT GIVE
THIS A FEW EXTRA PEEPINGS & I
THINK YOU FEEL
THE HEAVY CHILLS
AS YOU COME INTO
SOMETHING BLEED-
ING & ALIVE. I FELT
REALLY SAFE WATCH-
ING THIS THE FIRST 4 OR 5 TIMES
I WATCHED THIS, BUT THESE DAYS
I'M WATCH'N IT WITH A STING
IN MY SIDE. IT GIVES ME
A SAFE PLACE TO DEAL WITH

HEAVY IDEAS. WHAT ARE SUPPOSED TO DO
WHENE YOU FALL INTO A MOVIE LIKE
THIS. I HAVE NO IDEA. STILL, I FEEL
LIKE EVERYONE SHOULD GIVE THIS
A FAIR SHOT. AT LEAST ONCE. YOU KNOW
WHAT? MAYBE I'M JUST BEING SOME
AMERIKKKN GOTHIC STAMP COLLECTER
TYPE, BUT G-WHIZ YALL. I DIG IT.

WRITTEN BY JOHN ROACH & MARY SWEENEY
DIRECTED BY DAVID LYNCH

ALEX COX'S

STRAIGHT TO HELL RETURNS

YES, RETURNS. SO IT'S THE SAME BUT, THERES NEW FOOTAGE CUT IN; THAT WAS FROM THE SCRIPT BUT DID'NT GET SHOT FOR **MISC.** REASONS. I THINK. IF YOU DON'T LIKE THE ORIGINAL THEN THIS AINT GONNA CHANGE THAT. ESSENTIALY THE SAME W/ MORE OVERT CARTOONY'NESS & A FEW C.G'S. MORE BLOOD. THINK IT TOOK ME 3 WATCHES {OVERTIME} TO DIG THE ORIGINAL. NOW I DIG IT & THIS NEW CUT IS COOL TOO. I THINK IN SOME INSTANCES COX HAS PLAY'D DOWN HIS CARTOONYNESS FOR CERTINE MOVIES, & I LIKE THOSE; BUT HE'S MORE MY JAM WHEN HE'S OFF THE "CHAIN". SO TO ME THIS IS A PREFERABLE VERSION. AS FAR AS I CAN TELL, THERE DON'T "SEEM" TO BE ANY OMISIONS. IT'S A GANGSTER WESTERN SATIRE MADE W/ BY THE ROCK'RS WHO PARTY &/OR RULE THAT COX KNOWS/DIGS.

SY RICHARDSON JOE STRUMMER DICK RUDE COURTNEY LOVE THE POGUES ELVIS COSTELLO DENNIS HOPPER GRACE JONES EDWARD TUDOR-POLE &

MIGUEL SANDOVAL JENNIFER BALGOBIN

WRITTEN BY DICK RUDE & ALEX COX

DIRECTOR ALEX COX

RUNNINGTIME 91 MINS. COLOR 1987 & 2010 5.1 DVD R

MICROMEDIA.COM ALEXCOX.COM

SY RICHARDSON
JOE STRUMMER
DICK RUDE
COURTNEY LOVE

ALEX COX'S

STRAIGHT TO HELL RETURNS

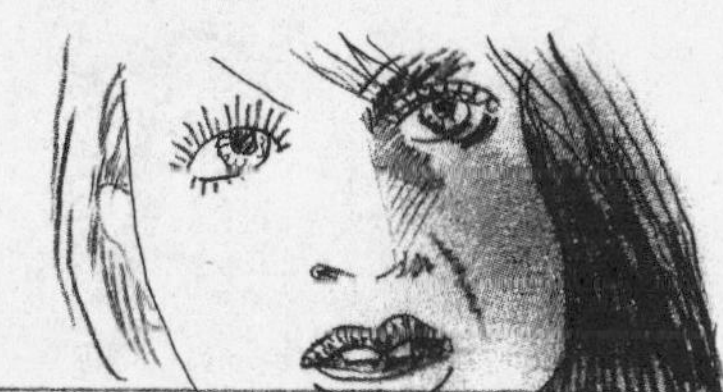

JOHN CLEESE in THE STRANGE CASE OF THE END OF CIVILIZATION AS WE KNOW IT

JOHN CLEESE in THE STRANGE CASE OF THE END OF CIVILIZATION AS WE KNOW IT

I LOVE THIS MOVIE. IT'S FULLY MY JAM. I DIG SHIRLOCK HOLMES SPIN OFF'S & FAKE HOLMES MOVIES. BUT THE ROOT OF MY ATTACHMENT IS JOSEPH McGRATH, WHO DIRECTED & CO-WROTE THIS. McGRATH IS AMONG A SHORT LIST OF DIRECTORS I'M OBSESSED WITH. HE DIRECTED "THE MAGIC CHRISTIAN" WHICH IS ALSO AMAZING. THIS MOVIE IS TONS OF FUN AND I GET THE FEELING IT WAS FOR TV SO MOST FOLKS COULD WATCH IT, BUT THS SENCE OF HUMOR IS VERY STONEY & POLITICLLY CONTRARIAN TO WHAT STILL IS THE ESTABLISHMENT. DOPE. I COULD & WILL WATCH THIS A BAZGILLION'Z OF TIMES FOR SURE.

PERFECTION.

WRITTEN BY: JACK HOBBS, JOSEPH McGRATH, JOHN CLEESE

PRODUCER: HUMPHREY BARCLAY

DIRECTOR: JOSEPH McGRATH

1977 RUNNING TIME: 55 Min. COLOR

A DIVISION OF KULTUR
121 Highway 36
WEST LONG BRANCH, NJ 07764
(908) 229-2343

STUART SAVES HIS FAMILY

YOU'LL LAUGH
BECAUSE IT'S NOT
YOUR FAMILY.
YOU'LL CRY
BECAUSE IT IS.

AL FRANKEN LAURA SAN GIACOMO
VINCENT D'ONOFRIO, SHERLEY KNIGHT, HARRIS YULIN
SCREENPLAY BY AL FRANKEN
DIRECTED BY HAROLD RAMIS

STUART SAVES HIS FAMILY

I WAS OPPTIMISTIC, BUT KEPT MY EXPECTATIONS LOW. IT IS AN S.N.L. MOVIE. THANKFULLY THEY MOVE PAST THE SKIT & JUST FOLLOW STUART DOWN HIS PATH OF TROUBLES.

SMALLEY

NOT A TYPICAL COMEDY. MORE OF A MILD FAMILY DRAMA WITH STUART AS THE BLACKSHEEP. I THINK MY MOM WOULD DIG THIS. THIS A GOOD SOLID COMEDY/DRAMA. NOT SLAPSTICK. THE CAST IS GREAT. ALL THIS NEEDS IS A NEW AUDIENCE. I'M DOWN TO WATCH IT AGAIN.

1995 PG-13 97 MINUTES

TROMA TEAMVIDEO
PRESENTS
Stuck on You!
TROMA
TEAM

THIS IS THE MELLOIST A LEAST SALATIOUS OF THE TROMA CATALOGUE I HAVE SEEN SOFAR. IT'S ACTUALY KIND'A SWEET & CHARMING. SOMEWHERE BETWEEN THE NEIGHBORHOODS OF 1970'S ZUCKER BROTHERS & WOODY ALLEN. THE BOX SAYS IT 1995 BUT THATS JUST UNLIKELY BASED ON THE AGE ATTITUDE & ERA. ACCORDING TO SHEAS PHONE IT'S FROM 1982. THIS COUPLE AREFILE'N FOR DIVORCE AND THEY NEED THE JUDGE TO SIGN OFF ON IT. BUT INSTED HE GRILLS THEM AND COUNCELS THEM AGAINST THEY'R WISHS. THEY WIND UP RECOUNTING THE SWEET, SILLY, STRESSY, ANGRY, HORNIE, BEST AND WORST MOMENTS OF THEIR RELATIONSHIP. ALL FRAMED W/THIS RASCALLY NOSIE LOVABLY SKAMP OF A JUDGE. IF YOU DON'T DIG TROMA THEN THIS IS THE ONE FOR YOU & VISAVERSA. I WAS HOPE'N IT WOULD BE ABOUT TWO PEOPLE GLUED TOGETHER BUT NO. PERHAPS ANOTHER DAY.

PROFESSOR IRWIN COREY VIRGINIA PENTA MARK MIKULSKI

BY MICHAEL HERZ & LLOYD KAUFMAN

~~1995~~ COLOR

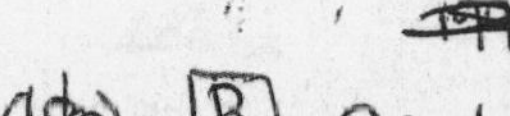

APPROX TIME 85 minutes

STUNTS

STARRING ROBERT FORSTER, FIONA LEWIS, RAY SHARKEY
JOANNA CASSIDY

DIRECTED BY MARK L. LESTER

SCREENPLAY DENNIS JOHNSON BARNEY COHEN

I DUG THIS. IT'S PRETTY CAPTIVATING DISPITE HAVING A TACKED ON SUSPENCE TYPE "PLOT" THAT SORT'A TAKES UP TOO MUCH TIME. STUNTPEOPLE ARE PRETTY AMAZING & CAPTIVATING TO ME AND I BELIEVE AT LEAST ONE OF THE SCREENWRITTERS IS A STUNTMAN SO THERES A NICE SENCE OF LIFESTYLE REPRESENTED. THEY LIVE IN VANS W/DOGS, JUMP ON HELICOPTERS, OFF TOWERS, 2-WHEEL'N CARS, ASSASSINATED BY MYSTERIOUS CREWMEMBER? A STUNTMAN DIES UNDER FISH'Y CIRCUMSTANCES & FORSTER IS DRAW'N BACK INTO STUNTS FOR THE REST OF THE SHOW. IT'S THE MOST COMMON PART OF THE MOVIE & THERES NOT MUCH TO GET INTERESTED IN THIS ELEMENT OF THE MOVIE, THANFULLY IT'S CUTUP INTO THE MOVIE LESS OFTEN THAN NOT. FORSTER HAS A GREAT LAYED BACK CHARISMA WHICH IS WHY HE CAN PULL THIS OFF, BECAUSE HE DOSENT HAVE THAT COWBOYISH QUALITY THAT THE STUNTFOLK SEEM TO. THIS MAY SEEM PRETTY MELLOW TO PEOPLE WHO ARE INTO MODERN ACTION/ADVENTURE MOVIES, THERE ACTUAL CHARACTERS WHO HAVE BELIEVABLE LIVES AND MOTIVES. A CASE OF "THEY DON'T MAKE'M LIKE THAT ANYMORE"

RUNNING TIME: 90 MINUTES
COLOR
1977
NEWLINECINEMA CORP.

TVB 1639

ACTION-ADVENTURE

Dying is one hell of a way to make a living.

STUNTS

A STORY ABOUT STUNTMEN.

SPECIAL
50¢
RENTAL

OJAI VIDEO
305 E. MATILIJA
OJAI. CA 93023
(805) 646-9652

Surf II
BUZZ
MEDIA

STARRING: EDDIE DEEZEN, LINDA KERRIDGE, CLEAVON LITTLE, MORGAN PAULL
Surf II.
RUTH BUZZI & LYLE WAGGONER
ALL KINDS OF DIFFERENT THINGS ARE HAPPENING TO ALL KINDA PEOPLE, BUT MOSTLY IT ABOUT THIS TOXIC SODA THAT MAKES YOU EAT GARBAGE & STUFF. MOSTLY JOKES, BUT THERES SOME GLUE ON PARTS. WHATA HOOT. CRAZYSHIT. I DIG IT.
PRODUCED by GEORGE G. BRAUNSTEIN AND RON HAMADY
WRITTEN & DIRECTED by RANDAL BADAT
COLOR
96 MINUTES
R
1984
BUZZ
BUZZ

THIS IS MY 2ND FAVORITE CRAVEN. ITS PAIRED DOWN NICELY. EVERYTHING LOOKS PRETT COOL EXCEPT FOR SWAMPTHING? JESUS WEPT. IT WOULD BE NICE TO CUT FOOTAGE FROM PART TWO OR THE SHOW OR EVEN THE CARTOON, INTO IT OVER HIM. NO DIS' ON THE DUDE IN THE HEFTYBAG. I FLIP FLOP ON THE SUIT. IS IT MENT TO BE AN ARTY THING. A BUNUEL TYPE THING? BACKYARD ROMANCE? ABSURDIST, I DON'T KNOW... MAYBE IT WAS SOME STUPID PRODUCTION CONFLICT.

THERES A NICE 50'S STYLE THING GOING ON HERE, A BIT OF JACK ARNOLD SPICE. IT'S CLASSIC TROPES, SECRET FORMULAS BEAUTY & THE BEAST. THE SYRUM MAGNAFYS YOUR TRUE SELF, ALEC HOLLAND BECOMES A WISE COOL PLANT. SOME TERRENCE McKENNA DEAL. ALL THE CREEPS TURN INTO VIOLENT BEASTS. THE SUIT AINT SO BAD. AND RAY WISE & DAVID HESS!

LOUIS JOURDAN ADRIENNE BARBEAU

WRITTEN & DIRECTED by WES CRAVEN

APPROX. FEATURE RUN TIME: 1 HOUR 31 MINUTES • COLOR • 1982

SWAMP
THING
SCIENCE MADE HIM A MONSTER

WIDE SCREEN

TALES FROM THE CRYPT

DEMONKNIGHT

TALES FROM THE CRYPT

I LOVE THE TALES F/the CRYPT BRAND. DUDE ERNEST DICKERSON, DUDE. THIS ONES A LITTLE TOO NORMAL BY CONTRAST TO THE HBO SHOW, BUT STILL A CUT ABOVE YOUR STANDARD FAIR. PROBABLY MY FAVORITE OF THE MOVIES FROM THE SERIES OF MOVIES. SO... HONESTLEY... A SOLID MOVIE. I WISH THERE WAS A CRYPT KEEPER FAIMING SEQUENCE W/ ASIDES & ALL THAT CRYPT KEEP'R STUFF. I SAW THIS AT THE CHEAP 'O THEATRE W/ MY BUDDY J-STONE. I THINK IT'S BILLY ZANE'S FIRST BALD ROLL OR IT WAS THE 1ST I SAW. THERES ELECTRIC NIPPLE CLAMPS. THE DUDE FROM "PEOPLE UNDER THE STAIRS" IS IN THIS, I THINK. GOTTA SAY IT'S BEEN TOO LONG FOR ME TO KEEP IT ALL STREIGHT. I DO REMEMBER THE TWISTS WERE'NT TOO GREAT COMPAIRED TO SOME OF THE EPISODES AND COMICBOOKS. BUT ITS FUN.

TALES FROM THE CRYPT, MOVIE

THOMAS HADEN CHURCH
BILLY ZANE · JADA PINKETT · JOHN KASSIR
DICK MILLER · WILLIAM SADLER · CCH POUNDER
SCREENPLAY BY
ETHAN REIFF, CYRUS VORIS, & MARK BISHOP
DIRECTED BY ERNEST DICKERSON
1995 92 MINUTES [R]

TOO HIP FOR SPIELBERG
ACTION
NEW RELEASE

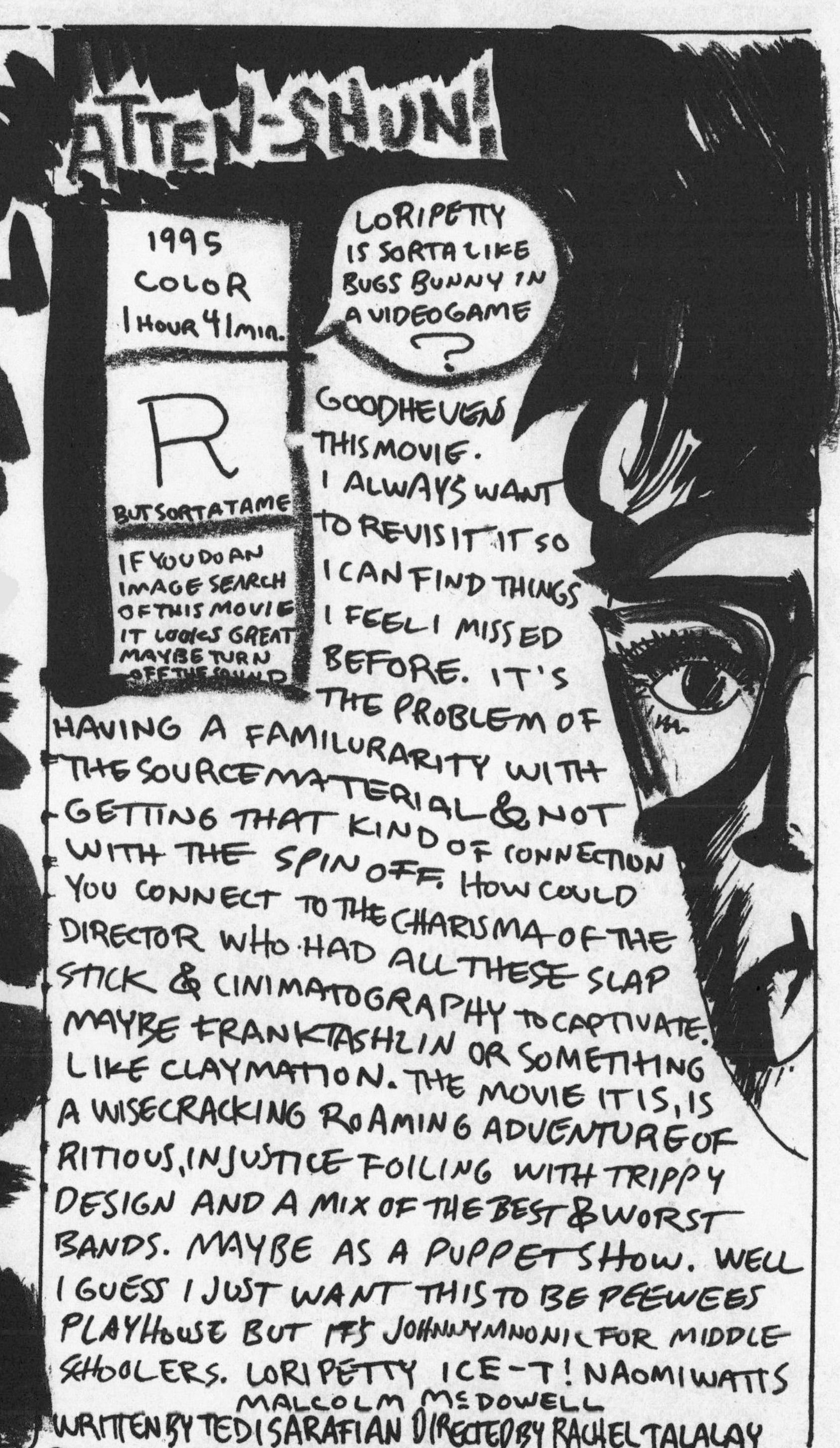
ATTEN-SHUN!
1995
COLOR
1 HOUR 41 MIN.
R
BUT SORTA TAME
IF YOU DO AN IMAGE SEARCH OF THIS MOVIE IT LOOKS GREAT MAYBE TURN OFF THE SOUND
LORI PETTY IS SORTA LIKE BUGS BUNNY IN A VIDEOGAME ?
GOOD HEVENS THIS MOVIE. I ALWAYS WANT TO REVISIT IT SO I CAN FIND THINGS I FEEL I MISSED BEFORE. IT'S THE PROBLEM OF HAVING A FAMILURARITY WITH THE SOURCE MATERIAL & NOT GETTING THAT KIND OF CONNECTION WITH THE SPINOFF. HOW COULD YOU CONNECT TO THE CHARISMA OF THE DIRECTOR WHO HAD ALL THESE SLAP STICK & CINIMATOGRAPHY TO CAPTIVATE. MAYBE FRANK TASHLIN OR SOMETHING LIKE CLAYMATION. THE MOVIE IT IS, IS A WISECRACKING ROAMING ADVENTURE OF RITIOUS, INJUSTICE FOILING WITH TRIPPY DESIGN AND A MIX OF THE BEST & WORST BANDS. MAYBE AS A PUPPET SHOW. WELL I GUESS I JUST WANT THIS TO BE PEEWEES PLAYHOUSE BUT IT'S JOHNNY MNONIC FOR MIDDLE SCHOOLERS. LORI PETTY ICE-T! NAOMI WATTS MALCOLM McDOWELL
WRITTEN BY TEDI SARAFIAN DIRECTED BY RACHEL TALALAY

THE TEXAS CHAINSAW MASSACRE
4/5
Young Fry'endz A-typical summer afternoon drive becomes a terrifying nightmare

PLEASE, TELL ME YOU HAVE NOT SEE'N THIS.

IF YOU HAVE SEEN IT THEN JUST SKIP THIS BECAUSE YOU'V ALLREADY HEAR'D IT.

SO, SOME CITY FREAKS DRIVE A VAN INTO THE COUNTRY & RUN INTO SOME COUNTRY FREAKS WHO SERIOUSLY DESIMATE THEM. COOL.

THIS IS A SUPER ART'Y MOVIE WHICH FOLKS REAIZE AFTER SEE'N IT BUT THE TITLE IS SO GOOD THAT I THINK IT'S A BIT OF THE "COAT THAT WEARS YOU" TYPE CINARIO.

I DEFINATELY FEEL VERY ALIVE AFTER WATCH'N IT.

THIS MOVIE IS A GOOD RORSHOCK TEST ON PEOPLE. IT SORT'A PUTS EVERYONE IN A MAD LIB OF THERE OWN TRIPPY MINDSET & WHAT YOU COME OUT WITH SAYS MORE ABOUT THEM THAN THE MOVIE. OR, MAYBE I'M AN ASS.

TOBE HOOPER HAS MADE SOME OF THE BEST MOVIES IN HISTORY, & THIS IS HIS FIRST ONE. NO COMPLAINTS.

IF YOU FIND ANY FLAW IN THIS IT ONLY BECAUSE YOU ARE A FOOL LET IN TO THE LIGHT, & MUST RETREAT BACK TO YOUR FOOL CHAMBER TO EXPLAIN YOUR FAILINGS WITH FINGER POINTING

DO YOU FIND MURDER CAPTIVATING?

COOL MOVIE. CHECK THIS OUT Y'ALL. BELIEVE.

MARILYN BURNS PAUL A. PARTAIN EDWIN NEAL JIM SIEDOW

& GUNNAR HANSEN

WRITTEN BY KIM HENKEL & TOBE HOOPER

DIRECTED BY TOBE HOOPER

DIGITALLY REMASTERED COLLECTORS EDITION

FUCK DUDE.... WHAT?IT'S ONLY ONE OF MY MOST FAVORITE SEQUELS. PEEP THIS OUT.

A TOBE HOOPER FILM

THE TEXAS CHAINSAW MASSACRE PART 2

THE TEXAS CHAINSAW MASSACRE PART 2
DIRECTOR: TOBE HOOPER
DENNIS HOPPER
WRITTEN BY
L.M. KIT CARSON
I DON'T KNOW WHAT ELSE YOU WANT BUT IF THIS AINT IT PLEASE DON'T TELL ME

LEATHERFACE

THE TEXAS CHAINSAW MASSACRE PART III

ORIGINAL UNCUT CLASSIC

THE TEXAS CHAINSAW MASSACRE III

THE TEXAS CHAINSAW MASSICRE III

ORIGINAL UNCUT CLASSIC

IF THIS MOVIE HAD A DIFFERENT NAME I THINK FOLKS WOULD DIG IT A LOT MORE. I THOUGHT IT WAS GOOD. NOT REALLY IN LINE WITH THE FIRST TWO, AND NOT REALLY TOO DIFERENT THOUGH. VIGGO IS IN IT, BUT NOT ENOUGH. KEN FOREE IS AWESOME & FUNNY. BUT A LITTLE TOO AWESOME. HE STARTS SHREDDING & JUST WON'T STOP. IF YOU HAVE THE ABILITY TO SEPERATE THIS FROM THE FIRST TWO, I SAY WATCH IT. I'V ALLWAYS BEEN A BIG FAN OF THE PREVIEW FOR THIS MOVIE.

KATE HODGE WILLIAM BUTLER
KEN FOREE TONI HUDSON JOE UNGER
VIGGO MORTENSEN R.A. MIHAILOFF

WRITTEN BY
DAVID SCHOW

DIRECTED BY
JEFF BURR

COLOR

NOT RATED

LETTER BOXED

RUNNING TIME APPROX. 85 Mins.

YOU SEE THEM ON THE STREET. YOU WATCH THEM ON T.V.
YOU THINK THEY'R PEOPLE JUST LIKE YOU.
YOUR WRONG. DEAD WRONG.
JOHN CARPENTERS
THEY LIVE
RODDY PIPER
KEITH DAVID MEG FOSTER
SCREENPLAY by FRANK ARMITAGE
DIRECTED by JOHN CARPENTER
MCA
HOMEVIDEO
STEREO

JOHN CARPENER'S THEY LIVE

I LOVE THIS MOVIE. FULL ON PIPER/CARPENTER ITS A PERFECT FOLLOW THROUGH FROM PRINCE OF DARKNESS. OF THE TWO, THIS IS THE FUN ONE W/ SOME HOPE, IT END W/ SEX & THE DEATH OF T.V. AND ALL. CARPENTER GETS A REAL HONEST HARDWORKING LOVE-ABLE BLUE COLLOR HERO W/PIPER & IT'S PERFECT. I BELIEVE IT'S BECOME A TRUE STORY TOO... I HOPE THE BULLSHIT THING WILL COME TO AN END SO FANTASTICLY. THE QUIETMAN STYLE FIGHT FEELS GOOD STILL. I WISH THESE DUDE WOULD DO MORE MOVIES TOGETHER. PIPER HAS THAT REAL DEAL SHIT. UNBEATABLE.

COLOR 1 HR. 35 MIN. R

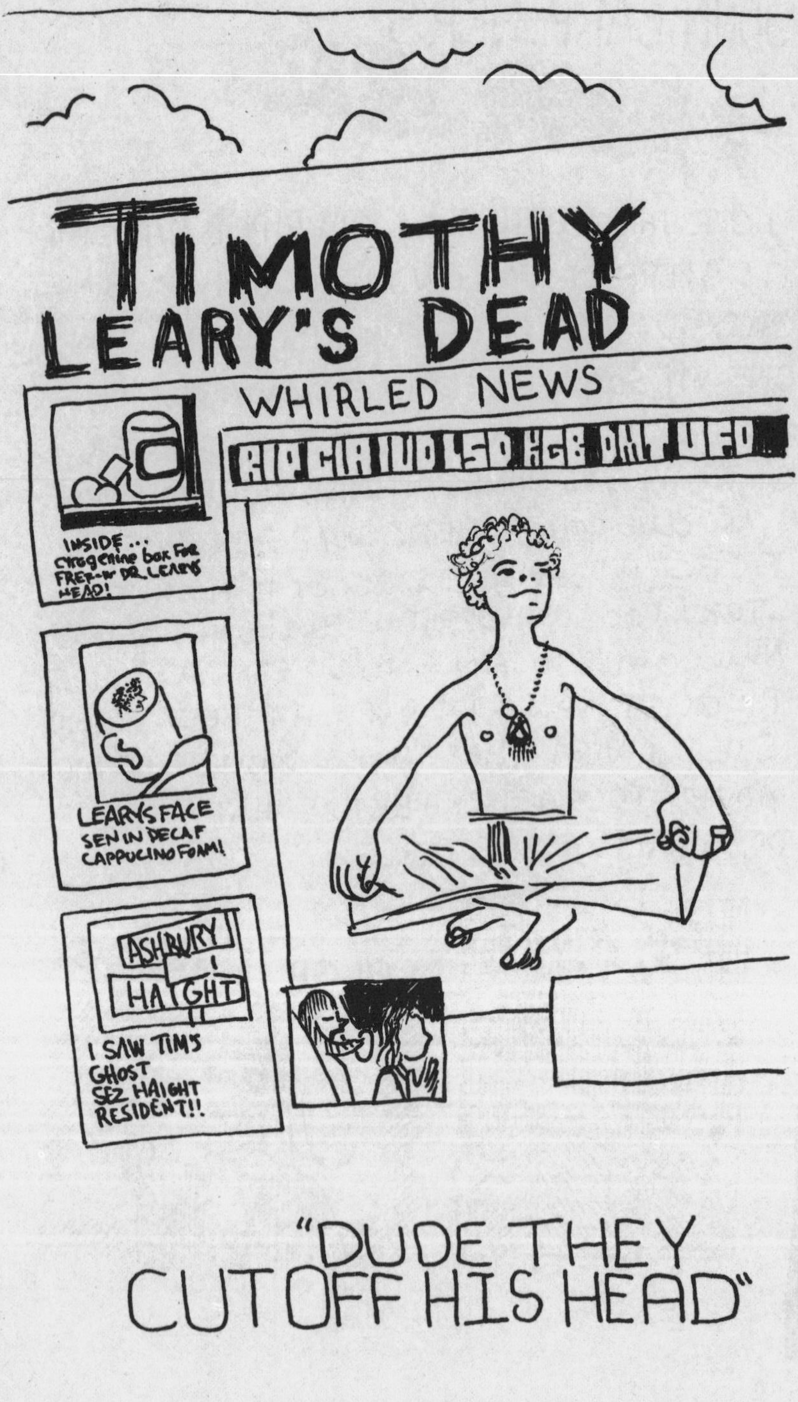

TIMOTHY LEARY'S DEAD

WHIRLED NEWS

RIP CIA IUD LSD HGB DMT UFO

INSIDE...
Cryogenine box For FREE-zr DR LEARYS HEAD!

LEARYS FACE
SEN IN DECAF
CAPPUCINO FOAM!

ASHBURY
HAIGHT

I SAW TIM'S GHOST SEZ HAIGHT RESIDENT!!

"DUDE THEY CUT OFF HIS HEAD"

LEARY'S DEAD

A LOW BUDGET DOCUMENTRY OF THE LAST DAYS OF DUDE'S LIFE. PRETTY INTERESTING BUT NOT THAT GOOD. THEY GIVE A LIFE HISTORY, "TALK" WITH LEARY, TAPE HIS DEATH & DECAPITATION, BUT DUG THE INTERVIEW WITH RAM DAS THE MOST. I CAN'T GET REALLY INTO MAKING LEARY A BIG DEAL. HE SEEMS TO BE TOO MUCH OR NOT ENOUGH OF A PAIN IN SQUARES ASS'. MAYBE THE STAN LEE OF DOPE.

TIMOTHY LEARY & RICHARD ALPERT

DIRECTED BY

PAUL DAVIDS

WESLEY
SNIPES
PATRICK
SWAYZE
JOHN
LEGUIZAMO
To Wong Foo
THANKS FOR Everything!
Julie Newmar
WESLEY SNIPES PATRICK SWAYZE
JOHN LEGUIZAMO STOCKARD CHANNING
BLYTH DANNER ARLISS HOWARD CHRIS PENN
WRITTEN by DOUGLAS CARTER BEANE
DIRECTED by BEEBAN KIDRON

FOR ALL THE PROMIS THIS MOVIE HAS IT'S A BIT MILD FOR ME. USUALLY SNIPES &/OR SWAYZE ARE THE ONES CARRY'N A MOVIE BUT ZEGUIZAMOS THE MOST BELIEVABLE. SORT'A BIG CITY GIRLS ON A ROAD TRIP GET STRANDED IN A SMALL TOWN & THEY CHANGE THE TOWN & VISAVERSA. YOU KNOW THAT FORMULA RIGHT? STILL IT'S ALLRIGHT THOUGH. CHRIS PENN IS PRETTY AWESOME TOO. FOR A MOVIE W/SUCH A SPACIFIC & NERDY TITLE I WISH IT HAD MORE OF AN OBCESION W/ JULIE NEWMAR. FEELS LIKE THE BALANCE OF THE CHARACTERS IS IS OFF. MOSTLY BECAUSE THERES NOT REALLY MUCH CHEMISTRY JUST LEGUIZAMO GO'N OVER THE TOP. I LIKE IT IN A HALLMARK/DAYTIME T.V. WAY. THE IDEA & CASTING SEEM LIKE GOOD ONES BUT SOME WHERE ALONG THE LINE THIS ALL GOT OFF FOOT & JUST RUNS AT ROOM TEMPRITURE.

COLOR 1 hour 49 Mins. PG-13 CC

SOME TIMES KNOW AS...

"TOPAZ"

I USED TO THINK OF THIS AS AN ART MOVIE ABOUT A PROSTITUTE. WHICH IT IS, BUT NOW'A DAYS I SEE SO MUCH IN IT. UNENPOWERED, ALIENATED, BROKEN HEARTED, IMPRESIONABLE, AMBIVELENT, SHE ENCOUNTERS TIME & AGAIN IMOUTIONAL SOCIAL ABUSE FROM START TO FINISH & S to M. SHE SEE'S A FORTUNE TELLER & PARTYS W/A DOMINANT CO-WERKER. DRAWING HER DIRECTION FROM THEM SHE FOLLOWS A DARK NITE OF THE SOUL SHAMANIC PATH TO... WELL I SHOULD'NT BLOW IT FOR YOU. I RECOMEND THIS FULLY, IT'S LITE & HEAVY. BEAUTIFUL SLEEP-DEPRIVATION PSYCHIDELIC PHOTOGRAPHY. SOME REALLY COOL HAIR/WIGS. DRUGY BUT NOT THE FUN STYLE. LEATHER. I LOVE THE SCENE WHERE THE DUDE SAYS HE'S KERMIT THE FROG. ALSO THERES AN AKIRA COMIC ON A STERIO.

WRITTEN & DIRECTED by RYU MURAKAMI

1992 112 MINUTES  NC-17

TOKYO
DECADENCE

2004 FEATURE RUNNING TIME APPROX 94 MINUTES CC R

ANGELA BETTIS BRENT ROAM JULIET LANDAU
GREG TRAVIS MARCO RODRIGUEZ SARA DOWNING
ADAM GIERASCH SHERI MOON ADAM WEISMAN
RANCE HOWARD

WRITTEN BY
JACE ANDERSON & ADAM GIERASCH

DIRECTED BY
TOBE HOOPER

WIDE SCREEN
TOOLBOX
MURDERS

SCHWARZENEGGER

GET READY FOR THE RIDE OF YOUR LIFE

TOTAL RECALL

O'BANNON & VERHOEVEN! HAVE YOU NOT SEEN THIS? THIS... ONE OF MY ALLTIME FAV'Z. YOU OUGHT TO. SEX, GORE, SCI-FI, PARANOID, MARS, AKTION OUT THE ASS. GET YOUR ASS TO MARS. PRIME AMERICAN VERHOEVEN, THE ONLY THING MISSING IS A COCK SHOT. TOP OF THE LINE IN MY BOOK. SEE YOU AT THE PARTY RICHTER.
APPROX RUNNINGTIME 113 MIN
02
ARNOLD SCHWARZENEGGER
RACHEL TICOTIN SHARON STONE
MICHAEL IRONSIDE RONNY COX
INSPIRED BY "WE CAN REMEMBER IT FOR YOU WHOLESALE"
BY PHILLIP K. DICK
SCREENPLAY BY RONALD SHUSETT &
DAN O'BANNON & GARY GOLDMAN
DIRECTED BY PAUL VERHOEVEN
STERIO
R
1990©

RAD. CHUCK CONNORS IS SO COOL. WITHOUT BEING TOO UNIQUE, IT'S STILL VERY GOOD. HOT YOUNG FOOLS GO OFF THE BEAT'N PATH, HAVE TROUBLE WITH THEIR VW THING. THEY RUN INTO CHUCK WHO TAKES THEM TO HIS RUN DOWN AUTOMATED MANAQUIN FREAK FARM. MYSTERIOUS THINGS START GO'N DOWN & FOOLS DIE. SIMPLE. AWESOME. A TASTY CLASSIC.

CHAPTERS
<Spoilers>

STRANDED
ANYBODY HOME
CLOSED TO THE PUBLIC
HELPFULL STRANGER
CURIOSITY KILLED THE CAT
A GOOD WIFE
AN UNNATURAL ATTACHMENT
LOOKING FOR EILEEN
CAPTIVES
PLASTERFACE
DAVEY REFLECTS
RUN LITTLE GIRL RUN
GOOD GOLLY MISS MOLLY
AN INTIMATE DINNER
SUCH A PRETTY GIRL
GETTING AWAY
GUESS WHO
IT'S TIME
THE STORY UNFOLDS
A KNOCK ON THE DOOR
SLAUSON CUT-OFF

STARRING CHUCK CONNORS
Jocelyn Jones Jon Van Ness Robin Scerwood
& Tanya Roberts

WRITTEN BY DAVID SCHMOELLER & J. LARRY CARROLL
DIRECTED BY DAVID SCHMOELLER

CULT VIDEO

20TH ANNIVERSARY SPECIAL EDITION

TOURIST TRAP

EVERY YEAR YOUNG PEOPLE DISAPPEAR...

I WAS OPTIMISTIC & UNSURE OF THIS. IT'S GOOD, FUN, STRAIT & SPOFFY W/OUT CRASHING. IF ANYTHING I'DA HOPED IT'D BE WEIRD'R. DAVID A. IS A GOOD DIRECTOR
THE CASTING IS REALLY GOOD. THE SHIT HEADS ARE POLITICAL TYPES BUT THE COPS ARE COOL. THE "TEENS" ARE MOSTLY LIKE-ABLE WHILE THE TOWNIE HICKS ARE NOT. EXCEPT FOR THE MOUNTAINMAN, BUT HE'S NOT A TOWNIE. PAUL REUBENS IS DOPE & I WISH WE GOT TO SEE MORE OF HIM THESE DAYS. NOT REALY CRAZY BUT NOT A BORE. I WATCHED IT 2 OR 3 TIMES SO FAR
PAUL REUBENS
RICHMOND ARQUETTE PAZ DE LA HUERTA BALTHAZAR GETTY
LUKAS HAAS BRAD HUNT THOMAS JANE
JAIME KING JASON MEWES MARSHA THOMASON
WRITTEN BY DAVID ARQUETTE AND JOE HARRIS
DIRECTED BY DAVID ARQUETTE
UNRATED
20 FOX
2007
ENGLISH
97 MINUTES WIDESCREEN
COLOR
DOLBY
CC

THE TRIPPER

SEX DUGS &
RONNIE

TRIPPY SORT'A POSITIVE ABOUT MODERN PASSIVE LIFE STYLE. NOT SURE IF IT'S MENT TO BE A FEEL GOOD MOVIE BUT IT DOSE THE JOB FOR ME. SPALDING GRAY IS GREAT & OWNES EVERY MOMENT HE'S ON SCREEN. JOHN GOODMAN IS THE JIMMY STEWERT OF THE SHOW & SOMETIMES BRINGS A TEAR TO MY EYE... WHAT A SAP. NICE USE OF NARARATION, LOTS OF QUESTIONS & UNCERTINTY. MAN, THERES THIS PART AT THE DINNER TABEL WHERE SPALDING DOSE AN EPIC PRESENTATOIN OF THE NEXT STEP IN SOCIAL EVOLUTION THROUGH THIS NEW CITY. SORRY, I FORGOT WHAT MY POINT WAS ON THAT BIT.

DIGITALLY PROCESSED

1986

89 minutes

TRUE STORIES
JOHN GOODMAN ANNIE McENROE TITO LARRIVA
SWOOSIE KURTZ SPALDING GRAY POPS STAPLES
DAVID BYRNE
WRITTEN BY
STEPHEN TOBOLOWSKY BETH HENLEY & DAVID BYRNE
DIRECTED BY DAVID BYRNE

SOME FOLKS SAID TO ME THAT SEASON 2 WAS LESS THAN THE FIRST. WHAT? I DON'T GET IT. THIS IS 100% BANG'N DUDE. I COULD USE A FEW MORE SEASONS TOO. I GUESS SOME FOLKS CAN'T GET WITH THE SHIFT TO EXPLORING BEYOND THE WHOLE LAURA INVESTIGATION. WHILE THE FIRST ONE FOCUS'S ON AN ELEMENT, HERE WE SEE THE BEGINING OF A BIGGER PICTURE. ALSO THE SOAP ELEMENTS HIT THIS GREAT PACE WHICH OPENS UP A TON OF AMAZING CANS OF "WORMS". ANSWERS COME INCONSIQUENTIALY AND THE QUESTIONS COME IN HAZY COMPOUNDED SUCSESSION. STILL, SO GREAT IT'S "ALLMOST" A JOKE HOW THE REST OF T.V. SHOW CAN'T GET WITH IT ANYWHERE LIKE THIS. SURE. OTHER SHOWS IN TV HISTORY CAN RUN HEADS UP BUT THERE IS NO SUCSESSOR FOR ME SINCE. SHIT, WHO CARES; I'M SURE YOU LOVE SO NEW JAM I DON'T KNOW OF. BUT DAMN DUDE, HOW CAN YOU STEP TO LEAVE IT TO BEAVER? NOT WORTH GETTING BENT OUT OF SHAPE OVER YOU KNOW? IT'S JUST NOT REPLICATABLE, SO IT IS IN IT'S OWN SPOT. I CAN & WILL PEEP THIS AT THE DROP OF A HAT

BY

DAVID LYNCH & MARK FROST

TWIN PEAKS

RR

Cafe

HORROR/SUSPENSE

ARE YOU A CAT LOVER? HMMMM... WELL THERES SOME NICECAT STUFF HERE & THERES ALSO SOME NOT SO NICECAT STUFF HAPPENING HERE. MORE NOT SO, SO YA KNOW. A FOOLISH CRIMINAL HENCHMAN INVITES A CUTIE PIE ON A CRIME BOSS MEETING BOAT TRIP & SHE INVITES HER FRIEND & A DUDE OR 2 WITHOUT ASKING. AT THE DOCK THEY FIND A CAT IN A TRASH CAN & HEY WHY NOT BRING IT OUT TO SEA TOO? OKAY. WELL, NOT EVERYTHING GOES SMOOTH. THERES SOME PERSONALITY CONFLICTS BUT IT ALSO THE CAT IS A DEMONCAT THAT WEARS THE THE BODY OF A CUTE FLUFFY CAT. I THINK THAT IMAGE ABOVE IS OF SAID DEMONCAT "SHEDDING" IT'S DISGUISE. I THINK IT'S A SCULPTURE SHUVED THREW A PUPPET. THEN ITS A DIFFERENT CAT WHO JACKS UP FOOLS.

TONI HUDSON ERIC LARSON ALEX CORD
GEORGE KENNEDY & CLU GULAGAR
PRODUCED, WRITTEN & DIRECTED by GREYDON CLARK
NR COLOR 90 MINUTES NTSC © 1988

THE UNINVITED

Cheech & Chong's
Up in
Smoke

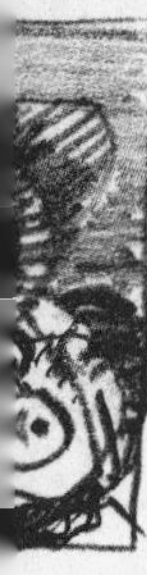

THE CLASSIC. THE GOLD STANDARD OF GRASS. YOU DON'T EVEN NEED TO SMOKE WEED TO DIG ON THIS MOVIE. PROBABLY. IT'S JUST A PERFECT FEEL GOOD. MOVIE WITH TWO A-SIMETRICAL MOUSTACHS. SOME KIND OF HALF-BAKED PEACE SIGN. BACK WHEN I FEEL FOR THE BMG RECORD SUBSCRIPTION THING I GOT THIS SOUNDTRACK. I MEMORIZED EVERY SECOND. THERES A LOT OF COOL CARS & STUFF. THE T.V. SET IT SELF IS THE MARIJUANA.

CHEECH MARIN — TOMMY CHONG

TOM SKERRITT · EDIE ADAMS · STROTHER MARTIN & STACY KEACH

WRITTEN BY TOMMY CHONG & CHEECH MARIN

DIRECTED BY LOU ADLER 1978 (R)

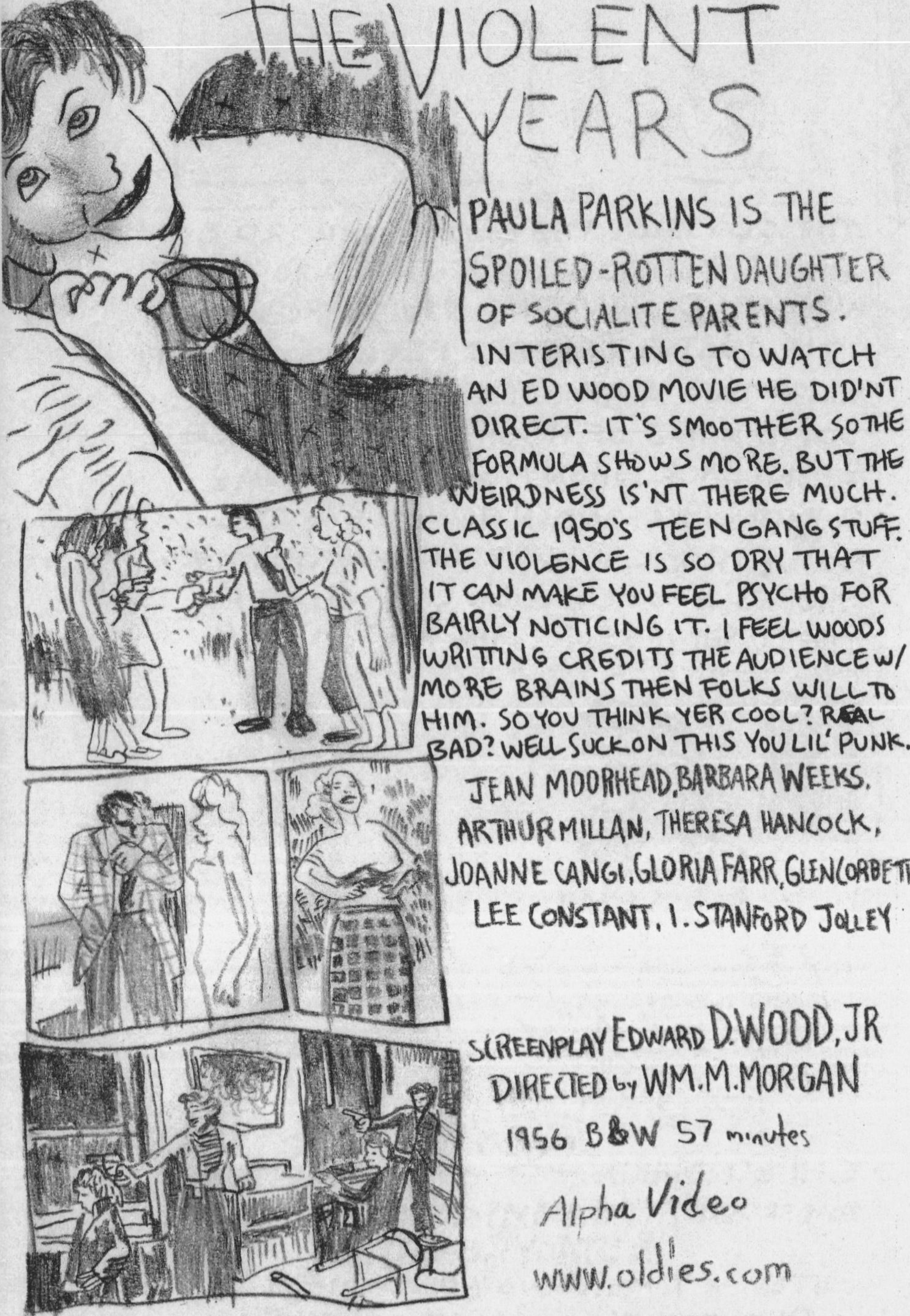
THE VIOLENT YEARS
PAULA PARKINS IS THE SPOILED-ROTTEN DAUGHTER OF SOCIALITE PARENTS.
INTERISTING TO WATCH AN ED WOOD MOVIE HE DID'NT DIRECT. IT'S SMOOTHER SO THE FORMULA SHOWS MORE. BUT THE WEIRDNESS IS'NT THERE MUCH. CLASSIC 1950'S TEEN GANG STUFF. THE VIOLENCE IS SO DRY THAT IT CAN MAKE YOU FEEL PSYCHO FOR BAIRLY NOTICING IT. I FEEL WOODS WRITTING CREDITS THE AUDIENCE W/ MORE BRAINS THEN FOLKS WILL TO HIM. SO YOU THINK YER COOL? REAL BAD? WELL SUCK ON THIS YOU LIL' PUNK.
JEAN MOORHEAD, BARBARA WEEKS, ARTHUR MILLAN, THERESA HANCOCK, JOANNE CANGI, GLORIA FARR, GLEN CORBETT LEE CONSTANT, I. STANFORD JOLLEY
SCREENPLAY EDWARD D. WOOD, JR
DIRECTED by WM. M. MORGAN
1956 B&W 57 minutes
Alpha Video
www.oldies.com

THE VIOLENT YEARS

91 MINUTES?

SPAWNED FROM LOST FLESH NUGGETS OFF OF FRANKENSTEIN {CONQUORS THE EARTH/WORLD}. ONE GROWS UP IN THE SEA. THE OTHER IS RAISED BY SCIENTISTS. BUT THEY ARE NOT LIKE FRANKENSTEIN THEY ARE SHAGGY. GREEN <SEA> & ORANGE <SCIENCE>

MADE IN JAPAN

THEIR LIKE DEVOLUTIONS, BUT THE ORANGE IS CHILL WITH HUMANITY. GREEN STOMPS ASS ON CITYS, BOATS, AIRPORTS. THEY TUSSEL BUT START TO BE COOL W/ EACHOTHER. IT ALL GO'S SIDEWAYS THOUGH. SO GREAT. RUNNING THROUGH HILL SIDES POPPING HOUSES OFF BARE TOES. CATCHING HELICOPTERS IN FORESTS. RUSS TAMBLIN DUBED W/ JAPANESE.

VHS

WRITTEN by ISHIRO HONDA & TAKESHI KIMURA

DIRECTED by ISHIRO HONDA

フランケンシュタイ

サンダ対ガイラ

WAR OF THE GARGANTUAS

War Of The Gargantuas

Bernie Lomax would be the perfect host
except for one small thing...
He's dead.

Weekend at
BERNIE'S

Weekend at BERNIE'S

IT HAS BEEN A LONG TIME SINCE I SAW THIS LAST. I PROBABLY SAW IT 10 or MORE TIMES BACK IN DAY. BACK THEN I DIDN'T KNOW BERNIE WAS ON BLOWCAIN. I FORGOT HOW LONG HE STAY'D ALIVE TOO. NOT AS EPIC AS I REMEMBERED, BUT I STILL DIG IT. NOW I'M INTERESTED IN SEE'N PART TWO. TYPICALLY ANDREW McCARTHY BUGS ME, BUT THIS ROLL SUITES HIM PRETTY WELL HE'S A GOOFY, ANOYING, LAZY SLOB; BUT THATS A GOOD CONTRAST TO SILVERMEN WHO CHARACTER IS... DUMB DESPITE BEING SMART. AND, THE GIRL HE FALLS IN LOVE WITH IS JUST HORRABLE, AND VAPID. BERNIE IS THE BEST PART

APPROX RUNNING TIME

101 MIN

IVE

LARRY DAVID IS THE WOODY CHARACTOR IN THIS ONE. HE'S THE ONLY ONE IN THE MOVIE WHO CAN SEE THE AUDIENCE & SOMETIMES ADDRESES US. HE FAILS AT A SUICIDE & LOSES HIS OLD LADY. HE'S GOT SOME FORM OF NEHILISTIC NY BUDAHISM THING A.K.A "WHATEVER WORKS". HE HELPS A SWEET NAIVE FARM GIRL WHO CRASHS HIS APT. AND HE SHOWS HER HOW TO AVOID THE SHITTY CREEPS OF NY. SHE'S IN LOVE W/ HIM BUT HE KNOWS BETTER. BUT WHAT CAN HE DO? GIVE IN. HER MOM POPS UP & STARTS COCKBLOCKING THEM. CHARACTERS COME & GO MOSTLY WEIRD NICE TYPES. IT HAS A "LOVE OF LIFES RICH TAPISTRY" KIND OF STYLE WHERE THERES MUCH BEAUTY & NOT MUCH HARSH DAMAGE. SORT'A BRITISH MOM POSITIVITY KITCHEN SINK DRAMA TONE. IN THE END IT ALL WORKS OUT FOR WHATS BEST FOR MOST. THIS' ONE OF WOODYS LITE DRAMAS AND I DIG IT. PROBABLY THE NICEIST CHARACTER LARRY DAVID HAS PLAYED TO MY MEMORY.

ED BEGLEY, JR. PATRICIA CLARKSON LARRY DAVID CONLETH HILL
MICHAEL McKEAN EVAN RACHEL WOOD
WRITTEN & DIRECTED BY WOODY ALLEN

LANGUAGE	ENGLISH 5.1	1.78:1
CC	APPROX 92 mins.	COLOR

PG-13

2009 SONY

Ed Begley, Jr. Patricia Clarkson Larry DAVID Conleth HILL Michael McKean Evan Rachel Wood

WhateverWorks

a new comedy

AKA THE CONQUEROR WORM

THIS IS ONE I'D KIND'A HEARD ABOUT BUT FOLKS DID'NT REALLY TALK ABOUT. THEN IF YOU LOOK IT UP, EVERYONE WHO WRITES ABOUT IT IS REALLY DETAILED & ATTENTIVE. SO IT'S A NERD CLASSIC. WHICH MAKES SENCE, IT IS A PERIOD PIECE; BUT ALSO A CORMAN. I THINK IT'S FANTASTIC. I THEN PEEP'D OUT THE OTHER 2 MICHAEL REEVES MOVIES & THEY'R DOPE TOO. PRICE IS A PROFESIONAL PERSACUTER, POWER TRIPPER, CREEP, SADIST... YOU KNOW, A WITCH FINDER OF HIGH RANK. DUH. HIM & HIS FLUNKY ARE THE 2 EDGES OF RAPE'O's. OGILVY IS A YOUNG BAD ASS OF HONOR WHO'S OLD LADY'S FAMILY IS SET UPON BY PRICE. HE TRACKS HIM & EVERYTHING GETS WORSE ON A REVENGE/JUSTICE TRIP W/ POETIC BRUTAL RESULTS. NO ONE COMES OUT ON TOP. THATS THE KIND OF ENDING I LIKE. ALSO IT HAS A NICE AXE MURDER AT THE END TOO. DISPITE IT SAY'N IT'S FROM EDGAR ALLAN POE IT'S NOT. PRICE READS THE CONQUEROR WORM ALOUD SO I GUESS THEY GET BY TECHNICLY. THERES A FAIR AMOUNT OF VARIETY IN THE TORTURES INCLUDING TIE'N "WITCHS" TO LADDERS & TIPPING THEM INTO BONFIRES WHICH I HAD NEVER SEEN DONE IN A MOVIE IN MOST INSTANCES PRICE WOULD STEAL THE MOVIE & THE AUDIENCE INTO ROOT'N FOR HIM BUT IT SEEMS REEVES GOT HIM TO PLAY IT DRY AND EVIL W/ NO BIG CHARISMAFICATION. AWESOME. PEEP IT OUT.

VINCENT PRICE
IAN OGILVY HILLARY DWYER ROBERT RUSSELL
PETER WYMARK RUPERT DAVIES WILFRID BRAMBELL

WRITTEN & DIRECTED by
MICHAEL REEVES

COLOR 1968 TIGON/AIP 86 MINUTES MONO DVD

LEAVE THE CHILDREN HOME!
...and if YOU are SQUEAMISH
STAY HOME WITH THEM!!!!!!!

EDGAR ALLAN POE'S

Witchfinder General

VINCENT PRICE • IAN OGILVY • RUPERT DAVIES
HILARY DWYER • WILFRED BRAMBELL

THE WIZ
COLOR/2 hours 13 Min
G
MCA
UNIVERSAL
HOME VIDEO

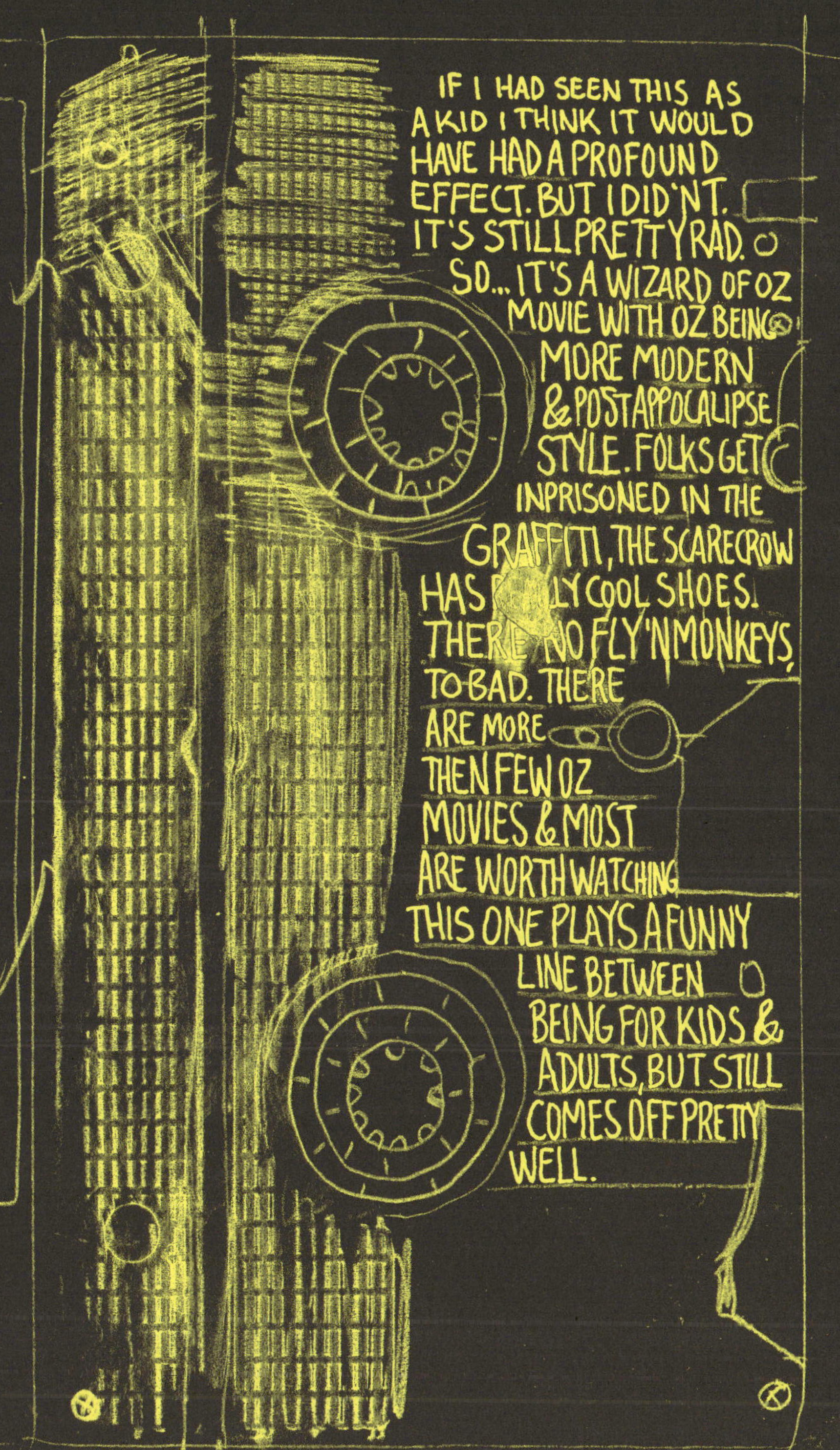
IF I HAD SEEN THIS AS
A KID I THINK IT WOULD
HAVE HAD A PROFOUND
EFFECT. BUT I DID'NT.
IT'S STILL PRETTY RAD.
SO... IT'S A WIZARD OF OZ
MOVIE WITH OZ BEING
MORE MODERN
& POST APPOCALIPSE
STYLE. FOLKS GET
INPRISONED IN THE
GRAFFITI, THE SCARECROW
HAS LLY COOL SHOES.
THERE NO FLY'N MONKEYS,
TO BAD. THERE
ARE MORE
THEN FEW OZ
MOVIES & MOST
ARE WORTH WATCHING
THIS ONE PLAYS A FUNNY
LINE BETWEEN
BEING FOR KIDS &
ADULTS, BUT STILL
COMES OFF PRETTY
WELL.

TWENTIETH CENTURY FOX

SELECTIONS

MEL BROOKS

YOUNG

RANKENSTEIN

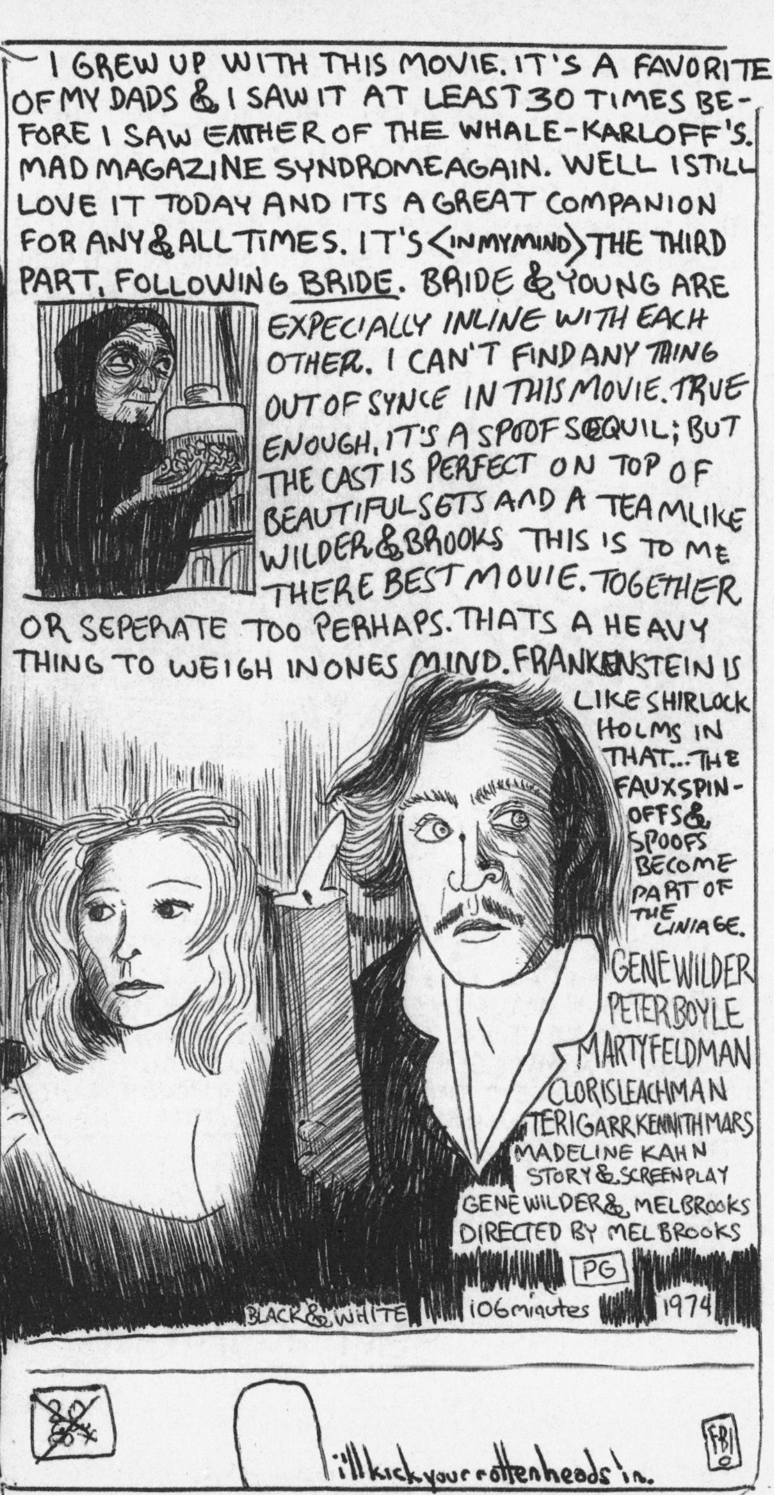
I GREW UP WITH THIS MOVIE. IT'S A FAVORITE OF MY DADS & I SAW IT AT LEAST 30 TIMES BEFORE I SAW EATHER OF THE WHALE-KARLOFF'S. MAD MAGAZINE SYNDROME AGAIN. WELL I STILL LOVE IT TODAY AND ITS A GREAT COMPANION FOR ANY & ALL TIMES. IT'S <IN MY MIND> THE THIRD PART, FOLLOWING BRIDE. BRIDE & YOUNG ARE EXPECIALLY INLINE WITH EACH OTHER. I CAN'T FIND ANY THING OUT OF SYNCE IN THIS MOVIE. TRUE ENOUGH, IT'S A SPOOF SEQUIL; BUT THE CAST IS PERFECT ON TOP OF BEAUTIFUL SETS AND A TEAM LIKE WILDER & BROOKS THIS IS TO ME THERE BEST MOVIE. TOGETHER OR SEPERATE TOO PERHAPS. THATS A HEAVY THING TO WEIGH IN ONES MIND. FRANKENSTEIN IS LIKE SHIRLOCK HOLMS IN THAT... THE FAUX SPIN-OFFS & SPOOFS BECOME PART OF THE LINIAGE.
GENE WILDER
PETER BOYLE
MARTY FELDMAN
CLORIS LEACHMAN
TERI GARR KENNITH MARS
MADELINE KAHN
STORY & SCREENPLAY
GENE WILDER & MEL BROOKS
DIRECTED BY MEL BROOKS
PG
BLACK & WHITE
106 minutes
1974
ill kick your rotten heads in.
FBI

"BEAT" KITANO

SORRY Y'ALL I CAN'T TELL WHAT THE INFO IS. ABOUT 2 HOURS. COLOR. 2000-2005 'ISH?

Zatoichi
DVD

INDEX

C

D

N

O

P

Q

R

U

V

W

Y

Z